# DISCOVERING FRANÇOISE DOLTO

This psychobiographical study of the renowned French pediatrician and psycho-analyst Françoise Dolto introduces both her theories of child development and her unique insights into language and identity.

A friend of Jacques Lacan's, Dolto believed that we are all humanized through language, and that the words we use carry unconscious traces of our early histories of love, suffering and desire. Suggesting that infants unconsciously symbolize and that a continuous circulation of unconscious affects—the transference—prevails in all language-based relations, her findings challenge assumptions about autism, autobiography, linguistics, literacy, pedagogy and therapy.

Dolto's own corpus—a rich archive blending the personal and professional— demonstrates this, with echoes between Dolto's constructs about the child and her own challenging childhood. This fascinating book will not only introduce the work of Françoise Dolto to many readers, but will be a valuable resource for all psychoanalytic researchers and theorists interested in childhood, language and identity.

**Kathleen Saint-Onge** is a Canadian researcher interested in the role of language in identity-formation and the question, "What is a word?" Saint-Onge follows Freud as she taps Françoise Dolto's notion of the *phonème* to explore the unconscious work of the transference (in texts) in psychical development. Saint-Onge is also the author of *Bilingual Being: My Life as a Hyphen* (2013).

# DISCOVERING FRANÇOISE DOLTO

## Psychoanalysis, Identity and Child Development

*Kathleen Saint-Onge*

Routledge
Taylor & Francis Group

LONDON AND NEW YORK

First published 2019
by Routledge
2 Park Square, Milton Park, Abingdon, Oxon OX14 4RN

and by Routledge
52 Vanderbilt Avenue, New York, NY 10017

*Routledge is an imprint of the Taylor & Francis Group, an informa business*

© 2019 Kathleen Saint-Onge

*British Library Cataloguing-in-Publication Data*
A catalogue record for this book is available from the British Library

*Library of Congress Cataloging-in-Publication Data*
A catalog record has been requested for this book

ISBN: 978–0–367–14428–9 (hbk)
ISBN: 978–0–367–14430–2 (pbk)
ISBN: 978–0–429–03198–4 (ebk)

Typeset in Bembo
by Swales & Willis, Exeter, Devon, UK

Printed in the United Kingdom
by Henry Ling Limited

I dedicate this book to my mother, Thérèse Dumont, in recognition of our shared history in Quebec City, such as it was.

*RUBY*
*an elemental phrase*
*mined deep in trauma*
*becomes the simplest*
*stone through which a*
*broken hand makes a*
*life into a thin bracelet*
*patterned from the un-*
*ending repetitions of a*
*blood-red ruby bead*
*(ks 2011)*

# CONTENTS

ACKNOWLEDGMENTS

# ACKNOWLEDGMENTS

I extend my deepest gratitude to Françoise Dolto (née Marette) for her astonishing generosity in sharing such a bounty of intimate materials, by which she bequeaths to human literature a truly unprecedented gift.

I thank her daughter, Catherine Dolto, for her lifelong efforts in curating Dolto's legacy, and Anne-Marie Canu, also of the Archives Françoise Dolto, for her thoughtful correspondence during the writing of my doctoral dissertation.

This project would have been impossible without the strong support for interdisciplinary studies and psychoanalysis in the Faculty of Education at York University (Toronto) in 2008–2016, in particular the influence and contributions of Deborah P. Britzman.

And though words will never be enough, I thank my three adult children, Peter, Jacob and Sarah, for sharing their love, strength, wisdom and humor with me—while indulging my passion for Freud for many years now—and my small canine companion, T., for his enduring loyalty.

# ABBREVIATIONS

**AI:**     Potin, Y. (Ed.) (2008). *Françoise Dolto: archives de l'intime.* Paris: Gallimard.

**APP:**     Dolto, F. (1956). "Introduction au dessin d'enfant." *La vie médicale: arts et psychopathologie, Numéro spécial,* Noël 1956, 27–39.

**ATP:**     Dolto, F. (1989b). *Autoportrait d'une psychanalyste 1934–1988: entretiens avec Alain et Colette Manier.* Paris: Éditions du Seuil.

**CD:**     Dolto, F. (1971). *Le cas Dominique.* Paris: Éditions du Seuil.

**CE:**     Halmos, C. (Ed.) (1994). *Françoise Dolto, articles et conférences, II: les chemins de l'éducation.* Paris: Gallimard. (Original work published 1946–1989.)

**DQ:**     De Sauverzac, J.-F. (Ed.) (1987). *Françoise Dolto: dialogues québécois.* Paris: Éditions du Seuil. (Original work published 1983.)

**D&R:**     Dolto, F. & Roudinesco, E. (1986/1988). "Des jalons pour une histoire: entretien." In J. Aubrey et al., *Quelques pas sur le chemin de Françoise Dolto* (pp. 11–42). Paris: Éditions du Seuil.

**DV:**     Dolto. F. (1986a). *La difficulté de vivre.* Paris: Vertiges du Nord/Carrere.

**DW:**     Dolto, F. & Winter, J.-P. (1986). *Les images, les mots, le corps.* Paris: Gallimard.

**EF:**     Dolto, F. (1978/1998). *L'enfant et la fête: entretien avec André Parinaud.* Paris: Mercure de France.

**EM:**     Halmos, C. & Dolto, C. (Eds.) (1994). *Françoise Dolto, articles et conférences, I: les étapes majeures de l'enfance.* Paris: Gallimard. (Original work published 1946–1988.)

**EN:**     Dolto. F. (1986c). *Enfances.* Paris: Éditions du Seuil.

**ES:**     Dolto. F. (1989a). *L'échec scolaire, essais sur l'éducation.* Paris: Ergo. (Original work published 1980–1986.)

**EV:**     Dolto, F. (1987/1998a). "L'enfant dans la ville." In *Françoise Dolto: l'enfant dans la ville* (pp. 9–52). Paris: Mercure de France.

**IIC:** Dolto. F. (1984). *L'image inconsciente du corps.* Paris: Éditions du Seuil.

**JD:** Dolto, F. (1981). *Le jeu du désir: essais cliniques.* Paris: Éditions du Seuil. (Original work published 1946–1978.)

**JP:** Faure-Poirée, C. & Djéribi-Valentin, M. (Eds.) (1999). *Jeu de poupées.* Paris: Mercure de France. (Original work published 1949, 1964.)

**LF:** Djéribi-Valentin, M. & Kouki, É. (Eds.) (1998). *Françoise Dolto, articles et conférences 5: le féminin.* Paris: Gallimard. (Original work published 1959–1988.)

**LO1:** Dolto, F. (1977a). *Lorsque l'enfant parait, Tome 1.* Paris: Éditions du Seuil.

**LO2:** Dolto, F. (1978). *Lorsque l'enfant parait, Tome 2.* Paris: France Loisirs.

**LO3:** Dolto, F. (1979a). *Lorsque l'enfant parait, Tome 3.* Paris: Éditions du Seuil.

**MA:** Marette, F. (1940). *Psychanalyse et pédiatrie: le complexe de castration, étude générale et cas cliniques.* Paris: Amédée Legrand.

**MF:** Djéribi-Valentin, M. (Ed.) (2008). *Françoise Dolto: mère et fille, une correspondance (1931–1962).* Paris: Mercure de France.

**NE:** Dolto, F. (1977/1984). "Heures et jours qui suivent l'accouchement." In E. Herbinet (Ed.), *Naître et ensuite?* (pp. 187–266). Paris: Stock.

**PF:** Djéribi-Valentin, M. (Ed.) (2001). *Françoise Dolto: père et fille, une correspondance (1914–1938).* Paris: Mercure de France.

**PJE:** Lévy, D. M. (Ed.) (2002). *Parler juste aux enfants: entretien de Françoise Dolto & D. M. Lévy.* Paris: Mercure de France. (Original work published 1978–1988.)

**P&P:** Dolto, F. (1940/1971). *Psychanalyse et pédiatrie: les grandes notions de la psychanalyse, seize observations d'enfants* (quatrième édition). Paris: Éditions du Seuil.

**PM:** Dolto, F. (1985/1998). *Parler de la mort.* Paris: Mercure de France.

**PS:** Kouki, É. (Ed.) (2005). *Françoise Dolto: parler de la solitude.* Paris: Mercure de France. (Original work published 1975.)

**QS:** Dolto, F. (1988b). *Quand les parents se separent.* Paris: Éditions du Seuil.

**SF:** Djéribi-Valentin, M. & Kouki, É. (Eds.) (1996). *Françoise Dolto, essais: sexualité féminine, la libido génitale et son destin féminin.* Paris: Gallimard. (Original work published 1960–1985.)

**SP1:** Caldaguès, L. (Ed.) (1982). *Françoise Dolto: séminaire de la psychanalyse d'enfants, Tome 1.* Paris: Éditions du Seuil.

**SP2:** De Sauverzac, J.-F. (Ed.) (1985). *Françoise Dolto: séminaire de la psychanalyse d'enfants, Tome 2.* Paris: Éditions du Seuil.

**SP3:** De Sauverzac, J.-F. (Ed.) (1988). *Françoise Dolto: séminaire de la psychanalyse d'enfants, Tome 3.* Paris: Éditions du Seuil.

**SS:** Guillerault, G. (Ed.) (1997). *Francoise Dolto: le sentiment de soi, aux sources de l'image du corps.* Paris: Gallimard. (Original work published 1956–1957.)

**TL:** Dolto. F. (1987). *Tout est langage.* Paris: Vertiges du Nord/Carrere.

**VC1:**  Percheminier, C. (Ed.) (1991). *Françoise Dolto: correspondance, 1913–1938.* Paris: Hatier.

**VC2:**  Djéribi-Valentin, M. (Ed.) (2005). *Françoise Dolto: une vie de correspondances, 1938–1988.* Paris: Gallimard.

**VO:**  Manier, C. & Kouki, É. (2003). *Françoise Dolto: la vague et l'océan, séminaire sur les pulsions de mort (1970–1971).* Paris: Gallimard.

# 1
# SUBJECT

## Introduction

Françoise Dolto (1908–1988) is arguably the most famous French psychoanalyst ever to have lived, and one of France's most respected and beloved historical figures. Yet relatively few people in the English-speaking world know anything about her. Until October 2012, I didn't either. By then, I had been teaching for 25 years, mostly ESL or FSL.[1] I am a French-English bilingual, and while French is my mother tongue, I have always read voraciously in English, my language of schooling. In 2011, I completed a Master's in Education, focusing on bilingualism, after which I undertook doctoral studies to delve into the sequelae of infantile trauma and the role of words in early child development. But through all of these adventures in learning, I had never come across Dolto's name—not once. It stuns me now to recall this, given that Dolto may well be *the* most indispensable thinker on language and identity. With this book, I hope to show the reader why, and to introduce Dolto to new English audiences. By my approach, it may also be that readers who have met Dolto in French will hear something novel about this iconic woman who believed that the «désir de vivre» is the foundation of human health, and who repurposes the "early Freud" for a whole new century.

## Rue Françoise Dolto

In the French-speaking world, Françoise Dolto is widely regarded as France's most influential psychoanalyst in terms of popular appeal and longevity. She leaves behind a legacy of hundreds of publications, and Dolto-inspired facilities for young children and their carers—*Maisons vertes*—number over 100 worldwide, of which the three in Canada are in Quebec. Her network of connections reads like a names index to psychoanalysis, and her posterity includes hundreds of hours of radio broadcasts and a half-dozen movies. Through her brother, at one time the Minister of Posts, Dolto was the author of Santa's responses to children in more than 100 countries. And throughout France (a country where psychoanalysis is prominent), countless locations and events are named after her—schools, colleges, parks, gardens, adoption centres and conferences. There is even a street that carries her name along the Seine, adjoining the Bibliothèque Nationale de France, right in the most privileged heart of that auspicious city.

Around Rue Françoise Dolto are streets honoring Marguerite Duras, Albert Einstein, Primo Levi, Claude Levi-Strauss and Thomas Mann, among others, so that even the casual journeyer in Paris can comprehend just how highly Françoise Dolto is held at the national level. Dolto is so well-respected that her manuscripts and memorabilia are now housed in the greatly esteemed Archives Nationales de France. And via the largest second-hand book source on the Internet at this time,[2] there are currently almost 3500 books by Dolto in circulation for resale. If I can be forgiven the comparison for just a moment, that is actually more than Lacan (about 2800 books), her much-respected «confrère.» But somehow, in English, Dolto is nearly untranslated and rarely cited—a virtual unknown. So Dolto's life project arrives from the start as a problem of translation, a point that offers a clue to Dolto's work on subjectivity *as* translation— the human as a work of language.

Yet Dolto's corpus should invite biographers across the world, from every tongue, if only because it is so unique—like no other in history. For Dolto, who was both a medical doctor and a psychoanalyst, leaves behind not only mountains of clinical examples and remarkable insights on her observations, but also a treasure trove of intimate artifacts, including family stories, artwork and volumes of correspondence dating back to the turn of the 20th Century. And in this fusion of personal and professional materials, I believe we can experience something quite uncanny that I am calling *the transference in texts*. The transference in texts is a phenomenon at the core of the issue of language and identity because it implies (ensures, in effect) that our adult thoughts, our theories and our creativity will be rooted in (and disclose traces of) the particular language experiences of our earliest childhood.

At issue in the transference in texts is what Dolto herself aptly calls "latent speech"—the unconscious register of language:

> At the same time as we live our relation to the other, logic, referring us to the meaning of words, we also live on another register a relation to which we do not pay attention, from (in) the domain of the unconscious, and this one has always existed. But we retain, in daily language, only what is logical, recoverable, in our exchanges with people. Therefore, there is much that is illogical between people who communicate, but we no longer know this. And we need to reawaken to this acceptance, to this intelligence of the illogical, often much more dynamic than what is logical

and what exists. Clear language carries, when it is spontaneous, at the same time as what is manifest of its speech, a latent speech, the language of the unconscious.[3]

As Dolto will elaborate it, the unconscious is our (p)reserve of affect, and language is entrusted with the circulation of unconscious desire. Further, what Dolto will show is that because of the early association between our dreams on sound and our survival—as infants—we will need lifelong to maintain unconscious continuity with that first condition of human life: our precocious symbolization.

Dolto's main point is this: humans are structured psychically by words long before ever speaking that precious first word—when each of us is but an *infans*, one who cannot speak. Mind you, it is not the word as a whole that the child hears, but what Dolto calls its phonemes—its audible syllables, often in confabulation for the child with its homonyms. For example, the phoneme «père» ["father"] has three perfect homonyms in French that suggest (i.e., mean) something very different: «perd» ["lose"], «pair(e)» ["peer"] and «paire» ["pair"]. Adding to the audible soup of homonymic plays for every child, as reality slowly arrives—augmenting both perception and definition—word boundaries are an artificial construct in every language. In a long string of babble, sounds follow fluidly. So the infant could care less about the words. But each invested phoneme has a meaning for any infant that is deeply personal, spinning a phantasy of suggestions—and indelibly associated with a unique environment of love that secures survival. Dolto's original theorization of the phoneme is, I believe, her most determinative contribution to scholarship. For Dolto reveals that while we will teach language to a child, language is always teaching the child.

## Inscription

By way of a prelude to Dolto's unusual material, I would like to offer a glimpse of her conceptual cartography. I believe her project begins with her near-death as an infant in 1909 following the departure of her beloved nanny. From here, her history moves through the losses of a dear uncle and older sister, two World Wars, the madness of a grieving mother and the ironic trappings of the bourgeoisie. She would conduct 50 years of clinical work as a doctor and respected authority on children, right up to her death only months before turning 80. Dolto dedicated herself to the regressed, troubled, traumatized, psychotic, autistic, mute and preverbal—even the nursling. So doing, she became a fine witness to the sequelae of precocious learning—learning so early that even the smallest patient already has a complex history. And via her incomparable corpus, a radical narrative emerges from Dolto's work: *the infant dreams in a long-established auditory world*. The implications are staggering. So we pause for some scaffolding: five points.

*First*, the fetus hears. And the later the gestational age, the better that hearing is. After all, newborns hear and premature babies hear. So when does the fetus begin to hear? To avoid debating fetal development, we will settle on "sometime." Sometime in the womb, the baby begins to hear the world at least somewhat, and that hearing gets better closer to due dates. This is a seldom-discussed fact.

*Second*, the fetus is unconscious. All humans can maintain primary processes in the absence of consciousness—such as during comas or dream life, for example. Diverse physiological and neurological functions (along with nascent proprioception) are being installed progressively in the fetus, so that within about six months of conception, an infant may be born too soon yet live. Those assisting feel the unique presence of a small subject, however unwell, who deserves a name. Growing under glass, the preterm infant is witnessed having likes and dislikes—and most certainly, dreams. In fact, premature infants observed around the world each day certify clearly that at some point in uterine development—who knows precisely when—a subject begins unconscious activity. That it is uncomfortable to think about (or acknowledge) this is a hallmark of Dolto's project, for what she says is deeply unsettling.

*Third*, the fetus is a symbolizing being. Within moments of his birth, the tiniest human reacts to sensations and some vital objects (e.g., the breast). Within days, he begins to show love and fear, and he responds to a few more objects. Within weeks, he attends in ways that reveal a growing capacity for familiarization, recognition and differentiation. The question of how early symbolization starts is a popular topic in the literature on infants, while precocity during this developmental process is widely considered to be a sign of intelligence. But what Dolto does that is so distinctive is to carefully ponder how the human child is born into a world where things have names, and words matter. So the baby comes equipped to engage language and wants to be part of languaged relations. In a sense, Dolto's entire project narrates how the desire for language is so essential that it is through language that we are humanized. Thus the infant instinctively seeks «la parole.» And, needing language, the infant is lured into using words as very early "objects." Symbolically, then, the word is a kind of food—satisfaction—for the infant's oral-stage inclinations during a time of utter passivity. From these first unconscious experiences with words, when we all first feel life, we remain susceptible to taking in words passively.

*Fourth*, the fetus is indissociable from the mother. Optimal development dictates that the infant is designed to stay this way for months. It is "co-narcissism," as Dolto will explain, wherein the baby *is* the mother, beginning life psychically *as* this other. So not only the mother's health but her happiness impacts the fetus. For here is another ordinary fact: words make us feel love and fear. Some words are securing—they help us fall asleep. Other words wake us up—they cause us to act quickly, or to experience trauma. So the co-narcissistic baby enjoys an affectively filtered hearing inside a language bath of the mother's tongue. And it is another common observation that our bodies affect our dreams. If my alarm rings, I may dream of a phone. If I have a sore neck, I may dream of a guillotine. And a long, convoluted dream may be spun upon a single word I heard. Freud has dozens of examples in his opus on dreams. Freud shows how ambient conditions—including sensations and conversations—are material for dream-work. Dolto's turn is simply this: she discovers that the mother's body and her soundscape are audible to the infant at *some* point, and they inscribe *something*. So the young subject is literally engaged in a *bi*ography: a writing by two.

*Fifth*—the last point in our scaffolding—the fetus weaves his first thoughts from his dreams upon words. In linguistics and philosophy, arguments thrive on the question of how it is that the words in anyone's head ever begin. Yet there is general agreement that adults do most of their thinking with words. And Freud will provide us with much evidence that thought is nothing other than the emancipation of dream-work in the service of reality—dreams restrained by secondary revisions made necessary by the demands of consciousness. In other words, dreaming and thinking are continuous processes. What Dolto does that will matter so much is to provide evidence that the words infants encounter will affect how, and what, they later think. Thereby, Dolto shows that precocious infantile audition legates to adult thought and creativity.

With Dolto, the reader will learn about the "archaic"—a period of about 18 months where birth is roughly halfway. But the archaic is not merely a developmental passage. Rather, the archaic is the soft grounds of our being, permanently remaining like a water table beneath the soil of our selves. Dolto shows that invested phonemes promise a phantasy of archaic continuity, as the infant slowly "presentifies," as she will call it—coming to reality two steps forward, one step back. Word-play while dreaming helps the infant with the monumental task of overcoming an onslaught of input and formidable fears. For it is each baby's burden to surmount, well-enough, what is anxiogenic about reality—its delays, disappointments and discomforts. After all, perfect phantasies are hard to leave behind. Therefore, for Dolto, the infant is an honorable, dignified and melancholic subject engaged in a deep existential struggle.

## Passive stor(y)ing

Dolto awakens us to how a hodge-podge of repeated, affectively charged phonemes will inscribe themselves unconsciously: the mother's name, the names of those mother talks to (father and others), or mother talks about (including the deceased). Added to these are the phonemes associated with a mother's security or fear, and phonemes from the landscape of natality—place names and cultural idioms. And, of course, any phoneme can return in multiple permutations, in wildly different words. Thus playing with phonemes while dreaming—in associations, displacements and reversals—the infant is destined to take in words as things. For it is among the facts of infantile thought that it is concrete. In other words, children are predisposed to entrusting literal suggestions on phonemes.

And that auditory prehistory of unconscious affective investments will resonate lifelong in each one of us. With Dolto, then, an ordinary question becomes incredibly complex: *What is a word?* Dolto's answer will be that words are the best mediating objects for the transference.

In turn, for each one of us, archaically invested phonemes will be synonymous with the beginnings of our survival, when our unconscious play with words seeds our fetal dreams. This fetal dream-work then seeds thought, through the gradual encroachment of perception and proprioception. And this legacy to thought cannot help but become an unconscious inscription in our works, calling us to ask, *What is writing?* Furthermore, the unexpected arrival of these archaically invested phonemes, as echoes in our encounters with an other, cannot help but deliver unconscious security—an as-if proof of life—through a return of the phantastic biography in which we begin. And if we are driven to be passively lured by our auditory pre-investments, then, *What is reading?* Dolto compels the realization that literacy invites unchartable flows of restorative objects that none can help but leave behind, that others cannot help but find—in continuous, rogue exchanges in the social that entirely resist predictability.

Thus, unpredictably, while working through my research on Dolto—as I slowly came to terms with the archaic position about which (and from which) she speaks—I accidentally came upon a powerful conveyance in her corpus that adds unexpected significance. For just as Dolto provides countless examples of words as mediating objects in the transference of unconscious material in the life trajectories of her patients—their thoughts, words and work—her own writing is replete with the traces of her infancy. After spending three years sifting through Dolto's archive, I became aware of some peculiar repetitions in the use of names for patients or theories—and, most of all, in homonymic word-plays that seemed to offer their (highly credible) suggestions to theory: «bleu,» Brande(n)b(o)urg, Deauville, Marguerite, Rousse, Secrétan, Trousseau, Vava etc. As it turns out, this unconscious register in Dolto's corpus is an uncanny yet elegant demonstration of precisely what her theorizing proposes: children are marked unconsciously by the earliest words they encounter repeatedly and invested affectively—and this legates substantively to their speech, ideas and writing.

Conveyance from this unconscious register—the transference—arrives in Dolto's texts as an unstoppable countersignature. And by following this transference of unconscious material—her "latent speech"—we will uncover something unparalleled in human literature. For in this fluid place for thinking-as-dreaming, it will be oddly possible to begin to hear the fine counter-narrative that Dolto tells beneath the stories that she tells, as archaic echoes resound in her project. Even more curious, the transference in texts in Dolto's corpus is instrumental to elaborating her thought in new ways, with the most surprising examples being the most suggestive. Dolto's texts offer the transference as wild correspondence: a movement of traces as testimony to dream-work, and an access to a silent referent originating in private audition long ago and far away—a ruin and a «rue» in.

Further, the blurring of subject and object in the transference, in this project, will help to explicate how (and why) we will need Dolto to explain Dolto. For the richest archaic investments legate the most to thought, just as she predicts, in a "sonar heritage,"[4] that makes us all perpetually subject to wild transference. As Montaigne once said, "We are but human, and we hold on to one another but by our word."[5] Dolto will demonstrate that nothing could be truer.

With Dolto, then, I submit that we will find (as much as it is findable) what Freud once described as, "proof that what we are dealing with are impressions from childhood [that] must therefore be established by external evidence, and there is seldom an opportunity for doing this."[6] Dolto gives us such an opportunity. Yet the precocious relation between the unconscious and the phoneme that is central to elaborating her work emerges slowly, piecemeal, across her lifetime. It travels along a winding trail from her infancy to her dissertation, published in 1940, wherein Dolto relates how the child "passively stores words and sounds … to which he reacts according to their associations, agreeable or disagreeable."[7] From here, the phoneme infiltrates critical formulations throughout her career, until her very last publications. And in the powerful evidence that emerges from Dolto's extraordinary corpus, I believe we will observe the rather indisputable (though profoundly enigmatic) transference of the autobiographical in the theoretical.

## Trace

I am awakened to my method of study by Freud's singular text of less than 100 pages on Leonardo da Vinci, which is largely relegated to the margins of his corpus.[8] The publisher of a re-edition warns that, "Freud never repeated the exercise,"[9] and the book "seems to have been greeted since its publication with an unusual amount of disapproval."[10] This is our first hint that we have come upon what disturbs and disrupts: the unconscious cannot be far. For biography is normally a densely annotated timeline, but Freud writes something deceptively short that almost passes unnoticed, then becomes trivialized. Yet Freud's text on da Vinci is the first-ever demonstration of the path of instinctual activity towards thought in one person's life.[11] The key to understanding future achievements, Freud explains, is to be found in childhood phantasies.[12] I believe that what Freud opens is the notion of the transference in texts—a trace. At issue is a kind of record of the irrepressible transit of unconscious material from our early affective history to our later works—one that human beings cannot help but leave, seek and find.

While interpreting da Vinci's works, Freud also explains that nature has a way of forcing its way into experience,[13] causing repetitions of childhood patterns. So Freud advises biographers to look for the signature of the primary processes,[14] especially where there is overdetermination.[15] Freud then follows his method logically: if our earliest dream life affects our future, then later achievements should disclose traces of these phantasies and the work of the unconscious. And by way of a demonstration, Freud traces the phantasy da Vinci experienced in the cradle—that of a visit by a vulture[16]—to his theoretical work on flight. Through the influence of his unconscious, Freud explains, da Vinci was "destined from the first to investigate the flight of birds,"[17] being "bound up in a special and personal way with the problem of flight."[18]

Freud suggests that unconscious conveyance should be evident in an artist's technique too, for after his passion for the Mona Lisa, for example, da Vinci, "transferred its traits ... to all the faces that he painted or drew afterwards."[19] In other words, unconscious material particular to one's history will affect one's thinking about the world and one's work in that world—one's creations and innovations. Freud describes the transference as, "a universal phenomenon of the human mind" that "dominates the whole of each person's relations to his human environment,"[20] by which unconscious phantasies are externalized.[21] Yet while da Vinci refers to his childhood only once,[22] Dolto is the only psychoanalyst other than Freud to have left such a rich personal record. Through Freud's correspondence and his *Autobiographical Study*[23]—and critically, through the exposition of so much of his life and character in his study of dreams—psychoanalysis is itself accidental upon autobiography. Yet we will find few who are as willing to admit the unconscious into the human story as Freud and Dolto were.

By following the transference of Dolto's early libidinal investments in her texts, we will come upon an entirely new means of learning as we encounter what Lisa Farley beautifully describes as, "dreams as records of what is unthinkable about history."[24] We will also observe what Freud once theorized: "Psychic processes are essentially unconscious; becoming conscious, or being conscious, is not a necessary characteristic of psychic life."[25] Thus, while the present work may be considered an intellectual biography of sorts, it is not a classical example of the genre, wherein one person's life is rationally linked to a field's history of ideas— i.e., to intellectual communities. Rather, this original psychobiographical project on Dolto links her libidinal history to her remarkable theoretical notions—her genius. In other words, insofar as the psychobiographic genre normally aims to study one person's life in trying to understand a domain of thought, I have attempted instead to study one person's life to try to understand the ontogeny of thought itself.

## Enigma

Françoise Dolto's mark on the field of the psychoanalysis of children is so great that in France today, to follow psychoanalytic notions in parenting and/or educating children—or to speak of Oedipus—is widely referred to as «faire du Dolto» ["doing Dolto"]. Only one other female psychoanalyst has marked the 20th Century in this way: Melanie Klein, to whom we can assign ideas and practices as being *Kleinian*. These two women, both mothers of three, will define a wide body of thought in their field. Yet while the typical anglophone researcher in North America, for example, easily comes upon Klein during any study of the child's psychical world, the onset of symbolic functioning or the nature of narrative, Dolto is nowhere to be found.

And although Dolto enters the intimate spaces of family life in «la francopho-nie,» and she turns up on coffee tables and in public libraries all across her country, she has not yet entered many universities—anywhere. So begins a considerable problem of transmission that remains inexplicable. In English, for example, Dolto is effectively absent from a vast domain of study where she contributed actively for decades, as rich grounds for engagement continue to dissipate across the English Channel. So it remains true—despite translators abounding on both sides of that narrow body of water—that Dolto is little disseminated in the language of the present project.

Only one of Dolto's texts is easily available in English, a 2013 translation of her dissertation, *Psychoanalysis and Paediatrics: Key Psychoanalytic Concepts with Sixteen Clinical Observations of Children*, supported by the French Ministry of Foreign Affairs (translated by F. Hivernel and F. Sinclair). At this time, there is also one other book about (but not by) Dolto in English: *Theory and Practice in Child Analysis*, edited by G. Hall, F. Hivernel & S. Morgan (2009). Both were published by Karnac.[26] The attempted translation of *Flower Dolls: Essays in Psychotherapy* apparently never made it to press,[27] while another translation, *When Parents Separate*, either had a very limited run or was pulled prior to publishing, so it is unfindable in English (though available in Spanish).[28] *Dominique: Analysis of an Adolescent* was issued in 1973/1974, while a short piece by Dolto appeared in English in 1985, as did a collaboration with G. Severin (1979). And there are about a dozen independent articles about Dolto in English: N. Littner (1974), S. Turkle (1995/1997), E. Binet (1999), F. Gerrardyn and P. Walleghem (2005), G. Hall (2009), C. Reeves (2010), R. Bacon (2013), F. Hivernel (2013), S. Morgan (2013) and M. Paglia (2016). In sum, there is relative muting in English about a French researcher with a vibrant career a half-century long.

Of course, on Dolto's side of the English Channel, the French publishing world is full of texts by and about Dolto, many of them in multiple versions, and the legacy of Dolto's works to future generations is sizable. Materials left to posterity include not only clinical transcripts but also volumes of correspond-ence, family records dating back three generations, photographs, boxes of files and notes, a childhood journal, reflections on the 20th Century, both archived and unarchived memorabilia from her practice and samples of her artwork in charcoal, paint and clay.[29]

Paradoxically, this abundance of artifacts is met by a paucity of references. Dolto's published dissertation (in 1940)—the book considered to have started psychoanalysis in France[30]—will be, in the end, the only place where we will ever find a list of citations created by Dolto herself for any of her texts. In that work, she cites 21 texts by Freud; 17 by E. Pichon; five each by S. Morgenstern and R. Laforgue; three each by M. Bonaparte and R. De Saussure; two each by O. Codet, A. Freud and J. Leuba; one by E. Jones; and three other sources.[31] Yet even here, references appear in the first edition (only) but are entirely absent from all later editions—11 in French alone.[32] In contrast, the large number of references required to write a research text on Dolto now (about 500 sources and 2500 notes) is a witness to the breadth of her work and the productivity of her thought. Yet she remains largely uncited in academic publications, even in French—though French psychoanalysis has been operating for 80 years in the climate of Dolto. Symbolically, then, it is as if the problem of (the lack of) referencing in Dolto self-perpetuates.

And despite the staggering significance of Dolto's project, there are many today who categorize her as merely a woman of her time and place—though she herself never quite believed she was. They deem her to be insufficiently feminist, academic or political—or overly Catholic, normative or conservative. So doing, they lose the opportunity to hear what she has to say about the archaic, the phoneme, oral passivity and the unconscious "libidinal dialectic" between human beings. It is as if the abstractions of the intellect service repression on a social scale. And many others cast the judgment that could be heard even in her lifetime: that she was an over-glorified media star, or a theoretical lightweight, who happened to be intuitively good with babies. Dismissed out of hand, she falls conveniently out of sight.

I had the opportunity to run into a Parisian psychoanalyst with such an opinion at a conference years ago. Approaching him before his presentation, I asked him what he thought of Dolto now. He replied that Dolto was around before we understood all we do about autism, and that she was not relevant and no longer spoken of. He then volunteered that he had met her once, when she accompanied her daughter, Catherine,[33] and they all found themselves in an apartment for rent. So he laughed that his had only ever been a «rencontre immobilière» ["real estate encounter"; ironically, also "immobile encounter"]. I had to swallow hard to remain cordial. For so much of what Dolto has to say is directly relevant to autism today[34]—and yet the attitude of this highly respected colleague represents that of countless peers who have missed Dolto's theoretical resources while casually discarding her.

I often wonder, to be honest, if there is more than a touch of misogyny in the popular willingness—not his necessarily, but that of French academics in general—to discount the possibility that a pudgy older woman with a love of babies, with silver hair and sensible footwear, could ever be a genius. But sometime later, it hit me that this educated Parisian had produced a rather uncanny truth, at least metaphorically. Because by looking only at "real estate"—countable grounds on solid earth—it is so easy to miss the subtle offers in dream-work on the terrain of Dolto's thought. For as Freud once famously wrote, early in his project: "The interpretation of dreams is the royal road to a knowledge of the unconscious activities of the mind."[35] And what Dolto imparts, through her unprecedented forays into the unconscious work of words, is that a very long stretch of the royal road is on the landscape of the archaic.

## Languaged identity

Contrary to many received narratives about Dolto, then, my belief is that she can be put into a tremendously productive conversation on the finest points of theory with many prominent peers.[36] For as Élisabeth Roudinesco explains, "the most revolutionary aspect of the Freudian discovery [is] the relation between the unconscious and language."[37] And as Dolto theorized from 1940, the legacy of phonemes to linguistics is especially discernible. For example, Dolto seems to presage Julia's Kristeva's discussions of "displacements and condensations from phonemes,"[38] and how the unconscious predisposes a "narrative revolt" whereby the archaic can "overturn conscious meaning."[39] I think analytically inclined readers will also find a satisfying engagement between Dolto and (most especially) Melanie Klein, Jacques Lacan and Donald Winnicott—as well as others, such as Karl Abraham, Lou Andreas-Salomé, Susan Isaacs, Melitta Schmideberg, Hanna Segal, James Strachey, August Stärcke and Frances Tustin.[40] In addition, there is an uncanny relation between Dolto's work and the French philosophical current known as "deconstruction"—in particular, the project of Jacques Derrida,[41] whose notion of "trace" Dolto seems to incidentally but powerfully inscribe.

Derrida—who, like Dolto, walked Rue Saint-Jacques in Paris for 40 years (right around the same time too)—writes about the "hidden resource of homonymie,"[42] enabling «transferts homonymiques»[43] that tender their unconscious suggestions. And he offers this striking example: «sens blanc, sang blanc, sans blanc, cent blancs, semblant»[44]—phonemes that, despite appearances, are perfect homonyms.[45] In this phenomenon, Derrida locates a subterranean play of words,[46] and a "disposition to transference."[47] As a result, he says, we humans are all "autobiographical animals"[48]—anachronistic beings who sign everything we do with our unconscious history. Thus, language harbours what he calls a hypothesis from underneath,[49] a countersignature,[50] and a game in language[51] of reversibility and repetition[52] that "disorganizes and disturbs literalness"[53]—one that "overthrow[s] the landscape in (on) which the science of language has peacefully installed itself."[54] Dolto's work will deeply disrupt that installation.[55]

And while Dolto once said that she could live just as well not knowing where she was going,[56] her readers might not. So in the effort towards meaning-making with her difficult material, I propose an original movement that returns Dolto to Freud, the only theorist who really mattered to her, as I elaborate her very fine theorization on psychical development and the origins of the indelible, unconscious co-inscription of language and identity.

The role of the unconscious in human life was first widely disseminated in Freud's two most popular texts, with which he inaugurated both the 20th Century and psychoanalysis: his watershed work on *The Interpretation of Dreams* (in 1900) and his studies of the now-familiar Freudian slips, especially as found in *The Psychopathology of Everyday Life* (in 1901). That there is a lot of Freud here is an understatement. But Freud and Dolto are—as I will try to demonstrate—mutually elucidating. On the one hand, Dolto offers evidence of psychical life situated somewhere between Freud's early work on dreams and word things, and his later elaborations of Oedipus. Dolto thinks and writes, in other words, on the pre-Oedipal stage. On the other hand, Freud is needed to shore up Dolto's theorizations on oral passivity because what is crucial to comprehending her thinking is a strong grasp of the primary processes and Freud's drive theory.

Thoroughly original while loyally Freudian, Dolto finds a way to listen to the *infans*—the one who cannot talk—and the reader, too, will need to lend an ear to a subtle story. For Dolto's work will take us on a regressing adventure to the moment in human development before thought arrives on the scene—into a narration that is inferable as much by its silences as by what it says—onto a landscape far beneath consciousness where our encounters with words begin in precocious fetal audition. That reading and hearing Dolto can have this effect— that of regressing the reader and provoking anxiety—is something Freud was well aware of as one of the liabilities of psychoanalysis. But the uncomfortable psychical condition that meeting Dolto's work generates is precisely what enables the particular learning that her oeuvre disseminates. This in itself is a point of some significance on the deep psychical work of reading.

I suggest, then, that walking with Dolto is a journey where it is precisely by the loss of one's bearings that one can find what is lost. Dolto's project reveals that we are all lured to safety in reality by the veiled and necessary repetitions of our archaic sources of love. Hers is, in totality, a remarkable project on the uniqueness of each human being and the powerful role of the unconscious in learning—as well as an unrelenting defense of infants. For like no one before her, Dolto maps the prehistoric psychical terrain of the infant's emotional world.

## Beyond «Doltomania»

This research on Dolto is thus a work of the archive in all ways. I rely on artifacts from her childhood and treasures from the analytic archive, like her dissertation of 1940—its fragile pages literally leaving bits of dust on my desk, as if self-effacing while disseminating. With Dolto, I examine the human archive— the infant—primarily aided by Freud's archive, his dream book and other texts comprising the "early Freud." My work is also rooted in infantile ruptures of my own that left me questioning the psychical work of words.[57] And as pronouns slip from first to third in Dolto's project—engaging material that is not thinkable as "I," nor even "thinkable"—Dolto provokes the reader's othering, inviting us back to a messy time where (when) words begin in an "as-if" discursive space with an other.[58] So I effectively engage what Aparna Mishra Tarc aptly calls "primal scenes of reading":[59] the infant's, Dolto's, Freud's and my own.

The blurriness between subjects in my project—the loss of boundaries of a distinct self—is unavoidable inside Dolto's narrative space. This is the nature of the archaic pre-subjectivity to which Dolto draws our attention, and it seems that the transference affects even the means of transmission of her work. For the evidence suggests that the «je-nous» ["I-us/we"]—that «jeu de mots/maux» ["game of words/pains"] of the child, as Dolto describes it so creatively[60]— inscribes itself as a performative. This shared space of biography «à la Dolto» is an innovative offer to the craft of writing, then, as the transference opens up new experiences with literacy. But I would also like to alert the reader about the prevailing use of "us" and "we" in this biographic project that is the result (requirement?) of talking about the pre-subject. And serving a more practical rationale—but still impacting pronouns—I use "he/him" for the infant. For there is a technical requirement to avoid tiresome forms like "his/her," or "s/he," while clearly differentiating references to patients from those to Dolto herself inside sentences.

I also caution readers in advance that my study does not tender a history of child psychoanalysis in France, nor do I offer an account of every incident in Dolto's life, such as details of her marriage or her life with her children. Rather, I seek something different: the transference of affective investments from Dolto's childhood to her thinking about the child. Therefore, I explore themes based on some curious interlacing between Dolto's history and theory. And since Dolto is all about language and its unconscious register, I enlist word-association as a method of study, in the truest psychoanalytic tradition. As a result, each chapter is an essay in a field of encounters with language, wherein I hope the reader will experience Dolto's thought, her phenomenal productivity and the transference in texts in her corpus. In what may be a defining feature of my writing, the second meaning of the French word «essai»—what is attempted but may not succeed—seems most apt. For in each chapter, I can only try (again), in a psychobiographic exploration wherein circularity is more productive than linearity.

This unusual structure suggested itself sometime in 2013, in concert with my beginning to notice Dolto's invested phonemes. Thereby, the organization of the sea of Dolto's materials is driven by a few pivotal words that seem to condense material from every corner of her corpus. Elisabeth Young-Bruehl once explained it this way: "When you write a full-length biography, turning-point images slowly emerge to you and you use them to frame the book."[61] I agree with her completely. I am also encouraged to find a kindred approach in the most recent book about Dolto in French, by Caroline Eliacheff, who notifies her readers that she has used a, "circular composition ... to integrate to the present the past and the future, without pretending to write a biography."[62] For in the present project too, the reader will not learn what happened to Dolto sequentially, from birth to death, just like that. But I believe the reader will discover, through roundabout journeys, the essence and value of Dolto's startling theories. Writing on Freud, Deborah Britzman[63] speaks of, "the incredible and inaudible meaning, shards of history that compose and decompose psychical life,"[64] and how careful attention is needed to, "find a meaning in the forgotten word ... [so] stray thoughts can be linked to a forgotten history and narrated anew."[65] This is precisely the task to which I now invite the reader.

Admittedly, however, readers who know Dolto in French may wonder where the popular view has gone in my work: the Dolto of "Doltomania"; the Dolto vulgarized as an advice-giver on babies; the Dolto embroiled with Lacan in psychoanalytic societies; or the Dolto called to comment publicly on everything from abortion, to IVF to adoption—most of it when she was already ill and retired (or nearly) from decades of clinical work. Readers who purchase any Dolto book and read it from front to back will also probably give their heads a shake. For reading Dolto linearly like that, one merely encounters the busy collage of passages alternating between the professional, personal, clinical, anecdotal, serious, humorous, wise and wild. The full scope of her genius may not seem evident in such a structured approach, for the truth is that Dolto is not meant to be heard or read that way. Consistent with her preeminent message about the unconscious play through which we all first experience survival, associative thinking will necessarily be more useful than logic when studying Dolto. I believe this is, in itself, a revolutionary idea about ideas.

In fact, associative thinking—and the indispensable role of the word in it—has been at the core of the psychoanalytic project from its very first patient, Bertha Pappenheim (1859–1936), "Anna O," who gave the field its famous nickname: the "talking cure."[66] Unsurprisingly, then, the issue of translation has also been intrinsic to the psychoanalytic project from its origins. It is, as Élisabeth Roudinesco once called it, "the sea serpent of the history of the movement."[67] For example, in German, Freud's *wortgebilden* educate, form and construct, being neither mere "word-things" (objects), nor simply "word-presentations" (visual). In turn, the expression, "dream-interpretation," silences the *trau* (trust) embedded in Freud's *traumdeutung*. And of Freud's *trieb*—urge, sprout, desire, instinct and work—we translate only "drive," or in French, «pulsions.» So the word and the subject both begin with the inextricable problem of translation—the paradox of translation as both continuity and rupture.

## Word-things

By definition, then, any translation will necessarily be an imperfect rendering where much can be quietly scribed into the inaudible gap between the language of conveyance and the language of retrieval. For every translator knows that subtle meanings and affects can be changed—lost or added, accidentally or deliberately. And with regards to the safe transport of an eminent French thinker onto new English scenes, much more could be said about the arbitrariness of choosing one word over another, or about the relative merits of providing Dolto's original words.

All translations herein are my own, and I have opted for an economy of messaging geared to better understanding. First, I place translations in the main text (rather than in the notes), to reduce the need for shifting attention from the body of the work to its margins. Second, in the interest of precision, I provide Dolto's original phrasing whenever it impacts the main thesis of this work, as in notably homonymic passages. Third, to retain more of her voice than a normative translation would offer, I use her words whenever they are cognates: for example, «superbe» or «résonateur.» For at the heart of Dolto's innovative theorization is her belief (and evidence) that the phonemes that make up words are influential, and word-play offers unconscious suggestions. Therefore, I believe that considerable respect is owed to Dolto's own phonemes. Besides, we will need French to make sense of some suggestions along the way, though it may look and feel awkward at times. James Strachey, Freud's most respected translator, once remarked: "It is most unfortunate from the point of view of the translator that Freud chose slips of the tongue as his most frequent examples of parapraxes."[68] Strachey then explains why these are unique to a language, hard to translate and require notes and brackets. The problem with Dolto's corpus is exactly the same. So, like Strachey, I will need notes and brackets. For added clarity, I also enlist two forms of quotation marks: "English" and «français.»

However, despite my sincere attempts at simplification—including abbreviating about 40 oft-repeated sources—the reader will undoubtedly observe an avalanche of references. In fact, there are several thousand citations here, so despite my best efforts to be careful, a number of glitches will undoubtedly have slipped in. Any errors, oversights, confusions or weaknesses in this work are mine alone and should in no way reflect on Françoise Dolto, her estate or her publishers. In this regard, I offer my warmest and deepest appreciation to Dr. Catherine Dolto, Françoise's daughter and legatee, and to Dr. Anne-Marie Canu, a Dolto scholar and psychoanalyst, for extending so many kind and supportive sentiments.[69]

I also want to acknowledge all of the youngest patients of psychoanalysis, its children. In enduring gratitude for their passage in the literature, I offer this work as what Freud once called, in relation to his own, "an attempt to follow an idea consistently, out of curiosity, to see where it will lead."[70] For highly original play is bound to the origins of psychoanalysis by virtue of the particular task it undertakes, "to lift the veil of amnesia which hides the earliest years of childhood."[71] And acknowledging the one to whom I owe the most, I extend my inestimable appreciation, once again, to Françoise Dolto.[72] It is Dolto's free giving and her refreshing candor—her leaving the remnants of her extremely productive life for public viewing—that make possible the unique learning about the archaic and the transference that opens, like entirely new terrain, in her astounding project.

As I put the final touches on this manuscript, it is an anniversary year for Dolto, 2018, marking 30 years since her death (and 110 since her birth). In France, recent projects commemorating her include a televised documentary that frames her childhood between two wars and invokes the «nounou irlandaise» ["Irish nanny"] who changed the life of young Françoise—who then changed everything for children.[73] Its synopsis summarizes why Dolto remains so important today: "Françoise Dolto revolutionized how we speak to children, how we educate them and how we heal them."[74] I think it takes only a minute or two of live foot-age of Dolto (in this or any film)—or, in reading, a chapter or two—to sense her exceptional intelligence, her interpersonal warmth and her solemn respect for the child. But most palpable in any meeting is Dolto's inexhaustible hope. This hope is rooted in her predominant belief that the unconscious is a potent human resource whose dynamic is always in circulation as the source of individual vitality and liberty. Dolto's conviction is quietly persuasive: if you are still alive, then you are stronger than you think.

So without further ado, I welcome the reader to a wonderful new space for thought with (and through) Françoise Dolto—and to a revolution in common conceptions of childhood, education and the role of language in identity. It is not light reading, I admit. But it is, as I will try to show, absolutely imperative reading not just for educators or the psychoanalytically inclined, but for anyone interested in human development and human communication. It is an observ-able truth that the English-speaking world has a long-overdue meeting with Dolto. That such an encounter threatens to rattle more than a few paradigms and confound some comfortable theories may make acknowledging Dolto diffi-cult. Then again, is any adventure that's really worth having ever without an element of risk?

## Notes

1 English/French as a Second Language. I thank the many fine colleagues I have met throughout my career for their insights. I am also grateful to my students over 30 years, especially the youngest and the "identified," for enabling my learning about education.
2 Abebooks.com.
3 Dolto, 1985a, 283.
4 JD, 286.
5 Montaigne, 1580/1958a, 33.
6 Freud, 1900a, 189.
7 MA, 28.
8 Published in 1910. *Da Vinci* makes its first appearance as a work-in-progress in the *Minutes of the Vienna Psychoanalytic Society* on 1 December 1909 (Freud, 1909/1967, 338–346). Eighteen months prior (1 April 1908), the *Minutes* reveal Freud's attention: "Some day one should investigate how infantile impressions influence great achievements" (Freud, 1908/1962, 361). And nearly (exactly) two years earlier (11 December 1907), the *Minutes* record Freud's interest in the, "relation between the artistic creation and the poet's life" (Freud, 1907/1962, 265–266).
9 Freud, 1910b, frontispiece; re-edition in 1984.
10 Freud, 1910b, frontispiece.
11 Freud, 1910b, 136.
12 Freud, 1910b, 136.
13 Freud, 1910b, 137.
14 Freud, 1910b, 119.
15 Freud, 1910b, 93.
16 Freud, 1910b, 82.
17 Freud, 1910b, 92.
18 Freud, 1910b, 126.

19  Freud, 1910b, 110.
20  Freud, 1925[1924], 42.
21  Freud, 1914c, 150–151.
22  Freud, 1910b, 82.
23  Freud, 1925[1924].
24  Farley, 2011, 24. I thank Dr. Lisa Farley for her robust review of my dissertation (2016) and her interventions on Tustin and Winnicott.
25  Freud, 1907/1962, 124.
26  I thank Russell George, Elliott Morsia and the publishing team at Routledge (subsuming Karnac) for their support and their continued leadership in disseminating Dolto in English in the 21st Century.
27  The publisher (Marion Boyars, 1997/1998) reports that the translation may have been poor or incomplete (A.-M. Canu, personal communication, 8 March 2015); this problem is also noted in Hall, Hivernel & Morgan 2009, xx.
28  The publisher (David R. Godine, 1997) reports being unsure about how the book disappeared, and suggests it may not have been published (A.-M. Canu, personal communication, 26 February 2015). The translator hired for that project writes that she has no copies of it (D. Callimanopulos, personal communication, 26 February 2015). Curiously, Sherry Turkle (1995/1997) wrote an interesting introduction to it which is nonetheless findable (presumably through access to a pre-publication copy). Its "uncorrected prints" are in the Archives Françoise Dolto (A.-M. Canu, personal communication, 28 March 2015).
29  The multiple reprints of Dolto's texts, many in journals that are defunct and digitally unarchived (e.g., *Phot Anphar* and *Pratique des mots*)—as well as the diffusion of her work in countless conference proceedings—has made it advisable to use modern collections where these are regrouped (see Abbreviations).
30  Roudinesco, in Coronel & De Mezamat, 1997a.
31  MA, 269–271.
32  In 1940, 1961, 1965, 1971, 1976, 1979, 1986, 1988, 1994, 1998, 2008; see worldcat.org, 2015a.
33  Dolto had three children: Jean-Chrysostome ("Carlos") was an entertainer (d. 2008); Grégoire (Gregory) is a naval engineer; and Catherine (formerly Dolto-Tolitch) is a renowned pediatrician, psychotherapist and author.
34  I thank Dr. Paula Salvio for sharing my enthusiasm for Dolto's importance to educational interventions for autism, and for considering my dissertation to be, "a robust, complex intellectual history of Dolto that … is entirely original in the context of educational studies" (External Examiner's Report, June 2016).
35  Freud, 1900b, 608.
36  I thank my examiners for their rich engagement during my successful oral defense on 24 June 2016: Drs. Deborah Britzman, Lisa Farley, Jen Gilbert, Thomas L. Loebel, Aparna Mishra Tarc and Paula Salvio.
37  Roudinesco, 1975, 85.
38  Kristeva, 1974, 219.
39  Kristeva, 1996/2000, 15; her concept is productively taken up by Britzman (2011, 96). I thank Dr. Thomas L. Loebel for his insights on how Dolto's work relates to Kristeva's, following his close reading in 2016.
40  I will also draw some lines to Carl Jung and Otto Rank, but these will be more in the nature of a contrast.
41  I thank Dr. Mario DiPaolantonio for his unwavering support and generous words throughout my graduate studies (2008–2016), and for introducing me to Derrida's work in September 2008.
42  Derrida, 1993, 61.
43  Derrida, 1986b, 193f.

44 "White sense/direction, white blood, without white, one hundred whites, pretense/pretender."

45 Derrida, 1972/1987, 40.

46 Derrida, 1986b, 47.

47 Laplanche & Pontalis, 1967/2004, 498.

48 Derrida, 1997/2008.

49 Derrida, 2003, 167.

50 Derrida, 1991, 160.

51 Derrida, 1967a, 73.

52 Derrida, 1999/2004, 17.

53 Derrida, 1967b, 337.

54 Derrida, 1967a, 44.

55 I thank Dr. Heather Lotherington (York University) for our rich dialogues and her support of my masters degree (2008–2011). I am also grateful to other linguists at York for their input: Drs. Colette Granger, Razika Sanaoui and Sandra R. Schecter. As well, I thank Drs. Myrna Gopnik and Michel Paradis (formerly at McGill), for triggering my interest in linguistics 40 years ago.

56 ATP, 26.

57 Saint-Onge, 2013. I thank Mark Abley, my editor at McGill-Queen's University Press, and that book's kind reviewers: in particular, Claire Holden Rothman (*Montreal Gazette*, 18 May 2013); and Dr. Jatinder Mann (*British Journal of Canadian Studies*, 28:1, 2015, 126). For conversations that helped me move from that project to this one, I thank Dr. Fang Duan, Agnieszka Gozlan, Dr. Oren Gozlan, Dr. Alice Pitt, Dr. Carol Anne Wien—and my poetic cousin, Marie.

58 I thank Dr. Daniel Yon for his passionate lectures about messiness and fluidity, and for his kindness.

59 Mishra Tarc, 2015, 66; I thank Dr. Aparna Mishra Tarc for her critical feedback on the draft of my dissertation (2016).

60 IIC, 365; SP1, 217; SP3, 76; also Chapters 3 and 4 of this volume.

61 Young-Bruehl, 1998b, 24.

62 Eliacheff, 2018a, 13.

63 My doctoral studies were supervised by Dr. Deborah Britzman, Distinguished Professor at York University and a Fellow of the Royal Society of Canada. I am very grateful for her authentic appreciation of Freud, her attentive reading of my work in 2011–2016, and her provocations to a deep engagement with psychoanalytic theory. Her conversations, lectures, correspondence and publications on the emotional world in education have significantly and permanently affected my thinking, while her insights on Melanie Klein were instrumental. It was at her invitation that I attended a talk in November 2012 with Marie Normandin, of the *Maison Buissonière* (a *Maison verte* in Montreal). This is how I first heard of Dolto myself—how I came upon my subject—and I became an accidental biographer. I thank Ms. Normandin for bringing Dolto to Toronto, and Dr. Judith Hamilton, of the Toronto Psychoanalytic Society, for sponsoring that visit. In shaping this book from my dissertation (Saint-Onge, 2016), I completely revised its six chapters and citation style, and I composed extensive additional material (e.g., Chapter 8, new notes and an index).

64 Britzman, 2011, 5.

65 Britzman, 2011, 47.

66 Breuer & Freud, 1893a; also Guttman, 2001; Jones, 1953/1982, 223–224; Roudinesco, 1982, 30–33.

67 Roudinesco, 1982, 348.

68 Strachey, in Freud, 1916a, 31.

69 I had the good fortune to meet Anne-Marie in Paris in July 2014, when I shared a few hours with her at the Archives Françoise Dolto, and thereafter to sustain a nurturing dialogue by email. I also had the rare pleasure of meeting Catherine in

March 2017, when we spent about two hours in a coffee shop during her trip to Montreal to perform at the Théatre Outremont with her friend, «Emma la clown.» Catherine's works about her «drôle de mère» ["funny kind of mother"] (1986b, 79) are exquisite and crucial.

70  Freud, 1920, 24.
71  Freud, 1933a, 28.
72  Dolto's dissertation (1940) uses her maiden name, Marette; in the 1940s (e.g., in *Psyché* and the *Revue francaise de psychanalyse*), she is either Dolto-Marette or Dolto. By the 1950s, she publishes consistently as Dolto. Except where cited as C. (Catherine) Dolto (-Tolitch) or B. (Boris) Dolto—Françoise's husband (also a doctor)—the name "Dolto" in this work will refer to Françoise Dolto.
73  Miller, 2018a.
74  Miller & Feuillette, 2018.

# 2

# FILIATION

## Introduction

Dolto's corpus—almost equal parts autobiographical and professional, and continually rereleased—is characterized by texts that interweave brilliant insights and intricate clinical portraits with humorous anecdotes and self-deprecating remarks that her opinion is of no interest whatsoever.[1] Even in a casual encounter, one is struck by the word-play and frankness in Dolto's project. But in a slow reading, one begins to hear uncanny echoes between her childhood history and her theoretical notions about childhood, which alternately escape and attract her attention. Dolto's constructions—often punctuated by her favorite expression, «tout se passe comme si» ["everything happens as if"]—will unsettle our comfortable knowledge from the start. For she believes that the child just born has already been living a long life of shared desires.[2] She also insists that the fetus is a being in language,[3] one who is capable of ethical thought.[4]

Then, with few tributes to anyone but Freud, Dolto advances a novel project whose strength derives from her valuing what is childish and phantasmatic in herself[5] and, in her words, "this conviction that I have that the child *knows*."[6] Every child begins life in a story,[7] Dolto contends. And it is in the opening to her childhood story, so bounteously shared, that we will begin to explore the oeuvre of a human being who summarized her work by saying, "I have come for this, to witness for (before) you the unconscious."[8] In keeping this promise, she will assuredly succeed.

## «Vineuse» and «Vava»

Precisely as Freud was writing about da Vinci in 1909, Dolto had a brush with death,[9] falling into abject suffering when her young nurse was dismissed. The memory was repressed until 1937, by which time Dolto had been in psychoanalytic sessions with René Laforgue for almost three years. She was well after the first year, she recalls, but she insisted on another two because she wished to help others without thinking of herself.[10] The question begs as to the nature or origin of the feeling that something was being withheld. Yet years into her sessions, a word arrived in repetitions of faint recollections of fragrant red hair and clinking glasses: «Vineuse.»[11] Laforgue suggested that she ask her mother if «Vineuse» meant anything. So her mother reluctantly confessed that, «la Rue Vineuse, c'est une histoire.»[12] And a story it surely was—one that will slowly decompose in the most unusual way throughout our study.

For now, our awareness begins only with «la nurse,» an Irish nanny aged about 18, from a respectable family of judges, who found Paris in the spring of 1909 too hard to resist. She took her tiny charge to parties at nearby Hôtel le Franklin on Rue Vineuse,[13] parking the baby stroller outside the door. Her mother was angry that the incident was remembered at all, adding to her resentment of psychoanalysis. But Dolto remained thankful to Freud and Laforgue for all her years, for the chance to begin again after finally reaching the sorrow that had structured her life upon a "shaky foundation."[14] For as Freud said, "it is precisely these most important of all impressions that are not remembered in later years."[15] And yet, as Freud will theorize so decisively—and Dolto will illustrate so perfectly—these impressions are not exactly forgotten either.

Provocatively, Dolto believes that because the infant has an unobscured access to the unconscious, he is potentially stronger than the adult,[16] for reality extinguishes the richness of childhood.[17] Freud anticipates the resistance that Dolto's positions will trigger: "They arise from the fact that we are here touching on the generation of anxiety and on the problem of repression."[18] Hers truly is a landscape of radical uncertainty where, as she often repeats, "we don't know what we're doing."[19] Dolto will also be indebted lifelong to her analysis for how it helped her understand the troubles of children better than if she had only been a doctor.[20] Yet her brother, Philippe, suffered because she shared his analyst. It was very maladroit of Laforgue to take them both, she states[21]—«peut-être que Philippe a été malheureux que je vienne aussi» ["perhaps Philippe was unhappy that I came too"].[22] Yet listening carefully, we cannot miss the accidental word-play on Vienna by this dedicated Freudian.[23] And what we will learn is that Dolto's life and work reveal a continuous invocation of parapraxes as inevitabilities, as the unconscious interrupts the linear "progress" of reason to deliver unexpected creativity.

Perhaps Françoise was destined to be so frank from the start, born into biography we might say, as her name, «franc sois» ["honest be"], is literally the injunction to «parler vrai,» speak truth. Indeed, the ethics of speaking and listening are at the core of her project. Sifting, we learn that her childhood nickname was «Vava» ["gogo"].[24] Known for having boundless energy, Dolto reflects late in life that maybe she can't stop herself because, once married, Vava lost her surname, «Marette» ["stops me"].[25] She is only *half* joking. For we will discover the substantial share of play in her thinking—and her openness to surprise. In any event, young Françoise put her sleeplessness to good use, having liberal access to her father's library. By the age of 16, she had already read psychoanalysis through Régis and Hesnard (published in 1914),[26] when two works by Freud were translated: *On Dreams* (from 1901, translated by Hélène Legros in 1925); and *The Interpretation of Dreams* (from 1900, translated by Ignace Meyerson in 1926).[27] Dolto may also have read Freud in German, her mother's tongue—giving her even earlier access to his works—as Mlle tutored all the Marette children in German,[28] and a letter in 1931 suggests that Françoise could further tutor Philippe in it.[29]

Françoise was educated largely at home since her mother prevented her school attendance.[30] She was needed at home to keep her mother company, following the tragic death of the only other girl among seven children, lovely Jacqueline, much preferred, who died in 1920 at age 18. This death would be the second to devastate the family, following that of a maternal uncle, Pierre (b. 1886), a soldier killed in 1916.[31] Actually, the history of this bourgeois family quickly becomes far more nuanced than their material comforts suggest, exposing young Françoise to deep struggles, as some have noted publicly: "She spent her youth in a climate of grief and guilt; a serious neurosis was the result."[32] Despite Dolto's candidness and jokes, then, we will discover that the question of death was already troubling her since the age of four: "The question ... mustn't forget ... after death."[33]

In 1924, after years of arguments, Françoise enrolled at Lycée Molière to get her «bac» in philosophy, after which she trained with the Red Cross and began studies at l'Hôpital-école des Peupliers[34] in 1929 to become a nurse.[35] Then, against her mother's adamant belief that it would make her unmarriageable, Françoise won the right to go to medical school[36]—ironically, so she could accompany Philippe.[37] Dolto half-jokes again: "I would have said that I was settling in a bordello, and it wouldn't have been worse."[38] Her mother was particularly disgusted at her plan to study psychoanalysis, insisting Freud was a "wicked man."[39] No wonder, then, that when Dolto completed her dissertation exam, on 11 July 1939, she registered as a physician only two hours later.[40] She was in a compelling hurry to work.[41] And her doctoral thesis itself is worthy of note, being the first with "psychoanalysis" in its title among French filiations[42]—and the text from which Dolto would go on to found the field of "the subjectivity of the child" in France.[43] Yet her mother put greasy laundry on her copy.[44] Such was the home environment of this early reader of psychoanalysis whom Roudinesco (fully aware of Lacan's reknown) deems to have been the "most popular person of the French psychoanalytic community."[45]

## «Un médecin d'éducation»

As a doctor, Dolto first worked under Édouard Pichon, who (with Damourette) wrote an epic study of French grammar.[46] So when Pichon joined the psychoanalytic movement, he and Laforgue steered its vocabulary.[47] Ironically,

Laforgue, the first French disciple,[48] had imperfect French.[49] As a result, psycho-analysis was, "greeted in France under the auspices of an obscure Germanic thought,[50] and tribulations multiplied. For example, Freud and Laforgue disagreed on "scotomization,"[51] and Freud disliked the «ça» for "the Id."[52]

Of course, we can never know how much of Dolto's interest in psychoanalysis was nurtured by some concordances around her year of birth, 1908, which marked the first psychoanalytic congress,[53] the first dissemination of Freud in journals[54] and the formation of both the Vienna and Berlin psychoanalytic societies.[55] By any measure, Françoise Marette was born at an auspicious time for psychoanalysis. And by the age of eight, she was already expressing a desire to be a "doctor of education." People would ask her, what is that career? And she would reply that she had no idea, but it had to exist.[56] She explains that she had begun to notice that when household staff had disagreements, the younger children would be chided, then vomit. She knew the (new) Irish nanny had been drinking and had had words with the cook, but the doctor would be called anyhow. Then Philippe or André would be put on a diet for eight days because of "indigestion"; they weren't ill, she explains, only there had been a scene between the cook and «l'Irlandaise» ["the Irish female"].[57] But in echoes, the lost «nurse Irlandaise» seems ever-present.

Lifelong, Dolto would value her years as a nurse since they allowed her to see the obverse of the medical scene[58]—a difficult world where she was, at one point in 1929, the only intern for 1200 patients.[59] Dolto grew her interest in being a pediatrician,[60] and in doing psychoanalytic consultations around surgery.[61] In a warm interview with Élisabeth Roudinesco in 1986, when Dolto is nearly 80, it is clear that she valued having had a practice that evolved out of the everyday life of a hospital.[62] For example, she felt displeased in 1946 with the first centre for psychoanalysis in Paris, at Claude-Bernard, refusing to join because some children could have used a doctor as well.[63] Yet after hearing from Jenny Aubry about the realities of being a hospital physician, Dolto says, "I fled the hierarchy."[64]

In this high regard for the ordinary work of hospitals is rooted much of Dolto's unmitigated respect for Freud. On the first page of her dissertation, she credits him with being, "a man of the laboratory" who prioritized examples,[65] and who was always willing to rework his theories.[66] And throughout her life, she considers the clinic as an opportunity to "illustrate the theory invented by Freud."[67] She attributes to Freud the genius of inspiration,[68] the heroic beginning,[69] and a fantastically supportive schema.[70] She also honors him as the first to have given the unconscious a prominent role in psychical life.[71] Repeatedly, Dolto emphasizes that Freud is her only reference, with the caveat that she has used Freud to think about the period before «l'age oedipien.»[72] And Dolto believes her purpose is to commit herself to the research Freud inaugurated—to "the truth that speaks, since Freud, through his suffering and that of others."[73]

Dolto despised polemics,[74] and she states that she was never deeply aware of the psychoanalytic controversies in England.[75] So she was happy when psychoanalytic institutions dissolved in France, believing they impeded freedom of thought.[76] She walked away from the Société de psychanalyse de Paris (SPP) in 1953[77]—though Philippe, also an analyst, stayed. And she quit the Société française de psychanalyse (SFP) in 1963,[78] impatient with its power struggles. She was also frustrated by political machinations at L'École Freudienne de Paris (EFP) prior to its closure in 1980,[79] and she was unfazed by being deemed inadmissible to the International Psychoanalytical Association (IPA) in 1953.[80] As for the actual war overtaking Europe, Dolto still met with André Berge, Juliette Favez and Marc Schlumberger every two weeks, rotating homes—defying bombings and black-outs—as the work of psychoanalysis carried on, she explains.[81] So it was that Dolto became an integral member of the second generation of analysts in France,[82] mingling with the elite of her time. Yet what would matter to Dolto lifelong was never status but solidarity with those "convinced of the dynamic of the unconscious."[83]

## Inner circle

Planted on the soil of war, the «noyau» ["kernel"] of French psychoanalysis was Marie Bonaparte, René Laforgue and Eugénie Sokolnicka[84]—the first two deep in Dolto's inner circle. Regarding the Princess, whom Freud rightly valued so highly,[85] I find the suggestion on the name impossible to refuse: «bonne à part» ["good on the side," or "good one with a share"]. Bonaparte controlled some of Dolto's cases during the training phase of her psychoanalytic practice,[86] and Dolto's correspondence includes a thank-you note from the Princess for expressions of sympathy following Freud's passing.[87] There is also an uncanny series of resonances, as the heroine of an unfinished novel by the Princess is «Vaga,»[88] who runs away to the Midi—a work paused when she decides to translate *Da Vinci* the same year, 1925.[89] Bonaparte is sympathetic towards Dolto, writing a poignant message in a gift of her published notebooks: "For Françoise Marette, psychoanalyst and woman, these echoes of the drama of a little girl."[90] For her part, Dolto is sympathetic towards Bonaparte, commenting on her difficult life with a sadistic father and grandmother.[91] Funny enough, like Dolto, Bonaparte was also familiarly known as «Mimi,»[92] and had a beloved nanny she considered «zinzin» ["dingdong"].[93] The Princess was a neighbor, at Rue Adolphe Yvon,[94] a five-minute walk away. Dolto would be invited to her home on 12 (or 13) July 1939, hours after her thesis, for she had just been accepted as a member of the SPP (the first of two required cases had been submitted earlier, in 1937–1938).[95] Attendees that day apparently also included Ernest Jones and Melanie Klein.[96]

The other member of the French kernel, René Laforgue, would not only be Dolto's analyst but Bonaparte's too; and by 1925, Laforgue is dining regularly with the Princess.[97] When Dolto defends Laforgue against charges of anti-semitism, Bonaparte supports Dolto and Laforgue unequivocally.[98] Dolto credits Laforgue for being the first to practice psychoanalysis in France, at l'Hôpital de la Pitié-Salpêtrière, in 1914;[99] and the first meeting of French analysts was at his home in 1926.[100] However, Roudinesco believes his dissidence cost Dolto support by association, as she "inherited the hostility" directed towards Laforgue.[101] For Freud apparently questioned the poor reception given to Sokolnicka, his representative in France (for a time) and Laforgue's analyst.[102]

Dolto sought Laforgue on the advice of her friend, Marc Schlumberger.[103] Her analysis began on 17 February 1934 and ended in March 1937.[104] Dolto appreciated that he valued intuition,[105] did not try to normalize her,[106] and allowed silent sessions—including her first three, when she only cried.[107] In turn, Laforgue felt her gift for analysis, lowering his rate[108] and obtaining a bursary for her from Bonaparte.[109] Dolto even vacationed in the Midi with Laforgue and his other analysands,[110] the «Club des piqués» ["Club of the Stung"].[111] So it came to be that the Marettes were among the first families in France touched by the potential for a revolt of one's narrative that is so inherent in psychoanalysis; her mother hoped (after six months) that she would stop,[112] and her father disliked her new personality.[113]

Of her generation, Dolto's record with Lacan is the richest. Yet Dolto unabashedly admits that she barely read Lacan,[114] and never adhered to his theories.[115] Further, she points out that she was formed long before Lacan came onto the scene.[116] Aubry agrees: "Françoise does not need *mathèmes* to hear the unconscious of the child."[117] Still, they shared warm conversations and correspondence for decades, and Aubry comments on his fascination for Dolto: "Lacan drank her words."[118] So we will have many opportunities to encounter Lacan.

We also owe a special regard to Sophie Morgenstern, who arrives in Dolto's texts on the nebulous edge of repression—"But I'm forgetting to say my principal teacher ... It's Madame Morgenstern."[119] A survey of Morgenstern's oeuvre does reveal her significant contributions to Dolto's. Morgenstern began her practice in 1924, when she arrived in France,[120] and she volunteered with Georges Heuyer for more than a decade.[121] She was the first in France to employ psychoanalysis with children,[122] and she recommended Dolto to Pichon.[123] She was analyzed by Sokolnicka,[124] but Dolto (at nearly 80) would recall—in a touching slip?—that Morgenstern said she was analyzed by Freud.[125] Morgenstern's was a radical practice centred entirely on listening, a witnessing "without any ethic of normalisation,"[126] Dolto notes, by which children reentered communication with other children and with themselves: "demutization by graphic expression."[127] It was very precious, an example in the medical tradition, Dolto says.[128] Morgenstern's suicide in 1940 clearly wounded Dolto, as the reference to trying to help, and being unable to, comes up often: "I had gone to see her to bring her with me out of Paris in June 1940 ... but she did not want to come."[129] It was Morgenstern who taught Dolto to help children to talk with trust, she says.[130] And with Morgenstern's guidance, Dolto listened to babies on hospital night shifts, returning regularly,[131] producing one of the most powerful observations of her corpus: "The child waits for you ... even if you never speak to him."[132] Dolto adds that Morgenstern was a "soft and generous woman,"[133] with a "silent, warm, human attitude."[134]

## Hospitalism

Dolto's connections beyond this point are dizzying, being a veritable "who's who" of psychoanalysis in France. Yet, boldly independent, she would eschew referencing these same peers. Still, a study of Dolto would not be complete without an acknowledgment of at least some of the famous names circulating in her corpus. And in the absence of any other organizing principle for this array, I offer an alphabetical arrangement from Aubry to Winnicott.

We first meet Jenny Aubry (É. Roudinesco's mother), a neuropsychiatrist who embraces psychoanalysis in 1948.[135] Dolto admired Aubry for bringing analysts into the hospital for consultations,[136] and for diagnosing "hospitalism" as being provoked by psychical trouble.[137] Hospitalism, Dolto explains, happened when Public Assistance removed children from their parents, in aggravated separations that, "if it did not kill them, made them autists."[138] These children, Aubry found, were prone to vomiting and green diarrhea whenever their hospital caregivers argued with one another—what Dolto explains as the consequence of the auditory trial they had heard.[139] Dolto reports that Aubry told the nurses, "go ahead and argue, but know that the children are with you."[140] The record is abundant with the mutual respect between these two women, both medical pioneers, whose lifespans overlap.[141]

Alice Balint's sister paints a portrait of Dolto.[142] Raymond de Saussure (son of Ferdinand, and Freud's analysand),[143] congratulates her on her thesis,[144] marriage and work;[145] he also solicits her help finding employment for two colleagues.[146] Dolto is recorded visiting Julia Favez-Boutonnier's vacation home in 1961.[147] She credits Sándor Ferenczi with teaching her much, the most after Winnicott,[148] for he was "an open man, not too stuck on theory";[149] like Dolto, Ferenczi believed in learning from patients, including children.[150] Ángel Garma and Heinz Hartmann provided supervision (control) for her analytic training.[151] Georges Heuyer reportedly gave her a tough time at her dissertation exam, since he thought IQ could not be improved with analysis while she argued the opposite;[152] with Heuyer, she says she learned what not to do, for he was a harsh man who wrote insults in children's files and sent the ill to detention centres.[153]

There are wedding greetings from Daniel Lagache,[154] whom she could not differentiate from Lacan for years because they were inseparable, like "siamese twins"[155]—or "two zombies."[156] In regards to Serge Lebovici, the comments are unusually negative for Dolto, who seems to find something good to say about most people; she apparently often commented that Lebovici was her enemy at the SPP,[157] and she remarks that he and Diatkine made her, "the object of continual aggressions."[158] "I didn't care ... I kept going along on my way," she explains— adding that while she never wanted to live with five brothers either, it helped her deal with the SPP.[159] From John Leuba, then the SPP's secretary, there are congratulations to "my little Mimi" (in 1938), recognizing her membership[160] (his name for Dolto recalling the Princess). And Rudolph Loewenstein names his daughter Marie-Françoise in her honor;[161] along with René Spitz (below), he had taken over the supervision of her early cases from Garma and Hartmann.[162] There is a pleasant dinner invitation in 1960 from Maurice Merleau-Ponty.[163] While in regards to Sacha Nacht, there is (again) Dolto's rare dislike, as she calls him «un lourd» [idiomatic: someone unbearable].[164]

In correspondence in 1961, Jean-Bertrand Pontalis requests articles for publications[165] and his letter to her in 1978 fondly recalls how she let him walk with her to Trousseau years before.[166] There are many letters back and forth with Élisabeth Roudinesco, in thanks for gifts of their respective books,[167] and a note of sympathy when Aubry died;[168] we will also learn that Dolto was Élisabeth's childhood analyst.[169] René Spitz is supportive throughout her career, advising her on her doctorate;[170] even after emigrating to the United States, he writes regularly and sends her "delicious" American baby food for her children.[171] And only months before Dolto's death, Spitz's daughter is still corresponding with her.[172]

As for Donald Winnicott, she says, oddly enough, "this is work as I would work if I were a man."[173] But Dolto bemoans the bandwagon of "doing the squiggle," and how the transitional object is a family obsession.[174] And in a comment fully intended as a compliment, she adds, "Winnicott is not theory."[175] Winnicott once reflected, "I shall not first give a historical survey and show the development of my ideas from the theories of others, because my mind does not work that way."[176] Dolto's mind did not work that way either. Yet the Winnicott reader new to Dolto is likely to experience an uncomfortable familiarity that might be called, "the problem of the English Channel." For it is as if that body of water perfectly represents the problem of translation in Dolto's project.[177]

## Charcot and Co.

We need to stop and double back, though, for we have forgotten four without whom Dolto's story cannot be told. The first is Jean-Martin Charcot, whose work was so instrumental to psychoanalysis. All who care about mental health can only be thankful for the revolution he inaugurated, beginning with his humane observations that the removal of organs was not helpful,[178] repetition is a symptom,[179] and family environments are decisive in hysteria.[180] Charcot's death in 1936 appears in correspondence from Dolto's mother.[181] But true to her lifelong rejection of mimetism, Dolto has little use for national illusions. Some female hysterics put it on for Charcot, Dolto explains, because they loved him, but Freud noticed and called him out on it.[182]

A short way from here, we come upon the second, Pierre Janet—Charcot's student—who pays homage to his master for teaching the study of hysteria «en savant» ["intelligently"].[183] But unlike Charcot, who is as charismatic in writing as he apparently was in person, Janet is a hard read—his sentences constrained by his belief that the human spirit does not accept contradiction.[184] So I leave him to Roudinesco, who pens him as the "philosopher of a shredded kingdom, aggressive, arrogant."[185]

From this point, our path around Charcot diverges. One branch follows Janet towards the third, Édouard Pichon, his son-in-law.[186] As Dolto's dissertation supervisor, he congratulates her,[187] and she reports favorably about his being her teacher,[188] visiting him at Fontainebleau,[189] and the chance to work at l'Hôpital Bretonneau from 1936 (or 1937).[190] But a dark undertone seeps through, beginning with the revelation, in a footnote, that Dolto had not sent him a copy of her thesis, in which his preface is absent.[191] True, too, Pichon clashed with Laforgue and Bonaparte, especially regarding the fledgling *Revue française de psychanalyse*.[192] Then when Pichon died in 1940, Dolto relocated to Trousseau,[193] as if his death allowed her escape. Roudinesco does not mince words, calling Pichon "Jekyll and Hyde."[194] And on his acute paralysis from rheumatism and delusions, Roudinesco diagnoses the "evolution of incurability."[195] Sifting, I discover that Pichon once dedicated an article, "Death, anxiety and negation" to Dolto.[196] And I muse that his name for her, «la petite Marette»[197] [homonymically: "the little one stops me"], manifests in his symptoms, as a contagion on suggestion returns us to Charcot's hysterics. But in her early (contentious?) relation with Pichon, Dolto's project seems destined to embrace and disrupt received language.

Here, a final branch follows the fourth, Angélo Hesnard, self-appointed interpreter of Freud who, as Roudinesco states, knew Janet's hypotheses did not concord with Freud's but tried to link them anyhow.[198] Hesnard's texts are a passive-aggressive monument to Freud right from the dedication, as he vows, "with his unjust criticisms to offer homage in pure admiration."[199] Two decades later, his mood has calcified, as he calls the unconscious a "postulate,"[200] and he attributes to Freud a "cold and superhuman lucidity."[201] Hesnard's sword strikes even Janet, "student of our great Charcot"[202]—and by implication, Charcot too—for adhering to Freud's project, which he calls a "monotony of rules and hypotheses."[203] So I gladly abandon Hesnard's reality for a dream.

## Unconscious energy

Freud opened his practice in Vienna in 1886, about a year after a trip to Paris to study with Charcot,[204] financed by a grant he dreamed about.[205] He wrote to his fiancé, Martha, on 19 October 1885, that his dream came true on his first visit to the Salpêtrière.[206] From this first dream inaugurating psychoanalysis on French grounds, Freud "devoted the first half of his life's work to clinical phenomena that come into evidence more or less against the will of the ego."[207] Freud's interest in the unconscious[208] is first mentioned in an unpublished draft in 1892.[209] And Freud's oeuvre on dreams (in 1900) reveals that the unconscious is responsible for "primary processes [that] are present in the mental apparatus from the first,"[210] as the "true psychical reality,"[211] which is continuously active, day or night.[212] Thereby, "what is suppressed continues to exist … and remains capable of psychical functioning."[213] The nature of that functioning is described as an "amount of psychic energy"[214] displaceable in, "releases of pleasure and unpleasure [that] automatically regulate the course of cathectic processes."[215]

As early as 1895, Freud observed that the "affective process approximates to the uninhibited primary process,"[216] so "where there is affect there is a primary process,"[217] and we can speak of a "quanta" of affect.[218] In 1962, the archive of Freud's thought from 1893–1899 would finally be published, in which he declares his debts to Charcot, whom he is translating, and to the Salpêtrière.[219] In that text, Freud introduces the notion of "deferred action":[220] unconscious repetitions in, of, as reality. This notion of «après-coup,» as it is more commonly known, disturbs the meaning of the present and dislocates rationality from its hierarchy as, "our ordinary thought, unconscious, with occasional intrusions into consciousness."[221]

And it is here, deep in Freud's drive theory—libido theory[222]—that we will root Dolto's project, as she explains how, "Freud described the libidinal evolution of the human being whose pulses of desire, active and passive, are organized during infancy in an unconscious structure."[223] Dolto refers to libido as unconscious "modifying energy,"[224] and to Freud's as a "theory of the unconscious dynamic of desire."[225] Her use of «désir» should be read as synonymous with "libido," consistent with her close reading of Freud. She elucidates:

> If needs must be satisfied in reality by consumption, there is something other in the human being, which Freud named libido, and that is desire. Desire which, at its origin, is always unconscious…and demands, too, the appeasement of its tension in an accomplishment, in a consumption for the sake of pleasure.[226]

The unconscious introduces enigma into our thoughts, Freud explains, because in "unconscious mental activity, processes operate that are of quite another kind from those perceived in consciousness,"[227] being "more comprehensive and more important than the familiar activity that is linked with consciousness."[228] And we will learn about the characteristics of these unconscious processes from studying dreams, the foundation of psychoanalysis.[229] Dream-work, as Freud shows, enables us to witness psychical processes of a "more primary nature,"[230] that make use of symbolism,[231] and, especially, of condensation and displacement.[232] Through a meticulous study of countless examples of dream-work, Freud discovers that "all dreams have meaning,"[233] precisely because "dream language … forms part of a highly archaic system of expression."[234] It is into this realm of archaic symbolization that Dolto will journey.

Dolto is entirely up to the task of engaging Freud's project at its most complex, and of using difficulty as an opportunity. She believes, for example, that while it is a problem to deny reality, it is a problem to be too much in reality,[235] for "reality and phantasy are a contract we all need to assume."[236] She stresses repeatedly that we cannot understand the "unconscious component,"[237] because while everything comes from the «ça,»[238] the «ça» never obeys reason.[239] Then again, Dolto says, that is what is so interesting about the human, that he is never definitive.[240] Dolto welcomes the enigmatic, observing that, "the unconscious never stops teaching us there where it most surprises us."[241] Further, since the unconscious is constituted of questions and answers[242]—as Dolto elaborates—the best interpretations are not statements but questions,[243] or help clarifying the questions the unconscious asks.[244] Here is work on the terms of the primary processes, wherein we will need to «travailler sans raisonner» ["work without reasoning"],[245] as Freud advised (in French), so as to encounter the transference.

The transference first enters Freud's texts in 1888—in French—as «transfert.»[246] Freud develops the notion through the next decade,[247] leading to his treatise on dreams, wherein the transference is a displacement of an infantile scene onto the present.[248] There is also the transference of dream thoughts to dream content,[249] that makes it both the centre and obstacle of clinical practice. In fact, the transference in dreams and in analytic cures, as we learn with Freud, is indistinguishable,[250] for both are means of displacement in the service of the primary processes that are susceptible to being witnessed in analysis[251]—to becoming perceivable as experience.

## «Résonateur»

The displacement of unconscious energy in dreams and in the transference is evidence, Freud says, that "stress is laid upon making the cathecting energy mobile and capable of discharge,"[252] so there is a "need of transference on the part of repressed ideas."[253] In meeting this need, the transference privileges the auditory,[254] so the analyst becomes, as Dolto says, a «résonateur.»[255] By enabling the discharge of a quanta of unconscious energy, the transference offers relief: "There are always phantasms, even when there is neither facial nor gestural expression … It is these phantasms, expressed or not, accompanying the transferential relation, that heal the sick."[256]

Yet typical of Dolto's corpus—where margins and subtexts are often the most revealing—this substantial contribution to theory is buried in a letter to Diatkine, in the footnotes of a third party referencing an unpublished text in her archives. Our path of learning is as perplexing as its content. In any event, right from the beginning, Dolto recognizes the transference as the means of hearing the unspeakable, explaining in her dissertation that the transference reveals «réactions affectives,» and that healing requires the intermediary of the transference[257] for «libération libidinale.»[258] And right to the end, in a letter marked "confidential" written only months before her death, Dolto explains that the transference enables the liberation of repressed libido by the reliving of an event in the history of a subject, and of "sterilizing repetitions of archaic processes,"[259] maladapted at the time and never spoken, that left "traces of trauma."[260]

Freud creates a dynamic opening for the transference as, "the personal influence of the physician in a haphazard fashion that has not yet been explained."[261] Dolto is equally content with not knowing, believing theory is only useful in helping you explain the transference to yourself, as all kinds of things happen in the transference that actually cure,[262] though we do not know what, exactly.[263] Ironically, the transference "creates and abreacts troubles,"[264] Dolto says, as evidence of the ontological priority of serving the vital requirement of displacing cathexis.[265]

Dolto credits Freud with discovering the transference, and she too believes it to be perpetually present in human relations,[266] adding that it offers a source of pleasure in its symbolic function of securing affect and remembrance.[267] And she takes on skeptics preemptively: "Do not think transference acts by suggestion," she states in 1940, with the remarkable force of authority, as "suggestion necessitates bringing something new" to the subject,[268] but the analyst usually brings "absolutely nothing new."[269] Rather, it is the old that returns in the transference, a reexperiencing of something missed of the past,[270] a transference of archaic relations.[271] And as the transference brings much-needed liberation, we remain unconsciously in a state of "alerted narcissism,"[272] destined to seek to engage the "operational fact of the transference"[273] as an unconscious dialectic,[274] an emotional resonance,[275] an infraverbal expression[276]—i.e., primitive human exchanges[277] that are "archaic witnesses of a system of affective relays"[278] animating unconscious associations.

Dolto's acceptance of anomaly, her humility before the transference and her conviction of the correctness of Freud's drive theory would define her practice. On this view, the "symptom is a condensation"[279]—a proof, or witness, holding unconscious memory,[280] by which the body, in health or in sickness, *is* language.[281] So when troubles are spoken, it liberates the symptom, returning the "peace of the body."[282] Like Freud,[283] Dolto believes treatment begins with repetitions,[284] as alienation is "overdetermined."[285] Unlike psychotherapy, she adds, psychoanalysis never aims to fix a symptom.[286] Rather, the analyst should feel sympathy[287] and be open to whatever phantasms arrive.[288] Even a baby is sensitive to such consideration, she adds,[289] asking, "What if we took seriously the suffering of the child?"[290]—instead of deriding libidinal suffering.[291] For Dolto, it is the belittling (dismissing, muting) of suffering, not its mere presence, that causes psychical disorganization. And right from her first publication, a natural grasp of Freudian theory would already be hers (what detractors call her "intuition"). We are dealing with an "affective economy,"[292] she says, and we need to seek the "economic reason for non-insertion."[293] From the start, then, Dolto is passionately engaging the emotional world.

## «Phonème»

By our travels with Dolto, we will arrive at a deep pool entirely without landmarks: Dolto's original psychoanalytic conceptualization of the «phonème,»[294] and the phantastic affective history of words it entails. The playful bilingual reader may hear a conveyance on the word itself—«faux» ["false"] name, and «faut n'aime» ["must not love"?]—as if it were a warning about reality itself. Dolto will show that the phoneme is the first mediating object between phantasy and reality, returning us to word-things in Freud's German—*wortgebilden*: words that build, form, infuse and structure. Words are offers of phantasy for our earliest audition, but we repress the legacy of this dreamscape, as if reality itself were a troubling journey from synesthesia to amnesia. Yet Dolto will bring us right back to the word-thing that is the blur of the autobiographic at the heart of analysis, beginning with Freud's book on dreams. For she will provide countless examples where words have marked a subject like "magnetic bands" with his first, unconscious significations of "narcissising joy" or "de-narcissizing anxiety."[295]

On 29 July 1987, about one year before her death, Dolto stated that, with *Tout est langage* ["All is language"], she had finished writing.[296] And in that book, she is asked: "So one word spoken in childhood can decide a whole life?" «Oui,» she responds, and silence hangs.[297] Yet this astonishing statement perfectly captures her thinking on the infant—and the phoneme. Paradoxically, what is at stake is not only what is said, but also what is not said. For in the auditory climate of primary narcissism, "what is not named is nothing."[298] In this way, Dolto explains, we are all born into "the language of our parents, a language sworn to silence,"[299] inheritors of suffering that "did not give its name."[300] Here is the word in tandem with its reversal, as two of Dolto's theories coalesce ironically: the «non-dit,» i.e., what marks because it *is not* said; and the homonymic «nom dit,» the "given name," i.e., what marks because it *is* said. Contradiction is thus installed right at a letter whose difference cannot even be heard. So words are "heavy with phantasms for intelligent children,"[301] and children experience language "in metaphoric, metonymic ways"[302]—playing with words, living words, and rooting truth in them.[303] The resulting "suggestibility of a child"[304] has staggering implications. For from the first moments of audition, Dolto declares, "we bequeath in legacy, as a debt or an inheritance, in the unconscious of our children."[305] Here again is the idea of an inherited education, and of an unconscious trace that always exceeds the subject.

A decade before publishing his dream book, Freud wrote about how a "sound image was not perceived as a sequence of letters ... [that] the word sound was a whole,"[306] and "word-associations [were] evoked by the spoken sounds."[307] We also recall how, with Freud, words are subject to condensation and displacement,[308] and the "invariable rule that the words spoken in the dream are derived from spoken words."[309] Here is a delicate tension in theory, then, where words are remainders of the day for dream-work; these then return, archaically reinvested, to our encounters with reality, "reviving once more the sensations to which the verbal expression owes its justification."[310] I posit that this tension is exactly how Dolto's project on the early human begins a remarkable reciprocity with Freud's earliest work, whereby she is supported by him and also provides evidence for him. The investment of words with unconscious affect begins precisely because of the, "credulity such as the subject has in relation to his hypnotist [as] is shown only by a child towards his parents," as Freud explained it, and this leads to "mental-physical behaviour corresponding to the idea's content."[311]

There will be a moving example from a friend who is dying, who dreams of "meaningless" syllables that filled her with a sense of being loved. Recalling that her friend lived in India from one to nine months of age (having had a local girl as a nanny), Dolto advised her to consult a translator. As it turned out, the words were from an Indian lullaby whose lyrics were along the lines of, "My dear love, whose eyes are more beautiful than the stars."[312] The phonemes said "nothing to her when she was awake," Dolto points out, but in her sleep, they gave her unspoken narcissistic joy.[313]

Freud theorized that, "intermediate ideas are looked for between two psychical dream-stimuli,"[314] to "transfer energy" by establishing connections.[315] Freud says this happens "with remarkable frequency ... in speech,"[316] because the word has "predestined ambiguity."[317] And central to Freudian theory is the notion that language is a privileged setting for transference.[318] Or, as Dolto puts it, the word is the best transitional object for the transference.[319] What is a word, then? A word is a signpost to unchartable regions of psychical life—and right off the sonar of linguistics.

## «Repères»

As Dolto explains it in her very first publication as a psychoanalyst, when pulses, upon their appearance, find an interdiction exterior to the subject, "*the idea is repressed but the affective charge remains and provokes anxiety ... which we call 'primary.'*"[320] Secondary anxiety, in turn, occurs when pulses "*enter into resonance ...* [by] an unconscious association being established between 'actual' ideas and ideas that had, in the first experiences of childhood ... provoked repression followed by primary anxiety."[321]

Thus, as she sees it, Freud opens a dialectic of the «don» ["bequest"][322] that returns liberty to humans deprived of it.[323] And reliving the enclave changes you.[324] She sums up her belief:

> This faith of mine is that everyone has chosen to be born and that if he survives, then that is already something. So is something unhealthy already, or is there something still healthy and he has a right to the auto-defense of his libido? «Ça» ["That"; "the Id"] is what I look for. And if he has the right to the auto-defense of his libido, and he suffers from not refinding this auto-defense of his libido, I try to help him to express his anxiety [anguish], because then he can refind his primary narcissism with a body that can experience joy sufficiently for life to be sufficiently good, and he can be happy—well, he can be sufficiently happy to continue to support the ordeal of living.[325]

So Dolto spontaneously lets theory spring from the clinic,[326] while she admits trouble in formulating her work.[327] She believes theory is moot without examples,[328] and that her work is more of a witnessing put into words,[329] a conversation rather than a schema:[330] «Je peux bafouiller des choses qui, pour moi, sont des repères» ["I can stammer some things that, for me, are landmarks"].[331] Yet we should pause to hear the spectacular homonymic echoes of «repères» [at once, "re-father/lose again/pair again/another peer/repair"]. Dolto tells us theory is not something to dwell on though,[332] so we follow her out from this place for now—from this enigmatic «repère»—but we will return. For the time being, we just accept the invitation to hear suggestions on (in, from) this word-thing.

We will also want to remember as we travel, exploring all that is accidental yet compelling about the movement of the transference in Dolto's texts, that the unconscious "affective roots of language"[333] are entirely idiosyncratic for individual human capital.[334] Freud notes how, "a combination of individual factors, physiological and accidental … determines how a person shall behave in particular cases of comparatively intense objective stimulation during sleep … to suppress … [or] overcome the stimulus by weaving it into a dream."[335] As Dolto explains it, then, the child engages, "continuous unconscious rapports to a past from which he cannot be disjoint to assure his future."[336] So it is not merely that the transference endures, but rather, that we endure because of the transference—as a resourcing by (in) unconscious primary processes.

In a television interview she granted Bernard Pivot in the last year of her life, Dolto is asked to imagine what story the walls in her office would tell. She replies, after a pause:

> It would recount the words, but it would not say what had passed that was intense, lived by the person who spoke, behind the words that served as mediators between the unconscious of the patient and the unconscious of the psychoanalyst, and that, because of this mediation, allowed affects to be relived and definitively enter a past that no longer draws interest.[337]

Thus, where the unconscious is concerned, she says, we are only witnesses—and this idea will infuse Dolto's entire project.[338]

On the one hand, being a witness seems uncomplicated: listening and giving trust is a lot, she says, and you need to say «courage,»[339] to try even when all seems impossible.[340] But beneath the surface, Dolto's notion of the witness is fathomless, tethered to her belief that the analysand has a lucidity that just needs to be awakened,[341] and witnessing "ennobles his existence that resisted difficulties."[342] It is as if the witness honours what survives, and so doing, reawakens a dormant capacity for self-defense originating in what is perennially well, the unconscious—the individual human resource conserving life. Dolto elaborates:

> I don't think madness is structural. I think it is a disorder due to the hopelessness of not having a «semblable» ["similar"] that deems you lovable and who «se reconnaît» ["recognizes himself," "is reborn"] in you. I think it is due to «ça» ["that," "the Id"]. I think that from the moment when we

speak about how we feel to a psychotic, he is already much less so and he can enter the process of accepting the difference between the imaginary and reality, which is merely an imaginary common to all the others.[343]

## Organizing silence

From 1940 onwards, right from her dissertation, Dolto would steer the future of psychoanalysis in France. And in the only direct quote from Freud in that inaugural work, her focus on the drives could not be more evident:

> Impulses that strive for pleasure are not all taken up into the final organization of the sexual function. A number of them are set aside as unserviceable, by repression or some other means; a few of them are diverted from their aim in the remarkable manner I have mentioned and used to strengthen other impulses; yet others persist in minor roles, and serve for the performance of introductory acts, for the production of fore-pleasure.[344]

Yet the acknowledgment due to Dolto remains unspoken as contemporary historians explain that the, "classical study of the relationship between the thing-presentation and word-presentation in Freudian meta-psychology continues to underpin the thinking of French psychoanalysis,"[345] rooted in "very early Freud,"[346] that "does not stray far from the focus on the drives."[347]

From this foundation, Dolto's corpus will offer an astounding demonstration of the play at the origin of thought, as digressions will take us, lost stories insist, sentences continue elsewhere and theory is inferable. Not only will unexpected material arrive, but unexpected processes too—dream-work and passive pulses—as "unconscious material … brings its own modes of working along with it,"[348] Freud explains. Therefore, as Freud states, "unconscious ideation"[349] or "unconscious thinking … is also active in the day,"[350] making each of us a "dreamer in daylight."[351] And any writing in the psychobiographical genre—as this project attempts—should value what Dolto calls, the "unconscious ruptures in spoken language and contradictions,"[352] because as she notes, contradiction [is] inherent in the human.[353]

Reading Dolto through Freud—because she did—will make experienceable the work of the primary processes. For Dolto's corpus will slowly reveal an intimate weave of what is remembered and forgotten, as an unconscious resonance testifies to a register, beneath and between words—latent speech, just as she predicts. Dolto believes that suffering inheres in the human condition,[354] and if we cannot yet sense that the transference offers securitization, we soon will. For Dolto will elaborate the transference as an "organizing silence"[355]—a potential for interhuman exchanges upon which our wish to live depends. She asks, "Who dreams? Is it 'me'? Is it 'I'? We are dealing with 'an unknown that remains unknown.'"[356] And of the transference, "Who, then, speaks to whom, and to what, from/about whom?"[357]

Privileging the story of another child in closing this chapter, we meet Marcel, a ten-year-old at l'Hôpital Bretonneau, brought for school delays and balding in 1938.[358] Dolto notices that she needs to wait 20–30 seconds for his answers, so "I take his rhythm," she says. And taking her dissertation to press after a year, she comments that Marcel is on the road to a recovery he may never reach. But at least he no longer thinks that work is «pas la *peine*» ["not worth it;" also "no(t) *suffering/pain*"].[359] In her italicizing is a hint of the word-play that would inform her life's work. In later editions,[360] we will also learn that Marcel visited Dolto in 1967, while he was passing through France, to introduce his ten-year-old son to her[361]—a concordance of age. Marcel is the only initial case we can be sure she saw again,[362] and his story lingers. Because walking with Dolto, we begin to feel that we are in the company of someone with exceptional knowledge, but we can never be sure how she came upon it—and we will need to take her rhythm.

With Dolto, it becomes patent that language exceeds our intention, as the unconscious infuses unpredictability into our narratives. For Dolto reveals how experience forms in curious stratifications—like dreams layered upon each other,[363] as Freud once suggested—compelling a reality that is never unitary. Dolto's unusual corpus also begs the question that a colleague of Freud's once suggested as the apt problematic for any psychobiographical study: "Why does a man solve precisely this problem and in precisely this way?"[364] And in the organizing silence wherein we will try to listen for answers, Dolto will tell not only the story of one woman, but the story of man: every autobiography begins in an idiosyncratic, unconscious, auditory prehistory as an indelible self-other with a witness—as the subject of a *biography*.

## Notes

1  CE, 369.
2  CE, 350; JD, 273; PJE, 71; SP1, 76.
3  CE, 43; NE, 208.
4  SF, 342 & 345.
5  DW, 22; EN, 90, 120 & 124; Nobécourt, 2008a; Ribowski, 1987/2004.
6  SP3, 9 (emphasis hers).
7  PJE, 23; SP3, 19.
8  CE, 328.
9  EN, 62.
10  ATP, 119–122; DW, 162–163; EN, 96.
11  AI, 144; Nobécourt, 2008a.
12  Nobécourt, 2008a.
13  A hotel/restaurant with this name still exists at this location.
14  PF, 105.
15  Freud, 1913, 183.
16  EM, 221.
17  EM, 223.
18  Freud, 1900a, 237.
19  E.g., CE, 329.
20  Nadal, 2006, 39f.
21  EN, 95; Roudinesco, 1982, 355.

22  ATP, 121 (emphasis mine).
23  In French, Vienna is Vienne.
24  E.g., AI, 74; EN, 24; MF, 19–20; VC1, 34–35, 160–161 & 327.
25  VC2, 453.
26  AI, 116; ATP, 104.
27  Douville, 2009, 117 & 123.
28  ATP, 88.
29  VC1, 331.
30  AI, 132; D&R, 16; EN, 92.
31  A minor error giving his year of birth as 1846 in VC1 (frontispiece) is corrected in VC2 (frontispiece). I feel comforted (but not absolved) by such typographical inevitabilities.
32  *Psychoanalytikerinnen*, 2013.
33  EN, 12.
34  Photo: VC1, 241.
35  AI, 28–29; EN, 82; VC1, 231.
36  AI, 118–119; EN, 77.
37  AI, 122.
38  DW, 157; Nobécourt, 2008a.
39  AI, 125; EN, 99.
40  The year of her dissertation was 1939, though it was published in 1940.
41  AI, 35; VC2, 16f.
42  Birksted-Breen, Flanders & Gibeault, 2010, xixi.
43  Birksted-Breen, Flanders & Gibeault, 2010, 24f.
44  AI, 125; EN, 99.
45  Roudinesco, 1986, 169.
46  Leroy & Muni Toke, 2007; also Roudinesco, 1982.
47  Roudinesco, 1982, 315 & 386.
48  Roudinesco, 1982, 290.
49  Roudinesco, 1982, 291.
50  Roudinesco, 1982, 397.
51  Roudinesco, 1982, 315 & 391–392.
52  Roudinesco, 1982, 376–385.
53  Gay, 1988, 184.
54  Gay, 1988, 157.
55  Gay, 1988, 174 & 181.
56  AI, 112; Dolto, 1985a, 231–232; D&R, 17; EN, 68–69.
57  AI, 112.
58  Nobécourt, 2008a.
59  ATP, 127.
60  EN, 84.
61  EN, 97–98.
62  D&R, 14–15.
63  D&R, 30.
64  D&R, 30.
65  MA, 1.
66  VC2, 672.
67  D&R, 33.
68  JD, 67.
69  DW, 22.
70  TL, 36.
71  MA, 14.
72  AI, 217; D&R, 32; DW, 27, 31–32 & 39; Nobécourt, 2008b; VC2, 796–797.
73  VC2, 655.

74  ATP, 19; LF, 300; VC2, 225 & 333.
75  VC2, 31.
76  ATP, 133; VC2, 24.
77  D&R, 23; VC2, 231–233.
78  Roudinesco, 1986, 365–367.
79  VC2, 669–672.
80  Roudinesco, 1986, 329, 356, 365 & 657; Turkle, 1995/1997.
81  AI, 169.
82  Birksted-Breen, Flanders & Gibeault, 2010, xx.
83  AI, 218; VC2, 796–797.
84  Douville, 2009, 116.
85  Bertin, 1982, 300; E. Freud, 1970, 158; Gay, 1988, 586.
86  Nasio, 1987/1998, 36.
87  VC2, 22.
88  Bourgeron, 1993.
89  Bertin, 1982, 295.
90  AI, 125.
91  SF, 313.
92  Bertin, 1982, 53.
93  Bertin, 1982, 189.
94  Douville, 2009, 177.
95  LF, 292–293.
96  LF, 292–293.
97  Bertin, 1982, 277; Bourgeron, 1993, 12.
98  Roudinesco, 1986, 175.
99  D&R, 17.
100 Postel, n.d.; also Bourgeron, 1993, 13.
101 Roudinesco, 1999, 186.
102 Bertin, 1982, 264; Douville, 2009, 109; Roudinesco, 1982, 288 & 294.
103 EN, 92; Roudinesco, 1986, 169; VC1, 349f.
104 VC1, 402; VC2, 13f.
105 SP3, 8; Laforgue, 1932/1963, 106.
106 EN, 119; PF, 70.
107 ATP, 118; EN, 104.
108 ATP, 118; EN, 104.
109 François, 1999a, 27.
110 MF, 95; PF, 61.
111 VC2, 526–527. In another context, Lou Andreas-Salomé incidentally offers a possible interpretation for the name of Laforgue's analysands, in her sharing of a proverb I either never knew or forgot: «Ce n'est pas le plus mauvais fruit que la guêpe choisit de piquer» ["It is not the worst fruit that the wasp chooses to sting"] (Pfeiffer, 1983, 168).
112 MF, 81.
113 VC1, 532.
114 D&R, 23–25.
115 Geissmann & Geissmann, 1998, 293.
116 DW, 65.
117 Aubry & Cifali, 1986/1988, 48.
118 Aubry & Cifali, 1986/1988, 45.
119 DW, 23; Nobécourt, 2008b.
120 Sédat, 2003, 9.
121 AI, 217; Geissmann & Geissmann, 1998, 149; VC2, 797.
122 Douville, 2009, 129; DW, 23; Nobécourt, 2008b; VC2, 797.
123 Nasio, 1987/1998, 37; VC2, 786.

124  Roudinesco, 1982, 344.
125  Geissmann & Geissmann, 1998, 140; Nasio, 1987/1998, 30; VC2, 786.
126  AI, 217; VC2, 797.
127  AI, 217; VC2, 797.
128  AI, 217; VC2, 797.
129  VC2, 786; also Geissmann & Geissmann, 1998, 150; Nasio, 1987/1998, 28.
130  D&R, 12; Sédat, 2003, 12.
131  D&R, 11.
132  DW, 24; Nobécourt, 2008b.
133  D&R, 18; VC2, 786.
134  Nasio, 1987/1998, 30.
135  Roudinesco, 1986, 222.
136  D&R, 27 & 29; VO, 233.
137  VO, 233–234.
138  VO, 233–234.
139  VO, 233–234.
140  VO, 233–234.
141  Roudinesco, 1982, 418.
142  VC2, 511f.
143  Birksted-Breen, Flanders & Gibeault, 2010, xx.
144  VC2, 17.
145  VC2, 153.
146  VC2, 153 & 369.
147  MF, 138.
148  DW, 23.
149  SF, 309.
150  Ferenczi, 1931/1980, 14–15 & 21.
151  EN, 104.
152  D&R, 19.
153  ATP, 123.
154  VC2, 93.
155  D&R, 19–20.
156  LF, 292.
157  VC2, 668n.
158  LF, 300.
159  LF, 300–301.
160  AI, 36.
161  VC2, 25.
162  EN, 104; Nasio, 1987/1998, 36.
163  VC2, 313.
164  LF, 294.
165  VC2, 351 & 622.
166  VC2, 622.
167  VC2, 585, 737, 818, 837 & 886.
168  VC2, 839.
169  *Psychoanalytikerinnen*, 2013.
170  VC2, 511–513.
171  LF, 293.
172  LF, 294.
173  DW, 27.
174  DW, 27 & 30.
175  DW, 27.
176  Winnicott, 1945, 137.

177 Nowhere is this familiarity more noticeable than in relation to Winnicott's "going on becoming" ("going on being") (1956/1992, 188 & 303). In 1957, Dolto refers to «continuité» (SS, 277, 285 & 288) and «allant-devenant continue» ["continuous going-becoming"] (SS, 267 & 286; also APP, 28 & SS, 291); to «continuation de l'intégrité biologique» (SS, 260); and to "continuity," as «sécurité d'exister» (SS, 265). Dolto's «allant-devenant» also appears in a paper from 1947 (JD, 124, 125 & 130), but it may have been added in a re-edition in 1981 (JD, 96f). At the risk of straining the argument for her originality, I suggest that there is a subtle difference whereby we feel with Winnicott the trajectory towards consciousness, whereas what is most appreciable in Dolto is the trajectory from a fully unconscious state. I also find particularly useful Farley's note that Winnicott stresses the visual realm (2011, 11), as it enables a contrast with Dolto's strong focus on the auditory.

178 Charcot, 1887/1971, 127.
179 Charcot, 1887/1971, 200.
180 Charcot, 1887/1971, 165 & 202.
181 VC1, 542.
182 SF, 326.
183 Janet, 1892/2013, 78.
184 Janet, 1892/2013, 16.
185 Roudinesco, 1982, 245.
186 Bertin, 1982, 301; VC2, 26f.
187 D&R, 19.
188 VC2, 228.
189 VC2, 26.
190 From 1936: D&R, 12–14. From 1937, Nasio, 1987/1998, 37; Roudinesco, 1986, 169.
191 VC2, 26f.
192 Bourgeron, 1993, 13.
193 D&R, 25.
194 Roudinesco, 1982, 297.
195 Roudinesco, 1982, 298.
196 Roudinesco, 1982, 382.
197 Roudinesco, 1986, 168 & 277.
198 Roudinesco, 1982, 262.
199 Hesnard, 1926, n.p.
200 Hesnard, 1946, 120.
201 Hesnard, 1946, 131.
202 Hesnard, 1946, 19.
203 Hesnard, 1946, 131.
204 Freud, 1886; Roudinesco, 1982, 60.
205 E. Freud, 1961, 166.
206 E. Freud, 1961, 182.
207 E. Freud et al. 1978, 30.
208 Laplanche & Pontalis, 1967/2004, 197.
209 Breuer & Freud, 1893a, 45f.
210 Freud, 1900a, 603.
211 Freud, 1900a, 613.
212 Freud, 1900a, 613.
213 Freud, 1900a, 608.
214 Freud, 1900a, 103.
215 Freud, 1900a, 574.
216 Freud, 1895, 357.
217 Freud, 1895, 358.
218 Laplanche & Pontalis, 1967/2004, 12, 325 & 448–450.
219 Freud, 1893c, 5 & 13.

220  Freud, 1895, 456.
221  Freud, 1895c, 373.
222  Freud, 1917b, 137 & 139.
223  SS, 26.
224  SS, 243; also LF, 9 & 11; SP1, 161.
225  LF, 60.
226  JD, 269.
227  Freud, 1913, 171.
228  Laplanche & Pontalis, 1967/2004, 197.
229  Freud, 1912b, 265, 1913, 169–170.
230  Freud, 1900a, 177.
231  Freud, 1900b, 352.
232  Freud, 1900a, 177, 1909b, 36 (also Laplanche & Pontalis, 1967/2004, 197).
233  Freud, 1913, 170.
234  Freud, 1913, 176.
235  SP1, 29.
236  SP1, 30.
237  DW, 30.
238  VO, 34 & 52.
239  JD, 326–328.
240  SF, 345.
241  SP2, 55.
242  SP2, 62.
243  DW, 54; SP2, 65.
244  SP2, 66; VO, 56 & 66.
245  Freud, 1886/1974, 307.
246  Freud, 1888, 48.
247  Freud, 1893e, 302 & 302f.
248  Freud, 1900b, 546 & 567.
249  Freud, 1901a, 667.
250  Laplanche & Pontalis, 1967/2004, 494.
251  Freud, 1900a, 184.
252  Freud, 1900b, 597.
253  Freud, 1900b, 563–564, 1905a, 116.
254  Laplanche & Pontalis, 1967/2004, 418.
255  SS, 77.
256  Nadal, 2006, 130f.
257  MA, 148.
258  MA, 202.
259  VC2, 853.
260  VC2, 853.
261  Freud, 1913, 165.
262  DW, 420; SP3, 21.
263  EN, 124; SP2, 78; SP3, 14.
264  DV, 162.
265  DV, 8; JD, 288; SF, 314; SS, 256.
266  DV, 8.
267  DV, 158–160; JD, 286.
268  MA, 148.
269  MA, 148.
270  DV, 8 & 189; LF, 185.
271  SS, 78 & 270.
272  CD, 193.
273  SS, 79; also CD, 201.

274 LF, 107; SS, 42, 244 & 269.
275 SS, 79.
276 CD, 195.
277 LF, 103.
278 LF, 90.
279 SP3, 17.
280 CE, 40; DW, 46.
281 CD, 200; DV, 48; IIC, 363, 365 & 367; PS, 79; QS, 52; SS, 253; TL, 130.
282 DW, 45; DV, 46 & 48; TL, 130.
283 Freud, 1914c, 150.
284 SP2, 183; SP3, 69 & 189.
285 CD, 183.
286 DW, 45; TL, 23.
287 EM, 316; MA, 60.
288 D&R, 28.
289 EM, 176–177.
290 MA, 153.
291 DW, 81.
292 MA, 12.
293 MA, 161.
294 E.g., IIC, 275; SS, 210.
295 Grignon, 1997, 16; also DV, 73; DW, 76; EM, 178; PJ, 15; SP2, 96; TL, 34.
296 VC2, 858.
297 TL, 91–92.
298 SF, 156.
299 NE, 191.
300 SS, 167.
301 VC2, 876.
302 SS, 181.
303 CE, 41; EN, 64; LF, 283; PJE, 14; VC2, 808 & 844.
304 JD, 58.
305 CE, 344.
306 Freud, 1891/2011, 36–37.
307 Freud, 1901b, 60.
308 Laplanche & Pontalis, 1967/2004, 418.
309 Freud, 1900a, 304.
310 Freud, 1893b, 181.
311 Freud, 1905b, 296.
312 Dolto, 1985c, 199; also DV, 77–81; EM, 177–178; SP2, 174–177; SS, 238–239.
313 SP2, 177.
314 Freud, 1900a, 228 & 235.
315 Freud, 1900b, 596.
316 Freud, 1900b, 596.
317 Freud, 1900b, 340.
318 Laplanche & Pontalis, 1967/2004, 497.
319 DQ, 195–196; SP1, 136; SP3, 133; TL, 109.
320 MA, 16 (emphasis hers).
321 MA, 17 (emphasis hers).
322 LF, 186.
323 DW, 86.
324 SP 131.
325 Nobécourt, 2008b. The French «angoisse,» which Dolto uses, means "anguish" and/or "anxiety."
326 Aubry & Cifali, 1986/1988, 44; Roudinesco, 1986, 170 & 519.

327 D&R, 23; VC2, 452–453.
328 CE, 343; VC2, 684.
329 DW, 31.
330 DW, 42; SP2, 93.
331 DW, 87.
332 DW, 41.
333 SP3, 192–194.
334 LO3, 170; NE, 205; SP2, 151.
335 Freud, 1900a, 229.
336 SS, 41.
337 AI, 220; Ribowski, 1987/2004.
338 E.g., CD, 194 & 199; Dolto & Dolto-Tolitch, 1989, 135; SP3, 14 & 162; SS, 154; TL, 49; VC2, 228.
339 CE, 61.
340 VC2, 292.
341 Dolto, 1985/1989b, 134; DW, 61; VC2, 678.
342 CE, 40.
343 ATP, 167–168.
344 Freud, 1933c, 98; cited in MA, 25.
345 Birksted-Breen, Flanders & Gibeault, 2010, 37.
346 Birksted-Breen, Flanders & Gibeault, 2010, 29.
347 Birksted-Breen, Flanders & Gibeault, 2010, 31 & 27.
348 Freud, 1940[1939], 167.
349 Freud, 1896d, 151.
350 Freud, 1900b, 613,
351 Freud, 1908a, 149.
352 CD, 206.
353 PS, 84; also CE, 320; Dolto, 1985/1989a, 68; SP1, 43; TL, 155.
354 JD, 57; JP, 41; SS, 234; TL, 46.
355 SP1, 163.
356 SP1, 13.
357 SS, 256.
358 MA, 218–227 (emphasis hers).
359 MA, 218–227.
360 Marcel keeps the name Dolto (then Marette) gives him in her dissertation, as do others: Gustave ("G"), Bernard, Roland, Gerard, Paul (age 14), Tote, Denise, Claudine and Monique. But the names of some in that first group are changed in future editions: Jacques becomes Sebastien, Paul (age ten) becomes Patrice, Denis becomes Didier, and Jeanne becomes Fabienne. Young Josette gains an entry in the Table of Contents (TOC) after 1940. Meanwhile, Jean (who keeps his name) has an entry in the TOC in 1940 and 1940/1965, but not in 1940/1971 (P&P). Tote is (mis)named Rose in the TOC in 1940/1965 (but not in the body)—an error corrected in 1940/1971 (P&P). Beyond other (mostly minor) changes between the dissertation and later editions, the slippery names seem to presage the word play essential to Dolto's theorization.
361 See re-editions after 1967: e.g., Dolto, 1940/2013, 192; P&P, 237.
362 P&P, 239.
363 Freud, 1900a, 219f.
364 Hitschmann, 1957, 65.

# 3
# FAMILY

## Introduction

During a famous interview in 1987, Pivot asks Françoise Dolto if one can speak of the existential anxiety of the baby. "Surely,"[1] she replies. For Dolto's infant is anything but the digestive tube of medicine. Nor is it mere rhetoric when Dolto tells Élisabeth Roudinesco that babies "invented everything"[2] in her practice, as only they bring "something really new."[3] But Dolto's conviction invites a question: how can anyone learn from babies? And in its wake, the transference arrives. For what possible teaching could the *infans* ever convey, if not via an unconscious conduit?

As if answering these vital questions, Claude Halmos perfectly describes Dolto as "an ethnologist in the world of children."[4] And what Dolto discovers in her explorations of the infant's world disturbs biography profoundly: the infant unconsciously "intuits his history,"[5] constructing his psyche on the truth he hears. From this arises the need for those around him to «parler vrai» ["speak truth"; homonymically: «par les vrais,» "by true ones"][6]—as a fine tension is bound to every word. For what we will slowly learn is that untruth disturbs structuration by provoking anxiety, inciting regression—whereas truth, even if it is difficult, enables progression.

Dolto theorizes that relational dependence is fundamental to humanization, for if a child hears others speak of his suffering, "it is taken from him."[7] So speaking to a baby changes the diagnostic,[8] especially speaking near the origin of the trouble.[9] But how can a baby tell what is true? Dolto explains:

> I don't know what he [baby] says to me, but I know that he says, that he communicates with me unceasingly. And I know, I try to understand him, and he knows that I don't understand him exactly. But that is the work

between us. With you [interviewer], it's the same…what I'm conscious of saying is a small part next to what I say unconsciously without knowing, and that these people [listeners] will hear with their unconscious, and that everyone in the world is like that…The greatest desire of every human is to communicate his psyche with another human psyche.[10]

Tracing Dolto's conviction will require a rapid descent into her history, wherein we will meet a potent psychical force tangible throughout her project, and we will source her theory in her infancy.

## Family neurosis

Dolto believes that an analyst cannot bring a patient to a place in psycho-affective development that he has not attained,[11] and that an analyst is someone capable of going backwards in his story,[12] because real psychoanalysis always revives archaic pulses.[13] Further, she says, the closer one has been to psychosis, the better the analyst.[14] Her words admit a difficult truth. For Dolto works "from her own experience," as Roudinesco says[15]—or, in the words of Michèle Montrelay, as a «revenant,» one "who came back fighting against death in an archaic state … wherein she reconstituted herself."[16]

Dolto begins each case with a detailed anamnesis, believing that therapy is much longer without it.[17] Critically, she seeks the names in a patient's history. It is curious, she notes, how "de-rhythming" and developmental delays occur in orphanages because so many adults have the same name[18] (i.e., "nurse" or "doctor"). The same happens in families, she adds, as children believe the wrong grandmother is married to a given grandfather.[19] In fact, World War I, which framed Dolto's childhood, inclined families towards using names as guarantors of the posterity of the dead.[20] Dolto's record includes a maternal grandmother and great-grandmother both called «Dan-Mé»; a homonymic father (Henry) and paternal grandfather (Henri); and a preference for names such that correspondence refers to dinner with "the Pierres," or "the Andrés."[21] And long after Jacqueline has died, the reader hears that "Jacqueline is still here."[22] Even Freud felt that his own children's names made them «revenants.»[23] But so pronounced was this propensity in Dolto's family that when her father went to register his baby boy (a replacement child for Jacqueline), with forceful instructions from his wife to name him anything but Jacques, that is exactly what he named him.[24]

Dolto's parents had standing in the bourgeoisie,[25] but all was not as it seemed. Her mother hit her and pulled her hair, in a maniac state triggered by her very presence.[26] She had had an inhumane mother herself, Dolto notes calmly,[27] and a father who told her that she was stupid, ugly and mean.[28] Then, when Jacqueline died, her mother lost her passion for life,[29] calling her children serpents and vipers,[30] and railing publicly about why her pretty daughter died while the disabled do not.[31] So Dolto says that she was already "somewhat of an analyst" listening to this mother.[32] But it was not until her analysis with Laforgue that she could talk back to her, telling her mother that she was too hard.[33] Dolto thus depicts a mother who suffered much and passed on suffering as a legacy. As for her father, he is remembered as good but too silent.[34]

World War I made mourning a reality for children, where it left over a million orphans in France alone and what scholars call "a codification of bereavement"[35]— one that impacted all societal relations. A touching letter to God by Françoise in 1915 asks for protection for her beloved uncle, Pierre.[36] And the family record is rich with war efforts, including her mother and Mlle (the governess, Élisabeth Weilandt) tending soldiers,[37] in a world of "women disguised as nurses."[38] Young Françoise tirelessly knit «cache-nez» ["mufflers"; homonym: "hiding-born"],[39] wetting and stretching them between chairs just to free up some play time.[40] Of her early childhood, Dolto remembers World War I determining everything. So when it ended, she wondered how one could live, as war was at the heart of social life.[41] And when she was caught daydreaming, she would defend herself by saying that she was thinking of the unfortunate soldiers in the «tranches»[42] ["trenches"; also, "slices" and (oddly), "psychoanalytic sessions"]. Women with wails that sounded more like laughter came to her home and cried as they talked of seeking a «fils disparu» ["lost son"; homographically: "lost threads"]—but he obviously wasn't at our house, she remembers thinking.[43] The literality of words is patent in so many of her recollections. Further, as so few widows had jobs,[44] many fell into pathological mourning,[45] driving her own push for an education.[46] For in the right kind of family, she was told, a widow never remarries.[47] And months before turning eight, a widow was precisely what she believed she was.

Oncle Pierre, the «oncle oedipien» she adored—twice-decorated recipient of the Military Cross, and Captain of the 62nd Batallion of elite «Chasseurs Alpins»—died on 10 July 1916, in Alsace, during his third tour of duty.[48] He was her godfather,[49] but far more than that, she believed he was her fiancé. The story cannot properly be understood without considering its powerful support in reality. His letters from the trenches address her as «ma fiancée Vava,»[50] he promises to marry her after the war,[51] and he writes that he dreams he is with her.[52] In addition, his sister (Dolto's mother) sends Françoise his Legion of Honour photo, telling her seven-year-old that to deserve marriage, she must never cry again.[53] And his mother (Dolto's maternal grandmother) sends Françoise two posthumous gifts: a diamond, as if making her officially his fiancé;[54] and a cross for her communion, following instructions he left.[55] But the night before that ceremony, Françoise learns that Jacqueline is dying of cancer. Suzanne pleads that since nothing is purer than a child before communion, Françoise should pray for her sister's survival.[56] So the deaths of Jacqueline and Pierre become co-immortalized, *as if* in a union—«*comme* union»—in a haunting homonymic tension wherein suffering and the promise not to cry, silence, intertwine. A letter to Mlle in 1928 still echoes mourning: "No one will know, perhaps not even myself, though I suspect it, the formidable influence upon me of the sadness at the death of Oncle Pierre."[57]

Dolto relates that she would never have become a psychoanalyst without the drama of Jacqueline's death in 1920.[58] Yet her psychical pain is patent far earlier, in her admission of transient schizophrenia around age four.[59] And one can only suppose that Laforgue (interestingly, from Alsace), conceived his theory of "family neurosis"[60] with at least some reference to Françoise and Philippe. Indeed, it is a home where much catches our attention on the scene of orality. For example, in the Marette household, children have no right to speak at the table,[61] and seven-year-old Françoise is punished for being rude to a valet with a month of eating from a chamber pot.[62] There are privations of dessert for dirtying her dress,[63] and a prohibition against eating anywhere but at the mother's or maternal grandmother's until she is 24.[64] In turn, hers is an oral (aural) curiosity, turning on words—for example, the funny way conversations jump subjects,[65] and the absurdity of idioms that suggest that shrimp ask to be boiled alive.[66] "I didn't understand (the) words,"[67] she states.

Young Françoise's persistent questions got her reassigned to Mlle, as the other «nurses» could not stand her.[68] And musing on how adults were like a different species,[69] she wished: "When I'm big, I'll try to remember what it's like when you're small."[70] In fact, Mlle herself was two nannies removed, following a Miss Brice, from that first English-speaking nanny—whose name is forgotten—in a home where nannies are cut from family photos anyhow,[71] as if they were never there at all.

## «Médiation langagière»

In this presence-absence, we come upon the Irish girl whose story, unlike her name, is broadcast widely across Dolto's project.[72] The vibrant 18-to-20-year-old enjoyed "coke and orgies"[73] at a local hotel by borrowing Suzanne's clothing and jewels, for which she was fired. Dolto explains her feelings for her as an archaic love,[74] relating how she stunned her family by first babbling in English at 18 months, after a long silence.[75] Dolto recalls the nanny dressing her fully in blue one day, dyeing even her shoes, calling her a beautiful "blue angel."[76] And she describes to Laforgue, "auburn hair that smelled very good … long tables … like the Romans, with very tall people dressed like Russian generals," and an elevator man in a uniform just like a "Brandebourg."[77] And it is here, on these words, that we will begin a deep dive into dream-work. For the Brandebourg style is actually a strong match to Pierre's uniform,[78] and also to the so-called "Greycoat" soldiers of the (then-recent) American Civil War.

In one direction, this daydream takes us to the proximity of Greycoat Hospital School—"doctor of education"?—a prestigious institute for girls in England that the nanny surely knew about (and spoke of to her tiny charge?). And in another, we somehow arrive at the American singer Billy Williams, whose huge hit in 1909 (played at Hôtel le Franklin?) was, "The Old Grey Coat," and whose role in that ancient scene is inadvertently also recalled by a street name right around Françoise's home—Rue Singer. And right around the song, in

1905, a risqué German novel, *Professor Unrat* ["Professor Garbage"] centred its plot on a fictitious cabaret, "The Blue Angel." So the nanny's soundscape, long silenced, becomes oddly hearable again as archaic echoes held in trust in the unconscious of the infant who loved her so. It is as if a word serves as a memorial preventing the forgetting of what can never, in infancy, be "remembered"—and precious syllables drenched in archaic affects inform and countersign the far later landscape onto which thoughts (thus, theories) emerge.

Dolto insists that the removal of any loved nanny is an act of violence, and that the loss of «médiation langagière,» being more traumatic than the loss of a parent,[79] causes «maladies langagières» ["languaged illnesses"].[80] Adding to the loss of that precious first nanny, Dolto's suffering was fed by potent guilt: not making enough scarves,[81] not praying well enough,[82] hurting those she loved,[83] asking too many questions,[84] crying,[85] making her mother anxious[86]—even having fun when her mother was bored.[87] Dolto describes her debilitating culpability as "narcissistic dereliction."[88] And she reveals that her rescue came via an angel named B.A.G.,[89] an acronym for «Bon Ange Guardien» ["good guardian angel"—but English slang for theft!]. Visiting her nightly, so that she had to negotiate fair space on her bed with his big wings, B.A.G. absolved her by explaining that her mischief helped adults to «gagner leur ciel» ["win heaven"][90]—in other words, that her way of being good was by being bad. "It was a very, very big consolation,"[91] she declares.

Dolto theorizes that the guilt originating in the "first preverbal physiological sensations of the difficulty of living"[92] produces a narcissistic wound that blocks later investments of erogenous zones.[93] "Family neurosis" is a structure, she says, whereby the child is prevented from healing because he is needed to assume guilt.[94] And the greatest source of the infant's guilt is that of hurting the mother[95]—though ironically, Dolto states, "you cannot ever live without hurting your mother."[96] So it is that guilt and suffering enter into our earliest relations of dependency, she says, wherein "we are punished hence we are guilty."[97] Guilt enfolds narcissism,[98] while the child will be alright as long as he is not guilty.[99] Dolto will also develop the idea that losing a libidinal investment suddenly, before it has been displaced, will cause an enclave «à bas bruits» ["at low noise"][100]—an "infirmation at the oral stage"[101]—which provokes disinterest in the exterior world,[102] and a vulnerability to frustration that can return the "oral autistic type."[103]

Dolto believes that a predominance of unresolved oral fixations leads to smoking, among other sequelae,[104] while a wet nurse can aggravate or correct the lacks in the «structure libidinale des parents.»[105] In fact, Dolto smokes in a film[106] and in two photos,[107] having apparently been a heavy smoker.[108] Yet her own mother nursed all of her infants for a full year,[109] preventing the loss of the actual breast. Here, then, erupts the odd, illogical thought that the suffering of Dolto's weaning has nothing much to do with her mother—but rather, that her rupture of oral-stage love is lived entirely inside the (hi)story of her lost nanny. An "impossible desire" arrives with weaning,[110] she states poignantly, a "suffering of abandon."[111] And by invoking the lost nanny, we can begin to comprehend Dolto's vital notion of castration as a symbolic loss informing a potent contradiction (the telltale signature of dream-work?), wherein the one who suffers an oral castration too early or too quickly has, paradoxically, no oral castration.

## Relative autism

Thus grounding her understanding of primary narcissism, Dolto believes that the infant experiences suffering as a threat[112]—a narcissistic trial or wound.[113] And in an original turn, Dolto insists on the risk of "relational trouble":[114] a "language of refusal" or of not being heard[115] as a «phénomène de resonance»[116]— that is, of a «histoire vrai» ["true story"] that ironically renders the child «pas vrai» ["untrue"].[117] At stake is "depersonalization" that is (enigmatically) caused by "affect stripped of valor."[118] So trauma is not always (or only) a real event for Dolto, but rather, any break in structuring relations that is "pregenitally inverting."[119] Dolto thus focuses her work on refinding and recovering children by telling them the origin of the rupture.[120] And a powerful idea emerges here whereby infancy and analysis share their roots: the talking cure works because suffering originates in the faulty insertion of a valorous young subject into the human story.

We will meet Josette, age three-and-a-half, early in the dissertation.[121] Josette is experiencing enuresis, nightmares, anorexia and a loss of play. Over three visits in a single month, Dolto speaks to the mother (with Josette), about how troubles commenced when parents made secret plans to move her out of their bedroom; and she explains to Josette (with mother), about wanting to stay a baby. Dolto recommends speaking about the room changes directly and valorizing progression. So, at home, the father talks to Josette about her going to school soon and his being proud of her. Then, on one page, the heart of a powerful theory is put on the table so unpretentiously that it may be missed altogether. What is overheard creates anxiety, Dolto says, causing «symptômes du négativisme»—a revolt against progress, sleep, food and games—that prompts regression to a prior stage in «évolution libidinale.»[122] And progression requires incremental unpleasure—a "sacrifice that reality imposes on you."[123] But, of critical importance, "pleasure can never be renounced without an exchange for another pleasure."[124]

What enables progression, then? It is "promises of unknown pleasures."[125] So words, as offers of pleasure, become the site-means—mediators—of unconscious affects that determine whether or not we can invest in reality. Not only is the ontogeny of the transference patent here, but also the "role of the transference is visible,"[126] Dolto notes, as the child insists on returning to tell her doctor that she is well. For emergence in reality is, as Freud describes it, contingent on continuity under the control of the pleasure principle. And in an invaluable footnote to Freud's work, Strachey adds: "An 'experience of satisfaction' is only a special application of Freud's general theory of the mechanism of wishes, as explained in ... *The Interpretation of Dreams* ... The whole topic links up with Freud's views on reality-testing."[127] So the word is foremost a consolation for an unnameable absence, rooted in time immemorial.

Dolto's career as an analyst had begun with Sophie Morgenstern, whose practice focused on «démutisation»: pulling children out of regressive states.[128] Morgenstern observed that unresolved traumas lead to a predisposition to return to anterior libidinal stages;[129] death and departure are identical for a child;[130] and what is psychogenic about troubles is also what is most hopeful.[131] Acknowledging Morgenstern to the end of her life,[132] Dolto recalls that many children became autistic during the evacuation of Paris in World War II.[133] And she believes of the child that, "autistic is not what he is, but what *he becomes*."[134] Autism is amenable to psychoanalytic treatment, Dolto insists, and she refuses the "fatality" of autism,[135] because it is both "relative"[136] and "reversible."[137] The autistic subject suffers from a break in relationality, Dolto insists; language did not "arrive on time," so the child felt unheard, left with unsymbolized desires and unspoken suffering.[138] The result is affective starvation,[139] as children enter autism passively, no longer asking for anything[140]—and by slow renunciation,[141] regress to anonymity and phantasy relations with sensations, in a private battle against solitude.[142]

Dolto even offers a remedy: explain the origin of the rupture to the autistic subject while he is half-asleep.[143] And in an influential work in 1957, Dolto proposes that the person with autism needs to go back far enough to find an other sufficiently «semblable» to feel secure in his presence.[144] Dolto is narrating an unconscious witnessing: a relation inhering in our infantile autism, the silent period of our developmental passage.[145] After all, she says, right at the inception of her project, "*the unconscious is not an obscure, mute receptacle* of useless psychical representations."[146] For Dolto, autism is "proof of the symbolic function in humans,"[147] and fertile for new psychoanalytic cures.[148] Yet thinking with Dolto, I believe we cannot shake the feeling that organization and disorganization work something like an elevator. We may have gone some distance along the road of theory, but it seems that the nanny's story is still nearby.

## Sonar heritage

In the apparent negation of destructuration is, paradoxically, a positive opportunity for recovery—one that Dolto believes makes regression a necessity[149]—because of the capacity of oral passivity (including sleep) for "re-narcissization by deculpabilization."[150] According to Dolto, regression is a right to live "larvally"[151] that enables healing because primary narcissism is an "automaterning":[152] a self-assumption of repair as we, "take ourselves as a relay object in the absence of another."[153] Dolto even prescribes that patients be allowed to live out a stage normally surpassed.[154] This valuation of regression to oral passivity[155] circulates throughout Dolto's project, from Josette's ordinary trouble with growing up to the most distressing cases:

There is residual libidinal health conserved intact in psychotics behind the regressive tableau of their symptoms…The reactivation, in psychotics, of a state remaining sane but very archaic was therefore possible and could be followed by a restructuration of the relation to themselves and to the world.[156]

Additionally, "regression is or can be a positive process … [since] every event that provokes a subjective disorganization returns the subject to the search for libidinal investments that were previously acquired and … imaginarily conserved as a place-time of existential security."[157]

And what is the nature of this restorative oral passive environment? It is defined by «aimance absorptive» ["absorbing love"],[158] where "having" is indistinguishable from "being."[159] The first form of the oral stage is passive[160] and auto-erotic,[161] being an unconscious existence,[162] the archaic stage of desire.[163] As language is present in fetal life "at least auditorily,"[164] the infant immediately organizes a "code of calls,"[165] since the symbolic function is "foundational of the human being"[166]—and the desire for communication precedes the need for assistance.[167] Further, as the phonemes encountered in fetal life leave in our memory a "sonar heritage,"[168] links in language are crucial to elaborating separation,[169] as we transition to "aerial life."[170]

Significantly, in the liquid dreamscape of the oral passive stage, there is no "splitting,"[171] and the infant has no notion of a world differentiated from himself.[172] So he is vulnerable to "ethical devaluation"[173] from the environment, "drinking anxiety with his milk";[174] or, if put to bed with a bottle, "swallowing the ceiling with his milk."[175] His only recourse is a "passive defense"[176]—returning to a prior state of goodness and safety. "Precocious libidinal stages" are a proven fact,[177] Dolto declares, as "the libidinal sub-basement of relations of dependence … that stays in later libidinal organizations."[178]

Dolto's practice is thus centred on regression from the start. In 1940, Marcel, age ten, is diagnosed with "libidinal regression";[179] and in 1943, Marie-Louise B., age 28, is diagnosed with a deeply "archaic regression."[180] In fact, the material on regression dominates Dolto's project quantitatively. Living is an encounter with "regressing tension,"[181] as the death of loved ones causes "momentary regression";[182] so does removing the mother or trying to,[183] and narcissistic trials.[184] Humans react by withdrawing, hiding their desire[185]—as an "anorexic jouissance of slowing down,"[186] an "archaic symbolic satisfaction."[187] In turn, sleep is restorative as a daily regression,[188] and as a defense against the loss of relational protection.[189] And we recall here Freud's observations on "attacks of sleep,"[190] and "the instinct to sleep."[191]

Implicit in Dolto's view of regression is the "continuity" of the subject,[192] wherein narcissism remains essential to his future well-being,[193] and the "narcissistic economy"[194] is supplied by a ceaseless "desiring force."[195] Dolto opens her dissertation with full credit to Freud for her belief that instinct and its physiological substratum characterize all that is life,[196] as she explains how pulses are subject to cyclical repetition;[197] developmental shifts in the "elective erogenous zone";[198] phases of excitation;[199] and mute rest cycles.[200] Further, all affect is linked to narcissism,[201] Dolto says, and constructed in passive pulses only.[202] So her notion of primary narcissism is as a perpetually reachable subterranean river, supplying what grows—and highly reminiscent of Freud's "reservoirs" of narcissistic libido.[203]

Dolto's narration of archaic prehistory cannot help but astound, as she relates how biological processes result in a "narcissistic symbolic" constituting language[204]—and language is described with the same tropes as pulses: "Language is made to bounce."[205] And wherever we search, we will find no one exploring the archaic with Dolto's dedication: "As for precocity, I really have no idea anymore where it is ... It really seems to be right from the first day of life."[206] The moral and social implications are astonishing.

## «Régression à l'archaïque»

Dolto credits Freud's concept of regression with allowing her to hypothesize «régression à l'archaïque.»[207] As she explains it, when life pulses are blocked from symbolic expression, the system complies for a while by inhibiting them.[208] But if pulses accumulate too much, regression to a more infantile mode of expression is made necessary to release tension.[209] After all, we are at a time prior to projection, when regression is the primary defense. We should also recall that at this juncture in development, as Freud's work makes clear, the pulses of conservation are indissociable from the sexual pulses.[210] So in the absence of a means of symbolic expression—for the preverbal child with "untranslatable anguish"[211]—regression becomes a trap that is seldom spontaneously reversible.[212] We pause to hear the depths of Dolto's thought: regression is a solution for a quantitative excess of affect, but it can be pathological in the absence of symbolic mediation. For recovery requires regression and "a call beyond."[213] The role of this call in the "processes of regression and their resolution" cannot be overstated,[214] and we will hear of it later, in Dolto's notion of a "third" to enable transference at the oral passive stage.[215]

Narrating the capacity for mediated reemergence, Dolto values regression as a healthy folding,[216] a dynamic involution,[217] a fall into passivity,[218] a fall back to restart,[219] and a refuge or passive defense.[220] For the symbolic function secures "granted desires ... necessary for the pre-subject's cohesive structuration."[221] And in this register of dream-work, we truly begin to appreciate that Dolto's «désir» [both "desire" and "wish"] is unconscious. Thus, Dolto says—as if it were not only the most obvious thing but also the most comforting—"Negation is not absence. In negation, the Id is there."[222] Puzzlingly, recent historians claim that a focus on regression characterizes French psychoanalysis,[223] yet still without crediting Dolto.

Dolto's view of regression marks not just a return to an earlier distribution of psychical energy, but also to what Freud refers to as primitive methods of psychical expression,[224] and this is critical. Freud describes regression as an involution or withdrawal of libido[225] and as a refuge or flight from stimulus[226] made possible because of the indestructibility of unconscious paths,[227] and the role of unconscious complexes in attracting the liberation of affects towards the interior of the body.[228] We also reinvest in Freud's greatest discovery, that wishes are the motives for dreams,[229] guarding sleep.[230] For functionally, the hallucination of satisfaction ends excitation.[231] Ferenczi also describes regression as a "hallucinatory reoccupation of the satisfying situation."[232]

Freud explains that the wish for satisfaction is present from the beginning of life, [233] emanating from an interior organic source,[234] and that the free discharge of excitation is sought to limit tension.[235] Freud finds that not only affect[236] but also somatic stimuli influence dreams.[237] Fear, rage, mental pain and sexual delight do too[238]—even "quietly thinking ... volition and attention."[239] How, then, could the mother's influences not affect symbolic mediation in the fetal environment? Yet Freud also declares narcissism a limit-concept[240]—and instinct, the frontier of biology and psychology.[241]

For as early as oral eroticism is,[242] its libido has already passed through an archaic scene. And, as our references to Freud become overly dense—as if we need to cling to something material before sinking even deeper into dreamwork with Dolto—we discover the near-impossibility of describing the archaic. So we might well give up hope of ever making meaning, were it not that this is precisely where hope for the human story originates. For in the sheer difficulty of speaking about it, a summation of the archaic ironically arrives: there is always a point before the loss of hope where hope actually was.

## Archaic identification

It is as if archaic love is findable deep in Dolto's theory, as a hearing within a hearing. Dolto describes regression as a "resurgence of unconscious affect that reactualizes the archaic object of fixation,"[243] as "all tension calls to the other or oneself as another remembered."[244] And what is the nature of this extremely "archaic epoch"?[245] It is a repressed "archaic emotional imbroglio,"[246] an "anterior lived,"[247] "archaic plans,"[248] an "archaic subbasement,"[249] and a "unitary structure in the interior."[250] Archaic, unconscious libidinal organization is idiosyncratic,[251] Dolto says, as a "souvenir of the interrelational language that is at the origin of the psychical structure of the libido."[252] And in a strikingly passionate expression, Dolto speaks of regression ensuing from, "a lack of love for silent sufferings and the teratological folding of the precociously banned."[253] A "tone of mourning colors the French understanding,"[254] claim some historians—yet, again, without recognizing Dolto.

And what about the nature of this archaic relation? Dolto describes it as an "archaic identification"[255] with "archaic parents,"[256] an "interior family"[257] that makes those a child calls his parents only his "first others."[258] Freud writes of the infantile roots of love,[259] and of a "prehistoric, unforgettable other person."[260]

But Dolto has an unmatched willingness to speak about the archaic, as if she were sweeping away ashes in the basement of psychosis with a bold Cinderella's broom. Dolto invokes an "archaic mother,"[261] or "oral phallic mother."[262] But more prominent still is a «père symbolique» ["symbolic father"],[263] since the "father in space-time is not the true father for someone."[264] Thus, Dolto believes that "the only parents that are important are those within us,"[265] and that what matters is living so as "to honour the parent inside ... so the internal parent is proud of you."[266] In sum, Dolto insists that, "the archaic always continues to exist within us, that constantly there is a level that is archaic."[267] So recovery, she explains, requires the recuperation of unconscious continuity: "What heals them, is to refind the symbolic father of their early childhood, and to be able to establish the relay with their actual symbolic father."[268] Dolto even speaks of a «père préhistorique ... père antérieur à la scène primitive»[269]—in a progression of interiority contingent on symbolic filiation.

Here is another hint of a fantastically dense yet subtle concept to which we will keep returning: the «repère» ["re-father" and "landmark"]. The «repère» is made possible by the father separating from the «co-moi papa-maman» ["co-me father-mother"][270] of dream-work, and the archaic identification of the pre-subject with the one who, like himself, is a part of the mother yet not. We will eventually understand this bit of dream-work as the first moment of the pre-subject. Meanwhile, our historians disclose the particular interest of French psychoanalysis in "subjectivation"[271]—this time, referencing Dolto in a single footnote.[272]

Then again, if all goes well, we are all too willing to forget the enigmas and paradoxes of the archaic. So at the risk of losing the wide doorway Dolto opens onto autism and psychosis, we witness the public tendency to relegate Dolto to a collective amnesia. For Dolto takes up Freud's narrative of precocious sexuality where(in) it is most provocative—at the dawn of the subject—and she seems to be engaged in a struggle for a hearing against the repression barrier itself. Without doubt, the archaic will challenge our capacity for understanding (and description), because of the slow forgetting that coming to reality imposes. What happens then, Dolto says, is that for the adult, infancy is as "foreign as the vital needs of a tadpole are to a frog."[273]

Tellingly, in teasing out Dolto's notion of the archaic parent, we will find not the super-ego or ego ideal, but what is ontologically prior: dream-work, a phantasy of a parent. For nascent proprioception informs a dream of provision under the pulses of conservation that, in developmental progressions (paradoxically in non-time), conveys a witnessing with an indissociable other that ensures survival. Repetitive sounds become richly invested in this association with our self-preservation. Henceforth, the child is unconsciously securitized by remaining, as Dolto describes it beautifully, in a continual "intimate affective mute colloquium" with himself.[274]

Deep in the womb now, we will at first barely hear the soft slide of meaning from physicality to something far more nuanced and dreamier: both maternal and paternal security are included in the mother,[275] every mother is also a father,[276] and the father is the one who occupies the thoughts of the mother.[277] Dolto adds that because symbolic filiation confers existential security,[278] the primal scene enriches primary narcissism.[279]

## Wild transference

For Dolto, the primal scene may be one's own conception.[280] Yet we are very far from Klein's primal scene, with its fearful combined figure—the mother containing the penis, and the father containing the breast.[281] Even Klein's good object is laden with maternal tropes, described with relation to a splitting between a good breast and bad breast.[282] In contrast, Dolto's archaic identification is a symbolic figuration devoid of any sense of bodily parts, informed solely by the fluidity of sound in an unconscious life, and the indivisibility of the «pré-moi» from its archaic environment. For if Klein discovers that the child has already repressed the infant,[283] Dolto discovers that the infant has already repressed the fetus.

In an interview in 1986, Roudinesco suggests that, in France in the 1960s, Dolto held the equivalent of Klein's position in London. "Maybe," Dolto answers.[284] Then in 1984, Dolto comments on her concept of the "bicephalic Ideal Ego" in parentheses: "(This may be what the school of Melanie Klein calls the combined parent)."[285] The "maybes" and parentheses signal Dolto's reserve in constructing a dialogue with this other pioneer who, in more ways than one, does not speak the same language. So we will need to close our eyes and cease imagining Klein's part-objects to fall, with Dolto, towards what is deep beneath and developmentally prior, onto a landscape described only by Freud: to the "combined figure" of dream-work, wherein common features unite persons.[286] Crucial to our understanding will be Freud's notes that one dream thought represents more than one dream element,[287] dream-content is overdetermined[288] and the amount of condensation is indeterminate.[289]

Dolto takes Freud as her invisible cloth, as she deftly weaves her articulation of a continuously accessible, unconscious, combined but de-combinable parent as a «repère» that opens up her theory to some landmarks for our travels. And what we find emerging powerfully is the notion of a means for progression to reality (along the model of decombining), and for regression to the archaic (along the model of recombining). The dream-work translating what permeates the fluid medium of primary narcissism makes possible the impossible, in the offer of a necessary path—one that enables us to theorize just how it is that projection could ever develop out of the passive domain of our archaic prehistory. I suggest that Dolto's thought also invites a homonymic masterplay on the declaration of subjectivity itself, «je suis»—meaning both "I am" and "I follow." I also believe that here Dolto answers (inadvertently) the incisive question posed by Laplanche and Pontalis in their dictionary of Freud's oeuvre: "How is it possible to pass from a monad closed onto itself to the progressive recognition of an object?"[290] For Dolto is indeed teasing out a critical question: how do object relations begin?

Dolto offers a working definition of the object in her dissertation of 1940, one rooted unhesitatingly in the oral stage: "Object: food, for example."[291] At the other extreme—yet, interestingly, still in keeping with the idea of alimentation—is the theoretical complexity of broader definitions of the object as a metaphor, for example: "The thing (breast), its invested meanings, and the interpretive psychosocial processes we bring to it."[292] Of decisive relevance to the nascent human subject (and to our understanding) is the fact that the object never exists strictly in the concrete or the metaphorical realm. Rather, the object always exists in both (and in between) realms. For as Freud tells us, the distinction between the reality and phantasy of an object is moot in our use of it psychically: "It is a matter of indifference whether this internal process of working-over is carried out upon real or imaginary objects."[293] So a lost object may be a real thing, or a phantasy once serving a wish. Similarly, milk is a reparative object—but so is an unconscious «repère.» Thus, when we invoke archaic objects, we cannot functionally distinguish (psychically) between a lost grandfather, his lost name, or the love of a «père symbolique.»

Dolto consistently evokes a passive pre-subject for whom there is no object that is not a part of the self. And the archaic's subtle objects are a path to the dream as much as to reality. Therefore, the notion of an internal object to be taken in or used, in coming to reality, is best set aside for a conception that is far more «anobjectal»[294] before we can think with Dolto—not about developmentally limited or transitory "infantile transferences,"[295] but, rather, about the infantile origins of the enduring human capacity for the transference. For the liquid dream-work of the narcissistic environment renders archaic identification as a securitizing witnessing in an ironic, continuous potential wherein the pre-subject and combined parents are inseparable yet dissociable—a kind of "two" that is also a "three," we might say.

Fundamentally informing this paradox, we come upon Dolto's notion of «prolongement» ["prolonging"], invoking both fusion and reversibility: "The human being is made such that he feels himself to be the prolonging of the being he loves, or else the being he loves is his prolonging. If he is at a distance, he believes himself to be the being he loves; he is not at his place, he is at the place of the other." [296] Dolto then effectively invokes something of the dynamics of prolonging in considering the work of the transference in her clinic: patients lend solutions to her while imagining what they would do if they were the doctor and she were the patient.[297]

Of interest, we learn that Dolto attended one of Klein's control sessions, reporting that she was "horrified" because "the subject was reduced to relations of parts of his body with other parts of partial bodies,"[298] in an "*amputation* of the theory ... of Freud"[299] (a subtle play on body parts?). So while Dolto credits Klein with working diligently to dephobize mental illness,[300] she believes Klein was too theorized and failed to appreciate how every child brings something new.[301] Further, she disagrees with Klein's notion of the internal object.[302] Dolto's view is clear:

One never constructs an internal object—fortunately for the subject!—
because the internal object is madness. It is the subject of desire who must
construct himself *for* someone, *with* someone and *by* someone. Never is
desire satisfied outside of the presence of someone—a presence sometimes
hallucinated, as for psychotics who have the illusion of hearing the voice
of the loved one. It is the «parole» ["speech"; "words"] of a third that presentifies, for a subject, an absent person. There is a presence restituted
only in language, but always by a third.[303]

Dolto apparently met Klein a few times,[304] commenting that one could "feel
the theory in her head,"[305] and that Klein's stunning charisma[306] and securitizing human contact[307] healed her patients, not her theory.[308] She seemed like an
English nanny, Dolto suggests.[309] And archaic echoes jump right through the
elusive gates of subjectivation, into the wild outdoors.

## Dynamic complimentary regulation

Dolto believes that all babies are fusional,[310] fusion happens better in sleep[311]
and children incline to "reversibility."[312] And where there is fusion, there is
"fusional transference."[313] As young Bernadette eerily remarks: "If I die, I will
go live in my daughter."[314] But if we listen to Dolto carefully, I believe we can
hear what Freud described as the dream-work's preference for reversal and
contraries,[315] what August Stärcke considered to be a lack of differentiation
between inner and outer world,[316] and the "repeated alternation between
becoming one's own and not one's own … [that is] a prototype for the process
of projection":[317] as well as the lack of distinction Karl Abraham noted between
the nursing child and breast.[318]

In fusional transference, we will locate the origins of projection (ironically) in
the passive pulses—and we will also find the theoretical beginnings of Dolto's
famous «poupée-fleur» (to which we will return).[319] At stake is a subject regressed
so far back that he cannot find in his surroundings any suitable "objects of
transference."[320] As a flower has life but no movement or speech,[321] and it is free
of "digestive dependence,"[322] the oral stage is "in resonance" with it[323]—as a
kind of similar-enough other, an as-if third. By this resonance is opened the possibility of projection to liberate oral affects[324]—securing abreaction even if it is
found accidentally.[325] Further, since it has no will, it is free of vengeance, enabling
the "recuperation of narcissism without anxiety":[326] a clean start for the subject.
And in an uncanny echo of Dolto's angel, B.A.G. (who is somehow still here),
Bernadette and Nicole, independent cases, each clearly state—while heaping
verbal abuse and guilt on their own «poupée-fleur»—that its way of being good is
being bad.[327]

Believing that a subject is constructed in relationality, Dolto makes potent claims
about unconscious transmission. The notion of unconscious inheritance is familiar on
French terrain, Roudinesco explains.[328] Even Freud writes of neurotics passing

disorders to their children,[329] "hereditary transmission,"[330] and "archaic heritage."[331] But Dolto's unparalleled observations lead to two phenomenal discoveries: first, infants serve an unconscious "regulatory complimentary dynamic role" for parents;[332] and second, an infant's libido wakes fragile adults and threatens that fragile state.[333] In brief, the infant is in a state of hypnosis with parents, always between consciousness and unconsciousness,[334] sharing phantasms with the mother.[335] So the mother's dreams and ideas structure the fetus,[336] and a newborn reacts to the unconscious projections of parents.[337] As a result, every child becomes an "anxiety sponge" for parents,[338] thereby inheriting suffering,[339] psychotic enclaves,[340] phobia,[341] guilt and fixations,[342] unconscious conflicts,[343] and "libidinal mutations"[344]—essentially, archaic history.[345]

Thereby, "what is silenced in the first generation, the second generation carries in the body,"[346] in a relation of complimentary "co-knowing or co-non-knowing,"[347] and "co-being or co-non-being."[348] Dolto even speaks of the "dispatching of libido in a family,"[349] of the "family economy,"[350] and of the regression of a whole family "by contamination."[351] "Destructuration is contagious,"[352] she explains, so "narcissistic devaluation is a simple operation"[353]—one, to stress, that is contingent on idiosyncratic prehistories of audition, affect and anxiety. Dolto further notes her witnessing of psychical instability in children whose parents over-use the word «on»[354]—a nebulous pronoun in French that can mean "I," "we," "everyone," and "no one in particular"—because nascent subjectivity in reality is impeded through "the problem of the non-castration of the other."[355] In sum, Dolto is unequivocal on a matter of staggering importance: we each inherit an unconscious education from our sources of affect.

## Floating narcissism

And upon Dolto's precious stories of the archaic, our ship sails. Yet where it goes from here will continually astound, in being an entirely non-locatable place for which our navigational coordinates will be suitably contradictory. For the geography of primary narcissism is watery, as Dolto explains it—"floating narcissism,"[356] in the "indifferentiation of the liquid mass,"[357] with stages that need to be "liquidated."[358] Yet there is also a warm hearth: a "hearth of reassurance,"[359] an "unconscious hearth."[360] Further, desire is born and reborn of ashes.[361] Dolto's thought blends seamlessly with childhood memories of war-era food lines outside the «fourneau» ["oven"; also, "soup kitchen"][362]—and (on the same page), collecting coal at the docks with her mother.[363] Decades apart—yet, somehow, affectively simultaneously—we find comments about how psychoanalysis needs to reach the archaic, to «aller au charbon» ["go to (the) coal(s)"];[364] and that without Laforgue, she would have always seen in the nanny fragment "only fire."[365] Talking with Pivot, Dolto even says that she admires «le charbonnier» ["coalcutter"], for whom she is "his student."[366] And amid Dolto's story-as-theory about ashes arrives the echoes of Cinderella—whose German name, *Aschenputtel*, resounds even louder.

And it is ironically "here," in this archaic "place," that we can begin to situate the problematic of organizing the inimitable material offered by Dolto's corpus. Misunderstanding first strikes as a symptom caused by the flush of details in personal stories that spin out from underneath key theories, set against the fact that Dolto seldom draws explicit connections between her history and her work. Casual remarks about being "somewhat of an analyst," or about her "archaic love" for the lost nanny, are about as close as we will get. And yet, the careful reader cannot help but notice after a while some rather uncanny associations, and how Dolto's ideas seem overdetermined on (by) the unconscious landscape of her infancy. Moreover, once one picks up the trail (so to speak) of the archaic heritage in Dolto's formulations, one encounters her thinking in ways that unexpectedly translate difficulty into clarity. It is as if one had unearthed a fragrance that gave its scent to everything downstream. And in countless unsettling moments, that peculiar sensation that is the transference—the arrival from somewhere, but where?—becomes Dolto's inadvertent telling of a moving story carried deep beneath the conscious stories that she tells.

Thus, Dolto's rare gift of biographical details is appreciated for the gracious gesture that it truly is: ample testimony to the unconscious as a living force on the scene long before consciousness, operating continuously from earliest infancy as a dynamic pressure subtending and countersigning our adult efforts, in an infiltration from a watery subterrain. So the biographical offers proof of (and desire for) the theoretical—and vice-versa. With Dolto, learning is not just *of* the transference but *in* transference, as subject and object blur entirely, and thought is co-opted by the primitive processes from which it originated. And as the transference becomes our best tool for engaging Dolto's complicated texts, research becomes a matter of waiting (wading) through much reading—taking her words as mediating objects to enable the arrival of the unconscious effect of compressed stories that eventually become discernible by the sheer force of repetition. In turn, the organization of her perplexing material only becomes possible thanks to word-things—phonemes—that become palpable through a quanta of associations that structure research notes like a dictionary, in a wild proliferation of dream-work from writer to reader.

Concluding this chapter, I offer that Dolto's corpus opens the possibility of finding the trace of an unconscious history. For in every sense, it is Françoise Marette, the inquiring child, who underwrites the work of Françoise Dolto, the woman of genius. And upon that very street Dolto walked each day, Rue Saint-Jacques, comes another hearing within a hearing as we depart. It is the call of a long-absent sister, Jacqueline, who returns on the name, as if our losses were never lost at all, and the porosity of time and space were our unconscious trust. Everything happens as if, as Dolto liked to say, it is the elusive transit beneath words—the boundless instability and unpredictability of dream-play that arrives via shared affect—that vouches for the veracity of human history, and makes possible the audacity of ingenuity.

## Notes

1  Ribowski, 1987/2004.
2  Roudinesco, 1986, 18.
3  Roudinesco, 1986, 13.
4  Meirieu & Kübler, 2001.
5  CE, 242; VC2, 770.
6  ES, 68; NE, 202, 204 & 208; PJE, 21; TL, 82 & 124.
7  DV, 37; also Nobécourt & Simonetta, 1978.
8  EM, 217; Le Péron, 2008; TL, 16.
9  JD, 129.
10  Interview with Bernard Pivot in Ribowski, 1987/2004.
11  MA, 166; also VO, 213.
12  Nobécourt, 2008b.
13  CD, 149.
14  DQ, 99.
15  Roudinesco, 1986, 518.
16  De Mezamat, 2008b.
17  LF, 180–183; SP2, 60–62.
18  EV, 62.
19  EV, 67.
20  Cabanes & Piketty, 2007, 7.
21  MF, 127–128.
22  MF, 146 & 145f.
23  Freud, 1900b, 487.
24  AI, 85.
25  AI, 86; Roudinesco, 1986.
26  AI, 130; DW, 157–161; EN, 99 & 103; VC1, 290.
27  AI, 130.
28  ATP, 1–18.
29  EN, 61.
30  ATP, 78.
31  DW, 132.
32  Nobécourt, 2008a.
33  AI, 130; ATP, 244; MF, 74; Nobécourt, 2008a.
34  AI, 122; EN, 91; PF, 113; Ribowski, 1987/2004.
35  Cabanes & Piketty, 2007, 2.
36  MF, 45–46; VC1, 45–46.
37  EN, 31; VC1, 2–30 & 256.
38  EN, 29.
39  AI, 74; EN, 29.
40  AI, 75.
41  AI, 66 & 74.
42  AI, 66 & 74.
43  AI, 74; ATP, 27–28; CE, 15; EN, 33.
44  AI, 69.
45  DW, 118.
46  AI, 118.
47  AI, 73; EN, 52–53; Ribowski, 1987/2004.
48  AI, 69, 73 & 78; EN, 16 & 35; MF, 142f; VC1, 29, 60f & 209–210.
49  MF, 141f & 142f.
50  VC1, 35.
51  VC1, 44 & 57.
52  VC1, 55.
53  MF, 23 & 51.

54  AI, 69.
55  AI, 73; VC1, 99.
56  ATP, 20; EN, 50; Ribowski, 1987/2004.
57  VC1, 215.
58  AI, 82.
59  EN, 10, 14, 82 & 93.
60  D&R, 21; also Laforgue, 1936.
61  ATP, 30; EN, 42.
62  EN, 46–47.
63  MF, 20; VC1, 41.
64  Ribowski, 1987/2004.
65  EN, 42.
66  ATP, 24. «Demander» can mean "ask" (literal) or "need to be" (idiomatic). So in hearing «les crevettes demandent à être cuites vivantes,» young Françoise understood the first rather than second (intended) sense; incidentally, in 1915, Françoise writes about fishing for shrimp in Deauville (VC1, 37).
67  ATP, 27.
68  EN, 65.
69  EN, 67.
70  EN, 67.
71  E.g., AI, 144.
72  E.g., AI, 144; CE, 272; DW, 40–41; EN, 64 & 117–118; Ribowski, 1987/2004.
73  AI, 144.
74  EN, 118–119.
75  CE, 272–273; also EN, 64.
76  EN, 64; Dolto & This, 1980/2002; Ribowski, 1987/2004.
77  AI, 144; Ribowski, 1987/2004.
78  AI, 79; EN, 35; PF, 35.
79  CE, 241; EM, 202–204.
80  EV, 61; IIC, 85.
81  EN, 30.
82  PF, 52.
83  ATP, 28; EN, 94.
84  EN, 47.
85  MF, 21 & 42.
86  VO, 199.
87  VC1, 305.
88  Nobécourt, 2008a; also DW, 163; EN, 84 & 93.
89  EN, 20–21.
90  EN, 20 (a common idiom).
91  EN, 21.
92  JD, 57.
93  SP2, 52.
94  D&R, 21; MA, 261.
95  VO, 199.
96  DQ, 116.
97  CE, 322.
98  CD, 239.
99  EV, 78.
100  SS, 143; also EM, 280; MA, 29; QS, 9; SS, 143.
101  SF, 140.
102  MA, 29.
103  MA, 29.
104  MA, 29; SP1, 155.

105 CD, 242f; also CE, 29; DV, 65; MA, 27; TL, 142.
106 Nobécourt & Simonetta, 1978.
107 VC2, 391 & 400.
108 AlloCiné, n.d..; Marie, 2008.
109 EN, 62 & 98.
110 SF, 250.
111 SP1, 213.
112 JD, 21; SF, 78; VC2, 14 & 702.
113 SF, 73–74; SP2, 45; SP3, 71; VO, 188.
114 SF, 73.
115 DW, 104; VC2, 641.
116 SP3, 81.
117 CD, 29.
118 CD, 215.
119 LF, 137.
120 CE, 328–329.
121 MA, 3–4.
122 MA, 153.
123 MA, 153.
124 MA, 153.
125 MA, 153.
126 MA, 153.
127 Freud, 1905c, 184f.
128 Morgenstern, 1927/2003.
129 Morgenstern, 1938/2003, 75 & 78.
130 Morgenstern, 1934/2003, 131.
131 Morgenstern, 1937/2003, 39.
132 VC2, 797.
133 SP3, 78.
134 SP2, 71 (emphasis hers).
135 Dolto, 1985c, 527–528.
136 SS, 221.
137 Dolto, 1957/1997a, 23.
138 ATP, 170; Dolto, 1985a, 527; DQ, 36; DV, 117; DW, 87 & 111; ES, 183–185; EV, 54; JD, 269; SP1,139–140; TL, 96.
139 JD, 23.
140 CD, 184; NE, 191.
141 CD, 70; SS, 37.
142 JD, 23; PS, 21 & 64; SP1, 148 & 151–152; SP2, 70.
143 Dolto, 1985a, 529.
144 SS, 24.
145 For a psychoanalytic study of the "silent period" in second language acquisition, see Granger, 2004. I believe Dolto further elucidates this phenomenon in terms of regression and the unconscious work of the phoneme.
146 MA, 15 (emphasis hers, contingent on French syntax).
147 Dolto, 1985a, 534.
148 VC2, 606.
149 DW, 110; EM, 140–144; MA, 224–225; SP3, 90; SS, 16, 42, 165 & 265; VO, 225.
150 LO3, 154; also SP2, 19; SP3, 175; VO, 42, 50 & 190–191.
151 JD, 126; also SP3, 156.
152 SP3, 26–29, VO, 162.
153 DQ, 196; also SF, 220.
154 JD, 149; MA, 17; Roudinesco, 1986, 497.
155 MA, 30.

156  SS, 23.
157  SS, 25.
158  MA, 27.
159  MA, 28.
160  MA, 28.
161  MA, 27 & 53.
162  JP, 41; MA, 15, 30 & 30f.
163  JD, 296–297; LF, 255; MA, 30.
164  JD, 270.
165  JD, 273.
166  JD, 270 & 296.
167  JD, 273.
168  JD, 286.
169  SS, 244.
170  QS, 9–10; VC2, 728.
171  DQ, 123.
172  MA, 27.
173  JD, 287; LF, 103.
174  EM, 111.
175  LF, 126.
176  LO1, 90; LO2, 50.
177  SF, 69.
178  LF, 103.
179  MA, 223.
180  SS, 89.
181  SS, 17.
182  JD, 226.
183  JD, 163.
184  SS, 24 & 144.
185  SS, 20.
186  SP2, 240.
187  SS, 42.
188  EM, 139.
189  SP2, 19; VO, 190–191.
190  Freud, 1896/1954a, 180.
191  Freud, 1940[1939], 166.
192  CE, 29; EM, 61.
193  JD, 123.
194  LF, 92.
195  DV, 9.
196  MA, 24.
197  MA, 24; also DW, 31.
198  MA, 11 & 24.
199  MA, 24–25.
200  MA, 24–25; also VO, 50.
201  JD, 256.
202  SF, 210.
203  Freud, 1905c, 218, 1917e, 252.
204  SS, 74.
205  ES, 107.
206  Coronel & De Mezamat, 1997b.
207  SS, 115–116, 142 & 265.
208  SF, 250.
209  JD, 30; LF, 113.

210 Laplanche & Pontalis, 1967/2004, 148.
211 JP, 38.
212 JP, 38 & 41; SS, 11, 26, 75, 114, 118 & 128.
213 VO, 225.
214 SS, 15–16.
215 JP, 39.
216 SS, 24–25 & 144.
217 LF, 97.
218 DQ, 261.
219 VO, 233.
220 Dolto, 1965, 16; EM, 140; LO1, 90; SP2, 154–155; VO, 233.
221 JD, 279.
222 SP1, 123.
223 Birksted-Breen, Flanders & Gibeault, 2010, 15, 33, 37 & 41.
224 Freud, 1900b, 542–543 & 548, 1905c, 240, 1909b, 49, 1917c, 342 & 417, 1917e, 250.
225 Freud, 1909b, 45, 1912a, 102, 1914b, 74–75 & 82.
226 Freud, 1895, 296, 1900b, 547–548, 1914b, 101, 1917e, 251.
227 Freud, 1900b, 553f, 1905c, 206, 1914b.
228 Freud, 1900a, 174, 1900b, 467, 1912a, 103.
229 Freud, 1895, 340, 1900a, 119, 120–122 & 133, 1900b, 553 & 589.
230 Freud, 1900a, 233–234, 1900b, 570, 1917c, 417, 1940[1939], 171.
231 Freud, 1900b, 565–566, 1905c, 213, 1914b, 80.
232 Ferenczi, 1913/1950, 218 & 220–221; also Dupont, 1985, 83.
233 Freud, 1900b, 603.
234 Freud, 1900a, 22–23, 64 & 280, 1900b, 525 & 603, 1915a, 123.
235 Freud, 1895, 297–298, 1900b, 599, 1917c, 356.
236 Freud, 1900a, 8 & 487, 1900b, 467.
237 Freud, 1900a, 235, 1913, 169.
238 Freud, 1905c, 287.
239 Freud, 1905c, 288.
240 Freud, 1914b, 85.
241 Freud, 1913, 182.
242 Freud, 1905c, 176, 205 & 233–234.
243 LF, 99.
244 SS, 42.
245 SS, 157.
246 SP2, 27.
247 SP1, 76.
248 LF, 283.
249 LF, 92 & 103.
250 CE, 29.
251 LO3, 170.
252 SF, 216.
253 EM, 283.
254 Birksted-Breen, Flanders & Gibeault, 2010, 37.
255 CH, 31; SP1, 90.
256 SF, 208.
257 DQ, 18.
258 PS, 22.
259 Freud, 1915b, 166.
260 Freud, 1896/1954a, 180.
261 SS, 41.
262 SP2, 130.

263  CD, 179; SP3, 204–206.
264  DW, 100.
265  SP1, 20.
266  De Mezamat, 2008a.
267  VO, 52.
268  SP3, 204.
269  CD, 179.
270  EM, 39; also CE, 27; QS, 14; DW, 166.
271  Birksted-Breen, Flanders & Gibeault, 2010, 15.
272  Birksted-Breen, Flanders & Gibeault, 2010, 24f.
273  AI, 192.
274  SS, 41.
275  CE, 172; LF, 87.
276  CD, 178; CE, 27; Dolto, 1988b, 14 & 77; DW, 166; SP1, 126.
277  SP2, 125; TL, 43.
278  CE, 243; also SP1, 37.
279  SP1, 216–217.
280  MA, 178; SF, 141; SP1, 123.
281  Bott Spillius et al., 2011, 271.
282  Bott Spillius et al., 2011, 348.
283  Roudinesco, 1999, 159.
284  Roudinesco, 1986/1988, 32.
285  IIC, 271.
286  Freud, 1900a, 112, 293, 321 & 324, 1900b, 342.
287  Freud, 1896a, 196, 1900a, 279 & 284.
288  Freud, 1900a, 284 & 306–307.
289  Freud, 1900a, 279.
290  Laplanche & Pontalis, 1967/2004, 263.
291  MA, 24.
292  Mishra Tarc, 2015, 135.
293  Freud, 1914b, 86.
294  Laplanche & Pontalis, 1967/2004, 262.
295  Rustin, 2008, 377.
296  CE, 262–263.
297  VC2, 206.
298  DW, 40–41.
299  DW, 40–41 (emphasis mine).
300  SF, 332.
301  D&R, 13.
302  Bott Spillius et al., 2011, 409–412.
303  DQ, 203 (emphasis hers).
304  D&R, 13; DW, 40–41.
305  D&R, 13; DW, 40.
306  DW, 40.
307  DW, 45.
308  DW, 41.
309  DW, 40.
310  Nobécourt, 2008c; PJE, 97.
311  SP3, 175.
312  EN, 96.
313  Dolto, 1985c, 197.
314  JD, 137.
315  Freud, 1900a, 326–327.
316  Stärcke, 1921a, 200; also Stärcke, 1921b.

317 Stärcke, 1921a, 198.
318 Abraham, 1924/1949, 450.
319 JP, 8.
320 SS, 72.
321 JP, 42.
322 JP, 40–42.
323 EM, 149; JD, 104; JP, 40–42.
324 JP, 47–48.
325 JP, 37.
326 JP, 48.
327 JD, 140 & 154.
328 Roudinesco, 1982, 108 & 210; 1986, 584.
329 Freud, 1905c, 224 & 236.
330 Freud, 1937, 240.
331 Freud, 1896/1954a, 180; 1937, 240 & 241,1940[1939], 167.
332 DV, 301; DW, 104; NE, 243; SP3, 176.
333 CD, 243.
334 CE, 16, 268 & 293.
335 NE, 243; SP1, 29.
336 DW, 34; SP1, 125; TL, 37.
337 LF, 98.
338 SP2, 213; EM, 220; LF, 206–208; NE, 190; SP2, 213.
339 SS, 167.
340 QC, 67.
341 JD, 19f; SS, 166.
342 CD, 19; EM, 28; LF, 98–99; TL, 150.
343 SS, 172.
344 JD, 202.
345 SP1, 31.
346 DQ, 113; also EM, 82; SP2, 191.
347 JD, 281.
348 JD, 282.
349 NE, 190.
350 EN, 108.
351 CD, 214; LF, 219.
352 CE, 33; also EM, 222–223.
353 VO, 197.
354 SP1, 217; also CD, 99: DW, 129; LF, 291; PM, 38.
355 SP1, 217.
356 VO, 162.
357 VO, 34; also AI, 120; SP1, 59.
358 DW, 34; MA, 258;SP1, 39; SP3, 92.
359 CE, 205.
360 SS, 15.
361 SS, 234 & 256.
362 EN, 54.
363 EN, 54.
364 D&R, 31.
365 EN, 119.
366 Ribowski, 1987/2004.

# 4

# LISTENING

## Introduction

If one word is repeated throughout Dolto's corpus more than any other, it is «Trousseau.» It appears in virtually all of her books, and a movie about her work has l'Hôpital Armand-Trousseau as its setting.[1] Dolto's daughter, Catherine, explains how this word stayed with her and her siblings all through their childhood because it came up so often, and because it was a place that drew their mother regularly for so long.[2] After all, Dolto worked there for almost 40 years, from 1941 to 1978.[3] She had received her medical certification in 1937, years after obtaining her nursing accreditation.[4] In her long career, there would be other hospitals, a private practice and countless seminars. But nowhere was her commitment greater than at Trousseau.

Yet we have only just entered the world of Dolto, where we meet a surface that impresses, only to discover that there is far more than meets the eye. For it turns out that Dolto was never paid for this work. Nonetheless, every Tuesday for nearly four decades, from 9:00 to 14:00, she listened to children's suffering.[5] "I never missed a consultation, I never missed a Tuesday," she says—«ça me portait.»[6] And here, a bilingual reader may feel the arrival of something, as if an unseen window has suddenly opened. For the common idiom, "it carried me," denotes what is fulfilling—but the «ça» is also "the Id." Dolto has just said, literally, that the unconscious carried her. Or has she?

Recent translators supported by the French government to help disseminate Dolto's work comment in their introduction about their difficulty with her language, explaining that she, "simply invents words, or slightly deforms them."[7] And one of her best interviewers admits to feeling "exhausted and haggard" after his dialogue with her, though Dolto was barely fatigued—at nearly 80.[8] For Dolto's rhetoric is a fluid mix of conversations and provocations from beneath that disturb, suggest and question, in interminable echoes that take some getting used to. Her translators also note the odd time-shifts in her storytelling, "from present, to future, to past."[9] Then again, why not? After all, Dolto says—as if it were commonly known—time is what is splitting.[10]

## Choral

But where is Dolto to talk like this? What is the vantage point of someone who speaks from a subject position prior to time? At the age of five, Dolto was already musing that she might have been "born too early in a century too old."[11] Even in adulthood, her location in reality seemed contestable: "Am I late? Or on the contrary, am I too early?"[12] Dolto's work is located on an archaic dreamscape where it is easy to lose space and time, just as invented word-things arrive to describe those experiences, like «mamelonnairement» ["nipplelingly"][13] and «chosifiant» ["thingifying"].[14] An availability for play and nuance is required if one is to be drawn by Dolto's discourse to the foremost element of her practice and theory: finely tuned audition. For the reader will need to be listening carefully to hear the *infans*—the voiceless one prior to speaking.

At Trousseau, Dolto maintained an unusual practice for which the lack of payment soon seems secondary. For one, she worked with a Madame Arlette for every one of those years—yet Madame Arlette is silent in the analytic literature.[15] She was an assistant installed in the hall outside, who served as a relay between (usually) the mother and Dolto. Letters and artwork, completed since the last visit, were handed to Madame Arlette, who came in with the mother and child—into a "minuscule office ... that barely fit five,"[16] Dolto recounts regretfully—and the remaining space was filled with trainees, typically two.

And while Dolto is widely known for the symbolic payments (rocks, stamps, snippets) that she asked of her young patients, what should interest us at least as much is the trademark greeting Dolto addressed to every child, welcoming him by his first name—and how everyone present repeated it, "in choral."[17] She reiterates throughout her corpus that you must always introduce yourself and address a baby by his name.[18] Here is the first hint that Dolto engages language differently, giving the name a unique valuation. Thus, her practice would include detailed anamneses, and every case would place the child in a story with family members and anyone else with a possible influence—all associated with their names. Dolto's cardinal assumption is that the child is a subject of language from conception, so his subjectivity is always at stake in the encounter with words. And her project, above all, will show that the human subject is conceived in languaged relations, thus destined to be inserted in these relations.

The assumption of a languaged being existing from the start takes us right to precocious audition, or the infant's pre-language. Human existence begins and continues because, "we are welcomed into language,"[19] Dolto explains. We need a long moment here to understand, then, that when Dolto says "all is language,"[20] she intends passive receptivity. It is not that the child speaks in every way possible (not yet), but, rather, that at the archaic stage she is narrating, the child is purely passive. And in that state of acute receptivity, he makes every experience into a communication because that is what it means to be humanized. For it is a fact that audition is prior to vision,[21] she notes, and the fetus from conception inhabits a "sonar climate."[22] Audition, then, is what "lures"[23] us onto a landscape of unconscious desires investing words. Further, when we speak of desire with Dolto, we are never speaking of conscious wants, but rather of a "pre-subject"[24] with an "unconscious desire" for communication.[25]

The fetus lives an "extraordinary social life," Dolto posits,[26] wherein his "audition is perfect."[27] Herein, he is in a "listening relation"[28] with his mother, as he is engaged in an "intra-narcissistic libidinal dialectic"[29]—a dream of discourse, we might say. His audition is his access,[30] and everything from the human heart to the mother's organic affects and respiration are his language[31]— one in which "organ peace," in a two-time (double) rhythm, represents the basis of life.[32] We stop to consider Dolto's remarkable offer: it is an engagement with sound in an entirely unconscious state of security.

## Precocious audition

We have arrived at the notion of a wish of perfect provision. As Dolto says: "Everything happens as if babies register the significance of what happens around them concerning them, and the emotional climate of the relation of their parents in their regard."[33] In this way, the phonemes of the mother tongue and even foreign languages are heard before nine months of age,[34] while the child is in a purely passive state of expectation, living out organic peace in a fetal, "purée of significance ... a purée of words"[35]—effectively, the nourishment of words and their affects—so audition is like eating.[36] The child is born waiting for human communication from the outside,[37] looking for "the road of a listening"[38]—using «repères langagiers fantasmatique sarchaïques» ["archaic phantasmatic languaged landmarks"][39] to refind archaic security—as perception slowly develops, and sensations that were first experienced as if they were words are replaced by actual words.[40]

This is a critical turn not to be missed. For on the word there is a migration to reality, and a conduit to and from the archaic. The body is a "mediator (but never a possessor) of this truth"[41]—access to a cultural-temporal history that the child is born into, that continues after him. So receptive is the passive child that he can intuit his filiation, having an innate sense of his story, including who his parents are,[42] being in a "telepathic relation"[43] with them. This symbolic filiation dominates over carnal filiation,[44] as "interpsychic communication,"[45] from fetal life through to birth, arising from "intuitive hearing"[46] from three or four months' gestation—or earlier, depending on his fetal history, what is heard and his affective reactions.[47] Therefore, Dolto believes unhesitatingly that birth brings possibilities for pleasure: "Birth is a liberation: we are born into liberty."[48]

With Dolto, then, the infant is an honorable human being who is already symbolizing, who merely depends on an other (as if himself) for his liberation.

To stress, Dolto's *infans* in the archaic stage is not only prior to speaking, but
prior to being present in the usual sense—a full subject who functions entirely
unconsciously, antedating birth. On this view, the mother and other adults may
grant or withhold their agreement to life, and it is "their duty to subsequent generations to sustain fetuses in their desire to be born."[49] As uncomfortable as
Dolto's words may feel, they compel a more careful listening, a second hearing,
and a playing with reversals. For the "fetus desiring to live" is none other than a
wishful being—alive unconsciously, subsisting blissfully in his dreams, in the jurisdiction of the instinct of conservation. And as Freud explains it, there is an auto-
erotic state at the origin of life: "Something must be added to auto-eroticism to
bring about narcissism."[50] In this state, Freud says, "auto-erotic sexual satisfactions
are experienced in connection with vital functions that serve the purpose of self-
preservation."[51]

Helped by Freud, we can follow Dolto more easily now when she muses
about how the mother's obligations confound pregnancy with illness and death
via the «interdit» ["prohibition"; homonym: «inter dit,» "spoken between"; and
near-homonym, «enterre dit»: "buried said"].[52] For her view of infancy is
rooted in the primacy of the instincts. Of course, this auto-erotic state *in utero* is
not "auto" at all: "There must be, actually, neither life pulses nor death pulses,
everything is absolutely linked to the mother,"[53] Dolto says. In addition, as
Freud noted, in exploring the onset of primary narcissism under the domination
of the pleasure principal, it is difficult "to find our bearings,"[54] so we "face the
possibility of error."[55] Yet Dolto's valuing of examples serves the Freudian
oeuvre extremely well, as "legitimate extensions of the theory of libido come
from observations of children."[56]

## Soma of understanding

Thus it comes to be that, in 1955–1956, the reader meets Lionel, an orphan,
age four.[57] Lionel likes to watch himself bleed, plays with his excrement and
destroys all that he touches. His symptoms include encopresis, incontinence and
insomnia, and he is covered in scabs and scars. Small for his age, his arms are
frozen to the touch and he smells horrible. Yet Dolto places him on her lap,
and they begin to model clay together as she carefully renarrates the confusing
story of his family—one where key men have the same name, and the mother
and grandmother share theirs too, so Lionel thinks his grandmother is his
mother[58]—whereby he has lost in his history his own dead mother. There will
be a remarkably rapid return of cleanliness and sleep, and Lionel will begin to
make friends in the public home where he will be placed in lieu of the psychi-
atric hospital where he was headed. Simply, Dolto had heard about Lionel from
hospital staff and insisted on a chance to see him, believing there was hope
because, "Lionel still speaks."[59]

In a dense sentence that could sum up her entire view of fetal life, Dolto states: "Everything happens as if gestation then infancy were periods of affective as much as somatic incarnation, as if the fetus constructs himself according to an organo-emotional register induced by his mother."[60] The words are vintage Dolto—a liquid flow of the puzzlingly phantasmatic with the radically new that challenges normative discourses. Here is a non-space, non-time where bodily sounds and syllables, "veiled" for now,[61] are auditorily invested as, "the child somatizes in the outlet of comprehension—ears."[62] And in Dolto's narration of the fluid dreamscape of self-sufficiency that is oral passivity, we refind Freud.

Freud was the first to note the imperative role of the word in our coming to reality: "Becoming conscious ... consists for the most part in the verbal consciousness pertaining to ... the associated word-presentations."[63] Freud's notion of the word-thing also helps explicate how words are subject to condensation and displacement, as if they were dream objects.[64] And if first syllables can do this, Dolto's work suggests, then all syllables can. For a sound in phantasy is entirely without a definition—free. So we locate the social life of the fetus in the nascent proprioception of sound that feeds the dream, as Freud describes it: "That the senses aroused during sleep influence the dream is well known and can be experimentally verified; it is one of the certain but much overestimated results of the medical investigation of dreams."[65] We also note that, "stimuli arising during sleep are worked up into a wish-fulfillment."[66] Freud explains how, "infantile experiences are ... sexual experiences affecting the subject's own body ... sexual intercourse (in the wider sense)";[67] and elsewhere he speaks of the "universally recognized influence exercised upon our dreams by states of excitation in our digestive, urinary and sexual organs."[68]

So we begin in a dream spun upon sounds, in the elaboration of the wish to which all stimuli encountered in an unconscious state are subject. As a result, language always locates the symptom for Dolto, being a mediating object of unconscious content. And though her corpus is rich with clinical cases (easily more than 100), one that merits special attention—not just because it is the only one with its own book (and one of the rare Dolto texts translated into English in her lifetime)—is that of Dominique Bel ["beautiful"], age 14. A footnote explains that "a few modifications of names and places were necessary,"[69] and enigma immediately arrives. For Dolto says he dominated his mother, conforming to his name;[70] and she would interpret "the sonar meeting of the patronym of the family and the adjective characterizing powerful specular seduction."[71] Yet, elsewhere, we learn that Dominique is a Russian restaurant in Paris,[72] and it was her favorite man's name in 1928.[73] And despite our attunement to the phoneme, Dolto adds that the modified names do not hamper the "significant associative value."[74] So has she changed his name, or not?

Through 12 sessions over a year-and-a-half—in snippets of observations scattered over 150 pages—her work with Dominique is centred on exploring the wild world of words and their psychical impact. Dolto discusses the relation between his surname, «bel,» and its antonym, «laid» ["ugly"]—which is itself a homonym of «lait» ["milk"]—and a regression to his nursery, «la salle» ["the room"], as a homonym of «la sale» ["the dirty one," i.e., his baby sister]. In turn, the name of that sister, Sylvie [homonymically: «si il vit,» "if he lives"], evokes (in contradiction) the death of an uncle (i.e., he who does not live). Dominique's desire to be a pirate, a «voleur de mer» ["thief of the sea"], is narrated in relation to its homonymic equivalent, a «voleur de mère» ["thief of the mother"]. And we witness Dolto's particular attention to a repeated phrase about an invisible river that Dominique names «Elmoru» [homonym: "she died"]. Dominique's eventual recovery is credited to his learning that there is such a thing as a «maire» ["mayor"], an exact homonym of «mère» ["mother"] but a male. Dolto concludes that he thus became entitled to «lait» ["milk"; homonym: «laid,» "ugly"], despite being «bel»—and, thereby, that he was authorized to assume life in his name.[75]

The freefall of logic is spectacular. And it is a bold testament to how the oral passive stage is a startlingly different setting for thought, as the symptom takes the word as an opportunity to express the affects of primary narcissism. Yet Dolto is always ready to risk herself for truth. Here is 12-year-old Tony, missing school for months due to acute pain in his «genoux» ["knees"; homonymically: "I we/us"]. Dolto comments: «*Genoux? Je, nous* … On dirait un jeu de mots ou de maux» ["Knees? I, we/us? … It seems like a game of words or pains"].[76] Disorientingly original, Dolto finds passages for archaic regressions and progressive renarrations right on the name. We also detect Dolto's unspoken awareness of the slippery pronouns that herald primary narcissism. Yet the healing is real. But, "Why *this* symptom?" Dolto is asked in seminars. "I have no idea," she replies—"I am asking if you have an idea."[77]

## «Mamaïser»

As a consequence of Dolto's foundational belief that the infant is unconsciously attuned to the flow of language around him, much of her work consists of untangling family stories, listening for the dream-work of words. "I listen otherwise," she says cryptically.[78] Working backwards along a regressive path to the archaic—not so far back for children—she searches for «malentendu» ["misunderstood"; but literally, "misheard" or "evil heard"]. For inherent in the notion that passive encounters with audition are formative to psychical structuration is the idea that such encounters can cause destructuration, too—knots of libido, condensations upon a word that need to be released, unspun.

This approach to the role of words in the psychical economy will inform Dolto's method in ways that cannot help but strike the unfamiliar reader as surprising: one must warn a child that he will be told lies;[79] one must never lie to a child;[80] every infant has a right to his truth, to know the trials he survived;[81] and if you speak to a baby as an equal, then you will have an equal with you.[82] Roger Bacon rightly says, "How odd, how 'other' [is] not just the direction of her thinking but the language."[83] Yet always, Dolto is candid and witty, professing that she is merely a «zinzin»[84] ["dingdong"], working with a «clientèle de zinzins,»[85] in a «zinzinnerie»[86] ["dingdongery"]. There is no pretension here—no sign of the «bourgeoise» from the 16th «arrondissement.»

Yet there is no sign of a theory of illness either. For, on the one hand, there is no coincidence: «Il n'y a pas de hazard.»[87] On the other hand, there are no generalities either: «Il n'y a pas d'en general.»[88] So the oral passive stage and its sense of no-place, no-time saturates the terrain of Dolto's discourse. Her translators point out the continuous "I-we" reversals, where the reader remains uncertain if "we" means colleagues or the "royal we," how the subject pronoun is often uncertain for gender (uncommon for French) and the slippery point of view.[89] So not just time is unsettled, as we have noted, but space (position) too. And in a story worth remembering under the giant clock tower at Trousseau, Dolto once commented that in the early century, «l'heure juste» ["the right time"] was a funny idea because no one actually had it.[90] Yet resounding here are powerful echoes on the homonym: «leurre(s) juste» ["just (ethical) lure(s)"]—as if the word itself suggested a beckoning to reality.

Wary of the tenuousness of making meaning from so much homonymic play, we might choose to refuse it. And yet, by this "play," we are led to the uncanny discovery of one of the most useful words in Dolto's entire project: «mamaïser» ["to motherify"]—a term "that says well what it says."[91] To "motherify" is to mark the present by the mother's voice, to lure to reality. Soon, like the fetus in his auditory climate, then, we too begin to detect sounds to which we can attach our phantasies as primitive ideas about Dolto's theories. Inherent in what is «mamaïser» is the mother, hopefully at her best, as an "auditory caress"[92]—the one upon whose rhythms the child is dependent[93]—leading Dolto to speak of "psychical vitality woven to organic vitality."[94] Our bodies rely on the «paroles» of our parents,[95] "more subtle than liquid,"[96] she says. In effect, Dolto is unraveling a narrative of life whereby we are drawn into reality by hearing, from early in gestational life, as language on the "outside" lures us into relations with the sources of those voices.[97] Language is what "humanizes the world,"[98] Dolto explains, making it worthwhile to engage because in utero, "audition tempers anxiety."[99]

Within the security of the "language bath that is our body,"[100] our wish to live is met by a dream of perfect provision that invests audition, whereby we are "conceived in language."[101] The subject thus survives by "a dialectic expressed ... by speech and by the phantasms subtending speech."[102] To stress, we are "lured towards reality by being spoken of."[103] Yet this address paradoxically needs no words, as Dolto will elaborate. And here, we are reminded of the momentary absence essential to any rhythm, by definition. Further, as Dolto puts it, there are mothers who speak to their babies in silence, and others who engage in empty discourses.[104] Here as elsewhere, Dolto is addressing the crucial investment of unconscious affect. So the mother can only be maternal in her mother tongue.[105] And the mother's death (or loss) will represent the "end of history," in that she is the source of «parole.»[106] At issue is a radical concept to which we will return:

mother and baby dream upon the same word in, "a continuous relation ... that creates a memory of myself-other."[107] Dolto explains that the baby begins to be spoken of when the mother starts to have «émois particuliers» ["particular affects"] for the child and speaks of him while pregnant.[108] But by now attuned to Dolto's condensations, we take a moment to reflect on her term here: «émois» [homonymically, "and me"].

## «Moi-mamère»

We might take this word-play as another bit of madness, except that it leads to another vital notion—the infant's indissociable "and-me" state with the mother —for which Dolto coins another word, «moi-mamère» ["me-mymother"].[109] Dolto conceptualizes an indivisible, fluid psychical entity that is not a child *and* mother—and this is fundamental—but, rather, the child *as* mother. In brief, the term signifies a narcissistic "prolonging."[110] This «sensorium,»[111] a term she credits to Pichon (in a highly atypical act of citation), is an environment Dolto elaborates lifelong as an undifferentiated liquid mass,[112] a liquid current,[113] a gestational interpersonal emotional rapport,[114] an unconscious fusional communication,[115] an unconscious continuum[116] and an emotional climate.[117] Thus Dolto elucidates the life of the infant as a rising sense of presence slowly encroaching on a most private residence.

Dolto describes the baby as being in a state of «covivance» ["coliving"] with the mother,[118] since primary narcissism is necessarily "co-narcissistic with the mother"[119]—with huge effects. For one, we will share dreams and have "complimentary phantasms with our mother" in unconscious life.[120] This alone is a shocking suggestion of "inherited education,"[121] as "archaic transference"[122]—a deep unconscious relation extending to those we encounter in words in our families, for about three generations.[123] Freud expressed in his earliest work how, "an unexplained hereditary predisposition may be accounted for as having been acquired at an early age."[124] With Dolto, the scope of "early" has merely shifted months back. And in this inseparable fusion of «moi-mamère,» as the mother is spoken to, the child becomes an unconscious addressee as words are first lived with soft, permeable boundaries between self and other. So archaic regression will necessarily entail an experience of the world through another that is as if the mother[125]—an inherent "reversibility of subject positions" upon the one to whom we speak[126]—in whom we recognize «mêmeté» ["sameness"].[127] Dolto asks: "Who speaks to whom, when someone refers to himself as 'you' in his *for intérieur*?"[128] Indeed.

For Dolto's work reveals that the transference subtends human relationality as a call to an-other-as-self, in an unconscious reversibility. And this, in a nutshell, is the archaic geography of primary narcissism. Inhering is the notion that the infant feels addressed within a text addressed to the «moi-mamère,» where the body of the *mater* is conducting matter—*materia*. Herein originates the passive experience of an address within language as an unconscious hearing-within-a-hearing rooted deep in an archaic prehistory where passivity dominates—conferring the symbolic continuity that we instinctively need, so unconsciously desire.

As a case for our consideration, in 1954, we meet le «petit schizophrène,»[129] during whose session something happened that Dolto says she will never forget, as it unsettled her so much.[130] At age 13, he is extremely phobic (especially of scissors), volatile, insomniac (never sleeping more than one hour) and illiterate. Dolto works with him every eight days, and in what becomes the penultimate session, she helps him move clay shapes towards a scraper on the table. Unexpectedly, she then helps his hand scratch the back of her hand with the scraper, saying, "You see, it is not you that is hurting, and this does not even hurt me." "That is all?" he asks, in a flash of lucidity. And then, from his mouth, comes a haunting discourse in two voices, one high and pleading, the other older and stern: "You slut, you will never have him ... Mother I want to keep him ..." The next day, Dolto receives an urgent request from the mother for a meeting, because when they got home from the session he slept all night and woke up calm, different. In ensuing conversations, Dolto learns that the child was adopted, and the «bande magnétique» was real—overheard by the adoptive mother as she waited in the hospital to receive the baby, in a private arrangement between families. She had never told anyone about the argument, and she was shocked to hear of how Dolto had learned of it. At his next session, the boy could not remember having said it. But cured of his phobias, he inserted himself in the social—and became a tailor!

## Narcissistic cohesion

What is most overdetermined in Dolto's practice, then, is a profound vesting of audition—a keen listening to words by which we will locate deep connections to Freud's earliest work. And what is foremost among Dolto's assumptions is her conviction about the value of a child's first name as a "symbol of primary narcissism" and "narcissistic cohesion."[131] Strong prescriptions issue from this belief: never change the first name of any child, including adoptees, as there is no way to predict the "toxic effect" on primary narcissism;[132] and beware of the unconscious effects of giving the name of the dead (as when names are handed down), whom the child now represents in language.[133] Furthermore, every child, even the profoundly deaf, must hear (feel) his name symbolized as early as possible,[134] for the absence or loss of a name leads to «déréliction narcissique,»[135] as "the saying of his name can wake up the subject."[136] We are dealing in dream-work here, and Dolto urges us to keep in mind the importance of overdetermination.[137] She then engages in wild discourses, staking her reputation to explain how the first name is "engrammed" like a magnetic band;[138] a midwife assisting birth can be an "evil-bearing witch,"[139] who marks destiny "as if it were written";[140] and "babies live from words."[141]

Amid the derision of nameless critics populating the edges of Dolto's project—and, sometimes, even through the warm laughter in seminars of the most informed—it is easy to lose sight (in an auditory world without vision) of the deft movements on the oral passive stage that are, quite literally, at play here. And while Dolto leaves drawing the connection to Freud to the reader, we will find it helpful to shore up her work on primary narcissism with Freud's, as we explore the pulses of auto-conservation on the elusive first scene of "oral eroticization."[142]

Thinking with Freud's paper on narcissism,[143] we consider not where the pulse is headed, towards the ego, but, rather, where it is coming from—a pre-history when the sexual libido that will eventually enable object relations is indissociable from primitive instincts. Oral passivity informs that liquid first scene of eroticization as an unconscious experience of audition sourced in the orality of the other—sounds that arrive through rhythms and silences in a phan-tastic weave with the affects they evoke—dream-work upon words in service of the wish. Freud's earliest studies on hysteria tell of Frau Emmy Von N., who called out her daughter's name—the same as her own—to "help her back to clear-headedness."[144] Elsewhere, Freud remarks that, "a sleeper is much more certain to be awakened by the sound of his own name than by any indifferent auditory impression";[145] and the "best method of waking a sleeper or a sleep-walker is to call him by his own name."[146] There is also an uncanny reference to hypnotism, where the "subject behaves to the rest of the external world as though he were asleep,"[147] while he hears and attends only to the hypnotist—a situation Freud precisely compares to "a mother who is nursing her baby."[148] Dolto's work confirms this relation eloquently. For our first encounters with words are right off the register of reality—and deep inside a dream. Morphology is marvellously murky.

Eventually, by listening to Dolto and to her patients, the reader becomes accus-tomed to the surroundings. And in that singular soundscape, in one analysis after another, we will find Dolto's distinctive attention to the unconscious play of invested words in an individual's history. For example, we will meet Isabelle, the trilingual little girl (age not given) who cannot add or spell in French because this represents a separation from her (non-Francophone) father;[149] an 11-year-old boy Dolto met in 1941, who becomes incontinent when he brings an English book home, as if the new language castrates his father;[150] Patrick, the eight-year-old who learns Italian from his nurse while in a coma for three months;[151] and Katia, the four-year-old whose analysis opens on her wanting a medal decorated with a «ficelle» ["thread"], for which Dolto takes up the homonym, the «fils-elle» ["son-she"], as a direction for interpretation.[152] We also encounter a nine-year-old who howls and eats dirt in identification with a beloved dead gardener, Robert, and who names himself «Robert tombé par la fenêtre» ["Robert fallen out the window"]—the window being, homonymically (and contradictorily), «feu naître» ["fire (of) being born"] and the «feu n'être» ["fire (of) not being"].[153] There was hope for Robert, Dolto states, because he could still "say the name," so she understood that he thought he was the gardener's dog. And her understanding is as hopeful as it is radical.

## Angles

We will also meet the 12-year-old boy who was (in keeping with Dolto's favorite adjective for her young patients) «superbe,» yet who had grave academic delays because his mother and father had the same last name, she explains. And because the maternal grandmother had died, he thought that his paternal grandmother was the mother of both of his parents. "What is the theoretical plan for an interpretation?" a seminar attendee asks; half-laughing, Dolto answers that "it interprets the «chosification» ["thingification"] of living beings."[154]

There is Jeanne (age 13), one of the 16 cases in Dolto's dissertation, whose pivotal symptoms are a reversal of syllable order and saccadic speech;[155] about a decade later, another child will be reported to have a similar symptom, Nicole (age five), who speaks only one syllable at a time.[156] Then there is Gilles, whose phobia of "murderous angles" is deemed by Dolto to be connected to the departure of a beloved uncle to war, in 1940, to join «les anglais» ["the English"] in «Angleterre» [homonyms: "angle-hush," "angle-earth"]; Gilles became anxious because of having to keep silent (hushed) about his family being collaborators while they were forced to host Germans.[157]

One hardly knows where to begin or end the examples, and there is no clear line between them either. For Dolto's oeuvre seems compelled to convey by its style a message of continuity and reversibility, as if it were an uncanny literary metaphor—an incidental performative—of primary narcissism as the condition of our origins in a non-space, non-time wherein there is fusion between self and other, inseparability. Thus Dolto opens very provocative questions about where a life, a subject or an autobiography begins—or ends.

With keen listening for manifestations of the oral passive stage, Dolto embarks on a career spanning 50 years, almost all of it overlapping with Trousseau, where she will begin uncommon observations: that the oral «pré-moi» stage is humanizing and marked by archaic desires;[158] as important as gestation is the first 10–12 months, being rooted in much earlier incidents;[159] and the intelligence of the infant is in the service of oral passive survival[160] until about nine months of age, the time of first teeth, when weaning is recommended,[161] as teeth suffering demands biting.[162] Here is a fine movement we should note carefully, for passivity suffices until there is suffering—and passivity is prior to suffering. Suffering at orality, then, necessitates exterior libidinal investments at orality.

Prior to reality, the baby hallucinates while sleeping,[163] and the entire oral passive stage takes place in a "dream-like, quasi-hallucinatory mode"[164] that avoids the devastation of solitude by the continuous delivery of unconscious pleasure. This dream of perfect provision secures what Freud described as the "wish to sleep"[165]—primitive auto-eroticism where "satisfaction is obtained from the subject's own body and extraneous objects are disregarded."[166] It is a perfect "continuum" or "habitus" of security and unity.[167] So pleasurable is this dream state that Dolto views anxiety as a "resistance to eroticization."[168] This is highly consistent with Freud's view that, "anxiety must enter the psyche from elsewhere."[169] As Dolto explains it, it is the remains of that prior libidinal organization, our preverbal internal language, that is "experienceable in transference."[170] For Dolto, the transference is a continuous interrelational phenomenon that begins at conception and is «perpétuellement présent» in human relations as a "receptive resonance"[171]—the continuation of what is living, unconsciously, as the source of life[172] that is the archaic origin of language.[173] Summatively, Dolto believes libido is "woven to the body but of the order of language,"[174] animating the «fonction symbolique.»[175]

## Continuum of security

Thus grounded, Dolto will privilege listening. Roudinesco describes it perfectly as a psychoanalytic method centred on hearing the unconscious.[176] And Aubry (Roudinesco's mother) calls Dolto «géniale» in listening for the unconscious.[177] I listen naïvely, Dolto admits, listening for the other,[178] unconscious language,[179] a human presence[180]—because learning is in listening,[181] and the analyst must put himself in parentheses,[182] refraining from impeding what the analysand says.[183] Dolto will listen slowly, quietly,[184] believing the analyst's "non-reactivity" is what reactualizes what is unknown or forgotten in history.[185] In other words, the listener is foremost a witness.[186] So she stresses, like Freud, looking at patients the least possible[187] as she works to decode unconscious fixations keeping the past alive, thereby allowing patients to recover libidinal energy that had been unusable.[188] Dolto explains it thus: "The elucidation of not-saids transforms [a person's] destiny … and the energy put back in play is irreversible. It is like a source."[189]

And that is how we come to value the peculiar case wherein Dolto explains the body as the "fruit" of speech exchanged.[190] The 15-month-old boy is "superb" during the day—in contact with others and objects, she says. But he is a profound insomniac, wailing all night, in full opisthonos, when he does not recognize his mother. Dolto sees him four times, biweekly. The last time, in a session that may disturb the reader, she explains to him that he wears the name of a stillborn son preceding him (along a family tradition of handing down names), and that his mother is sad not to be able to think of her dead child with a name, so perhaps he fears sleep as he is afraid to represent the dead child. The toddler pulls himself up to Dolto's chair and gives her a penetrating look, then quickly asks to depart. Other toddlers will say the same thing over the years, asking their mothers to leave. And yet, so typically, Dolto's intervention installs a rapid cure whereby he "refound sleep" and began to catch up in maturity— sitting, drawing and modeling. "But was this an interpretation or an intrusion?" a seminar attendee asks. "I don't know," Dolto answers. "It had a liberating effect … but I don't know."[191] And soft laughter follows, like warm water. Of course, the reader will naturally want to know his name, considering its centrality. Yet it is not given, in a case Dolto calls "The lack of a name in the Other."

Dolto's clinical approach to the child is to consider each one as a worthy "interlocutor" to whom we should tell the truth,[192] as invested words forced into hiding take with them countless associations. Consider the 14-year-old for whom a word arrived, «putain» ["slut"], by which he "refound his story"— details of visits by his mother (a prostitute) to his foster home—restoring his capacity for learning.[193] Or take Katia, the four-year-old hemiplegic psychotic in Dolto's choral clinics, whom we have already met. Katia insists she has «vinguit» friends [sic: "twenty-eight"], as Dolto tells the reader: "There is a condensation of something here, for this returns a name, Valerie, appearing later, and valgus" (her bone deformity).[194] Condensation is everywhere,[195] Freud points out. And since it is dream-work, the most archaic phonemes hold the most associations. Is this not why psychoanalysis is, as it is commonly called, "a talking cure"[196]— and words are its "tools of treatment"?[197] For "language is a substitute for action," Freud explains, "whereby affect is abreacted almost as effectively."[198] Or, as Dolto puts it, "communication ventilates everything."[199]

Further, because anxiety is released by using phonemes,[200] as Dolto notes, the "phantasms subtending speech are expressible only in the mother tongue,"[201] giving the mother tongue a "historicizing function."[202] And commenting on her clinical approach to mothers, in an interview with J.-P. Winter in 1986— appearing both in print and on film—Dolto states clearly: "It's never their fault, but it happens to be their fact."[203] For any infant's prehistory will be woven with the mother's history—even her unconscious history, as we are learning— and Dolto's deep (albeit unusual) conviction is that the fetus asks to be born. In other words, Dolto conceives of a full subject, from the start, who survives because of his own desire to live. I believe Dolto is interpreting the paradox of the infant as a subject—that is, of auto-eroticism in the absence of autonomy. She is also inscribing the role of the mother tongue in psychical structuration.

## Marguerite and Narcissus

We now move backwards in time, in the style of Dolto herself, to "not later than yesterday."[204] The year is 1949, when Dolto meets Bernadette, a five-year-old schizophrenic who issued blood from her anus and mouth for ten days perinatally.[205] She remains a hemiplegic schizophrenic who talks openly of her hatred of her mother, walks with her head bent to one side and speaks in a monotone voice. She is anorexic, phobic and very hostile, and she suffers from debilitating anxiety. "I had never seen such a grave case,"[206] Dolto says plainly. From the first, Dolto attends to Bernadette's language, as the child turns objects into verbs: «se luner» ["to moon yourself"]; «sapiner» ["to fir-tree"]; and «chaiser» ["to chair"].[207] In a typical session, Bernadette draws a tree and narrates that she «sapinait» ["was tree-ing"] or making «sapinades» ["tree-collectives"]. Dolto offers the noun «sapin» for the tree, and «ça prenait» ["it took/worked"; or "the Id took hold"].

Dolto saw Bernadette 18 times over 20 months in 1946–1948.[208] And while the hemiplegia remained as the sequela of birth injuries, she became a well-adapted child. In turn, Bernadette became the inspiration for the «poupée-fleur,» a doll with the head of a «marguerite» ["daisy"] that is cathartic for injuries at the oral stage,[209] Dolto explains. Bernadette expressed in an early session that she disliked animals and dolls. "Perhaps Bernadette would like a flower-doll?" Dolto inquired. "Oh, yes, a flower-doll!" the girl replied. "What in the world is that?" asked the mother. "I have no idea," answered Dolto, "but it seems that this is what she would like."[210] So Dolto requested that the mother make one, providing instructions.[211] The dolls would be used successfully to heal other children, becoming iconic of Dolto.

Here, then, is theory arriving in unanticipated moments made from unpredictable movements—and being welcomed. There is a lovely footnote 50 years later that a letter was found after Dolto's death,[212] forwarded by this patient, who became a speech therapist! In a strange circularity, she had found it after her own mother's death, by accident.[213] Dolto relates how she observed «marguerites» as identifications in primary narcissism, in clinic, perhaps because the idea came from herself (because it is her middle name)[214]—but without mentioning that it is her grandmother's name too.

Yet familiar by now with homonymic play, we hear the «marguerite» also as the «mère guérite» ["healed mother"?] and «mère guerre-ite» ["warring mother"], as we find ourselves returned to the construction of primary narcissism as a co-narcissistic state with the mother. Knowledge has gone rogue, as theory is prompted by phantasies informed by word-things, whereby there is a "change in the verbal expression of the thoughts concerned,"[215] as Freud once said. And pondering the «marguerite» on the soft ground between the biographical and the theoretical, I submit that we cannot but recall the narcissus, that other flower and myth, amid the echoes of primary love that return us to Oedipus.

Dolto's project narrates our difficult encounter with reality, and it explicates how continuous resourcing in the unconscious is the only thing that makes the strain bearable: "Once one leaves the womb … life is not always as one would want it,"[216] she states drily. Life is indelibly associated with suffering,[217] because the umbilical separation from archaic security is a wound.[218] Dolto's project flows with a powerful current in psychoanalysis, while also infusing its roots. For Dolto confirms that melancholy is constitutional, and that the purpose of psychical work is thus, "to heal our suffering, but not to replace it."[219] For Dolto, suffering is our undeniable heritage, and wellness means "transforming pathogenic suffering into useful suffering."[220] As Dolto explains it from the vantage point of oral passivity, the problem is that we have, in our archaic prehistory, «beaucoup de peine à s'exprimer.»[221] The phrase is a spectacular play on «peine» ["harm, hurt, hardship, sadness"] that relates, at once, our great difficulty in expressing ourselves—and our great sorrow. And near, somehow, are echoes of young Marcel's «peine.»[222]

For the infant, then, it is as if the transference teaches the sense of words and of the world. The transference is the infant's experience of being witnessed, protected, instructed, welcomed and securitized. And as phonemes are invested progressively, the mother functions as a kind of localization—like a city, a «Paris?» [homonyms: "no laugh," "wager"]. In other words, every mother is a highly productive mediating (common) object for the transference by being the richest conduit—effectively, the *mater* or matter—enabling the infant's archaically invested phonemes to transfer their investments to reality. So in her non-availability (protracted absence, non-responsiveness, death), the infant at risk searches psychically—as «on,» within a phantasy discourse of inseparability with an enigmatic other—through wild displacements and associations in dream-work, along any line, direction or transfer.

Yet because the unconscious is continuously operative (barring our own death), the capacity for the transference is never lost. At all times, we maintain a relation in phantasy with our unconscious, archaic investments. So while our gradual securitization in reality normally owes its efficacity to the mother, psychical survival is nonetheless possible by the «voie» ["path"]—«voix» ["voice"]—of the transference traversing words: mediating objects securing continuity:

> For the child, narcissism is linked to the well-being of his body, little-by-little valorized in relation to his unconscious and conscious perceptions concerning his person and his comportment; «j'entends» ["I understand/hear"] by that the speech and the attitude of the entourage — «provende» [archaic: "all-provider of life"] and protection.[223]

## Souvenir

Dolto shares that she kept a great «souvenir» all her life of Trousseau.[224] So we journey there in mind, in closing, with the help of a single photo that moves any witness,[225] and the difficulty of living that is patent in Dolto's project. A small girl touches the necklace Dolto is wearing, and Dolto's empathetic gaze, as she is bent to eye level, overflows words entirely. We are returned, as if in a dream, to her beloved nanny, fired for stealing a necklace, a "river of diamonds."[226] Dolto does not engage her homonymic play here, but by now we cannot miss it: «diamants»—homonymically, «dit à ma'an» ["word of mother," or "tell mother"], or «dit à ment» ["word for lying"]. And there is an uncanny presence of Dominique's invisible river too, «Elmoru» ["she died," "she received death"]—that loss of love—that we detect yet release (for now). For there is always more dreaming possible, and there is always something held in silence that we will never hear:

> Each child develops his autonomy as a function of words — from phonemes, their sonority, the timbre of a voice that is tense or amused, worried

> or joyous, with which the mother has accompanied his first initiatives...It
> is this interior audition, interiorized, that puts the child in security or
> insecurity.[227]

In sum, the word opens onto what is entirely heterogeneous to its origins. And
long before the first word we utter comes our phantastic unconscious prehistory
with words.

Elderly, Dolto will retell a personal story about nearly dying of double pneu-
monia at six months upon her nanny's departure, as their love was so great.[228]
The necklace the nanny stole had been the mother's most prized wedding gift,[229]
amid a rich «trousseau» ["dowry"], Dolto explains—as its echoes cannot but
resound for the attuned reader. Dolto regrets that no one remembers the nanny's
name,[230] as she recounts how the incident left a lingering «malentendu» with her
family[231]—and here again is that play on hearing and suffering, all on the word.
She spent long hours staring outside, she shares, when she was just four years old,
reflecting on death at the «fenêtre» ["window"]—the «feu-naître/feu-n'être»
["fire-being born/fire-not being"], she herself muses homonymically.[232] Word-
play invests her genius, all the while silently evoking little Robert for the reader
steeped in the reverberations of Dolto's astounding corpus. Poignantly, she offers,
"it was my guilt at the window."[233]

The nanny's departure left a big hole in her life, Dolto admits: «un profound
trou»[234]—as the echoes of that word seem to surround the entire telling of the
nanny's story, and return the listener (somehow) to l'Hôpital Armand-Trousseau.
Arriving here, I cannot help but muse on the name given to the child in her pivotal case, Bernadette: *burn-a-debt*? For the pseudonym of her famous patient is
decipherable only in the nanny's tongue. And we sense but cannot confirm that
we are teasing out the fragile but tenacious remnants of the deep sorrow of an
infant who would have gladly repaid what the nanny owed, in order to keep her.
Meanwhile, back in her twenties, when tensions ran highest and her mother kept
interrogating her, Dolto felt as if her mother took everything, believing then: "I
have nothing for myself ... So why live? I have not even a souvenir."[235] But that
single word too, «souvenir,» evokes a silent story of a rupture with the past, as if
being a suggestion emerging from language itself—«sous venir» ["under will
come"]—as if it held an indelible inscription of the unconscious.

In an earlier edition the same year of the most powerful autobiographical arti-
fact of her corpus, *Enfances*, Dolto muses that the desire for a retrospective had,
perhaps, something to do with «la magie des soixante-dix ans» ["the magic of 70
years"].[236] It is a mute play offered elliptically—in parentheses—while "70" is,
(near-)homonymically, «sois sans dit(s)» ["be without (a) word(s)"]. The line
appears in a striking two-page essay, one of her loveliest pieces of writing, that
is, ironically, the only bit removed from the second edition.[237] This flickering
sense of "here and gone," like little Ernst Freud's famous game,[238] pervades the
study of Dolto. Certainty gives way to surprise, rationalizations falter and con-
ventional ideas fall out of the window. Yet, somehow, the *infans* who cannot

speak gets to speak. Thus Dolto offers us a rich trade where, instead of standing on what is firm, one learns to float on topographies of dream-work. And though it is hard to see in the archaic, Dolto will teach us that it is nonetheless possible to hear.

## Portrait

Further, while time seems to split Dolto's project, as she warns, if her thought is gathered by its condensations instead—word-things that link notions from disparate regions of her corpus across the years—her work begins to tell its truly radical story: the unconscious quietly informs all psychical activity. There is no direct correspondence between any case and construct, nor any single book that can make sense of the whole. Our exercise in meaning-making will be hypothetical, inviting more questions—teaching us to value, as Dolto did, the importance of examples. For like in the clinic, interpreting Dolto requires an analytic reading, whereby we follow diffuse associations upon unusual grounds for thought, as sense issues in ironic returns.

Discovery with Dolto takes form through wild plays on words whose phonemes are unique to Dolto's "sonar heritage," to use her term. Yet even in twins, similarities in perceptual endowments and auditory environments are progressively nuanced by affective experiences that subtly impact dream-work, to give each one a distinctive archaic prehistory. So while geographic, linguistic and familial proximity enable common words to serve as mediating objects for the transference, what happens from here, during symbolization, is anyone's guess. The phoneme is inherently idiosyncratic.

Before leaving this field of hearing, then, we listen just a bit more. Dolto read Morgenstern's watershed paper when it was published in the first year of the *Revue française de psychanalyse*, in 1927 (and she was still rereading it in 1987).[239] It describes young Jacques (with his evocative name)—mute but fond of drawing.[240] Eleven years later, Morgenstern would become Dolto's kindly mentor. But back in 1927, Dolto herself was a young woman fond of drawing. Examples of posters she entered in contests in 1927–1931[241] include two gouache print advertisements: one with champagne popping, for Veuve Clicquot, and another with a huge alligator mouth, for Dentol.[242] The first seems like an odd reminder of the «veuve» ["widow"] she felt herself to be, and the second an uncanny prefiguration of the scene of orality that became her life's focus.

Yet the impact of these posters is dwarfed by two other pieces from that period. The first is, "Portrait in oil of two non-identified women," a classical image of two similar-looking females, in profile to the shoulders, and back-to-back.[243] Is one Françoise, or not? And if so, who is the other? So as Dolto asks of her patients ("Where are you?"), we too ask, "Where is Françoise?" The second piece is a bold art-deco print featuring a thin woman standing on a rooftop with nothing around it, her right hand shielding her eyes (though it is dark), as she looks out at nothing—as if scanning the ocean for someone's return.[244]

Its caption (in Dolto's cursive) reads: "Anne, my sister Anne, do you not see anything coming?" But by 1927, there is no sister, for Dolto's lifespan (at 19) has just surpassed hers. There is no Anne in Dolto's family tree,[245] and I believe it is not ever used as a patient's name either. It is as if, by its incongruity in the corpus, it looks nowhere too. And yet there is a Suzanne [homonymically: «sous anne,» "under anne"]—as the phoneme leaves its moorings and sets off alone. Here then is a condensation of two losses on (under) the mother's name: her sister, Jacqueline (whose name is silenced); and the beloved Irish nanny across the sea (whose name is forgotten). Do those who have departed from reality call for (to) each other in an archaic dream-scape—a searching in the dark? But who calls for whom? And, again, where is Françoise?

Lifelong, Dolto felt that she was "chasing a chimera."[246] And with Dolto, but without bearings, I believe we come upon abundant evidence of Freud's observations that, "the unconscious [is] a particular realm of mind with its own wishful impulses."[247] For the nascent psyche develops in an organizing silence, as Dolto puts it—a hearing-within-a-hearing, we could say. This early association between survival and sound makes of language what Freud found it to be: the critical inroad, via unconscious associations, for the interpretation and the cure. Thus our words will always carry the traces of our unspeakable prehistories, forever telling silent stories beneath the stories that we tell.

## Notes

1 Le Péron, 2008.
2 C. Dolto, 2001.
3 ATP, 195.
4 See Chapter 2.
5 AI, 224; ATP, 195.
6 ATP, 196.
7 Hivernel & Sinclair in Dolto, 1940/2013, xv.
8 DW, 17.
9 Hivernel & Sinclair in Dolto, 1940/2013, xvi.
10 EN, 40.
11 ATP, 46.
12 VC1, 215.
13 LF, 97.
14 SS, 147.
15 Rare photo of Mme Arlette: Eliacheff, 2018a, 138.
16 VC2, 413; office photos: VC2, 390 & 391.
17 CE, 74; QS, 11; SP1, 49; VO, 226.
18 E.g., CE, 64; EM, 185.
19 LF, 207.
20 EM, 230; IIC, 367; TL, 24.
21 JD, 277.
22 VC2, 239.
23 JD, 277.
24 JD, 275.
25 VO, 185.
26 CE, 350; EM, 178.

27  LO1, 26 & 130.
28  LF, 73.
29  JD, 274; LF, 95; NE, 192; SF, 48, 71, 210 & 334; SP1, 176.
30  JD, 276.
31  DV, 115; JD, 277; LF, 86; LO2, 79.
32  DV, 48; NE, 212; PJ, 105; SP2, 157 & 241.
33  SF, 153.
34  CE, 16; JD, 250.
35  PJE, 106.
36  JD, 275–277; VO, 234.
37  JD, 272.
38  CE, 17; VO, 154.
39  DV, 117; also SS, 41.
40  ATP, 170; DV, 300.
41  PS, 92.
42  CE, 16–17, 133–134 & 242; EM, 63 & 230; PJ, 95.
43  CE, 268 & 293; SP1, 120.
44  CE, 44.
45  TL, 23.
46  CE, 339.
47  CD, 7; CE, 350; SP1, 119.
48  SP1, 133. Otto Rank spoke first of what is "before the development of the Oedipus Complex" (1924/1993, 216), so he is credited for coining the "pre-Oedipal" period. But from this shared term, I believe Rank and Dolto depart dramatically. In brief, Rank believes, "every infantile … anxiety or fear is a partial disposal of the birth anxiety" (1924/1993, 17; also Laplanche & Pontalis, 1967/2004, 77). However, for Dolto, birth is an opportunity for freedom that merely introduces new sources of anxiety—and "anxiety is a result not a cause of the failure of *allant-devenant*" (JD, 199). Further, with Dolto, the infant is unconsciously symbolizing prior to birth (and its trauma), and has a relatively long history of managing impingements.
49  SP1, 225.
50  Freud, 1914b, 77.
51  Freud, 1914b, 87.
52  SP1, 225.
53  VO, 114.
54  Freud, 1914b, 78.
55  Freud, 1914b, 79.
56  Freud, 1914b, 75.
57  Full story: SS, 95–104.
58  SS, 95.
59  SS, 96.
60  LF, 90.
61  JD, 273.
62  SP3, 156.
63  Freud, 1896e, 232; also, 1915c, 209–215.
64  Laplanche & Pontalis, 1967/2004, 418.
65  Freud, 1901a, 680.
66  Freud, 1900a, 228.
67  Freud, 1896a, 203.
68  Freud, 1900a, 221.
69  CD, 8f.
70  CD, 71.
71  CD, 75 (i.e., «bel»).
72  VC2, 123f.

73  AI, 88.
74  CD, 8f.
75  CD, 9–172.
76  IIC, 363; also IIC, 365 & 371–372; SP3, 76 (emphasis hers; «mots» and «maux» are homonyms).
77  E.g., SP3, 43.
78  ATP, 24.
79  DV, 30.
80  PJE, 17–18.
81  CE, 40; SF, 156; SP3, 146.
82  CE, 255.
83  Bacon, 2013, 520.
84  VC2, 453 & 709.
85  SP2, 230; TL, 38.
86  TL, 39.
87  DW, 25; SS, 99 & 113; VC2, 495.
88  LF, 123 & 248.
89  Hall, Hivernel & Morgan, 2009, xv–xvi.
90  ATP, 32 & 41.
91  JD, 281; also LF, 126; SP2, 158; SS, 157.
92  SF, 359.
93  LF, 102.
94  PJE, 15.
95  LO1, 98.
96  SP1, 61.
97  TL, 15.
98  JD, 273.
99  VC2, 329.
100  CE, 16.
101  CE, 16.
102  NE, 249.
103  LO1, 111 (emphasis mine).
104  CE, 255.
105  LO1, 130.
106  JD, 252.
107  SP1, 197.
108  CE, 55.
109  SP2, 127.
110  CD, 224; CE, 262.
111  JD, 125; also DW, 78; JD, 299; JP, 24; PJE, 87; SP1, 57; VO, 222; Nobécourt, 2008b.
112  VO, 34.
113  SS, 184.
114  LF, 86.
115  Dolto, 1989a, 68; EM, 37.
116  CE, 29.
117  SF, 153.
118  JD, 280.
119  VO, 11–12.
120  NE, 243; SP3, 176.
121  EM, 222.
122  SP1, 31; SS, 78.
123  CD, 242; Dolto, 1985/1989b, 123.
124  Freud, 1896a, 202.

125 PJ, 95; SP1, 29; SP2, 18–19.
126 DW, 124.
127 JD, 256.
128 SP1, 75.
129 Dolto, 1985c; DV, 30–37; SP2, 167–170.
130 DV, 31.
131 CD, 198; CE, 239; DQ, 49; DV, 21; IIC, 46 & 93–94; JD, 125; NE, 202; PJ, 107; SF, 206; SP3, 145; SS, 117.
132 CE, 239–240; IIC, 46.
133 VO, 196–197.
134 PJ, 108.
135 VO, 42.
136 IIC, 46 & 94.
137 CD, 183.
138 IIC, 93.
139 TL, 35.
140 NE, 234–235.
141 PJ, 14.
142 Freud, 1905a, 181 & 205; also 1905a, 52.
143 Freud, 1914b.
144 Freud, 1893a, 80.
145 Freud, 1900a, 223.
146 Freud, 1907, 27.
147 Freud, 1905b, 295.
148 Freud, 1905b, 295.
149 SP1, 95.
150 SP1, 98–99.
151 SP1, 117.
152 SP1, 51.
153 SP3, 88–90.
154 SP3, 159.
155 MA, 244 (Jeanne is renamed Fabienne in re-editions).
156 JD, 150.
157 IIC, 53–55; also Bacon, 2013, 521.
158 JD, 296–297; P&P, 33; SS, 16.
159 DV, 169; DW, 87.
160 JD, 27.
161 EM, 311; IIC, 104; PS, 25.
162 P&P, 34.
163 JD, 274.
164 Dolto, 1940/2013, 17; also P&P, 1; PS, 75; SP1, 157 & 161; SP3, 146; VO, 185.
165 Freud, 1900b, 570 & 590, 1901a, 680.
166 Freud, 1909b, 44.
167 APP, 32; CE, 29; JD, 256, 290 & 299; PS, 22 & 86; QS, 17; SF, 209 & 362; SP1, 20; SS, 41 & 184.
168 SP1, 27.
169 Freud, 1911/1974, 318.
170 LF, 103; also PJ, 92.
171 DV, 8 & 158; PJE, 92; SP3, 11.
172 CE, 283; LF, 9, 11, 20 & 247; NE, 249.
173 CD, 189; LF, 68; SS, 117.
174 SF, 334.
175 SF, 48.
176 Roudinesco, 1986, 170.

177 Aubry & Cifali, 1986/1988, 44.
178 DW, 27.
179 CD, 196.
180 DV, 293.
181 DW, 24.
182 DW, 163.
183 DW, 30; NE, 207.
184 EM, 50.
185 VC2, 799.
186 TL, 16.
187 JD, 69; Nobécourt, 2008a.
188 VC2, 800.
189 VC2, 859.
190 SP3, 142.
191 SP3, 152–153.
192 NE, 210; SP1, 69; TL, 31.
193 SP3, 83–86.
194 SP1, 53–54.
195 Freud, 1913, 174.
196 Breuer & Freud, 1893a, 30.
197 Freud, 1905/1953c, 283.
198 Breuer & Freud, 1893c, 8; Freud, 1895, 365–366.
199 D&R, 39; DV, 66; JD, 22; PJE, 23; QS, 22.
200 IIC, 328; SS, 37.
201 NE, 249; also PJE, 95.
202 Chaperot & Celacu, 2010, 439.
203 Print: DW, 109; film: Nobécourt, 2008b.
204 JD, 273.
205 JD, 133–193; JP, 19–33.
206 JP, 25.
207 JP, 25.
208 JP, 86f.
209 AI, 56; JD, 158–159; JP, 40; SS, 21.
210 JP, 27; JD, 139.
211 AI, 57; JP, 46; VC2, 259; photo: VC2, 257 & AI, 54.
212 VC2, 258f.
213 VC2, 258 (on "Bernadette" being Béatrice L.).
214 AI, 56; JD, 139.
215 Freud, 1900b, 339.
216 EM, 21.
217 JD, 57; also JP, 41; SF, 362; SS, 234.
218 PS, 27; SF, 362; SP1, 213.
219 SP1, 52.
220 Dolto, 1989a, 133.
221 EM, 96.
222 See Chapter 2.
223 JD, 256.
224 ATP, 195.
225 AI, 225.
226 AI, 144; EN, 62.
227 IIC, 260.
228 EN, 62–65.
229 EN, 62.
230 EN, 64.

231 DW, 66.
232 EN, 14.
233 EN, 12.
234 MF, 21.
235 AI, 55.
236 Dolto, 1986b, 78–79.
237 Dolto, 1986c.
238 Freud, 1920, 14–15.
239 Dolto in Nasio, 1987/1998, 38.
240 Morgenstern, 1927/2003 (she reviews Jacques' drawings with him after he is "demuted").
241 AI, 120f.
242 AI, 121.
243 AI, 104.
244 AI, 104.
245 E.g., PF, 8–9; VC1, 16–17; VC2, 1016–1017.
246 AI, 157; also AI, 55; DW, 170.
247 Freud, 1916b, 212.

# 5

# READING

## Introduction

In the summer of 1913, Dolto learned to read when Mlle first arrived to help Suzanne with her fifth infant.[1] Dolto's rich retelling of this story of learning[2] makes patent her impressive capacity for autobiography. Mlle used a Fröbel-inspired method and, "what is funny, is that it is very important for me that psychoanalysis be a method,"[3] Dolto quips. The book selected for daily sessions—sounding out syllables, ten lines at a time—was a prize Dolto's scholarly father had won, *Les Babouches de Baba Hassein*, a collection of Orientalist stories by H. Balesta (1894/1902)—the last called «Le témoin» ["The Witness"]. This 237-page book that most marked her childhood,[4] she says, features 16 images, of which 10 are partially hand-colored. Dolto recalls a small donkey[5]—a scene where a mounted «passant» hears the faint cry of a rope-bound child named Abd-Allah.[6] Dolto hoped the book would explain how, as she opened and closed it repeatedly, its images seemed to move—though when she looked at each one, it did not. That it failed to do so became "one of the biggest deceptions of my life,"[7] she reports, revealing that "books were not at all what they promised from their images."[8] Devastated, she tried to *unlearn* reading by refusing to look, and she wept so profusely that she needed a «mouchoir.»[9]

## *Babouches*

After theorizing about this anecdote for two years, I notice one day that the boy on the cover repeats on page 35; the shoe on page 7 is thrown on page 35; the man on the title page returns on page 105; and so on, for a rosary (on pages 47 and 93), a rope (on pages 117 and 131) and a sun/moon (on pages 7, 145 and 151). Still, any explanation masks the great significance at play. After all, why is an inability to account for displacements discouraging? And why invest such promise in texts?

Freud believes misreading stems from "an intense wish to reject what we have read."[10] In obverse, then, Freud pens the perplexity of reading to which Dolto testifies: text somehow receives (and carries an expectation of returning) unconscious investments.

Dolto memorized pages of *Babouches*, convincing almost everyone she could read, sounding out "syllables that meant nothing," in a ridiculous exercise that "led nowhere."[11] But Mlle saved her, she vouches, by telling her to listen to herself.[12] She calls the moment sense arrived from her own voice a miracle,[13] as a sentence became "activated, enchained."[14] "They were separate syllables," she recounts, "but they meant something if you joined them while listening, linking them."[15] So another question beckons: why is securing sense from one's own voice difficult—and indispensable?

In any event, from that day on, reading was her happiness,[16] she was full of vitality,[17] and she never wanted to let go of a text.[18] Yet while the book's stories are, as she rightly puts it, «idiot»[19]—including the sixth and the eighth, both set in Algeria—I notice a stunning bridge to her reality. On one side of 1913, two generations lived through the colonization of Algeria, including Dan-mé Étan, the maternal great-grandmother born in 1839, when «Algérie» was named.[20] Its annexation was surely discussed in this educated family. On the other side, in 1915–1916, her mother sponsored a wounded soldier, Mohamed Ben Meckri;[21] Oncle Pierre's company was named the Sidi Brahim;[22] and Pierre wrote fiction for Françoise about a hero called Sidi Vava Ben Abdallah.[23]

So foreign words arrive, unconsciously registering in difference, repetition and affect, as reality plays with phantasy. And when Dolto asks gravely how anyone can live if they don't read,[24] insisting it is necessary,[25] she draws attention to its deep psychical work. Dolto calls that first book magical,[26] and my own copy of this rare text feels that way too—full of portents. Asking myself why, I become aware of my deep investment in Dolto. Is it possible, then, to detect in reading a kind of inheritance—the lure of a similar-enough other to follow? Can readers be unconsciously influenced in their ability to think with words—their capacity to take someone's word—by their affective investments in the witness of (to) that word? Is there in reading simply what any good psychoanalyst knows: the transference requires relations of trust? (And what would this mean for translation?) For with Dolto's help, it seems that we can invoke the notion of a chain of custody in texts.

## Écho de Paris

Writing the very year Dolto was born, Freud reminds us that, "creative writing ... is a continuation and substitution ... for the play of childhood."[27] And Freud begins his project by noting that reading is, "very complicated ... and entails a frequent shift of the direction of the association,"[28] sharing that while walking in a strange town, he reads "every shop sign that resembles the word in any way as 'Antiquities' ... betray[ing] the questing spirit of the collector."[29]

There is, in the treasure of Freud's example, in one direction, a "disturbance in reading ... utilizing a 'switch-word,'"[30] as "pre-cathected word-images provide a passage for discharge";[31] while in another direction, "reading ... provid[es] an abundant and not easily traceable source for ... dreams."[32] So reading emerges as a potent, archaic-systonic act offering an echo of our pre-cathected word-things—facilitating shifts that recall the reversals inhering in the archaic transference situation[33]—as a reparation that can return our lost objects.

Dolto savored reading each morning at dawn.[34] Flash ahead to 1940, and she advises a ten-year-old patient to read Jules Verne and science books;[35] and in 1952, she counsels a peer to prescribe stories with a free lion or tiger,[36] to invite "useful aggression."[37] Her dissertation even references Cinderella's passivity[38]—in a passage ironically deleted from later editions. Children "use fairy tales to construct themselves in reality,"[39] she states, as phantasms deform, develop—or help one escape—one's own story.[40] Dolto recommends "contradictory narratives,"[41] and reading fables without adding explanations,[42] in order to enable the author's presence.[43] And defending since childhood her right to phantasy—"Why do you call it imagination? Maybe it's true!"[44]—Dolto becomes a resonator of the archaic. For a child, a fairy "is not a story, it is true";[45] she takes seriously Bernadette's claim to be a wolf-child;[46] and she translates a child's problem with moving as a lack of a trail of crumbs.[47]

Freud notes that the relation of dreams to fairy-tales is not accidental[48] and he plays with their metaphors, explaining that he once experienced a beautiful fairy-tale;[49] titling a key draft "A Christmas Fairy Tale";[50] and once declaring himself, "delighted as the dwarf."[51] In turn, Bertha Pappenheim, who wrote fairy-tales after her passage in the analytic literature,[52] ostensibly derived from her prior relation with Cinderella the first definition of psychoanalysis: "chimney sweeping."[53] Yet as for the destination of the same childhood story for different subjects, no two paths will align. For early reading will legate elusive objects to dream-work, in idiosyncratic filiations with our archaic prehistory, as Dolto predicts. And while this type of material seldom sees light in academic writing—as if associating with primitivity precluded serious thinking—Dolto believes that just the opposite is true: phantasy drives trains of thought.[54]

Dolto remembers her subscription to *L'Écho de Paris*—a gift from her grandmother with a children's page[55]—and the weekly *La Semaine de Suzette* she calls "an enormous thing that helped me live in reality."[56] She reflects that texts arriving in her home enabled her to love society, since it meant that there were others (outside her family) who understood children,[57] and that there were children like her, since they were interested in the same things.[58] It also seems impossible to miss the echo (echo of Paris?) between «Suzette» and her mother's name, «Suzanne»—and its suggestion on the name of (as) identification. In any event, this "little donkey," as Mlle called her,[59] spent the prize money she won (mostly for good marks) buying more children's papers.[60] And upon her death, Dolto's children placed a wreath of flowers on behalf of the phantasy characters that populated their family life, such as Mr Passe-Passe and «petits êtres» ["small beings"].[61] For Dolto remained aware lifelong of the archaisms that subtended her childhood. And recalling time itself as a puzzling encounter, Dolto relates her frustration at age ten that one could study, in one year, both ancient history and Lafontaine.[62] She sought connections but found none,[63] she says, searching the dictionary for the meaning of literature,[64] only to find that it was about "people who spoke otherwise than ourselves."[65]

Chronology is a kind of "splitting," Dolto concludes,[66] and a text is an offer to read messages coming from persons alive in another space, another time.[67] But one should never attract readers by color or presentation, she warns, for a book only "brings something" as an experience of reality that can be put back into real life.[68] Dolto's careful musing draws attention to the work of phonemes in our coming to reality—«présentification»[69]—as "quantities of synchronous external and internal encounters take on the value of language signs,"[70] and the child constantly "imagines himself in an activity that valorises him" and sustains his «allant-devenant»:[71]

> Sounds … interweave with the perception of his body in tension with needs, or in phantasms of desire … These sonar signifiers … retain the child in reality through an ephemeral articulation of a perception that has come from the exterior world to which he remains attached, that is, fragments of phantasms.[72]

## Private theatre

Still in 1913, as the auditory landscape of *Babouches* arrived, Dolto moved with her family from 18 Rue Gustave-Zédé to the fifth floor of an even more prestigious address at 2 Avenue du Colonel Bonnet. The new building offered views of not only the Eiffel Tower and the Seine, but also of the renowned *Maison Blanche* ["white house"], where once lived Maupassant [homonym: «mot passant,» "word passing"].[73] Forbidden to look, she watched through a sheer as nurses served «thé spécial» in the garden to their patients, sometimes howling.[74] Even her building bore the "sign of syphilis,"[75] as she recounts.[76] For on the sixth was a man who periodically held a bag out the window, threatening to drop his (long-deceased) wife. A Russian princess-type lived on the fourth with her intellectually disabled daughter, a tall girl who "resembled Dante" or a "witch" with a yellow face; the daughter's husband, a giant hunchback dwarf; and a "caricature of a basset." Another daughter, a skeleton, had died at 18 of anorexia, while a gorgeous son twirled like a top to avoid clothes touching his skin. As the elevator was out during the war, families met on the stairs and Mlle advised not looking at him, as "the poor man has ideas in his head."[77] Meanwhile, on the third lived «Quatrebarbes» ["fourbeards"]—"but he had only one chin, it gave me something to think about!"[78] And on the second was a woman with mystical delusions, who screamed at the full moon and kept a heated table to lure children with warmth. "On the fifth," Dolto sums up drily, "I knew madness well, I lived in it!"[79]

Reality and phantasy have entirely permeable boundaries here. For the new home has an elevator, recalling the lost nanny; story characters share her building; the mad take polite tea; and what one reads comes into circulation on the table, or on the sidewalk. The child does not separate reality from a, "series of dreams continuing over weeks or months based on common ground."[80] Rather, he lives perpetually in the "neighbourhood of wish-fulfilment,"[81] that "playground of transference."[82] What makes Dolto extraordinary is her comfort on that archaic landscape:

> I close my eyes and see quantities of things … people who are walking about … I could, if I had the time, draw them all and represent them, they are not confoundable with any other, and yet, they are anonymous … I see landscapes that are very specific, characterizable … it is new all the time … But I ask myself this question: What is this, these people that I see, and that do not exist?[83]

Dolto accepts the richness of childhood that is her heritage in a manner highly reminiscent of Pappenheim's "private theatre"[84]—and she lets it influence her work. So she is happy living, "not knowing exactly where she was going,"[85] with one foot on the «terrain de l'inconscient,»[86] where "the echo of an archaic peace of one's being resonates, peace prior to the time of appearances."[87]

Grounded in the archaic, Dolto's cartography naturally adopts the water-and-road metaphors of Freud's drive theory, wherein geography informs biography: his tributaries and channels[88] of "an instinctual stream,"[89] and displacements along roundabout, connecting or indirect paths.[90] Humans live a life of exchanges (a current) in our dynamic participation with one another,[91] Dolto says, as libido flows like a sea[92] towards its dynamic creative goal.[93] If detoured, libido resumes a path previously employed,[94] or meanders, depending on the terrain and quantity of the flow.[95] Any excess flows through «brèches spontanées» at the point of least resistance.[96] And following the imaginary walk of Freud's dream book[97]—his own archaic coordinates—Dolto believes that archaic desires remain lifelong. So the child unconsciously projects them into vegetation and animals, as security is unconsciously represented by refuges in nature,[98] especially around water—and phantasy, not reality, is our originary security.

Childhood wishes can always return as experience is merely overlaid in «strates,» Dolto explains, extending from the "actual terrain to the most ancient terrain."[99] In the child, there are merely fewer layers, so the transference is easier.[100] As Freud states, "in a particular province … relics of the past still survive,"[101] upon which are structured "successive transcripts"[102]—in an overlaying (distancing) from an "archaic heritage."[103] Thus, reality is always a displacement from that first setting via progressive associations and substitutions.

## «Habitus de securité»

Regarding her new home and its liminal characters, Dolto shares another gem: her angel, B.A.G., arrived at Colonel Bonnet—he was not at Gustave-Zédé.[104] He appeared in the days when she asked Mlle, newly arrived,[105] hard questions about death and she felt «schizoïde.»[106] Associations to the beloved first nanny were surely left behind in the shift, but given any child's blur of reality and phantasy, we cannot know what was lost that mattered most. The child has a «habitus de securité,»[107] Dolto theorizes, and this emotional climate is unnoticed unless it goes away.[108] For the child is attached to a place recalling security[109]— context-bound.[110] And the present is layered upon the past in messy ways, as time itself is felt as splitting. So just how it is that unconscious security arrives is neither understandable nor rational. For example, Dolto's patient Dominique regains his voice upon moving[111]—while Morgenstern's patient loses it.[112] Can we only go so far at once from an archaic shelter? And how do we port our unconscious investments from one place to the other, in coming to reality?

After meandering along circuitous trails and libidinal rivers, we have refound some questions, though they seem to be a long way from our queries about reading. But are they really? In truth, lifelong, Dolto could not easily be still.[113] Even when vacationing at Laforgue's, she walked extensively, hand-painting arrows to mark trails.[114] And while working, she ran around her building between patients until one day, she says, she noticed that she could read a page of Racine and be refreshed enough to listen anew.[115] Her interviewer appears dislodged momentarily by what cannot easily be reconciled with reason, as Dolto tenders brilliance, then moves on. Yet in a seminar (elsewhere, years earlier), Dolto commented that to read is to «parcourir, courir» ["roam, run"] with the eyes.[116] Here again is this curious relation between reading and displacement, in a conjunction of statements that share neither time nor space.

So if reality and phantasy are blurred for the child, who lives comfortably with the logic of the wish—and if every landscape in reality involves a slow, uneven migration from the archaic—then how is a story setting any different from a real one? And if we are lured towards reality by being spoken of,[117] why wouldn't finding a strong identification in a story—as if finding oneself in it— help that process along? Why would a word from an author or character have a different capacity to hold and move affect than one spoken by family or neighbors? Is this not the "reality" of the peculiar terrain of childhood? That for the one whose dreams are many, but whose strata are few, Cinderella *is* true? For the unconscious is a "blind force"[118] with us from our passive origins, when a word was not easily assignable from inside the veils of our passage, and dreamwork played with whatever arrived. Why would we not retain the capacity to use any audition as a means of unconscious displacement: to vent by the transference in texts?

Further, it is a given of drive theory that excitation requires an outlet in motility, so we must keep libido circulating to be well.[119] Thus an intelligent child, traumatized into feeling schizoid, who had lost the love of her life and then, in a move, lost the tethers leading back to her, would need what reading could offer: a bridge between phantasy and reality upon the word, taught by a middling being who, by her role, linked those infant dreams to her new reality. Do we not start to feel here the restitution of a secure climate? At the very least, we are compelled to ask: what is reading?

Yet a sense of reality does arrive, eventually, so I muse about the role of the real parents as words echo in a dreamscape. Dolto believes that it is essential for children to be «alimenter en vocabulaire,»[120] fed words—especially if they are precociously intelligent. She relates how children need to «têter des paroles» ["breastfeed words"],[121] drink the words of a new teacher,[122] or devour books.[123] After all, she says, the gift of food is proof of love,[124] and the stories a mother tells are «lait culturel» ["cultural milk"].[125] I believe she is close to Melitta Schmideberg's view, that absorbing knowledge corresponds to oral introjections;[126] and to Strachey's thoughts on the oral influence in metaphors for reading,[127] such as "eating another person's words."[128] So I pause to daydream about how reading is, as it opens for us now, a feeding of oneself. Dolto states that every child needs to «s'automaterner dans les épreuves» ["mother himself during trials"] by age three.[129] On Dolto's view, then, learning to read would mean psychical self-sufficiency—"automaterning."

## Transferential coloring

But as Freud advises, "let us stop and look back, and consider whether we have not overlooked something important on our way hither."[130] For it was not her mother but her father whom Dolto credits for her liberty in reading.[131] Mlle was also instrumental, as she let her plan her own education from her seventh year of (home)schooling, giving her time to read.[132] But as Guy Hall notes, it strikes any Dolto reader as surprising that she valued literacy so much yet referenced virtually no one.[133] The human defends his liberty since small,[134] Dolto states, as liberty is what makes us human.[135] Liberty must, "promise and bring surprises ... and allow the refinding of oneself";[136] so we must not restrict a child's «liberté individuelle.»[137]

Freud places the transference in the service of free association, as Roudinesco notes.[138] And free association places words in the service of an "exteriorization that discharges anxiety," Dolto says.[139] So in refusing to suggest readings (as analysis refuses suggestion), does Dolto carry her conviction about freedom to its ethical end? And while Suzanne was a great reader,[140] Dolto recalls talking about books only with Henry.[141] He let her read everything in his huge library other than Zola, that "chamber pot."[142] Portentously, Zola's novel, *Une page d'amour*, mentions Rue Vineuse—something Dolto never notes, but that raises somber questions about his ban. As ever, it seems that the lost nanny is still right here.

So I take up the offer of play that inheres in that auspicious word, «Vineuse»: its near-homonym, «vie neuve» ["new life"]—a word «mamaisé» in its time, now threatening the return of the repressed (repressed because «mamaisé»?). What is at stake in the free circulation of words anyhow? Evoking an archaic terrain, Dolto describes the social as "a field of listening" for the "symbolic being,"[143] and a "road of listening"[144] in many directions, whereby the transference is diffused and diffracted.[145] By communicating with other psyches, in the "greatest human pleasure,"[146] she adds, we are «renarcissiser» in society.[147] Her view clearly endorses Freud's, that "outside analysis, it [transference] must be regarded as the vehicle of cure and the condition of success."[148] For the "wish-fulfilment's power of representation is diffused over a certain sphere,"[149] Freud writes, and the transference prefers our "diffuse general sensibility."[150]

Thus, the analyst listening for the work of the primary processes must be an attuned witness, freely available[151] through "floating attention,"[152] Dolto states. And grounded in her conviction, she innovates a "mode of working with witnesses."[153] This «coeur antique» ["ancient choral"][154]—or choral assistants[155]—become confounded with her in "transferential coloring."[156] For the witnesses (analytic trainees and doctors) greet the child together,[157] then typically hold silent, taking notes as Dolto does. Dolto's application of diffusion is original, and her preference for this setting is at least partly accounted for by her belief that "interrelations take you out of narcissism"[158]—in a splendid tension whereby we are not just nurtured (renarcissized) by the transference, but also externalized.

The anomaly is left unresolved: "Speech passes between us without us knowing how."[159] Dolto believes the transference happens even in sleep or a coma,[160] when we lack only the capacity to react.[161] And as it does, it heals,[162] offering fruit.[163] Dolto's metaphor evokes a gift devoid of any predefined sender or addressee—what Freud called a "stimulus from the transference"[164]—in an exchange by association to unconscious material in the listener: a silent translation from one to another operating somewhere in the vicinity of language. As Roudinesco explains it, for Freud, the transference is only a particular case of the displacement of affect.[165] And just as the transference is rogue for space, so it is for time too—being anachronistic, Freud says, as a "transfer of energy" originally belonging to an unconscious wish,[166] one that unpredictably repeats the past in the present,[167] as a refinding of lost objects.[168] Or, as Dolto puts it: "Every other is an object of the transference of relations that are much more archaic."[169]

Here is the social, then, as a hodgepodge of objects from different strata, vested or muted, until what finally appears as a shared reality (even for adults) is phantastically complex and idiosyncratically textured. Dolto explains that the symbolic function secures our capacity to wake in others a receptive sensory resonance attuned to our own, through a «simultanéité d'émotion» awakened by a «signal médiateur» that achieves the «reconnaissance» ["recognition"; homonym: "co-birth again"][170] of a «semblable,» as the transference testifies to the trial of separation being surmounted, all this while consciousness is not really awake.[171] So while the transference is an intermediate region between illness and real life,[172] Dolto compels the realization that we all inhabit this intermediate region in perpetuity, as the transference quietly puts libido back into circulation.[173] Thus, Dolto inadvertently ushers in a new theory of narrativity, as the social displaces affect haphazardly, and we each unconsciously seek the resonances that hold the promise of our liberation. Through the transference, then, humans are "lured … towards a unity that never existed in body but that exists … interpsychically,"[174] she believes, and this unconscious lure offers a consolation for our "perpetual suffering."[175]

## «Bain sonore»

Such are the "luring effects of the transference,"[176] enabling the restoration of continuity,[177] Dolto explains. Central to her view is the archaic root of our unconscious securitization in a rhythm of presence and absence—a dream of discourse where our call is answered by an indissociable other. So we "lure" one another to being present,[178] using an unconscious register that recalls (and returns) our originary safety, as we help each other out of "uncreative solitude."[179] Freud started his own project thinking about how sound directs attention[180] and how key phrases can initiate excitation,[181] or offer a passage for discharge.[182] And as Dolto declares inimitably: "Speech is thrown out so it can be taken up."[183]

Yet if her call sounds bold, its echo is so fine. For in this return of archaic objects upon audition—by listening or reading—we will discover a movement sufficient to symbolize the promise of the other to follow, "a semblance of wind,"[184] as Dolto puts it. And with Dolto's objects of transference, we will be returned to the basic economics of drive theory: what Freud describes as a "need of transference on the part of repressed ideas"[185]—one that is so critical to our health that release can happen, Freud explains, even under a "mild and unpronounced transference."[186] For the story of libido is simple at its core: insofar as humans are embodied subjects, venting is essential to regulating excitation.[187] In Dolto's words, our relations must manage «l'économie libidinale» towards «l'homéostatie.»[188] Thus the infant intuits that the «bain ["bath"] sonore du groupe»[189] is a source of securitization,[190] as auditory perceptions introduce reality[191] throughout the acquisition of autonomy.[192] In sum, Dolto asserts unequivocally that unconscious psychical development begins in a language bath.

Needless to say, wild transference makes wild things happen. I take but one example from Dominique, whose sessions started in the summer of 1962, five years after Mlle died—a span and season recalling learning to read—and six months after Suzanne died. Dominique's uncle, like Oncle Pierre, has been killed in the mountains.[193] Incidentally, 1962 also marks Algeria's independence[194]— and in *Babouches*, the story of "The three steers" features the boy named Abd-Allah, the picture of the donkey and a red steer sold to help widows.[195] Dominique draws «chameaux» ["camels"; homonym: «chat(s) mot(s),» "cat word(s)"],[196] and he makes a clay model he describes as a nomad pulling a cow that he names Mlle.[197] He explains how the cow was sold[198] and "has just awakened from dreaming it belonged to a nomad."[199] Then, in two consecutive sessions, Dominique tells this story, ostensibly about «Fifi Brin d'Acier» ["Pippi Longstocking"][200]: "'He' had red hair, and the mother died when 'she' was a baby. She did a lot of nonsense[201] ... She put on the big high heeled-shoes of her mother[202] ... She left ... and when she knew her friends cried, she wanted to stay ... the boy said, I will keep this one [red pup], but the father sent it away."[203]

But how in the world have the lost nanny, Mlle and *Babouches* been displaced from Dolto's archaic history to Dominique's phantasies? Small wonder, then, that it is a problem if an analyst takes members of the same family, as Laforgue had with Philippe (Philippe's uncanny nickname being «Fifi»). For siblings encounter themselves as twins,[204] as Dolto puts it. Dolto's spectacular narrative of the transference—as well as how she never draws conscious attention to it—poses vibrant questions about what Freud called, the "production of common means,"[205] that is, the "how" of the transference. Roudinesco believes Freud's exposition of the transference is an "epistemological and theoretical act as important as the discovery of the unconscious."[206] And as we begin to grasp, the transference and the unconscious testify for each other.

I offer that we should also understand, with Freud, that the chief "characteristic of libido is mobility, the facility with which it passes from one object to other";[207] that "mediating ideas" are needed;[208] and words serve as "nodal points,"[209] enabling affect and ideas to "call up the other"[210]—even if we cannot always figure out how bridging happens since "the *tertium comparationis* often eludes us,"[211] as Freud points out. Dolto's most significant contribution, I submit, is precisely here, in the articulation of the common means: "Words are the mediators between the unconscious of the patient and the unconscious of analyst,"[212] she states, being «objets transitionnels subtiles.»[213]

Yet as we explore, with Dolto, the "mediating object's role in bringing affect to consciousness,"[214] we will need a loose notion of the word: "What is needed are verbal signifiers, not always a hearable spoken language, but a code of relations between two subjects."[215] Not necessarily worded nor even hearable, our relations are nonetheless "verbal" exchanges subject to dream-work. But how?

## Archaic phonemes

By a vigorous walk in archaic woods, our question returns us to the phoneme. A selection of cries valorizes mother tongue,[216] as "archaic phonemes [are] taken up, or not in the mother tongue,"[217] learned sometime during the suffering of dentition,[218] after weaning.[219] We should be attentive to the pain coinciding with the "vocal and auditory selection coupled with mimicry" of the «langue *dite* maternelle» ["tongue *said to be* maternal"].[220] For the mother tongue arrives on an auditory scene of long duration, as "libido weaves with the body, being of the order of language."[221] Archaic history is a phantastic play with bodily sounds and phonemes arriving in difference, repetition and affect, in a dream of discourse rooting our security. The infant is thus already the "translation of a subject,"[222] emerging from a phantastic prehistory with words. From here, he begins a "verbal apprenticeship" in the "physiological habitus" of his group's code,[223] as his relations are "unconsciously mediated by the first humans who welcome him."[224] In time, he adjusts to "this spoken or secret discourse going on prior to [his] arrival,"[225] thereby learning the mother's tongue.

The child needs maternal mediation for all that is new,[226] Dolto states, as what is «mamaïsé» delivers securitizing continuity.[227] So the mother tongue (if all goes well) offers «mamaïsation sécurisante,»[228] as unconscious affect is invested in the phonemes of our individual prehistory. On Dolto's view, then, the loss of (access to) the mother (or beloved nanny) would diminish this luring to reality through a reduced audition of archaic phonemes, hence slowing or stalling the developmental process of "presentification." Here, I believe Dolto quietly theorizes an origin for projection, while also presaging the value of old literature, maps, inscriptions and dictionaries (invested texts). For as the mother tongue offers mediating objects and the unconscious recognition of similitude, the mother facilitates libidinal displacements, enabling abundant associations on a field of archaic phonemes—a transferential harvest.

And wherever we place our feet on this terrain of thought, Freud's river runs. Freud notes how the preconscious comes about by thing-presentations being hyper-cathected through links with word-presentations,[229] and how dreams use residues of verbal presentations.[230] It follows, then, that the phonemes of the mother tongue will become remnants of the day for dream-work and be richly cathected with libido. Adults in analysis dream in their mother tongue,[231] Dolto states, and an analyst needs to speak to a child using the archaic phonemes of his mother tongue.[232] We should understand better now why a detailed anamnesis is so necessary for Dolto, for unconsciously invested phonemes are idiosyncratic.

For example, we learn that Mlle[233]—dearly loved[234]—was from Luxembourg,[235] and she sometimes spoke German on their walks, reciting German poetry.[236] So Dolto's own prehistory was lived and formed in a confluence of German, French and English, as her archaic phonemes become unfathomable—unique and unrepeatable. Besides, the child's phonemes may not have sense for us,[237] Dolto explains— and under the same words, people have different experiences.[238] Therefore, in Dolto's notion of the phoneme as a mediating object for the transference inheres a profound regard for all that is individual in the notion of liberty.

"Syllabic chemistry"[239] is also central to Freud's project. Beginning in 1891, Freud describes the word as a thing, an object of dreaming;[240] and he shares a rich example from the literature, of a dream on "lo," with *kilometres, kilogramme, Gilolo, Lobelia, Lopez* and *lotto*.[241] Freud believes dream-work has a "susceptibility to homonyms,"[242] as words serve as intermediate links, bridges or switches in displacing affect.[243] Dreams also engage in auditory hallucinations[244] that rediscover suggestion,[245] Freud explains, working to get power over displacement[246]—just as corroborative dreams follow the analyst's suggestion.[247] And this idiosyncratic weaving—of phonemes, dream-work, hallucination and suggestion—is what is at play in Dolto's extremely productive notion of "pre-sentification" via the transference.

## Affective truth

Homophones are very rich,[248] Dolto concords. And believing in the unmitigated force of the unconscious, she is informed by them continuously. For example, she explains that the «nez» ["nose"; homonym: "born"] is critical to narcissistic libido;[249] and the analyst needs to search «sous terre ... sous taire» [homonymic pair: "under ground ... under hush"].[250] In a letter regarding a colleague's young patient named Clément, Dolto explores his name, «clément» [homonym: "key lies"],[251] in offering her insights into his case. And in another letter, she muses that a child's regression may be rooted in his believing that his name, «Romain»—a near-homonym of «gros main» ["big hand"]—suggests inability.[252] In turn, a 12-year-old at Trousseau who is ashamed of his father, a «boxeur» ["fighter"], is deemed to behave like a «boxeur» ["dog"];[253] and the «épicerie» ["grocery store"] in a child's drawing is read for its carry of «pisse» ["pee"].[254] More than once, Dolto also insists that reading as an act cannot be understood without considering the homonymy between «lit» ["read"] and «lis» ["bed"].[255]

For phonemes root words in a "biological, affective truth,"[256] Dolto says, informing her emphasis on speaking truth to children. Meanwhile, the "correctness of words"[257] that Dolto stresses evokes Freud's discussion of the "similarity between the stimulus and content of dream"[258]—and the paradox he himself notes, namely that stimuli may be misunderstood in a dream.[259] Thus the literality of phonemes heralds the suffering of the dreamer in the encounter with reality. And in her own keen witnessing of childhood, Dolto even remembers the first time she noticed this phenomenon, when World War I ended in 1918, and she paraded with her family down Avenue des Ternes [«terne»: "dull, drab"], only to realize that it was "full of color."[260] But planted on Doltoian grounds, the bilingual reader cannot help but hear something uncanny in her realization that it was not drab: i.e., «pas terne» («paterne»?)—what is of, or from, the father?—as, once again, a point of great theoretical importance arrives coincidentally, as a suggestion issuing from word-play.[261]

I believe Dolto's musing puts her in concert with two peers to whom she apparently never spoke directly: Klein, for whom "when it comes to the unconscious, there is no difference between adults and children";[262] and Susan Isaacs, who believes the inner world of the mind has a continuous living reality that is indispensable to reality thinking.[263] For the unconscious play arriving in random auditory encounters, to which Dolto draws our attention, suggests that not only children are context-bound. Such is the *"fort-da* game ... at the origin of language,"[264] Dolto states, as the child plays with words[265]—metonyms, metaphors, differences and displacements.[266] It is a "game of forces,"[267] as narcissizing phantasms play their structuring game,[268] and the "symbolic function is in play, constantly keeping watch over the child."[269]

Early on, Dolto discovers that this "game of forces" with phonemes assists our hard transition to reality, as we seek "precious compensations" in language for the loss of «jouissance,»[270] and hidden phonemes bring narcissistic joy.[271] After all, the opposite of play is what is real, Freud reminds us.[272] With Dolto, phonemes become a gift in a passive register, returning security by representing the wish as "fulfilled in a hallucinatory fashion,"[273] as "consolations."[274] Moreover, as we "only [ever] exchange one thing for another,"[275] since unconscious wishes are always active and cannot be influenced,[276] Freud notes, then reality must promise phantasy. Is this not the early lesson Dolto drew from Josette's incremental sacrifices?[277] Thus the transference is a powerful, continuously available means whereby, as Dolto narrates, "life repairs what has been wounded."[278]

So it is that by turning in circles, we somehow arrive somewhere new, where we can hear what whispers unceasingly across Dolto's landscape: a rare narration of oral passivity. Right from her dissertation, Dolto describes the libidinal passive mode as essential to social adaptation,[279] for oral passivity serves the "pleasure principle,"[280] and «fantasmes autoérotiques hallucinatoires»[281] return the subject to oral passivity where—though unable to communicate with the outside world—he is securitized. Still in 1940, Dolto describes the role of "seductive passive pulses,"[282] as the subject unconsciously attracts those who protect him,[283] registers everything arriving[284] and "ardently waits."[285] In sum, she believes "passivity exists"[286] and we should value the passive in a child,[287] for passive pulses foster intense intellectual activity and receptivity.[288]

In describing passivity as a powerful and continuous resource, I offer that Dolto follows Freud closely: his "quiescent cathexis" as energy inherent in the unconscious wish,[289] and instincts with a passive aim.[290] Even the renowned linguist Ferdinand De Saussure stated that every language has a fixed number of phonemes[291] subject to passive agglutination;[292] and resonance characterizes phonemes by absence as well as presence.[293] This is the game of *fort-da*—the play at the origins of our unconscious, affective security. Not without relevance, secret journals by De Saussure from 1906–1909 reveal his passion for anagrams in Latin poetry—a repetition of syllables[294]—and for prevalent homophony[295] as a game on phonemes.[296] It is also a fact that «phonocentrisme» abounds in the most archaic languages, such as in the "dense, rampant homophony" in Chinese.[297]

## Presentification

Here, I believe we have accidentally refound an old question for psychoanalysis, about how a subject of the passive pulses, secure in autoerotic hallucinations, ardently waiting, ever emerges from a closed monad. Dolto's theorization begins with time itself: the present is "now and a gift."[298] Yet unsaid, a «présent» is a gift only in English—or in archaic, or literary, French[299]—not in standard French, where the usual word is «cadeau.» In turn, a «fête» ["party"; homonym:

«faite,» i.e., "done" or "made"]—wherein presents normally arrive—is liberty in security,[300] a scansion of time[301] and an "eruption of what is free."[302]

I play now with the uncertainty that opens. For the child is always in the present,[303] Dolto notes, and the present is rooted in repeated exchanges with same person.[304] She stresses: "Audition exists *in utero*, not sight. Conditions of presence and absence … depend on audition only."[305] On Dolto's view, then, a beneficent arrival initiates a desire to follow onto the landscape of reality—the same process by which invested absence (suffering) nurtures phantasies we follow in reverse, regressing to archaic landscapes:

> On «les avenues de langage» conjugated with the knowing and the «recon-naissance» of the self and the other elected as co-being of pleasure … whose absence arouses his research … are supports for the presentification of the other in space and time, the other momentarily absent whose objects are a co-existential having(ness) of security in the solitude of the baby separated from the tutelary being he knows, and representatives of subtle communi-cation, albeit lured.[306]

With swirls more apt to a river, Dolto illustrates Freud's critical point that the "thing and representation of a thing are equivalent for the primitive psyche as the object perceived and invested in its absence."[307] Coming full-circle, then, we refind Freud's notions that dreams depend on waking life,[308] while associ-ations in reality depend on first being dreamed.[309] Yet Dolto is unselfconscious about how her phrase, "avenues of language," not only recalls the first time she noticed a suggestion on invested phonemes, on Avenue des Ternes, but is also a priceless example: «a venue» being, in archaic (or non-standard) French, "he/she/it arrived."[310]

The archaic is indeed an odd landscape where our floating attention helps, while our eyes confound us. For walking distance from Avenue des Ternes is Square Henry-Paté, Dolto's home from 15 July 1937[311]—at number 13, with Laforgue at number 8[312]—a five-minute stroll from Oliver Freud's (in 1933), at 36 Rue George Sand.[313] Laforgue analyzed Oliver's daughter, Eva, in the Midi in 1934–1938, the same years Dolto was in analysis, walking the same trails.[314] Henry-Paté is itself a strange address, for it is the name of her father (Henry) and grandfather (Henri)—and homonymically, «enrit» ["within laugh"], as if signed by the pleasure principle. It also humorously suggests, "food of the father." Here then is a radical education where the very nature of knowledge changes, and the last dream of our walk begins.

If a father is absent, the analyst must make him present in words,[315] Dolto explains, for words return the "reparative object,"[316] as the «repère» arrives like a transferential burst at the end of analysis. The father is discontinuous,[317] one who goes and returns,[318] who takes his value from «l'attente» ["the wait(ing)"; homonyms: "the aunt" and "latent"].[319] The homonymy evokes all that is latent in psychical life *in utero*, and the invested absence by which a passive being engages a phantasy of projection on a filiation of testimony. With Dolto, a father in reality is merely a «prête-nom» ["lend-name"][320] relative to the original transference situation that secures indestructible wishes. Dolto thus rejects Lacan's foreclosure of the father: "The name of the father who is the true father is never foreclosed"[321]—for through the work of analysis, "you can «déforclore» him."[322] And she theorizes continuity with the archaic as instrumental in recovery: "[We help a patient] become conscious that the father who engendered him is always in him and totally integral (intact),"[323] or [else] he [himself] would not be living.[324] She adds boldly: "The one who represents the model for his development is taken for the father, but he is not. He is only a resonator of the father that each one of us has in us."[325]

On this perennially viable, symbolic (prehistoric) father[326] rests Dolto's deep belief that any child can «autopaterner» by five or six,[327] being "auto-directed without being dependent on his mother or father ... as a sort of dialectic will structure his person."[328] All we need is the transference available in the open circulation of language, including texts—as free associations in reading, «relations épistolaires,» are "sufficient for the function of the symbolic father"[329]—returning venting despite our (perhaps pathological) relations of dependency. These notions of an indestructible archaic father and of reparation via diffuse transference guide Dolto's work with even the most traumatized infant—one who is "without associated desires, without landmarks."[330] Such is the economic role of the word, as the transference liberates affects in the social. So even the child deprived of a transferential harvest can find enough to eat. As Dolto puts it dramatically: "Speech alone can, by symbolic means, reestablish the internal cohesion of the child."[331]

## «Voies subtiles»

Throughout Dolto's oeuvre—via every meandering that takes us from her clinic, to her theory, to the silent margins of her history—what is most appreciable is her absolute compassion for the muted subject who is unable to insert himself in communicative exchanges because of his loss of the psychical landmarks upon which his symbolic filiation was dependent:

> Beings in language ... but misguided in(to) a mode of receptivity and expression that makes them difficult to understand ... precocious children who were not recognized as such in the first weeks of their life, and who became definitely discouraged from searching to communicate with an entourage that did not understand them.[332]

As Dolto puts it (in theorization decades ahead of its time): "It is the impossibility of symbolizing a disappeared link ... that is the case with autism"[333]—the loss of securing continuity.

At issue in reparation, then, is that once things begin to lose their dreaminess at the encounter with reality, the child is secured unconsciously as, "what he perceives of the interior ... is articulated with what is perceived as coming from the exterior world."[334] Dolto explains the power of the symbolic function and its immense reparative potential:

> The importance of the symbolic function resides without any doubt in the fact that it escapes all delimitation in time and space ... From every repeated signal, a human can make a symbol. Any human has then, by the symbolic function, a means of acting on other humans, by waking in others a receptive sensory resonance in accordance with his own. This simultaneity of emotion ... for it to take a valorized hierarchical place, there must be a reliving of a sensation that is «antérieurement» ["anteri-orly"; homonymically: «en terre ris heure m'an/ment»:"in earth, laugh, hour, mother/lie"] «éprouvé» ["experienced"; also, "tested/tried"] and linked to a relation known as inter-human and «semblable.» *The symbolic function therefore implies the notion of recognized similitude* ... it implies the notion of the «déjà vu,» that is[,] of time ... [it] *implies the trial of separation being surmounted.*[335]

And while the enigmatic, homonymic layers would be easier to ignore, their suggestions seem to reinforce the theoretical point at issue—about space, time, the mother and the trial of reality.

Yet unlike tireless Dolto, a reader begins to feel dizzy on the archaic land-scape, as if reading about presentification transmits something of the fragile sub-jectivity at the blurry edge of reality. With Dolto, we not only witness the archaic scene, but we experience archaic processes, as an intrinsic truth emerges: all that is new in Dolto, her genius, comes from all that is old in her—for she fully taps her archaic inheritance.

Dolto will make her way to Morocco—the neighbourhood of *Babouches*—in 1933, with a five-year plan to study medicine there.[336] But after a "12-day fairy-tale,"[337] as her father calls it, she will return to Paris for undisclosed reasons. A decade later, in 1943, a charming photograph will show her first-born, Jean, nine months old, dressed in a homemade tunic and turban, the cap-tion reading, "Asian prince taking a walk incognito."[338] So it is that lost stories tendering their truth in childhood become cryptic maps for an inimitable "road travelled"[339]—each human's unique traverse on the terrain of autobiography, where the transference transects on «voies subtiles» ["subtle routes"; homonym: "subtle voices"].[340] And through seemingly disparate notions coalescing unpre-dictably along wild associative pathways, if we are willing to invest Dolto's texts with promise, one thing leads to another, and another—though we will never know exactly how.

# Notes

1 ES, 10; VC1, 61.
2 AI, 114–116; ATP, 81–85; Dolto, 1985a, 214–226; ES, 9–14.
3 ATP, 85.
4 ES, 11.
5 ATP, 82.
6 Balesta, 1894/1902, 157.
7 ES, 11; also ATP, 82.
8 ES, 11.
9 ATP, 85.
10 Freud, 1916a, 71.
11 AI, 116; ATP, 84.
12 AI, 116; ATP, 84.
13 AI, 114; Dolto, 1985a, 214.
14 AI, 114.
15 ATP, 84.
16 AI, 116.
17 AI, 116.
18 ATP, 84; also EN, 80.
19 ATP, 84.
20 ATP, 84.
21 AI, 75.
22 VC1, 44.
23 VC1, 58–59.
24 AI, 116.
25 EN, 81.
26 ATP, 82.
27 Freud, 1908a, 152.
28 1891/2011, 75–76.
29 1901b, 110.
30 1901b, 274.
31 1895, 365–366.
32 1900b, 419 & 495, 1901a, 668.
33 The highly useful expression, "transference situation," was coined by Betty Joseph (1985).
34 ATP, 85; Dolto, 1985a, 215; ES, 12.
35 MA, 210.
36 VC2, 213.
37 VC2, 213; also EM, 209.
38 «Elle reste passivement à la maison» ["she stays passively at home"]; see MA, 109.
39 DQ, 123; also LO3, 37.
40 EM, 296; Nobécourt and Simonetta,1978.
41 SP1, 121.
42 CE, 324.
43 APP, 27; also ES, 107–108; LO3, 41; SP1, 79.
44 ATP, 21.
45 PJE, 15; also TL, 36.
46 JD, 142–145.
47 EN, 66.
48 Freud,1900a, 246.
49 E.1961, 29.
50 Freud,1896/1954a, 146.
51 1896/1954e, 322.
52 See Pappenheim (1888/2008).

53  Jones, 1953/1982, 224; for a study inviting a relation between fairy-tales and the analytic object, see; Propp, 1965.
54  I believe we also find evidence of the rogue transit of phonemes in Derrida's *Feu la cendre* [*Cinders*], as he reflects on his mentions of «cendres» ["cinders" or "ashes"] over 15 years: "I thought it was ingeniously calculated, mastered, subjected, as if I had appropriated it myself. But since then, unceasingly, I must admit the truth before the evidence: this sentence «s'était passé» ['got through' or 'happened'] without any authorization" (1987, 7).
55  EN, 73.
56  EN, 67.
57  EN, 68.
58  EN, 68.
59  VC1, 70.
60  EN, 73.
61  AI, 15.
62  EN, 39–40.
63  EN, 40.
64  EN, 39.
65  EN, 39.
66  EN, 40.
67  ES, 13.
68  LO3, 41; also CE, 94.
69  IIC, 278; also IIC, 35; PS, 21–22.
70  TL, 27.
71  TL, 31.
72  IIC, 276.
73  Murat, 2001/2013 (founded by Esprit Blanche, a psychiatrist).
74  ATP, 52.
75  Roudinesco, 1982, 210.
76  Full description: ATP, 52–64.
77  ATP, 61.
78  ATP, 62.
79  AI, 60; Nobécourt, 2008a.
80  Freud, 1900b, 525.
81  1900b, 562.
82  1914c, 154.
83  AI, 45.
84  1893a, 22.
85  ATP, 26.
86  SF, 38 & 216.
87  PS, 80.
88  1900b, 479–480 & 483, 1905c, 232 & 237.
89  1905c, 232.
90  1900a, 311, 1900b, 532, 1913, 167–168, 1917c, 350.
91  CD, 67 & 67f.
92  MA, 14.
93  VC2, 165.
94  MA, 19.
95  MA, 18.
96  MA, 19.
97  1900a, 122f.
98  CE, 351; SS, 59.
99  Ribowski, 1987/2004.
100  Morgenstern, 1930/2003, 291.

101  Freud, 1896/1954b, 175.
102  1896/1954b, 175.
103  1921, 127.
104  ATP, 71.
105  EN, 66.
106  EN, 66.
107  JD, 290.
108  JD, 289; also JD, 250–252; SF, 153.
109  SF, 105.
110  DV, 84.
111  CD, 22.
112  Morgenstern, 1927/2003, 10.
113  D&R, 18; MF, 29–30.
114  PF, 75.
115  DW, 166; Nobécourt, 2008b.
116  SP3, 47.
117  See Chapter 4.
118  MA, 14.
119  E.g., Freud, 1900b, 566, 1917b, 139, 1919[1918]a, 163.
120  SS, 194.
121  SP1, 83.
122  CD, 45.
123  ATP, 84; SP3, 47.
124  CE, 316.
125  JD, 281; SF, 88.
126  Schmideberg, 1930, 411; also, 1947.
127  Strachey, 1930, 324.
128  1930, 326.
129  EM, 26; LO3, 65; TL, 51.
130  Freud, 1900b, 511.
131  EN, 80; Ribowski, 1987/2004.
132  AI, 111; ES, 9.
133  Hall, 2009, 317.
134  EM, 344.
135  SP2, 114.
136  EF, 10.
137  MA, 58.
138  Roudinesco, 1982, 55.
139  JD, 189.
140  E.g., MF, 129.
141  AI, 116; EN, 81.
142  AI, 110; EN, 80; Ribowski, 1987/2004.
143  SP1, 41.
144  VO, 154.
145  CD, 5–7, 196, 207 & 211; EN, 120.
146  JD, 286, 1987/2004.
147  SP3, 172.
148  Freud, 1912a, 101.
149  1900b, 562.
150  1900a, 35.
151  CD, 193f.
152  CD, 193f.
153  CD, 5.
154  QS, 11; also SP1, 49.

155  JD, 168.
156  JD, 169.
157  SP1, 49.
158  CE, 78.
159  SP1, 115; also CE, 368.
160  SP1, 114–115.
161  SP1, 114–115.
162  SP3, 235.
163  VO, 39.
164  1919[1918]a, 162.
165  Roudinesco, 1982, 168.
166  Freud, 1900b, 594; also, 1900a, 141, 1900b, 546, 562, 589 & 596.
167  1914c, 151.
168  1905c, 222.
169  SF, 208.
170  Homonymically, «conaissance» is «co-naissance» ["co-birth"], and «renaissance» is «re-naissance» ["re-birth"]; so «reconnaissance» can suggest both. (The military associations in English are absent in French.)
171  DV, 158–161.
172  Freud, 1914c, 154.
173  APP, 34; also MA, 148.
174  SS, 234.
175  SS, 234.
176  VC2, 762; also VC2, 678.
177  SS, 146.
178  SS, 256; also CD; 198; CE, 78; PS, 63–65; SS, 185; TL, 15.
179  PS, 54; also DV, 117.
180  1895, 367, 1916a, 68.
181  1900b, 497.
182  1895, 365–366.
183  DW, 29.
184  SP3, 13.
185  1900b, 563–564; 1905a, 116.
186  1914c, 151.
187  Laplanche & Pontalis, 1967/2004, 12, 325, 329, 333 & 340.
188  PS, 64.
189  JD, 270.
190  JD, 59; also CD, 43.
191  JD, 285.
192  DV, 157.
193  CD, 113.
194  History World, n.d.
195  Balesta, 1894/1902, 135–160.
196  CD, 61.
197  CD, 61.
198  CD, 98.
199  CD, 60.
200  Interestingly, the translation of *Dominique* by I. Kats gives the name as "Fifi Wisp o'Steel" (see Dolto 1971/1973, 51), as Kats stays surprisingly close to Dolto's word choices, offering a literal rendering that seems to privilege her phonemes.
201  CD, 48 (story begins).
202  CD, 52 (story continues).
203  CD, 55.
204  SP1, 31; SP3, 179.

205 Freud, 1905c, 183.
206 Roudinesco, 1982, 168.
207 Freud, 1940/1939, 151.
208 1900a, 235.
209 1896a, 198f.
210 1900a, 236.
211 1913, 177.
212 AI, 220; also Ribowski, 1987/2004.
213 SP3, 128.
214 APP, 37.
215 PJ, 93.
216 JD, 251.
217 SS, 37; also SP1, 121.
218 MA, 28–29.
219 IIC, 102.
220 JD, 251; also LF, 112 (emphasis mine).
221 SF, 334.
222 SS, 210; also IIC, 246 & 275.
223 JD, 287; VC2, 702.
224 SS, 117.
225 Laplanche & Pontalis, 1964/2010, 326.
226 LO1, 145.
227 EM, 191.
228 LO3, 48.
229 Freud 1915c, 207–208; also, 1896e, 232.
230 Freud, 1900a, 49.
231 SP1, 120.
232 SP1, 120.
233 AI, 63 & 97; VC1, 23.
234 AI, 114.
235 VC1, 23f.
236 ATP, 86.
237 LF, 283.
238 DW, 22; also VC2, 844.
239 1900a, 297f.
240 1891/2011, 77; also, 1891/2011, 36–37 & 83, 1900a, 295–297 & 303, 1900b, 340.
241 1900a, 59 (emphasis his).
242 Freud, 1900a, 59f & 320, 1900b, 596, 1905a, 99.
243 E.g., 1900a, 177, 206 & 295, 1900b, 339, 375 & 605, 1901b, 30f, 58 & 109, 1905a, 65f, 90 & 105f.
244 1900a, 32 & 49–50.
245 1917c, 446 & 451.
246 1900b, 567; also, 1914c, 150, 1917c, 290.
247 1911a, 95.
248 DQ, 21.
249 SF, 320–321.
250 CE, 340; DQ, 21; Ribowski, 1987/2004.
251 VC2, 482.
252 VC2, 808.
253 SP3, 183.
254 APP, 32.
255 Dolto, 1979b, 17 & 21; ES, 19; VC2, 876.
256 CE, 41.
257 TL, 175.

258  Freud, 1900a, 24.

259  1900a, 221.

260  EN, 36–37.

261  In 1986, Dolto advises a colleague interested in Freud's "Wolf-Man" (1918/1914) to consider the work of Torok and Abraham (1976 in French, 1986 in English), "around the signifiers of the Russian language" (VC2, 812). These authors state, however, "We do not know Russian," calling it "good fortune" since it lets them, "follow better the avenues of our own listening" (1986, 34). Derrida prefaces that work, observing a "proper-name effect," as they posit the "word-thing *tieret*" to advance the "central importance for the Wolf-Man of the root *tr, tor*" (1986a, xlvii, citing Torok & Abraham). Without Russian, these researchers naturally could only follow the avenues of their own listening, as they say. Given this influence of the phoneme, *tor*, I add that "Tarok" was Freud's favourite card game (Boehlich 1990, 180; E. Freud, 1961, 99f). Derrida calls the phenomenon a "motivation ... no linguistic consciousness can deny" (1986a, xlvii)—a "*desire for idiom* or an *idiom of desire*" (1986a, xlvi; emphasis his).

262  Britzman, 2003, 63.

263  Isaacs, 1948, 81, 94 & 96.

264  JD, 7; SS, 220.

265  VC2, 808.

266  VC2, 702.

267  MA, 16 & 165.

268  VC2, 457.

269  JD, 292.

270  DW, 36; VC1, 542.

271  SP2, 177.

272  Freud, 1908a, 144.

273  Freud, 1913, 171; also 1900b, 566–568; 1901a, 647.

274  Freud, 1908b, 231.

275  Freud, 1908a, 145.

276  Freud, 1900b, 553; Freud, 1909b, 53.

277  Also Chapter 3.

278  PJE, 99.

279  MA, 266; also MA 89, 106 & 109.

280  MA, 253.

281  MA, 29–30.

282  MA, 91.

283  MA, 112.

284  MA, 109.

285  MA, 114.

286  VC2, 296; also SF, 305.

287  ES, 26.

288  ES, 14; SP1, 114.

289  Freud, 1900b, 594.

290  Freud, 1913, 181; also 1912a, 107.

291  De Saussure, 1959/1974, 34.

292  De Saussure, 1959/1974, 176–177.

293  De Saussure, 1959/1974, 43.

294  Starobinski, 1971, 30–31; also Bachner, 2003 & Starobinski, 1964.

295  Starobinski, 1971, 129 & 134; also Starobinski, 1964.

296  Starobinski, 1971, 125.

297  Tan & Perfetti, 1998, 37 & 40.

298  IIC, 93.

299  Greimas, 1969, 511.

300 EF, 9.
301 EF, 18.
302 ATP, 210; EF, 25; PJE, 59; VC1, 416.
303 LO1, 100; also VC2, 808.
304 JD, 251.
305 VC2, 329; also JD, 277.
306 PS, 21–22.
307 Laplanche & Pontalis, 1967/2004, 415.
308 Freud, 1900a, 19, 26, 39, 174 & 228; 1909b, 35.
309 Freud, 1900a, 206.
310 I.e., «a venu(e)» instead of the normative «est venu(e)» for "came."
311 VC1, back matter.
312 De Sauverzac, 1993, 91.
313 E.L. Freud, 1970, 54.
314 Geni.com, 2015; Systemique.be, n.d.
315 CD, 197.
316 DQ, 196; PJE, 15.
317 CE, 27, 29 & 172; EM, 63.
318 TL, 141.
319 SP2, 126.
320 ATP, 126; ES, 9.
321 DW, 100; also SP2, 125–130.
322 DW, 99.
323 DW, 99.
324 DW, 104.
325 DW, 142.
326 See Chapter 3.
327 EM, 26; LO3, 65; SP2, 14.
328 SP2, 115.
329 QS, 36.
330 SP3, 71; also Dolto, 1977/1998, 81.
331 IIC, 213.
332 IIC, 325.
333 IIC, 84.
334 1982a, 146–147.
335 DV, 158 (emphasis hers); also PS, 21–22.
336 VC1, 356.
337 VC1, 369.
338 AI, 178.
339 IIC, 275.
340 IIC, 69.

# 6
# SPEAKING

## Introduction

Françoise Dolto recalls the end of World War I as an inflation of the senses—"a fever of living"—though she missed the Armistice Parade, watching out the window (again) as her parents took her older siblings and the ladder.[1] She credits her love of a new commodity, radio, to her father, who sent her to hear what was new, including Édouard Branly's conference on the «transfert sans fil» ["wireless"].[2] Using tips she located in the *Petit Sans-Filiste*, she made her own crystal radio by age eight, and she taught herself the «ti.ti.ti.» with her *Larousse*.[3] Back in 1914, she had learned that war was declared by reading a notice board in Deauville.[4] Now, translating Morse, she told her family the news—"She's crazy! She's dreaming!"—yet the next day, the papers would confirm it.[5] Dolto notes that after Morse, time was added, then music, as she imagined sound rippling across space like a «caillou» ["pebble"] in water, and English signals from America faded and returned.[6]

The world opened after eight in the evening, Dolto explains, "bringing people not there before," like beloved Radiolo and songs from the «Chat noir» ["black cat"] and «Lapin agile» ["agile rabbit"]—two cabarets in Montmartre.[7] Movingly, she adds that radio in 1920 offered «du vivant» ["something of the living"] of Jacqueline.[8] For her pretty sister, who loved dances and had celebrated the Armistice at 16, was dead by then. She had departed at 18, the same age as the Irish nanny who so loved Paris nights, whose name was already lost.[9] Dolto's parents kept secret that Jacqueline was dying (even from her) for 18 months, inscribing a hidden drama—and dead, her name was banned.[10] But in the consolation of dance music, can we not hear two devastating losses (nanny, sister) echo jointly?

Moving ahead to 1947, to soon after the near-death of Dolto's third infant, Catherine,[11] Dolto's young patient Nicole asks her mother to make her a «poupée-fleur» with the head of a rabbit, after hesitating between a cat or rabbit; in parentheses, Dolto notes Bernadette also recently drew a rabbit.[12] Yet do we not hear an echo, in two identical animals (among so many possibilities!), of Dolto's new grief somehow reopening old chasms in her archaic history—that then facilitate wild diffusion in the transference? And in this fleeting «transfert» of the «transfert-sans-fil,» we also encounter interdiction: that potent tension between what is spoken—the «nom dit» ["noun/name said"]—and its ironic, homonymic reversal, what is prohibited, the «non-dit» ["not-said"]. For in these radio broadcasts transits the silent paradox of historicization: we release and we retain all that is loved.

## «Docteur X»

Forward 20 years to 1969, and Dolto is Docteur X in a phone-in radio program— *S.O.S.Psychanalyste!*—30 years after originally declining radio in 1939.[13] As Dolto insisted on anonymity, a text assembling its 187 programs does not even bear her name.[14] Medical colleagues complained to Europe 1 about her free advice—but the real reason for their resistance, she offers, is that it was painful to listen to the children.[15] A decade on, in 1976–1978, Dolto returns to radio, in her name, for *Lorsque l'enfant paraît* ["When the child appears"] on France-Inter.[16] Subject to wide coverage, its content proliferated.[17] Parents wrote letters of at least five pages—and many were helped just by that, Dolto notes.[18] Dolto then carefully chose letters for the program with her daughter, who recalls it as a rich collaboration.[19] In this way, psychoanalysis was put in the service of a whole society.[20] Dolto reports having experienced great anxiety before agreeing to the show,[21] for at stake was a complex history. After the evacuation of children from Paris in 1940, she saw 60 a day for treatment, and radio was a chance to help these kids, adults now, with their own.[22] But children listened too, like Sophie Chérer, who wrote in 2008 about how much it supported her. So it was that Dolto became as beloved as Radiolo. Yet in her professional history with radio, the reader cannot help but hear a resonance of her personal history with that device—and even of World War II as an echo of World War I. Can history simply be thought of, then, as what Freud once called "editions of transference"?[23]

Radio propelled Dolto—Freudian above all[24]—to the "center of a dramatic French infatuation with Freud."[25] France became the country with the most analysts in the world[26]—and Dolto its most popular analyst.[27] Hers is truly an immense heritage,[28] transecting her society. Hundreds of places are named after her, even a star,[29] and the web is flooded with Dolto-inspired blogs.[30] An American film festival showing *Le désir de vivre* (2008) declares that Dolto "invented psychoanalysis for children";[31] while the popular movie *The Class* is set at Collège Dolto.[32] There are publications by non-specialists[33]—and specialists too, such as one that places Dolto with Hannah Arendt, Marie Curie and

Eleanor Roosevelt.[34] For Dolto is as likely to be talked about in *Télérama*[35] as she is by Roudinesco, who notes her "fantastic optimism and vitality."[36]

Known above all for her "utter respect for the autonomy and intelligence of the child,"[37] Dolto—this "great woman of her time"[38]—still met ordinary visitors, like one Canadian who recalls: "After meeting Madame Dolto, we don't listen to a child or speak to him as we did before."[39] And while Dolto is famous for her "humor and auto-derision,"[40] her writing is remarkably "difficult for its density."[41] So Dolto's words late in life seem prophetic: "I am beginning to be a bit known."[42] Then again, maybe an ordinary reader says it best: "She gave me a love of my own human condition"[43]—or little Justine, who holds her new mother's pen, as they sign her adoption papers together.[44] For this is «l'héritage Dolto» in its totality: "Human dignity is a precocious sentiment."[45]

Of course, Dolto's project carries liabilities, too. Foremost is a vain search by some for a debt to Lacan.[46] Dolto can also seem more religious than she actually was, just for being "comfortable within the tradition of Catholic moral philosophy," as Sherry Turkle notes.[47] Dolto's marketability is also exploited, with catchphrases like «doltomania» and «enfants-rois» ["baby kings"], since her project is "gadgetized because it disturbs,"[48] as Halmos astutely observes. Strangely enough, another Kathleen from Quebec City became Dolto's official biographer in 2004, but the project somehow vanished.[49] True, Dolto's generosity in giving interviews at 78 (on an oxygen tank) was not always to her advantage, and she could be "naïve," as her daughter admits.[50] But supporters note how she is labeled "crazy" or a "witch" by certain of her peers[51]—deemed to be, as Roudinesco puts it, "too charismatic"[52]—or accused of having "too much intuition and not enough method."[53] "Witch" is a telling epithet, suggesting Dolto is branded by her groundbreaking work on the archaic, as if it provoked an «interdit» of its own.

## Reinterrogation

Roudinesco suggests that Dolto never understood the hate she aroused[54]—but perhaps she did. For hate is a dynamic originating in fear and it is a "form of suffering,"[55] Dolto states—a means for individuals to express, "an intolerable relation in them that makes them want to destroy themselves."[56] So Dolto recognized that society needs those who can tolerate hate, and that hate is not the opposite of love—indifference is.[57] Further, Roudinesco herself rightly concludes that Dolto "incites a reinterrogation of the archaic."[58] And as Dolto puts it, "jealousy of the puisne is actually a regression."[59] Additionally, in her own work on the «jalousie du puîné» ["puisne"],[60] Dolto explains how, "listening about regression regresses listeners and incites defenses," against an "enigmatic intrusion" that tempts destructuration, being an identification offering a "danger of involution."[61] And given that regression returns the archaic security in dream-work that is prior to reality, "humans are jealous of those who don't need a mother or father to be happy."[62]

But are not Dolto's statements an offer of a genuinely divergent perspective—
an entirely new sound issuing from someone who was not present before on
our side of the English Channel? So the difficulty with Dolto is not merely in
translating her from French to English (or any other language), but in translating
her non-temporal material into temporality. The work is akin to deciphering
dots-and-dashes—an as-if «rhythme binaire»—as we make ourselves available for
endless echoes in Dolto's wildly busy social oeuvre, and we become receptive to
affect arriving in all directions via that most archaic conduit, the «transfert,» in
Dolto's transmission of a prehistory that is not, yet is, being spoken.

Seeking help with the problematic of dissemination, I locate another dissertation
on Dolto—uncannily written by another «Québecoise,» Marcelle Gauthier,
in 1995.[63] Gauthier's research team apparently met Dolto briefly in France, in
1983.[64] Supervised by Arlette Mucchielli-Bourcier, a French scholar on dyslexia,
Gauthier inquires into «ce que *fut* » ["what *was*"] the «phénomène Dolto»[65]—as
if it has passed. Gauthier samples 132 parents and specialists in Nice and Montreal,
collecting some 8000 responses in all. The strongest finding is that
respondents convincingly praise Dolto's simple language,[66] her advocacy for
children,[67] her clinical experience,[68] her courage, humility and honesty[69] and
her concern for the public good.[70] Respondents refuse only two of Dolto's
teachings: evicting children from the parental bed, and granting them autonomy
by age eight.[71] The biggest contrast is that Niceans, who listened to Dolto's
radio programs, want help raising their children; while Montrealers, who did
not, seek help working with children.

Gauthier avoids in-depth discussions of the unconscious in her project, but
her Catholic roots are patent in her decidedly religious approach to "psychoanalysis
and spirituality"[72]—and in her inclusion, for example, of an intricate
table comparing the conception of the human being between Dolto and
Thomas Aquinas.[73] Her own respondent, "PP," astutely remarks, "I find it painful
to see her [Dolto] classified as a Catho[lic]"[74]—though the irony escapes
Gauthier's attention. The researcher is unsurprised to discover, then, that Gauthier
apparently wrote a Master's thesis on children's relation to God (1962),
along with a research paper (thesis?) on a prominent Catholic figure (1953); further,
she was employed by a large Catholic school board.[75] For Gauthier's
"silent" history is as readable in the (sub)text of her dissertation as it is in publishing
catalogs.[76]

And while mainly keeping to an examination of Dolto's social oeuvre, Gauthier
mentions the transference once, unfortunately crediting it to the psychoanalyst
René Morichau-Beauchant in 1909.[77] That a stumble of this magnitude
would escape her esteemed supervisor leads to a wholly unanticipated discovery
binding Morichau-Beauchant and Mucchielli-Bourcier on French soil. For this
so-called "first transference" recalls (uncannily and homonymically) the first
(postal) "transfer [to] France." Freud writes to Jung on 3 December 1910: "I
have received my first letter from France, from a Dr. Morichau-Beauchant."[78]

Even in a purportedly quantitative study, then, unconscious affects countersign conscious works, as objectivity eludes us all.

## Libidinal life

Dolto kept up a dazzling conference pace from the start to the end of her long career—from Geneva in 1936,[79] to Rio de Janeiro in 1979,[80] and Canada in 1983.[81] She held seminars at the EFP in 1971[82]—two granting university credits[83]—while 600 attended the Institut Océanographique in 1972,[84] and 400 were registered at the Institut National des Sourds ["Deaf"] in 1981.[85] There were waiting lists for her training clinics, prompting Olivier Grignon to offer to be her driver just to attend, believing she, "pushed furthest the place of trauma in psychogenesis."[86] As late as 1988, she saw in her office on Cujas infants from the «Pouponnière d'Antony»—an orphanage whose children she had once received at the Centre Étienne-Marcel—and she continued seminars and supervisions, as many as she could manage with two hours of oxygen (from portable tanks).[87] From her bed in her last weeks, she read manuscripts sent to her,[88] and she collaborated intensely with her daughter to help adolescents and families,[89] covering everything from incest to fetal audition of the "rumor of the world."[90] Even her husband's book on kinesiotherapy concludes, "It is in speech that the true relation is effected"![91]

There are elusive legacies, too, like Anna Freud's reading of two Dolto papers Spitz sent her in 1949,[92] and Dolto's support of the next generation of analysts, like Piera Aulagnier[93] and Maud Mannoni,[94] with whom she was in regular contact.[95] Yet months before dying, Dolto insisted: "Remember, I don't have any students!"[96] In fact, she is right. For 30 years on, there is no particular method or training for following Dolto, and only rare adjectivization—«doltoïenne.»[97] And while Dolto's work continues to influence so many people, she does not command close adhesion. Then again, she did not wish to: "If to live well we had to identify with our parents ... we would still be Cro-Magnons."[98] Dolto herself declares that any child who always wants to please his parents and thinks they are correct is in bad health,[99] for imitation is "simian" and "inhuman."[100] There are, instead, innumerable minds worldwide inspired by Dolto, in the absence of any prescription for "doing Dolto."

Dolto's propositions would also revolutionize education in schools,[101] which she deems to be a "prophylaxis of psychosocial morbidity."[102] She rejects civilizing for useless things,[103] and the sacrifice of independence to groups,[104] believing that "good habits are a violence against the liberty of living."[105] Expecting others to please you extinguishes their potential,[106] she says, so adults should not impose ideas on children.[107] The problem, she adds, is that when obsessional symptoms are shared, we consider ourselves well.[108] Her solution is to open up spaces, age groups and curricula—and to reduce the years of forced schooling.[109]

Besides, a real education should awaken our critical sense,[110] she says. For while "we all live upon what is false, it is important to make the child aware of the false that is important for us."[111] Dolto's views invite a lively uptake,[112] and they inspire the praxis at L'École Neuville (outside of Paris),[113] where students inscribe their individual grievances, issues and wishes in a community book shared aloud at weekly meetings.[114] On Dolto's view, educators need to grasp the "role of libidinal life,"[115] and give children autonomy by age seven to nine, as "Oedipus is resolved."[116] And Dolto's boldest words for educators arise from her work: do not wreck the education of a child who almost dies but lives;[117] and schools overvalue conscious motivation and active pulses, missing the genius of unconscious motivation and passive pulses.[118] With Dolto, psychoanalysis serves democracy, the child is a citizen,[119] and the unconscious is always at play in the most serious way.

## «Interdit» and «inter-dit»

But of all of the Dolto offshoots, the *Maison verte* ["green house"] is her key legacy.[120] A *Maison verte* offers precocious socialization for under-threes and their caregivers.[121] Opened collaboratively by local stakeholders, *Maisons vertes* are now found throughout the world, with 154 in France alone[122]—and three in Canada, all in Quebec.[123] The web is full of *Maisons vertes* news[124]—and blogs, like one from Armenia with huge matryoshka dolls[125]—as groups culturally mark and name each one. Research on 15 *Maisons vertes* in France in 1984–1992 noted 1000–1500 visitors each[126]—that is 200,000 yearly! "Françoise liked doing good," Roudinesco notes.[127] Dolto won a prize from Lego for the concept[128]—money she reinvested in children—and she continued to attend the flagship site she helped open in 1979.[129] Each *Maison verte* is staffed with at least three analyzed persons, among them one male and an analyst. But if we enter for a moment that «maison»—homonymically, «mes sons» ["my sounds"]— Dolto says she dreamed about for 15 years,[130] I suggest that we cannot but hear Dolto too, in what she called, unassumingly, its "echo and ricochet effects."[131]

The original *Maison verte* was named by children in a story Dolto fondly repeats, explaining they called it "green" though it was blue.[132] Like another of her readers, I wonder, does the "green house" echo the (lost nanny's) Emerald Isle?[133] And I recall that Dan-Mé's mother, Cécile Secrétan, went to America to marry an Overnay, Irish-born,[134] a name akin to another ancestor's, Duvernoy[135] [both homonyms for "of green born"]—as the lost Irish nanny beckons. As children socialize, staff depathologize ordinary baby behavior, "drinking" or "sponging" adult anxiety[136] that would risk a child becoming a "symbolic hemiplegic."[137] For a subject enters the world with his own desires, and our task, Dolto says, is not to become human but to remain so.[138] "You feel stronger as a parent when you leave,"[139] an ordinary attendee at a *Maison verte* aptly remarks.

Dolto cites the importance of telling the two rules at any *Maison verte*: wearing a waterproof apron to play with water, and not crossing the red line with vehicles. So the "interdit becomes the inter dit."[140] (But are we also hearing an echo of «m'arrête» ["stop myself"], her name, in that red line?) At a *Maison verte*, communication confirms who a child is, and basic prohibitions aid his becoming,[141] as he "uses his libido in social activities that are tolerated or stimulated."[142] There is also the "technology of the ladder"—climbing play.[143] (Is this an echo of the missed Armistice parade?) Questions flow freely, with neither tracking nor reporting to outside agencies. For there is anonymity at a *Maison verte*,[144] as only the child's name is written on the board at the entrance. (Is this an echo of the big wartime board in Deauville?) The project offers infant-caregiver pairs a transition from being home alone, aiming to prevent sharp ruptures at the entry to daycare or preschool. (Is this an echo of children being evacuated during the war?)

True to form, Dolto is incredibly serious with infants at the *Maison verte*. There is no baby talk, only intense attention and respect. Yet even as we leave that «petite maison»[145] ["small house"]—an echo of a fairy tale?—we hear three potent notes on theorization in chit-chats about it: the way we greet children wakes up a child's attention, as the child is a taker if he knows he is with some-one listening;[146] the dead object (toy) does not become living until someone takes hold of it, as the child ignores that he himself has the power to give life to the toy, but accords that capacity to his similar;[147] and the fact that we speak to a child in front of his mother signifies that we accord him an identity that is relational to her, but not fusional.[148]

Awaiting for the deeper meaning of these three points to evolve, we simply "accumulate signs for later use,"[149] as some of her commentators elsewhere advise. In fact, transferential effects at *Maisons vertes* are so common that some even write of «transfert sur le lieu» ["transference on the site"],[150] while others note rightly that "transference on place" requires a witness.[151] Dolto is unequivocal that the transference requires a human presence: "Healing takes more than displacement, it takes a relation for the transference to put libido back into circulation."[152] And elsewhere, Dolto states clearly that, "the transfer-ence necessary for referencing oneself ... must be lived on a socially integrated human being"[153]—and that in her own work, for example, transference is effected through what is communicated to her as a person.[154] So a *Maison verte* offers attendees opportunities for a "narcissizing link."[155] Can it properly be called, then, a place of witnessing?

## «Transfert fantasmatique»

Freud explains that the transference is an exchange of affect that is present in all relationships,[156] and language is its privileged setting.[157] True to Freud, Dolto describes her therapeutic role in terms of a, "phantasmatic transference of past relations,"[158] wherein she serves as a "temporary prosthesis," as she "lends herself" to the subject[159] during difficult work that is «déréalisant.»[160] She believes effect-ive analysis revives the archaic,[161] so the subject can "express repressed pulses while reducing his guilt."[162] Her disposition is thus to be "available" to receive projections,[163] becoming a "resonator" to "wake" the subject's "own analyst."[164]

In effect, is she not elaborating how self-healing requires an analyzed witness—a resonator of the archaic? Does this not return the notion that a child is a taker if someone is listening? For is not psychoanalysis always about listening for the child in the adult? And, repeatedly, Dolto notes that the child listens better while busy, as if he were not listening[165]—when he is passive, as a third in the conversations of others. Is the child a taker, then, when someone else is listening (too)? Is this why a witness matters?

But our questions need to stay open because still more echoes arrive. For the child needs a «fil» ["wire/thread"],[166] Dolto says, until he can be «sans-filet» ["wireless"].[167] And Dolto is optimistic for all of her patients, even psychotics or infants engulfed in "mortifying anxiety":[168] "As the child has managed this long without you ... there is no reason to assume he will do less well now that he has your support."[169] But in this business of wires and wireless, is there not a silent telling of her history with radio? Funny enough, too, Dolto's first office (in 1936) was in a tiny flat on Dupuytren: "I often forgot my key ... I had to climb ... up the ladder to the little window."[170] How can the reader attuned to Dolto not hear more echoes bouncing from the *Maison verte* to the missed Armistice parade (and window)—and back again?

True to form, Dolto is not bothered by the hatred that can arise in analytic relations, as it is a "duty to show tolerance for what others do not tolerate."[171] For Dolto, as Grignon says, "the analyst is for life."[172] She is horrified to hear of any hate in the counter-transference, believing that one cannot work under those conditions.[173] And specifically to address hate, she invents her famous "symbolic payment":[174] patients bringing a stamp, stone, coin, ticket, etc. Forgetting it, she says, means an unconscious refusal of treatment.[175] The payment also prevents a patient from "mythologizing" the analyst.[176] So while it is always desirable, she explains, it is decisive with young children still resolving their «Oedipe.»[177] Dolto employed it from 1968 to 1988,[178] and an uptake seems to be starting.[179] But is there an echo here of details overlooked until now—about her wartime hobby of buying medals, and of a medal ceremony for Oncle Pierre?[180] And can we not also hear an echo of little Katia's desire for a medal with a «ficelle» on it?[181] For like the analyst, the symbolic payment works in phantasy, representing something unique for each person.[182] Most curiously, too, Dolto is widely known for having inspired the children's character *Caillou*—which, while being named by someone else, somehow echoes Dolto's own daydreams about radio waves.

In 1981, ironically at the Institute for the Deaf (situated next door), Dolto comments on the political discords around her: "There are stories happening in all of these transactions, but I have only vague echoes."[183] Could we not say the same? For what Dolto's uncanny corpus reveals is that no moment in time stands alone. All is ricochets, «reconnaissance» and «après-coup»—later editions of the transference of infantile history. Thereby, the transference is the «interdit» and the «inter-dit»: what is banned from consciousness but endures as an «articulation vitale» between us,[184] an "affective exchange that is a resourcing of vitality."[185] She explains:

There is somewhere a subject with his own desire, veiled, who watches in his passive pulses for the moment when he will be found by someone ... It is this availability towards the encounter with the most archaic pulses of a human being that is the *a priori* transference of the psychoanalyst.[186]

So emerges a remarkable unsaid narrative, as primary processes secure self-regulation lifelong, and language (including its silences and slips, and eluding time) enables us to take in and release affect. By this, we can conceive of the transference as a passive operation serving a kind of unconscious circulation that sustains our survival by managing the libidinal economy.

## «Témoin» and triangulation

Herein arrives Dolto's complex theory of the «tiers» ["third"; homonym: «tes hiers,» "your yesterdays"]—or «témoin» ["witness"; homonym: «tes moins,» "your lessers"][187]—silent and hidden in the "thickness of her propositions,"[188] as Halmos puts it. I do not claim a full grasp but offer only my interpretation, as meaning arrived gradually over the years. We begin with a fact: the fetus "cannot lose continuity" to survive.[189] This causes a need for "mediators that are other beings in language,"[190] as the securing of pleasure calms pulses and "abolishes a moment of time and space."[191] Developing, the "symbolic function ... permits the substitution of pleasure from a short circuit of desire, immediate, to a longer circuit that mediatizes pulses."[192]

So the fetus is referenced to an enduring sense of unconscious security within a unique archaic transference situation consisting of a co-narcissistic «pré-moi» and an other(ness) in (of) dream-work as a third. Near the horizon of space-time, through birth, substitutions of pleasure and the reversible circulation of affect will effect a slow, uneven, anxiogenic migration to reality, as the «pré-moi» remains unconsciously fusional with the mother. Meanwhile, restorative dream-work that invests audition secures ongoing continuity with the archaic—returning as (an) otherness or third—as the symbolic father provides (inherits), by unconscious associations, an offer of a «fil» (up and down, we could say) to the social.

Triangulation is then observable in the relation of an infant with his mother and (usually) his father, as progressive substitutions enable longer circuits for taking in and venting affect from diffuse sources. Somewhere here is the porous place of introjects. The reversibility inhering in triangulation means that a «pré-moi» holds shifting positions between himself and his mother, and between himself and the other, resulting in a blurry, liquid subjectivity. Crucially, then, "two" is always one, as a young human in a pair returns to «prolongement.» So the child needs a third, a witness, in order to be one—or, as Dolto puts it succinctly, "one and one makes three."[193] In other words, triangulation is indispensable for individuation. And it is as if the father indicates the secure direction to follow in the child's capacity to exit the monad to engage object relations— from his condition of «prolongement,» to language and its unconscious register.

As Dolto further elaborates it, the father is "separated out" from the mother,[194] emerging from a dual relation from the "heart of the mother to the body of the child."[195] The "other of the mother"[196] offers the invaluable potential for separability that inheres in his perpetual continuity with the subject, along which path the subject can develop symbolic relations in reality.

Dolto explains: "We are born in a triangular situation ... [so] the child needs this triangular situation to continue[,] to develop."[197] The triangular situation is constructed completely unconsciously[198] as, "any other perceptible by his mass or by effecting emotional variations on the mother ... is, like him, felt to be in dyad with the mother ... qualifying and quantifying her dyad."[199] She adds, "a common interest unites them emotionally. It is the beginning of a situation of three ... [that is,] two united relative to a third (the thing)."[200] And this «situation triangulaire»[201] is the source of «sécurité intérieure.»[202] Here is a critical notion: the child's first «semblable» is the other of the mother. Therefore, a word-thing is a confirmation restoring triangulation, a phantasy of a common interest—a mediating object—while a «repère» is an archaic landmark in reality. So witness, third, «repère» and confirmation condense.

As triangulation securitizes, the child wants to be witnessed,[203] phantasizing trees, birds, nature and even anthropomorphized objects as his witnesses:[204] "The child is always an interlocutor with an other, who is an interlocutor with an other. It is always a triangle."[205] So, Dolto stresses, "you need to be careful that there is always a third, always a third, when you have relations with children."[206] Is a powerful recommendation not implied here: always securitize a child via a triangular situation? And since triangulation is driven by passive pulses, I believe we refind those "toys in the hand" (from her chit-chats at a *Maison verte*) whereby a child is unaware he can enliven (himself) until he follows a «semblable» who can. For children need "proof of existence," Dolto explains, and they use each other for identification.[207] Thus, the libidinal dynamics of passivity are installed in triangulation.

In turn, a "social third" or "lateral person" prevents fusion, i.e., the loss of individuation.[208] Thus the analyst enters as a third, freeing the child[209]—theorizing Dolto's work with witnesses.[210] A choral clinic is "more operational," "radically curative" and an "extraordinary accelerator" of work, as it "returns the original triangular relation."[211] So too for presentification, as the "child needs to hear the mother speak to an object other than himself ... to access language."[212] This nurtures a "mediated relation instead of a dual one"[213]—theorizing a *Maison verte* as a triangular rather than fusional scene, and the "social milieu as a witness."[214] Of note, Dolto discussed the third as a «présence affective de "témoin réactif," sensible, passif et impartiel» as early as 1940.[215] Dolto thus narrates the dream-work by which we engage reality as a relational echo of the archaic and the transference tempers the anxiety of historicization. Her notion of triangulation also invokes the «interdit,» since individuation requires the interdiction of fusion that facilitates separability.

We pause for air, and for more of Dolto's rich examples. In 1942, she marries Boris, a Russian.[216] She recalls seeing the Russian Church from her kitchen at 13 Square Henry-Paté (in 1937), as if it were "written in her destiny."[217] Boris first dined with the Marettes to replace her brother, Pierre, then serving in Morocco.[218] Upon hearing about Boris, her father exclaimed: "Of course, she couldn't help bringing us a Tartare!"[219] But how can the bilingual listener not hear (amid the echoes of *Babouches* issuing from Morocco) the homonym, «tard tard» ["late late"],[220] in wild play against her old nickname, Vava ["gogo"]? She also explains that *Do l'oto* means "sculpting tool" in Old Slavonic[221]—and we cannot stop its homonym, «l'auto,» from evoking the wheels at *Maisons vertes* that «m'arrête» (Marette) at the red line.

We also recall the nanny's elevator man, dressed as a Brandebourg, like «généraux russes» (and Oncle Pierre).[222] Brandenburg Province actually joined the Weimar Republic after World War I. But how can this not, in turn, return Freud, "born [in Weimar] amid a slav population"[223]—and Brandenbourg (in Luxembourg), home of Mlle, that dear nanny replacement? Dolto remembers worrying about Boris meeting Laforgue, feeling tremendous anxiety on Boulevard Delessert as they walked over[224]—its near-homonym evoking those 15-day privations of dessert[225] for naughtiness. Here, then, are abundant substitutions on familiar names as the phoneme—gaining or losing the odd letter—serves as a mediating object. So when Dolto says that her love of Boris was "not in time and space,"[226] how can we not agree with her?

## Identification and interprojection

Further elaborating fusion, this first "captive mode of object relations" remains throughout life.[227] So a child cannot make contact with anything that interests him without "anthropomorphizing it" and experiencing «un transfert.»[228] Dolto adds a crucial note that, "it is also possible that the affects of pregenital stages ... need, in order to be expressed in the transference, a reciprocity of behavior."[229] And as our first means of engaging an other requires a «semblable,» then "[primary] narcissism is reversible on whom we speak to."[230] Dolto thus theorizes, beautifully, that "the protean child progressively weds the forms he faces."[231] At work is a primitive psychological process whereby "the human identifies himself with his entourage."[232] Yet this sustaining start makes it hard to learn the limits of self, leading to "over-identification in a transference that is more and more sticky."[233] In other words, fusion can cause an "infernal cycle" of interprojections, trapping both people.[234] And in this mode where to love is to be like, Dolto stresses, the "child unconsciously loses."[235]

Dramatically, Dolto adds that outgrown identifications to parents are «fatale» by age six or seven,[236] being a contamination by identification.[237] For symbolic communication requires distance.[238] And if the mother never separates from the child, he will not know that he exists.[239] Here we pause for another fine example of substitution, still on the name. For Dolto relates learning, at age seven, the good news that Saint-François (Francis of Assisi) was her patron saint—not Saint-Françoise (with its added "e").[240] She loves Francis of Assisi, calling him a «hippie de la Renaissance» who "invented ... a psychodrama of nativity,"[241] of a "non-fusional generous maternity."[242] But isn't what is at issue not Dolto's so-called religiosity, but, rather, an indissociability between her own identifications and her work on the role of language in identification?

Dolto's difficult writing on incest is also informed by her notion of fusion. Incest means "not separated,"[243] as separation calls for "assuming one's identity while renouncing the identification to the object of pleasure and desire for the parents."[244] Thus, incest "on all levels is deadly,"[245] and a principal cause of regression.[246] Even being phantasized as incestuous is "terrible for the child ... [i.e., his being] the prey of a possessive or excessive identificatory love."[247] Furthermore, "the practical sexual initiation of adolescents and children by an adult ... even if this partner is not incestuous ... is *always a profound psychological trauma.*"[248] Dolto even recalls a five-year-old traumatized by a "parody of marriage to his mother."[249] But how can Oncle Pierre not echo here? Dolto explains that if there is no phantasm of incest, there is no humanization; but if there is an actualization of that phantasm, there is no society.[250] So the most determinative education of all is to tell a child by age three about «l'interdit de l'inceste.»[251] Dolto credits Freud for articulating the incest taboo, stressing its universality[252]—reminding parents to share that they suffered [it] and survived.[253] But by this instruction, is the «interdit» of incest not also a kind of witnessing by a «semblable»?

Recovering a psychotic child requires helping him to find a «semblable» to liberate his expression.[254] Conversely, the mother perfectly identified to a child, dressed as an exact copy, is a "superb creature from the veterinary point of view,"[255] Dolto says drily. So we return now to Robert, her psychotic nine-year-old patient, the mute wolf-child who howls:

> There were in him two positive identifications: the animal identification [gardener's dog], and the identification to a dead man [beloved gardener dead of a heart attack]...This identification to the deceased was very beneficial because ... he could relive the trauma of dying by falling out of the window, that is, of having been separated at 15 days by forced weaning from the mother who birthed him, then at about two months, having almost died of dehydration [as his mother lost her milk during the war].[256]

And from her own life, Dolto offers a tip: "If you remain vigilant and question, you will not identify."[257]

## Languaged filiation

At stake in Dolto's theorization is the endurance of the archaic. If phobia or loss preclude security in reality, then resourcing by regression delivers the return of continuity. The transference then (later, eventually) facilitates a return to reality through phantasy. So continuity with the archaic harbors a phenomenally reparative potential. Dolto first spoke about continuity in 1940, in relation to the "acquisitions necessary to the normal continuation of psycho-affective development."[258] And in 1949—at the 16th International Congress (Zurich)—discussing cut flowers in children's drawings, she described «la solution de la continuité.»[259]

Dolto's notion of true archaic identification is a solution by means of a return, via symbolic filiations, to the prehistory of each «pré-moi» on a landscape constructed in dream-work. So we each need to keep something archaic and stable when identity is changing too quickly[260]—as in war[261]—Dolto says. She adds that she has always been interested in what is continuous that links what seems discrete.[262] We also recall that our first «semblable» is the other of the mother, in the archaic transference situation representing our "libidinal wealth,"[263] the "source of life,"[264] our "languaged filiation."[265] As a result, what Dolto analyzes in her clinic is identifications,[266] finding that a child often lives out "archaic object relations" with his entourage without anyone noticing.[267]

Dolto's theorization incidentally finds strong corroboration with the highly respected philosopher and political theorist Hannah Arendt: "All my life I considered myself Rahel [Varnhagen, 1771–1833] and nothing else";[268] and with Bertha Pappenheim, who became an inspired social activist dedicated to the defense of women,[269] and who was "identified so deeply with Glückel [von Hameln, her ancestor, 1646–1724] that she commissioned a dramatic portrait of herself as Glückel."[270] Also at issue here is Dolto's own unexpected identification with Lou Andreas-Salomé: "Later, only, when I read her and I read some works about her, I thought that she was like Françoise Marette or Françoise Dolto. I felt myself to be entirely «de la même veste» ["in/of the same vest": same cloth? same (affective) investments?] as Lou Andreas-Salomé."[271] Beneath Dolto's admission are unspoken returns of Weimar (where Lou first met Freud in 1911),[272] as Lou is transferentially colored with that returning word—Brande (n)b(o)urg—in a fine example of the diffusion of affects in the social. Further, as lovely Lou was «la russe» ["the Russian female"], she also returns the lost nanny with the auburn hair[273]—«la rousse» ["the red-headed female"]. So as we listen to Dolto explain how, while walking in Nimes (in the Midi) one day, she thought of her «semblables» 2000 years ago, [274] do we not begin to feel the fluidity of identifications—and how space-time is much more porous than we think? An affect of wounding and loss also comes through Lou's texts—one that invites a powerful question about the legacy of infantile suffering to a particular approach to psychoanalytic theory. For the faint echo of a little Russian girl with a hard history informs a haunting loneliness that suffuses Lou's texts and cannot help but lure the wounded reader. Maybe it drew Dolto too.

## «Castration symboligène»

Dolto writes that a second language is a way to "run from yourself,"[275] as she herself is reading Katherine Mansfield "to escape."[276] Dolto was also competent in Latin, English and Italian.[277] In 1931, she even writes of thinking and speaking "in the accent of the Midi";[278] and, in 1934, of reading in Provençal.[279] Truth be told, it was a second language that had brought that beloved nanny to her home,[280] always staffed with «l'anglaise des petits» ["the English girl for the little ones"].[281] Musing on second languages, Dolto relates how a French psychiatrist, a victim of incest, found peace in Australia[282]—for a new language may make the incest taboo redundant, Dolto says.[283] This is its advantage for those who cannot continue to use the mother tongue without finding themselves "trapped through this language."[284] And we recall Pappenheim, who, though German, was "at her best and most free" in French and Italian[285]—and who, at the depths of her illness, could only speak in English nursery rhymes.[286] The "salvific language" just needs to not conform to the mother's rhythm,[287] Dolto explains, so even an accent helps,[288] offering security in "camouflage."[289] The problem is, however, that the second language "risks breaking filiations"[290]— essentially, losing innumerable unconscious tethers to the archaic. Then again, is this not the very risk (and grave responsibility) of any act of translation?

The "as-if severing" inhering in a second language takes us to Dolto's notion of «castration symboligène» ["symboligenic castration"], elaborated from 1940. Enjoying a steady uptake, symboligenic castrations are aptly described by Grignon as "permitting access to sublimations"[291]—while «symboligène»[292] is a prime example of Dolto's non-traditional terms. Dolto explains that while symboligenic castrations are ongoing, psychical development hinges on the major castrations agreed upon in the literature, the oral and anal,[293] while she has merely added the prior "umbilical castration" of birth.[294] An entirely unconscious process is at stake in symboligenic castrations,[295] wherein the frustration of a desire impels the subject to transfer investments to subsequent objects, allowing a wider field of exchanges[296]—migration from short to longer circuits.[297]

Do castrations, then, serve as a continued elaboration of how the subject substitutes pleasures in triangulation? For every trial is a springboard that ruptures fixity,[298] Dolto explains, and a "drama for the one who lives it."[299] But growth requires risks,[300] so we are "fragilized" by a «non-castration»[301]—as play on its homonym, «nom,» softly invokes birth as the umbilical castration that delivers the name. So there is, Dolto notes, a "need for aggressive energy to detach oneself from what fascinates."[302] Thus, progressive symboligenic castrations comprise a "mutation process,"[303] one that "reinforces desire in front of an obstacle,"[304] yielding a richer symbolic life[305]—i.e., symbolic fruit.[306]

In brief, "all separations have a narcissizing value for the one who survives,"[307] being "liberating,"[308] as long as the restriction is "partial and compensated" with greater pleasure.[309] Dolto compares the process to pruning a tree,[310] or a flower,[311] for better growth. Intended to dovetail Freud, whom she credits,[312] symboligenic castrations do seem to elaborate his notions about temporary unpleasure making possible an attainment of greater pleasure;[313] instinctual demands being forced from direct satisfaction to substitutive satisfactions;[314] libido being in a "complemental series" with frustration;[315] and a "fruitful source of disappointment and renunciation … [being a] stimulus to dreaming."[316] With symboligenic castrations, Dolto theorizes human survival as hinging on a tension of endogenous castration anxiety.[317] She expands: "The unconscious economic objective (purpose) of these states of powerlessness is the neutralization of castration anxiety … The castration complex is a … success for the libidinal dynamic of the subject."[318]

On this view, trauma is a "failed castration,"[319] while health requires successive "bereavements": of fetal sonority,[320] of identification with one's mother,[321] of childhood,[322] even of the preceding hour[323]—to "separate from the oneself of yesterday to seek the oneself of tomorrow."[324] In effect, Dolto is narrating human suffering in the encounter with space-time, and deriving from castration a compassion for our sacrifice to the material world—melancholy as the cost of living.[325] Dolto's emphasis on symboligenic castrations being given in language is well commented: "Another human being signifies to him that the accomplishment of his desire, in the form he would like to give it, is prohibited."[326] So symboligenic castrations return the notion of a witness to suffering, as a loving other speaks upon an existential trial.

## «Après-coup»

As we linger a little longer on Dolto's notion of symboligenic castration, we come upon another vendor in Deauville who sang about sharpening scissors and knives,[327] and her sewing teacher, Suzanne (whose fiancé was a «chasseur alpin» like Oncle Pierre and died the same year), who gave her certificates for excellence in cutting.[328] To this, we add a somber fact: Jacqueline died of a hematoma 18 months after a bad fall; her leg needed amputating, but her mother had refused.[329] Published posthumously, the revelation evokes the tragic irony of the dance music on the radio. It also testifies to Dolto's notion of the «interdit» from the intimate grounds of her own bereavement, in the «après-coup» ["aftercut"] of her losses—and to the «transfert sans fil» that offered a balm on her suffering.

Dolto's texts leave little doubt that, just as she theorizes, our childhood histories inscribe an unconscious trace that is detectable. And this readability of the unconscious of (in) a corpus leads us to her most public theory, to which we will return:

> The *unconscious image of the body* … depends on the affective commerce with the mother and familiars. It is a structure that results from an intuitive process of the organization of phantasms, of pregenital affective and erotic relations … in particular, sensations of appeasement and of tension due to vital needs.[330]

Needless to say, though, phonemic play and condensations in the service of unconscious affects, rooted in the archaic, make impossible the adventure of translation. Even trying to read Dolto's theory becomes an "interpretation akin to a translation,"[331] to quote Freud—one where dream-work is indispensible to our comprehension. And although, for Dolto, the "only true transitional support is the word,"[332] Dolto's words are, as she says herself, «pas classiques»[333]—and the wild plays porting their transferential effects are, like slips of the tongue, highly resistant to translation.[334] So the English versions of *Dominique* (1973/ 1974) and her dissertation (2013) cannot help but somewhat disorient the reader seeking Dolto. It is as if the rebus is gone.

And here we come to the tragicomedy of the present project. In but one of countless examples, we find Dolto's anecdote from Deauville, that departure point for Britain where the family summered.[335] The bilingual news seller stuttered, saying 15 as «cinq–dix» ["five–ten"]—instead of the correct French, «quinze»—and calling out *mititi*, as she announced news at «midi» ["noon"].[336] But how can the attuned hearer not recall the «ti.ti.ti.» of the Morse code Dolto learned from the radio—or the dictionary decoding it, the *Larousse* ["female red-head"]—and the Midi [homonym: «mi-dit,» "half-said"], her adult refuge? Yet the word-play is entirely lost in translation: What is "noon"? What is "red-head"? It is nothing. Just like *Do l'oto*—that sculpting tool in Old Slavonic—no longer means anything as "dolto," as she explains: «Dolto ça ne signifie rien»[337] ["dolto it signifies nothing"]. As an autobiographical note (in the year of her death), it is the humblest of statements. Yet we watch helplessly from an English shore as Dolto's French messages recede like radio waves, and a sense of abandon—invoking the lost nanny—prevails.

## *Otitis*

In 1932, Pierre visits Deauville, and his infant (Dolto's godchild) almost gets *otitis*[338]—a "defense against hearing"[339]—as the first grandchild encounters repressed stories of war, death and departure. I submit that her suffering aptly symbolizes our own. For listening to Dolto is a non-linear engagement with theoretical density defying logical exposition, where echoes begin in a place unseen and never end. Dolto's texts are, as other scholars explain it perfectly, "a rendez-vous with a voice, words that ressemble nothing that we have heard until now"[340]—"another regime of communication than that which bends to the dominant discourse"[341]—while the "true dimension of her word remains largely unknown."[342]

As our habitual means of thought are supplanted by binary rhythms of presence and absence, we cannot help wanting to open a few paradoxes, to expand into time-space along some segues, seeking lures to reality. But regression calls for precisely the reverse; it requires sieving by compressing as, in Freud's words, "elements as allow any point of contact are condensed into new unities."[343] By this slow, unplannable process of compression, coordinates without «raison» ["reason"]—but (in perfect homonymy) with «ré-son» ["re-sound"]—reveal the other-ness that is also our selves, as the transference invests associative thinking with an archaic legacy. Further, I believe that the beauty, subtlety and complexity of the transference in Dolto's texts makes patent the interconnectedness of her ideas, and the (counter)signature by which her prehistory becomes audible.

At the very least, we should value the undeniable witness that is the infant: the auditory record by which Dolto attests to an early history wherein she was—like all infants—deemed to have been barely present at all. Maybe, as a female from the prestigious 16th «arrondissement,» Dolto is an unlikely witness to the unconscious. Then again, the unconscious is an unlikely witness by definition, as Roudinesco reminds us: "neither hereditary, nor cerebral, nor automatic, nor neural, nor cognitive, nor metaphysical, nor meta-psychical, nor symbolic."[344] For working inside Dolto's corpus, we learn that texts and theories are accidentally but necessarily countersigned by the unconscious, as the word is inscribed by (in) an unending dream attesting to its prehistory. Thus, the edifice of reality is only ever a stor(e)y.

## Notes

1 ATP, 43; EN, 36; LF, 273.
2 ATP, 31 & 43; EN, 81.
3 ATP, 31 & 42; EN, 74–75 & 115; VC1, 167.
4 AI, 66.
5 LF, 273.
6 ATP, 32–33, 41 & 49; EN, 74–76; VC1, 154.
7 ATP, 33 & 42; EN, 75; Radiola, n.d.
8 EN, 75.
9 EN, 106–108.
10 ATP, 74; EN, 106–108.
11 AI, 183; C. Dolto, 2005b.
12 JD, 142 & 156.
13 Frémeaux & Guéno, 2006; Vasquez, 1976; VC2, 25.
14 Vasquez, 1976.
15 D&R, 35.
16 D&R, 34.
17 E.g., LO1, LO2, LO3; Marc-Pezet, 2004; VC2, 192–193 & 197.
18 D&R, 36; DW, 154–155; Nobécourt & Simonetta, 1978.
19 C. Dolto-Tolitch, 1998.
20 AI, 228–229; Delphine, 2008; Nobécourt & Simonetta, 1978.
21 D&R, 34; DW, 152.
22 Nobécourt, 2008a.
23 Freud, 1905a, 116, 1915b, 168.
24 Golder, 2002b, 122.
25 Turkle, 1995/1997.
26 Roudinesco, in Coronel & De Mezamat, 1997c.
27 *Psychoanalytikerinnen*, 2013.
28 Berger, 2006.
29 Fédération Nationale du Patrimoine, 1988.
30 E.g., Freixa, n.d., and countless others in diverse languages.
31 Leonard, 2009.
32 Cantet, 2008; Hamelin & Rabaté, 2011b.
33 E.g., Chapsal, 1994.

34 Adler et al., 2006.
35 Portevin, 2008, 40.
36 Ina.fr, 1988.
37 Reeves, 2010, 318.
38 Ribowski, 1987/2004.
39 Camaraire-Santoire, 1983, 81.
40 Grellet & Kruse, 2004, 142.
41 Halmos, 2000, 34.
42 In D'Ortoli & Amram, 1990, 28.
43 Respondent "IC" in Gauthier, 1995, 246.
44 Coronel & De Mezamat, 1997c.
45 IIC, 26.
46 E.g., Guillerault, 2003; Ribas 2006, 24; Sudaka-Bénazéraf 1987/2012, 26–27.
47 Turkle, 1995/1997 (e.g., Binet, 1999; Guillerault, 2012; Dolto & Severin, 1977, 1978, 1979).
48 Halmos, 2000, 35.
49 Kelley-Lainé (e.g., 1997). See AI, 188; Beuve-Méry, 2008.
50 AI, 14.
51 Reported in François, 1999a, 34.
52 Roudinesco, 1999, 186.
53 Roudinesco, 1986, 496.
54 Roudinesco, 1986, 657.
55 DW, 139; also DW, 123; LF, 20.
56 DW, 139.
57 Dolto, 1988a, 218; DW, 140.
58 Roudinesco, 1986, 518.
59 SP3, 176.
60 E.g., Dolto-Marette, 1947.
61 JD, 49–50 & 124–126; SS, 13.
62 SP1, 18; TL, 130.
63 BNF, n.d.; Worldcat.org, 2015b. Olga Souslova Spiridonov (2015) has produced the only other dissertation in Dolto studies up to now. Writing in French (like Gauthier), her detailed analysis (over 500 pages) examines the history, establishment and work of a *Maison verte*, with particular reference to one in Saint Petersburg.
64 Camaraire-Santoire, 1983.
65 Gauthier, 1995, 15 (emphasis mine).
66 Gauthier, 1995, 254–257.
67 1995, 258.
68 1995, 264.
69 1995, 264.
70 1995, 265–266.
71 1995, 259.
72 1995, 100.
73 1995, 103–104.
74 1995, 246.
75 E.g., Féger & Gauthier 1987.
76 Gauthier may have been born in 1910 (almost the same year as Dolto), so she may have been 85 during her doctoral work. But as there were two Montrealers named Marcelle Gauthier alive almost concurrently, I cannot be certain.
77 Gauthier, 1995, 28 (on Morichau-Beauchant, see Moreau Ricaud, 2005).
78 Hoffman, 2011; also Douville, 2009, 50.
79 VC1, 508.
80 VC2, 629.
81 VC2, 859.

82   VC2, 495.
83   VC2, 732.
84   VC2, 523–524.
85   VC2, 698.
86   Grignon, 2002, 37; also VC1, 557–559.
87   VC2, 820 & 890. On ceasing to take new patients in June 1978 (but continuing other engagements), see VC2, 602 & 606. On the deterioration of her health from August 1979, see VC2, 639, 855 & 890.
88   C. Dolto, 1989, 9; C. Dolto in François, 1999a, 5.
89   Dolto & Dolto-Tolitch 1989; also C. Dolto, 2007; Dolto & Faure-Poirée, 2008.
90   C. Dolto, 1985, 37.
91   B.1976, 356.
92   For Spitz's letter, see VC2, 174; for the two papers sent, see EM, 94–107 & JD, 96–132. (A paper by Anna Freud appears after Dolto's on the «poupée-fleur» in an issue of the *Rfp* in 1949.)
93   E.g., Aulagnier, 1975/2001.
94   E.g., see Dolto, 1965 for her long preface in a book by Mannoni.
95   E.g., D&R, 24; PM, 9; VC2, 465, 486 & 585.
96   De Mezamat, 2008c; also D&R, 33.
97   Guillerault, 2002, 1.
98   Dolto, 1983.
99   EM, 21.
100  CE, 330–331; EF, 31; EM, 175; JD, 40 & 128; VC2, 885.
101  Louchart, 2008; also Meirieu & Kübler, 2001.
102  EM, 309; also Dolto, 1965, 43.
103  CE, 25; EM, 373.
104  APP, 39.
105  EM, 313.
106  De Mezamat, 2008c; Dolto, 1979b, 15.
107  DQ, 120; EM, 106; JD, 99.
108  SP3, 18.
109  Dolto 1985/1989b, 130; EF, 27–28; Ina.fr, 1978; SP1, 201–202.
110  CE, 24 & 95–97; IIC, 17 & 346.
111  PJ, 103; also DW, 73.
112  E.g., Binet, 2005; Chébaux, 1999b; Wittwer, 1992.
113  Dolto, D'Ortoli & Amram, 1973/1990; D'Ortoli & Amram, 1990, 2009a, 2009b.
114  Also C. Dolto in Monteiro, 2009, 94.
115  MA, 60; also EM, 99.
116  CE, 20; DV, 29 & 87; PS, 44 & 67; SS, 134; VC2, 889.
117  Ribowski, 1987/2004; SP3, 138.
118  ES, 14.
119  EF, 48–50; JD, 285; PJE, 18.
120  Canu, 2009, 144; Nobécourt, 2008c.
121  De Mezamat, 2008a; Dolto, 1985b; D&R, 38–42; Hamelin & Rabaté, 2011b; Malandrin, & Schauder, 2009; Nobécourt, 2008a (see also CE, 378–380; Dumas, 1997; EF, 12; Ina.fr.2, 1998; PM, 19; Ribowski, 1987/2004; TL, 95; VC2, 627, 715–716 & 876–877).
122  Archives Françoise Dolto 2001a & 2001b.
123  Krymko-Bleton, 2012; Maison Buissonière, 2014; Maison Ouverte, 2011; Normandin, 2012.
124  E.g., Rekhviashvili, 2008; also Administration of the President of Georgia, 2016.
125  Larajan, 2012.
126  Neyrand, 1995.
127  D&R, 39.

128 VC2, 876.

129 D&R, 38; Maison verte, n.d.; VC2, 793.

130 D&R, 40.

131 Hamelin & Rabaté, 2011b.

132 ATP, 192; CE, 380; Dolto, 1985b; Malandrin & Schauder, 2009, 368.

133 This, 2007.

134 EN, 57.

135 Genealogy: AI, 236; Provence, 1995, 30–38; VC2, 1014–1017.

136 VC2, 641; 1985b; also Malandrin & Schauder, 2009, 213.

137 Hamelin & Rabaté, 2011b.

138 Hamelin & Rabaté, 2011b.

139 Ina.fr.2, 1998.

140 Canu, 2009, 152.

141 Hamelin & Rabaté, 2011b.

142 MA, 19; also EM, 340; JD, 159, 283, 302 & 336; LF, 108; MA, 10 & 58; SS, 234.

143 D&R, 40.

144 The anonymity at a *Maison verte* precludes the infant observations of the Tavistock Model (e.g., Harris & Bick, 2011; Rustin, 2008).

145 PM, 19.

146 Hamelin & Rabaté, 2011b.

147 Dolto, 1985b; also SP3, 13.

148 Dolto, 1985b.

149 In AI, 189f.

150 E.g., Souslova Spiridonov, 2015, 32, 219, 239 & 246; This, 2007, 147 & 158–162; Vasse, 2006, 95, 269 & 301.

151 Durif-Varembont et al., 1999, 305.

152 APP, 34; also Dolto, 1940/1971, 239; Dolto, 1977b, 43; DV, 188–198; JD, 269.

153 VC2, 228.

154 VC2, 799.

155 IIC, 69.

156 Freud, 1900a, 177, 1909b, 51.

157 Laplanche & Pontalis, 1967/2004, 497.

158 SS, 157; also Dolto, 1985b; IIC, 33; SS, 113.

159 DW, 165; SP3, 173; SS, 16, 113–115 & 128.

160 SS, 16; also AI, 104; Dolto & Hamad, 1984/1995, 13; MA, 60; SP3, 192; VO, 173.

161 CD, 149; DW, 104; SS, 127–128.

162 APP, 37; also MA, 161.

163 Dolto, 1985c, 197; Dolto & Nasio, 1987, 66; DW, 163; MA, 22; Ribowski, 1987/2004; SP2, 157; VC2, 200; VC2, 762.

164 Dolto 1985/1989b, 134; DW, 61 & 143; SS, 77; VC2, 219.

165 DQ, 80; SP2, 219; SP3, 35, 144 & 146; TL, 24; VC2, 728 & 808; VO, 226.

166 SP1, 229; SS, 113.

167 VC2, 706.

168 AI, 218; VC2, 796–797.

169 SP1, 43.

170 AI, 146.

171 VC2, 763.

172 Grignon, 2002, 142.

173 SP1, 80–81.

174 E.g., ATP, 196; CE, 371; DW, 139; SS, 124–125; TL, 112; VC1, 342; VC2, 890.

175 DW, 139; TL, 112.

176 SS, 124.

177 SS, 15 & 125f.

178  CE, 371.
179  E.g., Puskas et al., 1991.
180  MF, 22; VC1, 43 & 175.
181  See Chapter 4.
182  VC1, 342.
183  VC2, 698.
184  IIC, 275.
185  JD, 57–58.
186  IIC, 275.
187  SS, 15.
188  Halmos, 2000, 34.
189  SS, 144.
190  CD, 194; also Dolto, 1985d, 15; DV, 64–65; VC2, 496.
191  JD, 286.
192  JD, 286; also IIC, 83; PS, 29–30.
193  ES, 39.
194  CE, 172.
195  SP2, 125.
196  TL, 43.
197  CE, 333.
198  SP1, 216.
199  LF, 87.
200  SF, 84; also SF, 373.
201  SP1, 215–217.
202  SP1, 215–217.
203  Hamelin & Rabaté, 2011a.
204  AI, 204; CD, 53f; SS, 39.
205  Ribowski, 1987/2004.
206  CE, 333.
207  Dolto, 1985c, 190; Hamelin & Rabaté, 2011b; PS, 41; SP3, 13; TL, 31; VC2, 762.
208  CE, 263; Hamelin & Rabaté, 2011b.
209  SP3, 36.
210  E.g., Nasio in Authier-Roux, 2000, 21–22.
211  Charial, Eliacheff & Valentin, 1999, 50–53; also Coronel & De Mezamat, 1997d; Dolto, 1977b, 28.
212  SF, 210; also Dolto 1985/1989b, 126; EM, 180; QS, 10; SP2, 126.
213  SP3, 179.
214  JD, 20.
215  MA, 166.
216  AI, 162; VC2, 88.
217  AI, 161.
218  EN, 99–101; VC1, 427f; VC2, 85.
219  EN, 100.
220  The «d» is silent.
221  AI, 27; VC2, 453.
222  AI, 144; Ribowski, 1987/2004, etc.
223  Freud, 1900a, 196.
224  ATP, 148.
225  EN, 21.
226  DW, 170.
227  MA, 28.
228  Dolto in Guillerault, 1989, 137; also CE, 63; PS, 86.
229  JD, 191.
230  DW, 124; also Charial, Eliacheff & Valentin, 1999, 53.

231 CE, 78.

232 JD, 124; also DW, 98; SP2, 193.

233 VO, 170; also CE, 263; SP2, 193.

234 CE, 263; EF, 31; IIC, 231; PJE, 43; VC2, 220, 703, 762 & 807.

235 DQ, 130; also CE, 270; EM, 205, 333 & 348–349; VC2, 808.

236 CE, 243 & 330–331; PS, 39; SS, 51; VO, 109.

237 CD, 211; JD, 50; SS, 38.

238 CE, 33, 244, 277 & 355; IIC, 71–77, 99, 102 & 326; JD, 189 & 301; LF, 113; PJE, 103; PS, 23, 85 & 89; SS, 73 & 124.

239 Dolto, 1985/1989b, 126; DW, 106.

240 ATP, 71; VC1, 85.

241 JD, 247.

242 JD, 248.

243 PJ, 44.

244 SP1, 37; also JD, 126–127.

245 PJE, 44; also LF, 51; VO, 206.

246 CD, 94.

247 CE, 167; also NE, 212.

248 VC2, 589 (emphasis hers). Despite such clear statements, when Dolto was in her seventies—retired and ill—she became the object of slander because her notion of the child as a full subject was misappropriated by individuals seeking to legitimize pedophilia. A half-dozen quotes were taken primarily from two interviews: one from 1983 (Dolto & Ruffo, 1983/1999)—conducted when Dolto was 75 and published (without her oversight) 11 years after her death; the other, a text she ostensibly revised, "a few days before rejoining her husband on the other shore," as its editor puts it (A. Coutin in Dolto, 1988a, 8). Yet as such slander persists, largely through self-publishing, Catherine is periodically compelled to intervene to set the record straight (e.g., C. Dolto, 2018b). It should be obvious to any educated person that Dolto's psychoanalytic project narrates unconscious—not conscious—desire. Further, Dolto's work is a formidable defense of each child's right to truth and dignity. Of course, a person with self-serving intentions can always find something to distort or quote out of context in anyone's corpus. But any victim of pedophilia— as I was—will attest that such experiences are traumatic and formidably anxiogenic (Saint-Onge, 2013). Pedophilia is a tired game between the radically unequal, wherein the elder's searches for sexual objects and self-absolution are equally pathological, relying on opportunism and the persistent distortion of reality. Pedophilia is a deeply selfish act. Dolto argues unequivocally in the letter cited, in November 1977: "Many young people are victims of it ... this trauma becomes a destructuring dynamic force ... children must be instructed to refuse the role of consenting object" (VC2, 589). In April 1981, Dolto asks patently, "Did you know that children have very great modesty that is ceaselessly violated by adults?" (VC2, 705). Then, in January 1987, she stresses that, "especially, the adult must give by his chaste behavior the example that the law is the same for all" (VC2, 843).

249 SP3, 104.

250 LF, 255; also CE, 243; DQ, 19; LF, 54; VO, 207.

251 CE, 73; DW, 167; JD, 260; PJE, 35.

252 CE, 354; DV, 22; JD, 228–229; IIC, 181 & 186–199; LF, 51; SS, 144.

253 PS, 46–48.

254 Nobécourt, 2008a.

255 TL, 185.

256 De Sauverzac, 1993, 170.

257 EN, 120.

258 MA, 69.

259 JP, 24; also Chapter 2.

260 CE, 31.

261 VC1, 252.

262 EN, 42.

263 MA, 58.

264 DW, 126.

265 CE, 44; SP1, 67.

266 LO1, 124 & 128; VC2, 208.

267 D&R, 12.

268 Goldstein, 2009, 1.

269 Pappenheim, 1924/1986.

270 Guttmann, 2001, 191.

271 D&R, 32. I believe Lou Andreas-Salomé is an exemplary subject for a psychobiographer fluent in Russian. Readers are alerted to her infantile suffering in a story about her lost name, Liola ou Lolia (Pfeiffer, 1979, 29), or Lyolya (Livingstone, 1984, 12). She refers to Freud as the, "father-face that presided over her life" (Pfeiffer, 1972, 241), and she writes extensively on primary narcissism (1977). Further, she admits to a "strong infantile regression" (Pfeiffer, 1979, 19), and she believes creativity thrives best in «récepteurs passifs» (Pfeiffer, 1983, 158). Further, like Dolto, she holds psychoanalysis as the gift of a lifetime (Leavy, 1964, 90). Coincidentally, Andreas-Salomé was with Rilke in Paris in 1902–1910 (Stieg & Michaud, 2001)—during both the birth and near-death of the infant Françoise. Oddly, too, the preface for Lou's autobiography, «Ma vie» ["My life"] (Pfeiffer, 1979), is written by Jacques Nobécourt, whose daughter, Emmanuelle (Who's Who in France, n.d.), produced a film series (Nobécourt, 2008a, 2008b, 2008c, 2008d) and movie (Nobécourt & Simonetta, 1978) about Dolto.

272 Leavy, 1964, 131.

273 AI, 144; Ribowski, 1987/2004.

274 PF, 35.

275 AI, 140.

276 AI, 140.

277 AI, 119; ATP, 75, 80 & 99; EN, 86; VC1, 322 & 330–331; also Chapter 2.

278 VC1, 473 & 478.

279 VC1, 306 & 311.

280 Ribowski, 1987/2004.

281 EN, 44 & 50.

282 LF, 54.

283 SP1, 99.

284 SP1, 21; also APP, 34.

285 Freud, 1893a, 25.

286 Freud, 1893a, 39.

287 TL, 16.

288 Psychotherapy is beginning to consider multilingualism as clinically significant. Some practitioners acknowledge that, "the patient's second language served an adaptive coping function, fending off both the affective components of early trauma and further psychotic disorganization" (Javier 1989, in Pérez Foster, 2004, 247)—and the "affective accuracy and intensity of the mother language ... the potential strength of the transference enactment that might be evoked when he [patient] enters the primal sensorial speech of his mother's speech" (Pérez Foster, 2004, 260). Recent research at McGill University provides first-hand accounts of identity reconstruction, as a respondent with childhood trauma in French shares: "It's creating an identity ... I feel more comfortable in it [English] ... When I'm back to animal instincts ... French takes over, and I get tired ... I cannot remember the last time I dreamed in French ... When I do think in French, there's always self-loathing ... I do feel more powerful in English." While a respondent with childhood trauma in

English shares: "When it's English ... I guess I'm probably afraid of not being safe ... and it's a really good way to avoid being emotional by speaking French ... [I] almost feel like a character of myself when I'm speaking French ... I feel like I sound sort of like I pieced together, you know, parts of other people's intonations and the way they spoke" ("Marilyn" and "Shelby," respectively, in Shepherd, 2018). I thank Jessica Shepherd for generously sharing her research by correspondence. For a personal account of the affective experience of appropriating language in (as) identity following trauma, see the fine memoir of Dr. Susan J. Brison: "Ten years after the assault, I still almost never speak French, even in Francophone company" (2002, 115). I submit that Dolto is instrumental to informing these vital new conversations about language in post-traumatic identities and therapies.

289  SP3, 237; TL, 33; VC2, 213.
290  SP1, 99.
291  Grignon, 1997, 21; 2002, 66 & 179.
292  E.g., MA, 78–90.
293  E.g, IIC, 90–147.
294  VC2, 516.
295  MA, 11.
296  E.g., D&R, 29; IIC, 78; SP1, 47–48; SS, 124.
297  IIC, 83.
298  De Mezamat, 2008c; JD, 131; PJE, 46; PS, 37–38; SP1, 16.
299  DW, 70.
300  Ina.fr, 1978.
301  DW, 99.
302  LF, 307.
303  IIC, 79; JD, 302.
304  IIC, 78.
305  D&R, 29; JD, 301; PM, 55; PS, 85; TL, 72.
306  DW, 71.
307  SP2, 161.
308  Nobécourt, 2008c.
309  DW, 46; JD, 29.
310  LO3, 120.
311  IIC, 79.
312  LF, 263; VC2, 516.
313  Freud, 1905c, 209–211 & 211f.
314  Freud, 1915b, 170; 1917c, 349; 1940[1939], 210.
315  Freud, 1917c, 347 & 347f.
316  Freud, 1900a, 130.
317  JD, 227.
318  Dolto, 1940/1965, 7; this key passage is not in the first edition (MA) and represents a refinement of her theory.
319  IIC, 345–346.
320  SP1, 147; SP3, 11.
321  JD, 215; SS, 210.
322  PJE, 42.
323  PJE, 42.
324  PJE, 46.
325  Karl Abraham describes patients in a "passive mode" (1924/1949, 450), experiencing an "archaic form of mourning" (Abraham, 1924/1949, 437). And citing August Stärcke, Abraham reiterates that coming to reality requires the successful withdrawal of the breast as a "primal castration" (Abraham, 1924/1949, 463). Despite such concordances, I believe Dolto comes to her notion of constitutional melancholy on her own and contributes something original. And given Abraham's

belief that melancholia is "not as yet sufficiently understood" (Abraham, 1924/1949, 434), I suggest Dolto can add much to our comprehension.

326 Dollander & De Tychey, 2004, 258.
327 EN, 32.
328 ATP, 55–56; EN, 37, 65 & 77–78.
329 AI, 83; EN, 108.
330 IIC, 49 (emphasis mine).
331 Freud, 1900a, 277; 1907, 60 & 93; 1913, 176.
332 Guillerault, 2007, 56.
333 MA, 13.
334 Freud, 1916a, 31f & 40f.
335 AI, 66; EN, 25; VC1, 69, 91 & 157.
336 EN, 32; VC1, 92 & 115.
337 AI, 27.
338 PF, 38 & 118f.
339 SP1, 213.
340 Halmos, 2008.
341 Louka, 2003, 149.
342 Halmos, 2000, 33.
343 Freud, 1933a, 20.
344 Roudinesco, 1999, 70.

# 7

# WRITING

## Introduction

"Sir, I am the little Françoise Marette who would really like to have something: 1st, a doll car; 2nd, a bear; 3rd, a *Tir du Père Fouettard*; and 4th, a *cantinière* costume I think of you."[1] Such is the letter of our young analyst to Santa in 1910, scribed by an unknown other. By 1913, she pens what her mother, Suzanne, annotates as her first copy: "The little Françoise asks the good Noël to bring her a doll car (still?), a small mailbox and a doll cradle. She promises to always be obedient."[2] By 1916, with Pierre dead, she writes to Santa unassisted, asking for no toys but only for «sagesse» ["obedience/goodness"], the war to end, to please Dan-Mé, and to be nicer to her sister, Jacqueline.[3] Accompanying a "magic potion" for «sagesse,» a «tableau» ["board"] and stamps, Suzanne composes a reply from Santa warning that if she is not tidy, the «tableau» will disappear into the night.[4]

## Père Noël

For the reader attuned to Dolto's history, the board evokes Deauville and the *Maison verte*—and the stamps, the symbolic payment. But Dolto is mute on these links, as she cautions simply that a Santa who threatens to retake gifts is "perverse,"[5] advising caregivers to give only what is asked for, to demonstrate listening.[6] Yet in this precious correspondence resides a history of desire and suffering, along with a narrative of an education in writing—from being scribed, to copying, to authoring. This story also takes us to some of the most compelling material in Dolto's entire corpus: the theorization of writing as a conduit for invested phonemes, whereby the transference facilitates an insertion into languaged relations even for a passively regressed subject—that is, even in the absence of a sufficient capacity for projection.

Flash forward to 1962, and the Minister of Posts, Jacques Marette,[7] asks his sister, Françoise, to compose a letter from Santa to be received by 5000 children in its inaugural year:

> My beloved child, your nice letter gave me much happiness. I'm sending you my portrait. You see, the mail carrier found me, he's very crafty. I received many orders. I don't know if I'll be able to bring you what you've asked me for. I'll try, but I'm old and sometimes I make mistakes. Forgive me. Be good, work hard, I'm sending you a big kiss. Le Père Noël.[8]

By 2012, following two minor revisions over the course of half-a-century,[9] as a free service of the Ministry of National Solidarity, Dolto's message would be delivered to 1.7 million children in over 120 countries,[10] recalling *La Semaine de Suzette* that she credits for her psychical survival. Dolto's letters from "Santa Claus" are a paradoxical writing in the name of the father by what many have called a "dreamed mother"[11]—they are contradiction personified. And in Dolto's esteem of Santa as a supportive myth,[12] her theory, at first as fine as snowflakes, slowly begins to arrive. For Santa holds archaic value that secures reparation: being without parents, accepting that the child cannot conform and being an adult outside of actual time on which to discharge guilt.[13] Moreover, Christmas trees are timeless, retaining their needles—being symbols of an "eternal childhood."[14] Dolto adds that we can all play Santa for each other, offering an "eruption" of the «gratuit» ["free"][15]: the delivery of joy as surprise. And silently, passivity and its ardent waiting return—along with the «repère» as a "present" essential to the present.[16]

## Script-girl

On the other hand, Dolto's abundant letters to her mother are largely confessional, addressing the minutiae of daily life, seldom conveying real emotion. Suzanne begs her daughter not to write so much[17]—while the daughter, likewise, asks her mother not to write so much.[18] Dolto also overwrites to continue a message, ostensibly to save paper[19]—but symbolically, as if to cross it out. These performances of *contra*diction as counter-narrative are also locatable in 1915, when Dolto writes to her father on the back of letters to her mother;[20] in 1934, when her writing is so microscopic as to be unreadable;[21] and in 1938, when a 25-page letter to her father about her suffering—the very great difficulty she experienced living in the family home—was perhaps never even sent.[22] For Suzanne was a meticulous record-keeper,[23] yet this long letter (15 June) "disappeared" and only Dolto's copy remains[24]—while a letter only weeks later (25 August) from both parents bears no hint of any rupture but only good wishes, even from her mother.[25]

Contradiction also returns us to 1913–1914, when young Françoise wrote Vava (or drew cats and flowers) on her legs—but never her real name;[26] and to 1925, when the girl banned only from Zola (that transporter of the muted street, Rue Vineuse), took class notes at Lycée Molière in a distinctive alexandrine style.[27] Curiously, Alexandrine was the name of Zola's wife, who spent her life looking for a lost child and reportedly died that very year. Is biography, thus history, formed by such enigmatic passages of what is in, yet exceeds, language—by rogue, unconscious correspondences from somewhere beneath the horizon of coincidence?

What is gained by a reading open to unconscious plays and conveyances is an unintended message that, ironically, the letter's recipient may never have heard—while years later we, who are not addressed, may hear in the «après-coup» of anachronistic associations. Slowly, we become aware in reading that something accidental but influential—elusive yet significant—has happened in writing. Of course, Suzanne's careful record of the family correspondence is invaluable as corroboration of her daughter's childhood history. But the act of writing against and behind the correspondence also alerts us to a presence transiting the text—one that struggles for articulation and succeeds paradoxically in, yet despite, the text.

More attuned, we will begin to hear the extraordinary unconscious foregrounding of Dolto's future professional work—as well as the echoes of her childhood—in her written exchanges with her trusted friend, Alain Cuny, the renowned French actor.[28] Like Dolto, Cuny was a member of Laforgue's «Club des piqués,» and he also worked with her in 1935–1936 at l'Hôpital de *Maison Blanche*[29] ["white house"]. This adult asylum was oddly near the junction of Avenue Secrétan (named after Dolto's paternal grandfather) and Rue de Meaux—homonymically, «rue de mots» ["words"] or «maux» ["pains"]—as if somehow evoking (presaging?) Tony and his sore knees.[30] Coincidentally, that hospital bore the same name as the *Maison Blanche* near Dolto's childhood home, though it was unrelated to it. And in but a few among many examples from their letters, Cuny tells Dolto that he is braided with her because she supports his mutism,[31] and she helps him overcome the interdiction against breathing.[32] For her part, she confesses to him that she is afraid of death, and that she always holds something in reserve.[33]

Then, in 1939, as Dolto stared at copious clinical notes, feeling unable to start writing her dissertation, she told Cuny she needed, "someone, eyes looking at me, obliging me to talk ... waiting for me to talk."[34] So he sent her two panther eyes,[35] and she began writing the book that changed everything—for her, for psychoanalysis and for children. Hence the woman known as a child for her own «yeux ronds» ["round eyes"; idiomatically, "great curiosity"] began her career with a need for an other who would hear her words, even in phantasy[36]—a call for a witness that is uncannily years ahead of her theory. Yet in another unpretentious self-reflection, Dolto adds that within a few years, she had put the eyes into some games for her children and no longer had them.[37] For, once the dream has done its work, it is so easily forgotten by consciousness.

We will also hear uncanny echoes in Dolto's epistolary relations with Madame Chapdelot—an old family friend who "heard my hopelessness," as Dolto puts it.[38] Unassumingly, Chapdelot writes of continuity with the archaic,[39] the need to let things arrive,[40] the mystery of refinding[41] and our unconscious differences with those we seem identified with.[42] The alerted reader also hears the near-homonym on her name, «chat de l'eau» ["cat of the water"], with echoes in another direction towards the «chameau» ["cat-words"] of *Babouches* (and Dominique);[43] and Chapdelot's fairy-tale nickname, «Milou» [homonym: «mi-loup,» "half wolf"],[44] inviting echoes of the Midi [homonym: «mi-dit,» "half-said"]—evoking even *Mititi*.[45] Chapdelot's mail indeed offers a huge "field of nuance,"[46] as she herself calls it, where Dolto's theory-as-life seems grounded. Even Dolto's love of owls[47] (and needing eyes to witness her writing?) returns us (in 1930) to Milou's admission about her own «hiboux amoindris» ["diminished owls"; colloquially, "reduced eyesight"].[48]

Dolto believes that letter-writing is necessary for humans,[49] as an expression at a distance with those whom one loves.[50] Small shifts evoke Freud's Hans, the first analysis by correspondence;[51] Bernadette, whose letters to her absent mother in 1947 (scripted by her father) reduced her anxiety;[52] Dolto's radio subscribers, who improved by writing (believing she would read their letters); and Dolto herself, in her casual observation that "treatment continues in letters."[53] And in this blur of sender, addressee, word and dream-work that is the transference, we reinvest in Dolto's comment that, at first, as a young child, she could not read her letters but others could,[54] as we start to follow the slow articulation of «le rôle de script-girl»—which, as Dolto tells us, "seems lowly," but is «après coup» of "very great critical interest."[55]

## Quartier Muet

We slip through time again to Dolto's first house, where she hid coins and small objects to forget them on purpose, for the sheer pleasure of refinding them, or as a surprise for others—what she calls "playing at who loses wins."[56] Deep within a field of nuances too, this game offers thoughts as play: the value of the lost consciousness of objects, and the accidental passing of objects in the social. By this game, we will also sense the nanny who is the not-said rooting Dolto's inimitable trails into infancy.

Regarding Rue Vineuse—a near-homonym of «rêve vie neuve» ["dream new life"], and a homonymic, inverted play on «vie rêveuse» ["dreaming life"]— Dolto comments that the street was without importance in her «quartier,» yet "it awoke in me an interesting climate, without my knowing why."[57] "Was it a great chagrin of love?" her interviewer (Pivot) asks. "Absolutely," she replies— and she looks sad still.[58] Yet while admitting the role of that ancient street in her life, Dolto unselfconsciously theorizes 50 years earlier about a six-year-old boy made «muet» ["mute"] due to "passing along streets rendered taboo by phobias."[59] And we cannot help but register that Dolto herself lived in Quartier Muet (in Paris) for decades.

It is as if Dolto's theory is engaged in a timeless correspondence with her history, receiving wild messages that somehow find their way into her writing. And we encounter, near her death, this stunning reflection from a conference in 1987—seemingly told in two parts, 36 pages apart, as if performing its slippages, as both time and subject are entirely porous:

> We discover the root of the illness in a first story that took place, for example, at the departure without explanation of the young girl that took care of him until then. No one enlightened the child on the strangeness of the lived sensation. Suddenly, he found himself without the reference that gave him what he knew himself to be ... Sometimes it's not the mother they lost, it's a person that took care of them completely.[60]

Here again are unconscious resonances perceptible to the familiar reader, of a silenced story that insists on a telling—that of the beloved lost nanny—whatever the actual (apparent) subject.

In fact, Rue Vineuse dates to 1693,[61] and it begins at 1 Rue Benjamin Franklin, marked by his statue. Dolto's second house, at 2 Avenue du Colonel Bonnet, bore a plaque attesting that it had once served as Franklin's home, where thunder had been, she says.[62] The house itself is an address for some curious correspondence around Franklin, who was—oddly enough—a postmaster keen on saving time.[63] And time is soft indeed in the game of "who loses wins":

> I remember very well the place where I discovered the ignorance of adults. It was next to the passerelle that crosses the Chemin de fer de [Petite] Ceinture, at the end of Rue du Ranelagh ... Each time ... I hoped a train would pass underneath ... The smoke made the world disappear ... we could not see ... [only] hear this big sound that passes and that frightens without frightening ... At that moment, I always said to myself, coming back down, she [governess] will have to tell me what happens after death.[64]

The passerelle was before reading, Dolto adds, among "ancient perceptions that return when reality is obscured."[65]

As a further return upon a field of sounds without boundaries of space or time, Ireland's Ranelagh Road happens to be next to its own Ranelagh Gardens.[66] Did the lost nanny ever speak about it? And when she was dismissed, did she leave Passy by train, boarding at the Gare de Passy-la-Muette? This daydream also evokes Dolto's paternal grandfather, Henri Marette, who died a hero saving five women from a train fire, making her father, Henry Marette, an orphan—as the homonymic play loses to speaking what can only be (re)found in writing, the "y" and "i."[67] So when Dolto says in an interview (in 1978) that a «passerelle» (under tracks) is a place of unusual acoustics,[68] advising children that if they want to play there, they can[69]—or that the "bridge" between beings is made by language[70]—she taps the archaic echoes of her past, and the wild passage via audition by which unconscious associations awaken unpredictably and thought arrives as (in) a present.

We also learn that the passerelle made her feel called.[71] And if we let ourselves drift almost to the point of sleep, we will hear Dominique (in 1963) telling Dolto about a good man who died saving another from a fire.[72] It is the same session wherein he speaks of a man with a lung eaten by microbes—the symptom that almost kills Dolto as an infant, and decades later does. As it turns out, then, new understandings are securable through the transference via haphazard languaged incidents in the social, as words move between us in a fluid, rogue network of correspondences. We come across echoes (familiar, yet othered) of our idiosyncratic archaic auditory prehistories—an offer of what is neither consciously intended nor sought. So we all play "who loses wins," continually, unconsciously, as our means of securitizing while coming to reality. It is the game at the origin of thought. Thus, any thought is necessarily the «aprèscoup» of a forgotten dream of love, engaged in a slow translation from the latent to the manifest.

## Rue Saint-Jacques

Within walking distance from the plaque about Franklin is another on Rue Kleiber about the «Frères Marette,» for Dolto's *paternal* grandfather, Henri, and his brother were architects for Queen Isabella II[73] and designers of Place des États-Unis.[74] In 1929, the place name would draw the son, Henry, to New York, to convince the Americans to join World War II.[75] Dolto remembers believing the USA was celebratory because her father brought back *Ô Solé Mio*, which he sang daily.[76] "I dreamed of it [the USA]," Dolto volunteers[77]—and we will follow this dream soon. For now, we muse only on the coincidence of the American *Maison Blanche* ["white house"] and the one near her home (also echoing the later *Maison Blanche* where she worked with Cuny)—and how her father purchased there a stainless knife that cut badly and could not be sharpened,[78] so goods were not «coupable» ["cuttable"; also, "guilty"]. Does this evoke *symboligenic* (i.e., not actual) castrations? It is intriguing play, but we must let go because the material calls otherwise, through her *maternal* great-grandfather this time, Auguste Demmler. This officer of the Wurtemberg Court, who fought in 1870 with the French,[79] left correspondence addressed to himself in a game of names, encouraging his descendants to seek their ancestors as «points de repères.»[80] Yet again, familiar theories seem grounded in archaic terms and experiences.

Some distance from Rue Kleiber, in the «5e,» is Rue Saint-Jacques, where Dolto lived from 1942 to her death. Walking there, we will pass (on the «15e») a plaque commemorating the late senator Jacques Marette, our other postmaster, and that other family recipient of the Military Cross. Dolto helps raise Jacques when Suzanne rejects her replacement child for Jacqueline for being a boy. She recounts being part of a tag team with Mlle for his care,[81] and how with Jacques, whom she loved dearly, she discovered the intelligence of a child, as she read to answer his questions about statues and tried to understand his suffering.[82] There is name play here, too, as Dolto (Jacques' godmother and fiancée of the deceased Pierre) walked baby Jacques with her older brother, Pierre—like a family of revenants—and how Jacques would eventually marry a Jacqueline.[83]

An astute researcher notes the "consequences of the death of Jacqueline are multiple and durable ... re the signifier Jacques."[84] And in this history incidentally written on land—streets, plaques and statues—we find not only a relation of the transference to place, but a circulation of stories in that other kind of displacement, walking. We recall the arrival of the transference, for Freud, at the Acropolis[85]—and his passion for his "Italian Moses ... that love child,"[86] the statue he contemplated for weeks. For in the inscriptions of words upon geography, and our random reading as we move about, we meet a question we cannot ignore: are we addressed by the address?

Over the years, Dolto will travel a long way to another plaque, this one in the mountains of Alsace, at «Sphinx de la Tête des *Faux*» [" ... head of the *false* ones"],[87] where Pierre was mortally wounded in 1916, and which became a pilgrimage site for the family.[88] Its name is portentous with Oedipal echoes, as well as clear resonances of the «phonème(s)» in a bilingual warning on two perfect homonyms—«faux» ["false"] name(s) and «faut n'aime» ["mustn't love"]. But the most prominent statue in the Jardin du Ranelagh, which young Françoise passed by each day (sustaining its overdetermination), is Léon Eugène Longepied's oeuvre (from 1883) in white marble depicting a young fisherman dragging a net holding a human head. The statue seems like an uncanny presaging of Dolto's belief in the unconscious strength of the child—and her emphasis on the emotional over the intellectual.

Thus, Oedipus, when Dolto refound it with Freud, would have offered silent returns from her childhood of a work of art by a man whose name also recalled her patriarch: Pierre-Eugène (Secrétan). Those resonances travel via curious echoes on "head" and "sphinx," bridging back to Pierre's death, and even further back to the beloved lost nanny from the land in echo on "Ranelagh"—as the grandfather's first name seems to literalize a union between Pierre and that nanny in a dreamscape. For it was with her that Dolto first strolled in those gardens daily for months, after which other nannies (and Pierres), with their «faux» names, walking there too, would tender critical paths for identification along symbolic filiations, eventually forward to lovely Mlle. But always, these identifications harked back to that young girl from Dolto's archaic landscape who was neither remembered nor forgotten—that «faut n'aime» she was no longer allowed to love.[89] And in that repeated «fau» [*pho*: a nonsense syllable], we cannot but hear the phoneme—as if it were announcing itself.

## Liquidation

In 1928, Dolto paints the scene in Alsace and writes to six-year-old Jacques, back home, about Pierre's death,[90] calling it the trip that opened her eyes.[91] Moving ahead to 1941, in a waking dream, Dolto sees a "young man of pain" who says she has to "go farther."[92] Meanwhile, the «chasseur alpin» leads to rich homonymic plays of its own: «chasse heure» ["chase hour"]; «chat soeur» ["sister cat"]; and inverting, «lapin» ["rabbit"]—all familiar phonemes by now, repeated in Dolto's corpus in permutations. Then without any personal reference, in 1980, she gives this clinical advice: "Why ... do you make a mountain thinking of the past? ... Go farther."[93]

Dolto aptly asks, "This lived trajectory that, in my solitude, I apprehend as my history, am I its object or its subject?"[94] In fact, her uncanny question is the query posed of any biographic project, as the transference becomes a kind of correspondence between the texts one reads and writes—and one experiences a suggestion in the suggested readings. So, much like her patient, Didier, we too "learn to read with Madame Dolto."[95] But it is a different kind of reading that reading Dolto teaches: one open to what traverses but exceeds the text—to what is hearable precisely because it is other, yet recognizable. So the game of "who loses wins" becomes a perfect trope for the uncanny, that "return of what is familiar but repressed,"[96] as Freud called it, embedding an indescribable sense of place, a "homesickness."[97] And here, the game seems to reveal that the function of the repression barrier is to ensure the *dis*remembering of the archaic—a becoming-unconscious, we could say—so echoes (when they inevitably return) will feel as if they are arriving from elsewhere, thus securing us like our dreams on sound first did.

Coming to reality, then, contradictorily requires that tethers from the latent to the manifest be unbroken yet forgotten, through the slow mediation of dream-work, in what Dolto theorizes from 1940: the "liquidation of the castration complex is translated by the dream,"[98] and a child's symbols reveal the affective age of the subject.[99] I believe that Dolto's thinking prefigures Hanna Segal's "symbolic equations";[100] and that Dolto and Segal (without intersects in reality) reveal something of the «après-coup» of precocious trauma through their compatible theoretical orientations—i.e., the legacy of that particular infantile record to adult thought. Segal's honesty (and humor) are noteworthy:

> I had a very traumatic childhood. I think that if I had turned out to be schizophrenic, people would have said, "No wonder, with that child-hood" ... The loss of the breast was combined with the loss of the person ... Some of my bloody governesses were French ... What kind of girl would go to Poland to be a nanny?[101]

What we learn with Dolto is that the passive operation of the transference depends on the surprise of refinding archaically invested phonemes—unconscious echoes across a gap—recalling our originary dreams of discourse *in utero*: that call-and-response with an indissociable other(ness), an enigmatic first «semblable» that secures the enduring experience of a witness.[102] Dolto's corpus also makes the eminent point that symbol formation is a dynamic process that requires human relations. And all those with whom we exchange words—even through texts—cannot help but return a letter whose transport they were not aware of effecting.

## Alimentation

Dolto's difficult language reaches its arc in her notion of the unconscious image of the body,[103] what many consider to be her "most important theoretical work,"[104] for which she is widely known. Like art, the *image* is but a mediation for the «dires» ["sayings"],[105] a game of words,[106] as Dolto explains it: "i" for *identité*; "ma" for *maman*; and "ge" for *je* [I].[107] But unlike its simple (?) name—with its recourse to the explanatory potential of phonemes and their suggestions—the unconscious image of the body, "mediatized by language,"[108] is "almost unintelligible in a theoretical register,"[109] therefore best engaged passively, as one scholar describes it: "We understand nothing at all and then, we let ourselves go freely and end up receiving it in a quite curious manner."[110]

Yet while it is taken up by some Lacanians,[111] the unconscious image of the body marks a "real divergence with Lacan,"[112] being the "articulation of a subject who is neither temporal nor spatial ... a subject of desire not only as a witness, but as an actor in his own history by the intermediary of the body."[113] I believe that the unconscious image of the body offers a boldly original narration of primary narcissism with reference to the passive pulses continually informing an unconscious self-as-otherness. For there is a tremendous power, a «pregnance»[114] of the most archaic phonemes, Dolto says, as if the fetus were woven with the word:

> The unconscious image of the body is the structural trace of the emotional history of a human being. It is the unconscious location (and present where?) from where is elaborated all the expression of the subject: location of the emission and reception of interhuman languaged affects.[115]

At a colloquium in 1958,[116] Dolto first suggested the unconscious image of the body as the «médiateur de présentifications» that is (ironically) outside of space and time.[117] It is this tension of presence and absence that alerts us to 1956–1957 being a watershed year in her life: Mlle died; Dolto went to Egypt (*Babouches*) and to Vienna (Freud);[118] and she wrote key papers on art (her passion)[119] and regression (her focus).[120] Further, in 1958, Catherine (b. 1946) turned 12, her own age when Jacqueline died. At another colloquium (in 1985), Dolto states that what someone lived at a certain age will play on his child of the same gender at the same age.[121] Thus, I submit that Dolto's theory of the unconscious image of the body divulges deep traces of her own archaic history of love and loss—and evidence of regression as resourcing.

It is a fact that the death of loved ones severs a crucial source of invested phonemes. Dolto notes that mutes lack semiotic elements for their alimentation;[122] and sudden weaning (losing a source of affect) causes mutism,[123] as does suffering.[124] In other words, one's (fear of) near-death is a regressing event. The mutism entailed offers a passive defense,[125] and a metamorphosis to passivity,[126] as we continue with another to exist[127] in a dream of existence[128]—a subtle link beyond space and time,[129] a refuge in "our mute sayings in the silences that scan them."[130] And she expands on symbolization in a description that is "signature Dolto":

> Verbal pre-language transitional phonemes have something paranormal … at once perennial thing and confused language of the relation child-mother or child-father: materialized language, phantom of unspeakable words, unconsciously conjugated with a sensory havingness that seems to answer from a beingness in a passive state that would passively conduct to the subject being.[131]

Barely translatable, Dolto's genius speaks at the nebulous edge of understandability, as writing laboriously relays archaic material—offering, like art, a means of demuting the subject.[132]

## Secrétan

Valuing art, Dolto saw 2–25 children daily, millions of drawings,[133] and her legacy to art in analysis endures.[134] Yet she always sought the auditory in the visual: «ce qui est dit en dessin» ["what is said in drawing"].[135] She joined art classes as a child,[136] and she produced self-portraits whenever she didn't know what to take up,[137] she says. We learn that the lost nanny was an artist too.[138] But more than the making of art, what matters to Dolto is its witness[139]—a "putting into resonance of affect by a witnessing"[140]—as true art is private.[141] In sum, graphic expression calls for a witness who looks only to hear. Does it call for a reader, then?

Feeling our way to the archaic along symbolic filiations, we now relocate Dan-Mé's father, Pierre-Eugène Secrétan [homonym: «secret temps,» "secret time"; near-homonym: «sacré temps,» "sacred time"]—a socialist-leaning industrialist whose telegraph address was «Tansecré» [homonym: "time sacred," or "time secret"].[142] His factory (near Deauville) made the Statue of Liberty, so that at his death in 1899, New York City gave Paris the replica that is now located beneath the Pont de Grenelle, and Dan-Mé donated the copper casts to the Louvre. Then, when Jacques died, his widow gave the artist's model to Paris City Hall.[143] Secrétan's letterhead was «Toujours tout droit» ["always straight ahead"],[144] and his art collection included the «Angelus,» which was sold in 1889 to an American buyer when copper markets sank. It returned to the Louvre in 1909—strangely enough, the year Dolto almost died.[145]

One of his factory workers wrote a grand funeral hymn for Secrétan to «La Marseillaise,» for he had saved his company with the French patent for electrolysis: the «procès Elmore» ["she dead"].[146] Dominique will speak about an invisible river, «Elmoru» ["she died"], five times in 1963[147]—a momentous year when Suzanne has just died, Algeria gains its independence, Dolto quits the SFP and she begins writing the Santa letters. Dolto muses unselfconsciously on «Elmoru»: "Is it a country? ... The problem of the mother?"[148] As for Dominique, he insists simply that «Elmoru» is a secret.[149]

We also learn that the sense of the sacred is inherent,[150] so a child "can identify with another who keeps secrets,"[151] as another field of nuances invokes repression—that secret history lost to consciousness in which every child invests, as young Françoise did. Further, children should be told about family deaths, which provoke regression,[152] for the notion of death is what gives life meaning.[153] Cemeteries offer peace,[154] Dolto says, even maternal security.[155] And finding one in Passy,[156] barely one block from Rue Vineuse, it seems possible to muse that the nanny (who stole the "river of diamonds," and whose name and existence became secrets) was very likely said to have died.

Then, in five pages that shift quickly between death, Francis of Assisi, Santa, hope, language, the unsaid, the sacred, witnessing, identification, presentification, emotion, splitting, repetition, naïve art, securitizing vegetation, the «gratuit» ["free"] and babies being right,[157] Dolto states that the «sacré» [homonym: «ça créé,» "it/the Id creates"] exists "by the sheer fact that we pronounce it."[158] Digressions thus mark the experience of reading Dolto, like visiting the Louvre— while correspondence from Secrétan somehow moves straight ahead in her texts. Yet her astounding examples clear a wide theoretical opening: in any wild circulation, where reversibility and multidirectionality inhere, any notion of *counter*transference is moot. There is just transference.

## Blue

In March 1911, the Flemish writer Maurice Maeterlinck debuted in Paris his grand fairy-tale, «L'Oiseau bleu» ["Blue Bird"].[159] While it is unclear if Dolto's siblings attended, her prominent family is certain to have discussed the spectacular event, whose blue bird could not but have affected little Françoise—then a two-year-old who had just been a "blue angel."[160] Besides, the tale itself is full of phonemic play: My*l*tyl (a girl), her brother *Tyl*tyl, Mother *Tyl*, Father *Tyl*, *Tyl*ô the dog and *Tyl*ette the cat. In her twenties, in Deauville, Dolto would read Maeterlinck's *Les Sentiers dans la montagne* ["The Trails in the Mountain"][161]—and a decade later, she would mark trails in the mountains at Laforgue's.[162] Then, in her seventies, she would describe her Grandfather Demmler being like the one in «L'Oiseau bleu.»[163]

We also recall the «train bleu» to the Midi[164]—a play on «mes dits» ["my sayings"] and *Mititi*—and the blue spot Dolto reports to her dentist (in the early 1960s): "Look, I have a hematoma!" (and the dentist's curious reply, "You have an

Amerindian stain in your mouth ... a blue stain").[165] Then, in 1963, Dominique (speaking of «Elmoru» and a train) describes a man sickened by a *«piqûre au bleu»* ["blue sting," i.e., infected]—«Club des *piqués*»?—as Dolto notes: "Is it a souvenir of a «hématome»? ... Or of the «maladie bleu» of the dead cousin when Dominique was eight?"[166] Thus, by example, the transference teaches that invested phonemes inhabit an uncanny gap between the literal and symbolic across which forgotten but indelible histories find their way into thought.

The transference in Dolto's texts is encountered passively: not by thinking, but by floating attention while reading. As Halmos counsels, Dolto's is an oeuvre in need of «passeurs»:[167] "How do you read her? Without method and haphazardly."[168] So doing, thoughts arrive in the «résonance émotionelle» that is the "operational fact of the transference."[169] For language effects a continuous "transference of things past, archaic things,"[170] "through the words proferred by him and the emotion experienced by me,"[171] Dolto explains—as originary events reappear in the «après-coup» of a «dire transférentiel.»[172] "Each time I speak with people, there is always a transference, and the other does half the road,"[173] she offers. And, as if anticipating the present project, Dolto adds, "I transmit clinical documents concerning the transference, that of patients and my own ... with hidden meaning I myself have not seen."[174]

By signposts barely audible at first, correspondence via the transference arrives along uncommon roads. For example, Dolto's note that Yvette Guilbert sang for Pierre's twenty-first birthday (in 1924)[175] gains our attention because Freud befriends Guilbert from 1929.[176] And following the trail by reading Guilbert—a «dame rousse» ["red woman"] in «satin vert» ["green satin"] who performed at the «Chat noir» ["black cat"]—I find a song in her corpus about a «nurse anglaise.»[177] Whether or not that song was featured, the party serves up a counter-narrative of deep losses: the nanny (red hair, green island), Jacqueline ("black cat" cabaret) and (the lost) Pierre. Likewise, Freud's interest in da Vinci's vulture returns an anxiety dream of him and his own mother, "carried ... by two (or three) persons with birds' beaks."[178] Its quanta for our interest increases when Freud's patient, Emmy von M., also dreams of a monster with a vulture's beak.[179] For the transference experienceable through texts releases potent affects, and we suddenly "see" only because we *hear* again—as «déja-vu» seem born of «déja-*entendre*.»

## «Linotte»

As dream-work prescribes the itinerary for the transference, writing serves what Dolto calls the duty of testimony,[180] as the act of leaving a trace.[181] We recall Freud's ardent desire for a plaque to mark where the secret of dreams was revealed.[182] And Dolto, too, is keen on inscriptions,[183] even self-publishing the book that started psychoanalysis in France.[184] She observes: "Some are capable of going back in relation to those of their time, probably as a result of their history or of their belated understanding of their history."[185] And by leaving behind clinical notes, the "mediation of psychoanalysts who expose their work

[,] ... patients ... come to the help of future analysands and practicing analysts."[186]

Besides, every child is written from the first, as Dolto explains, "inscribed in the civic record"[187] (like young Jacques). Dolto's childhood art was often printed in *L'Écho de Paris*[188]—and even with Boris, she notes, "I was first a person who had written an interesting book."[189] Fittingly, then, an unfinished autobiography[190] set against a final flurry of prefaces Dolto wrote for others,[191] and a biography of Dolto for children crafted only from line drawings and sparse text,[192] deliver her most vigorous message: the not-said always exceeds the said.

Dolto's testimony offers rare "proof that we are dealing with the impressions from childhood,"[193] to quote Freud, as her corpus confirms the radical truth of her theories: the infant has a vibrant unconscious life. Thus the human constructed in symbolic relations harbors an otherness that he can never contain: "This other, that is myself, I love him too,"[194] Dolto writes to Cuny in 1939. Moreover, as an indelible countersignature, the transference testifies to authorship—as Freud said of *St. Anne with Two Others*: "After ... some time, it suddenly dawns on us that only Leonardo could have painted it ... the picture contains the synthesis of the history of his childhood."[195]

We turn now to consider Dolto's diary entry of 27 February 1934: "Phone Milou. Lunch at Pierre's with Philippe and Marc. *Good*."[196] And we listen to excerpts from the same day, of her "four dreams on Laforgue," written on the back of a wedding invitation on 27–28 February 1934:

> *One*, a young woman predicts that all marked with a symbol is *good* and her tea service is so marked ... *Two*, a salon full of dancing people, including a thin, nebulous female ... Philippe arrives, angry, with an older man who wants to be a doctor. The doctor has ugly, sinking eyelids but shows that her own eyes are not properly opened ... So I am ashamed and say, "This man is strong who has guessed my life from this «mois» ["month"; homonym: "me"]." But I laugh to hide from him that I am «piquée au vif» ["deeply stung"] ... *Three:* Father at Deauville ... me at L[aforgue's]. Father and Mother. *Four:* A narrow boat leaves for England.[197]

Written in a rush on a pre-used surface (rather than in her journal), here are remnants of the day in use by the dream, as the lost nanny and analyst are brought together on the occasion of a wedding. There is also an uncanny marking of orality with English (tea set, *good*), as we hear the slide of identifications from Laforgue to father, and from mother to nanny, and the departure across the English Channel seems reconstituted.

Playing in a field of associations now, we shift to 28 July 1988, when Dolto says she was "dead for a laugh," i.e., in a coma.[198] Waking after three days, she rushed to write to a colleague because, while dreaming, "the thought of you and of your request, refused by me, came back ... I authorize you to use my name Françoise Dolto to sponsor your social realizations."[199] So it was that

Philippe Béague, a Flemish educator and psychoanalyst,[200] became the conduit by which the right to Dolto's endorsement passed to HRH Queen Mathilde of Belgium, who currently supports a parallel Association Françoise Dolto (since 1989). Beyond the faint Flemish echo bridging Maeterlinck and Béague, and the «nom dit»—Dolto—passing between these two nations, is an uncanny statue located at Place de la Reine Astrid (on Avenue Montaigne), honouring their joint efforts in World War I. It movingly depicts two women, representing France and Belgium, who hold hands and harbor children safely between them.

In countless forays, Dolto's corpus conveys the unbreakable tether of text to dream, and the radical unforeseenness of the transference. So she takes care to scribe in the clinic almost word-for-word:[201] "When you heal, which I hope, we will understand the road you followed."[202] For on Dolto's view, being a psychoanalyst means noting down the most that you can:[203] "It was a method I applied, that is all,"[204] she offers. Thus she describes herself to Dominique as, "the one who writes what you say."[205] I submit that this is not unlike young Sammy once telling his analyst, Joyce McDougall: "Write what I dictate."[206] Writing helps not only the patient but Dolto too: "What I received ... it was not at that moment that I made the connection. I made the connection writing my thesis."[207] And a rich return here takes us to 1938 and Jeanne (13), derided as a «linotte» ["linnet"; colloquial, "dodo"; homonym, "read note"]. "It's ... a little bird," Dolto explains, adding kindly that it, "knows enough to make its nest, cover its eggs and take care of its young."[208] Yet the "read note" makes a most uncanny (and helpful) suggestion on the word.

By scribing the "representative signs of phonemes,"[209] then, we too "arrive at thoughts that surprise [us],"[210] as Freud once noted—and the "writing ... by which the intensity of self-observation may be increased varies considerably according to the subject-matter."[211] Young-Bruehl, for example, experienced the transference while writing on Hannah Arendt[212] and Anna Freud.[213] She believes "biographers sometimes have a crucial dream in which their subject appears,"[214] as the "biographer relates in the medium of fantasy to the subject's fantasy."[215] Hers is an open "celebration of the subjectivity of biographers"[216]— one that endorses, I believe, the notion that something integral is learnable from the transference in texts. For as Freud put it: "It is a common event for a dream to give evidence of knowledge ... the waking subject is unaware of possessing."[217]

## «Lieux»

By writing, Dolto states, two beings communicate,[218] through "symbolic trans- mission ... speech, that is the mediator that permits us ... to have ... by his words some thoughts that are its inheritors."[219] For unconscious resonances in texts suddenly become hearable through our availability while reading. And here, we refind a comment (from elsewhere) that is so easy to overlook: "I accord much importance to the thought of neutral «lieux»"[220] ["sites";

homonyms: "read them," and "link (to) them"]. Dolto also remarks how a "fruitful encounter is produced only when both give and neither takes the given he received from the other,"[221] in a "giving to the other what one never possessed."[222] At issue is the non-ownership of the transference inhering in its non-intention, as those communicating "give of themselves in a presence that is ignored, rich with this life that inhabits them," that «ruisselle» ["trickles"; also echoing «rue»] from themselves.[223] And as thought is passively displaced in the transference, psychical energy is released in the «après-coup» of words. Thereby, crucially, phonemes reveal that they always harbor the potential energy of a displacement. After all, Dolto says, the unconscious is designed to show its effects much later.[224]

And in this liquid space of Dolto's texts—wherein the archaic insists and enriches us—we meet Jean Rostand, a famous biologist fascinated by life *in utero.*[225] Eight days after Dolto's dissertation, Rostand wrote her that it was his most interesting reading since Freud.[226] During regular visits, he prodded her, "What did you see?" "It made me work," she says.[227] And Sundays, she attended his salons for "biologists, writers, [and] theatre people."[228] Rostand helped publish the second edition of Dolto's dissertation,[229] he wrote an «homage» to Laforgue (in 1964), and he named his only son, François, in her honor. And in 1940, Dolto proposed a biologically inspired, delayed "larval" Oedipus Complex,[230] as unreleased, potential energy in the unconscious. But the uncanny circulation does not end here. For Marie Bonaparte's secretary, Anne Berman—an analyst herself and a translator of Freud—wrote her dissertation on «La famille des borraginacées» ["forget-me-nots"].[231] Also nearby is Gauthier—who may have been a mycologist at the start of her career[232]—as the larvae, fungi and plants arriving out of nowhere also return Freud's very famous dream, the "Botanical Monograph."[233] So, then, do we naturally seek a witnessing in archaic life?

Further, as continuity with the archaic is the aim of passive pulses, we will need the echo of an address («repère») to console our slow (never complete) passage to reality: "To perceive ... is to perceive the self-other that makes the unity of the subject,"[234] to refind familiar affect, as Dolto explains.[235] She expands:

> On the path of the hypothesis of regression of the affect of the subject ... an archaic image of the body without doubt resurges on the occasion of a trial of his history to which the subject cannot renounce without at the same time losing the notion of his continuity, his security of existing. He can neither accept himself, nor accept to communicate with others, in the conditions of his actual reality that do not permit him to recognize "the other" similar enough to himself to be in security with him.[236]

Through the transference, therefore, languaged encounters "produce resonances in the unconscious of one and the other"[237]—offers of «secours indispensable» to his «reconnaissance.»[238]

Thus, the phoneme is imperative: "The word is a transitional object that the child acquires to never be separated from it."[239] For it is through the phoneme that we transfer our attention to words, porting libidinal investments, as speech "demands to be awakened."[240] Conversely, the subject experiencing discontinuity in reality "exhausts himself" from not having any «rencontre faisant écho» ["echoing encounter"], which he needs "to give him coherence."[241] As Dolto puts it plainly: "Nothing is to repair, nor replace. It is to effect a relay all along."[242] Put another way, perception dissembles a melancholy born of our debt to an archaic witness, inscribing an incalculable culpability in the human condition. So the remainder of life is a narrativization of our living with forgetting—that is, the impossibility of a pardon and its necessity.

## Traces

Thinking with Dolto, we can now narrate the trace as a valuable «repère» to repair continuity—a relay to the father's library («récupération»?) we might say—circulation on a phantasy of a common interest in the word. The recovery of symbolic filiation through the transference in texts is possible because reversibility and inseparability inhere in the archaic, so the animated silence of reading effects, unconsciously, "I hear/I am heard." The trace thus offers a proof of life, a confirmation of unconscious continuity. Without that («ça»), we wait continually, exhausted, Dolto says—whereas the desire to die is greatly reduced if someone hears.[243] The trace delivers a letter of love in «après-coup»—"communication beyond space-time,"[244] whose "message can cover many centuries before meeting an other."[245] And while randomly talking about tadpoles (in another biological foray), Dolto notes a "putting into resonance of his affectivity, by a similitude of being, of the affect or thought evoked in him by this witnessing of the author."[246]

From 1940, Dolto finds traces of the complex of castration,[247] for we "keep a trace of the first link" that is «perdu» ["lost"; homonym: «père dû,» "father owed/expected"][248]—our ontological debt. Thus in "speech and hearing, a trace of archaic security remains,"[249] profoundly implicating literacy:

> Hic et nunc ... communication can also be deposited in traces on paper ... as differed and diffracted portions in effects parallel to verbal language, or substituted for it, that need to be heard. Psychoanalysis aims for the study and the deciphering of this unconscious language underlying consciously communicated language hic et nunc.[250]

Literally suspended between here and now, Dolto exposes a fine tension whereby not only do traces mark writing, but traces mark the subject. Thus, as she puts it, the infant's "most subtle functioning is marked by/of writing ... like a network of lines of force, of traces, left by interrelational language."[251]

Further, as the archaic is moot for space-time, texts "keep bearing fruit ... even if you are long dead."[252] So Dolto listens (and reads) for this:

> For hidden truth transmitted by the «fil» ["thread"] of associations in spoken language ... unconscious meaning ... truthful foundation of this "subject," for whom conscious discourse ... is the carrier of his irreducible authenticity ... Concomittant phantasms ... «transparaissent» ["transpire" or "appear in transit"] in silences, in jumps of theme, in lapsus, in brief, in «les failles» ["fault lines"or "fissures"] of conscious discourse. It is these phantasms that reveal the actual dynamic, unconscious, of desire.[253]

Simply put, "writing leaves traces."[254] Yet homonyms—despite acquiring phenomenal significance in her project—are paradoxically mute in Dolto's (conscious) list. Klein suggests that, "strokes, dots, etc. of the present script ... are the result of condensation [and] displacement."[255] And Freud, too, discusses an "unconscious psychical trace,"[256] and how "phantasy carries traces of its origin."[257]

As Dolto explains it, the «tissu langagier» ["languaged cloth"][258] of a text is a "witness to suffering or joy ... as proofs of the [author's] affect ... making us feel a similar emotional constitution."[259] There follows both a duty to leave testimony and the inevitability of doing so, in a moving return of Pierre (and a curious invocation of orality) that the slow reader cannot miss:

> The very fact of writing is for leaving a witnessing. The one who has written or has created, to witness his passage, does so for others. These are witnessings that we gather like blades of grass, everywhere! For example, someone goes to the high mountains, to repair a shelter demolished by a storm ... It's that, the human being! His behavior is always with rapport to a common oeuvre that, even if it is not in the same moment, is an oeuvre in time. Alpinists will return the next season ... because the conquest of the mountain is a common oeuvre, an oeuvre in time.[260]

The revolt the unconscious promises is inevitable because reality causes "contradiction [that] leaves traces in the libidinal economy,"[261] and "the archaic affect of the fetal epoch leaves its living traces in narcissistic organo-emotional representative associations."[262] So we each have a «rapport narcissisé (traversé de narcissisme)» to "sensory elements in resonance with vocabulary words,"[263] and a concomittant "hearing available to all significant traces."[264] We recall that with *Tout est langage* (published in 1987), Dolto felt she had finished writing, after nearly 50 years of scribing.[265] And querying with Dolto just how it is that "all is language," we come upon the libidinal story of ideas in powerful evidence that since "the unconscious is a fact of the human species,"[266] the word is a testament to discursive forces from somewhere entirely other. Language is neither fully real nor fully rational.

Via the trace, the nuanced «rôle de script-girl»—countersigned in the nanny's tongue—acquires staggering value in «après-coup» as a recollection of our young analyst pre-1913 returns with the cadence of theory. For Dolto tells us that when she first wrote letters, another could read what she could not. This dependence on a reader evokes Dolto's pivotal clinical observation that scribing a patient's words (spoken in the presence of a witness), then rereading these notes to him at a later date, secures the transference for him. Reciprocally, annotating a patient's words, then privately rereading these notes later, secures the transference for her. Can we say, then, that rereading witnessed notes facilitates the transference? And is there a return here of the early advice of Mlle, to read and listen to herself as she did? Or of that conspicuous suggestion on the word, «linotte,» to read notes and listen to yourself?

We also recall that the defining quality of the archaic transference situation (that original *bi*ography) is its fluidity: a timeless, spaceless, reversible, indissociable, unconscious subject-witness—when (where) phonemes of common interest in dream-work become mediating objects. But wouldn't archaic echoes naturally occur in one's own texts? So wouldn't rereading autobiographical fragments offer archaic-systonic play? And isn't reading to oneself a strong phantasy of feeding oneself—self-securing? Can archaic continuity be restored, then, by the surprise return of archaic investments (one's invested phonemes) enabled by the sufficient othering of one's words: by time (forgetting); space (rearranging); or an actual other («semblable»)? So it seems as if the script-girl enlists the transference to advance a startling provocation of pedagogy: can literacy practices be curative? And we are returned here to Dolto's momentous offer: that the human being, engaged in a phantasy of self-sufficiency[267] and symbolizing right from infancy, depends on an other, as if himself, for his liberation.

## Familiar shadows

In time, we will come to understand Dolto's true genius ironically—through word-plays and homonymic transfers that arrive in such quanta as to defy coincidence, and that become readable in an anachronological approach: condensing dispersed material around indexical phonemes that repeat haphazardly in the «après-coup» of her history. Dolto's corpus thereby reveals that we are all formed by (in) a dream of continuity that installs the most primitive bond of security we have: unconscious witnessing. And since long before we are seen in reality we are heard in phantasy, audition retains a place of privilege in unconscious securitization. Dolto also helps us realize, through her oeuvre, that the finest correspondence retrievable from the archaic is not knowledge per se—but rather, the desire to know that heralds the desire to live.

In her journal of April 1924, Dolto inscribes a poem: «Les morts» ["The dead"].[268] It is located in a text issued in 2008 for the one-hundredth anniversary of her birth, whose rare assemblage includes extracts from *Traversée du siècle* ["Crossing of the century"]—Dolto's unpublished co-autobiography with Boris.

The poem's time of writing should not be overlooked, being between two wars. Further, in 1924, Dolto was almost precisely between her birth (in 1908) and her "rebirth" in name, via marriage (in 1942). Jacqueline is gone (d. 1920), as is «Oncle Pierre» (d. 1916)—but Jacques has just arrived (b. 1922). And still alive are the elders of greatest influence: her maternal great-grandmother, Dan-mé Étan (Cécile Overnay, d. 1925); her maternal grandmother, Dan-mé (Henriette Marguerite Secrétan, d. 1938); and Mlle, her governess since 1919 (Élisabeth Weilandt, d. 1957).[269]

By 1924, Françoise—then the age Jacqueline was when she fell from the mountains—had already formulated a definition of psychoanalysis: "For me, psychoanalysis was the association of ideas, and the science of dreams, of which I had not understood much but a little; I spoke of the unconscious."[270] The 16-year-old's poem of 16 short lines is weighty, as she writes about seeking the calm of cemeteries and hearing the unceasing call of the departed—"invisible beings" forming "familiar shadows"[271]—and we encounter melancholy as the deeply personal human condition informing the difficulty of living.

By considering the work of the transference in assuaging our constitutional melancholy, via a restorative phantasy of filiation, I think we can also sense the extraordinary potential of the transference in texts as a consolation. Emmanuel Levinas once expressed a poignant hope for national literatures: "Not just that one learns words from it, but in it one lives 'the true life that is absent.'"[272] I submit that Dolto's corpus «sans pareil» can rightly be regarded as world literature. For Dolto compels our attention to the fact that our most primitive learning is scaffolded upon absence by an all-sustaining phantasy that we remain, despite appearances, continuous with what we have left behind but cannot bear to live without. Thus, while Dolto was admittedly not a philosopher, it seems impossible to ignore the profound philosophical provocations of her project.

## Notes

1 AI, 96. In French and Belgian folklore, the «Père Fouettard» ["Father Whipper"] accompanies Santa Claus to dispense coal and floggings (though he later repents); the game seems to have involved target-shooting with bows and arrows. The costume is an "inn-keeper"; its French phonemes will return later (italics not in the original).
2 VC1, 21; AI, 98 (this is the first letter in the two huge volumes of Dolto's correspondence, VC1 and VC2; parentheses mine).
3 VC1, 84.
4 VC1, 85.
5 PJE, 71.
6 PJE, 74.
7 Photo: VC2, 360.
8 Text: Notre Famille, 2015; enduring popularity: Le Point, 2012, 2014.
9 From 1965–1980, see VC2, 712; from 1981, see VC2, 713.
10 Chérer, 2008, 34.
11 AI, 236 & 237f; Provence, 1995.
12 PJE, 74; VC2, 563.

13  PJE, 72–73.
14  PJE, 78–79.
15  PJE, 59 & 61.
16  See Chapter 5.
17  MF, 52; VC1, 316.
18  MF, 88 & 96.
19  VC1, 50; also Malandrin & Schauder, 2009, 353.
20  VC1, 36 & 38.
21  Djéribi-Valentin in AI, 138.
22  Letter: PF, 90–115 & VC1, 560–574. Françoise chronicles problematic incidents in the Marette household—many involving her mother—in a tone likely to further inflame Suzanne. So it seems possible that she reconsidered sending it; by then, she had moved out of the family home anyhow.
23  C. Dolto in AI, 17 &VC1, preface; also EN, 60.
24  VC1, 559f;
25  VC2, 4.
26  EN, 24.
27  E.g., AI, 117.
28  Dolto met Cuny on her way to Laforgue's, likely in 1934. Cuny blocked the road, baring a revolver, apparently intended for Laforgue. Dolto said she wanted to talk to Laforgue first, joking that Cuny could eat supper with her and kill Laforgue the next day (ATP, 123–125). So they ate at L'Hôtel de la Loube in Roquebrussanne (PF, 119), igniting a friendship that endured until her death.
29  AI, 124 & 131; VC1, 490–491 & 507.
30  See Chapter 4.
31  VC2, 4.
32  VC2, 14.
33  VC2, 14.
34  AI, 124 (taxidermist's eyes).
35  AI, 124; also Chapter 10.
36  AI, 124; DW, 67; EN, 9.
37  AI, 124.
38  ATP, 209; VC1, 562; also Grellet & Kruse, 2004, 218 & 283.
39  VC1, 453 & 456.
40  VC1, 416.
41  VC2, 342.
42  VC1, 542.
43  See Chapter 5.
44  MF, 143; VC1, 381, 416 & 454.
45  See Chapter 6.
46  VC2, 94.
47  Owl art: ATP, 215 &1979c.
48  VC1, 378.
49  DQ, 115.
50  VC2, 681.
51  Freud, 1909a.
52  JD, 136.
53  SP3, 236.
54  AI, 95 & 98.
55  CD, 6.
56  AI, 17; EN, 115–117.
57  Ribowski, 1987/2004; also Destombes, 1989, 292.
58  Nobécourt, 2008a.
59  APP, 38.

60 EV, 16 & 52.
61 SHAP, n.d.
62 AI, 62; ATP, 45.
63 Schiff, 2005, 367 & 413–414; also Lemisch, 1961/2001.
64 EN, 10–12; also ATP, 70–71.
65 EN, 17.
66 See any map of Dublin.
67 AI, 240; ATP, 230–232 (also Chapter 8).
68 EF, 26–27.
69 EF, 26–27.
70 TL, 167.
71 EN, 17; also ATP, 70–71; EN, 10–12.
72 CD, 158–159.
73 AI, 240.
74 ATP, 230.
75 EN, 56; PF, 22; VC1, 26.
76 EN, 56.
77 EN, 57.
78 EN, 55.
79 AI, 243; ATP, 87.
80 AI, 236.
81 EN, 113; MF, 38.
82 EN, 109–111.
83 VC1, 427f.
84 De Sauverzac, 1993, 67.
85 Freud, 1936; Freud et al., 1978, 184.
86 E. Freud, 1912, 412 & 412f; also Freud, 1914a.
87 VC1, 60f (emphasis mine); also Lieux Insolites, 2010.
88 AI, 76–77, 79 & 207–211; VC1, 391.
89 See Chapter 2.
90 VC1, 205 & 209.
91 VC1, 210; also AI, 208.
92 AI, 155.
93 EM, 237.
94 PS, 61.
95 D'Ortoli & Amram, 1990, 53. The authors refer to a later Didier (1974)—not Denis (1940), renamed Didier in further editions of the dissertation. This Didier, a nine-year-old patient of Dolto's, was a student at L'École Neuville (also VC2, 616 & 622).
96 Freud, 1919, 241 & 247.
97 Freud, 1919, 245.
98 MA, 206.
99 MA, 53.
100 Segal explains:

> It is the time of hallucinatory wish-fulfillment, described by Freud, when the mind creates objects which are then felt to be available ... The subject in phantasy projects large parts of himself into the object, and the object becomes identified with the parts of the self that it is felt to contain ... [This is] the beginning of the process of symbol formation.
>
> *(1957/1981, 53)*

101 Segal in Quinodoz, 2008, 1–6.

102 Dolto's theorization contrasts with Klein's idea that, "the unrealistic nature of the extremely good or ideal object leaves it unstable and constantly under threat from reality" (Bott Spillius et al., 2011, 349). For the unrealistic, extreme goodness of the archaic transference situation at the origins of his conservation is what gives the subject, in a phantasy of continuity with it, security in reality. Further, the archaic landscape is never under threat by reality as it constitutes, by definition, a wish (phantasy, dream). Rather, the only thing reality threatens is reality itself, in that one will not come fully into it—withdrawing instead. For the primitive response to anxiety is to refuse, "to be distressed by the provocations of reality [or] be compelled to suffer," as Freud said (1927, 162).

103 See IIC. Dolto's dense theorization in that book is marked by prolific coinage: «absentéisation,» «autodéréliction,» «cohésir,» «décréative,» «démagicisant,» «désintimiser,» «érogénisation,» «eugène» (antonym of «pathogène»), «génitude,» «interparasitage,» etc. These words bridge English and French (bypassing translation), while disclosing the play in Dolto's thought. Two other words, «mimétiser» and «mythomaniser» (newer French terms), cite Dolto (IIC) to guide usage (e.g., Wiktionnaire, 2018a, 2018b).

104 Canu, 2009, 144.

105 IIC, 16.

106 Grignon, 1997, 19.

107 Dolto & Nasio, 1987, 13.

108 Esterle, 2011, 16; also Paquis, 2008, 6.

109 De Sauverzac, 1993, 245.

110 Petit in Grignon, 1997, 31.

111 E.g., Guillerault.

112 François, 1999b, 398; also Gerrardyn & Walleghem, 2005, 299.

113 IIC, 370.

114 IIC, 48.

115 IIC, 48.

116 Archives Françoise Dolto, 2001c; JD, 60–95.

117 JD, 72–73.

118 AI, 97; VC1, 23; VC2, 262–263, 267 &508.

119 APP.

120 SS.

121 Dolto, 1985/1989b, 123.

122 VC2, 701.

123 IIC, 215.

124 PF, 47; SS, 216.

125 CE, 21.

126 JD, 144.

127 SP2, 149; SS, 24–25.

128 IIC, 222.

129 PS, 53.

130 PS, 92–93.

131 IIC, 64.

132 AI, 217; also APP, 38.

133 Nobécourt & Simonetta, 1978.

134 E.g., François, 1999b.

135 D&R, 37; also Dolto & Nasio, 1987, 14; SP1, 26; SP2, 207.

136 AI, 119–121; EN, 79; PF, 26; VC1, 192 & 238.

137 AI, 101; ATP, 213.

138 EN, 65.

139 APP, 38; VC2, 467.

140 AI, 192; also APP, 27.

141  APP, 30 & 38.
142  AI, 238.
143  AI, 245–248.
144  AI, 238.
145  AI, 248.
146  AI, 246 (process: Western & Co., 1892).
147  CD, 109–100 & 156; see Chapter 4.
148  CD, 156.
149  CD, 109.
150  CE, 299.
151  SP1, 88; SP2, 91.
152  Dolto, 1976, 81; JD, 226 &252–253.
153  CE, 202–204; LF, 233; SS, 124; VO, 49 & 102.
154  PS, 100.
155  SP2, 232.
156  Landru, 2008.
157  PJE, 61–66.
158  PJE, 66.
159  ATP, 259n; also Albert-Buisson in Maeterlinck, 1908/1965, 264.
160  See Chapter 3.
161  VC1, 176; see also Maeterlinck, 1919.
162  See Chapter 5.
163  ATP, 69.
164  EN, 26 (local nickname for the train).
165  AI, 239; ATP, 247; EN, 25 & 57.
166  CD, 156 (emphasis mine).
167  Halmos, 2000, 35.
168  Halmos, 2008.
169  SS, 79.
170  LF, 304; also SP1, 31.
171  Dolto & Nasio, 1987, 63.
172  Dolto, 1985c, 197; Dolto & Nasio, 1987, 66.
173  Destombes, 1989, 296.
174  AI, 217; also VC2, 796–797.
175  ATP, 212. Freud met Yvette Guilbert in Paris in 1889, encouraged to her show by
     Madame Charcot (Steel, 1982, 84). They met again on her tours to Vienna, eight
     between 1892 and 1929 (Freud Museum London, 1992, 209–232). And when
     Freud passed through Paris in 1938, Guilbert was among the few guests at the Prin-
     cess's home (Steel, 1982, 89). Evoking Da Vinci, Freud explains to Guilbert how
     Saint-Anne can only be grasped, "if we understand the particularities of the infancy
     of Leonardo" (Freud, 1960, 443).
176  Douville, 2009, 179; Freud Museum London, 1992.
177  Guilbert, 1927, 59, 75 & 221.
178  Freud, 1900b, 583.
179  Breuer & Freud, 1893b, 62.
180  VO, 193.
181  SP1, 46; also PS, 101.
182  Freud, 1896/1954e, 322, 1900a, 121.
183  AI, 218; VC2, 796–797.
184  Roudinesco in Coronel & De Mezamat, 1997a.
185  DW, 140.
186  AI, 217; VC2, 796–797.
187  IIC, 94; SP3, 147.
188  EN, 73; VC1, 110–111.

189 D&R, 22.
190 Co-written with Boris in 1979–1980.
191 Dolto, 1965, 1967, 1977b, 1979b, 1979c, 1985d, 1985e, 1989c.
192 Farkas & Ratier, 2011.
193 Freud, 1900a, 189.
194 VC2, 14.
195 Freud, 1910b, 112 (St. Anne with the Madonna and Child).
196 AI, 140; in English in the diary (with emphasis).
197 AI, 142 (handwritten) and AI, 143 (typed). "Good" is in English in the first dream, with no quotation marks. In the diary, Dolto (twice) sketches a thin female. The first sketch is a loose set of lines; the second fleshes out a long, narrow dress and waist-length cape, a shoulder-length bob and high heels. In fact, the female in the dream, as drawn, does not look unlike the one in the portrait of "Anne" from 1927 (Chapter 4).
198 D'Ortoli & Amram, 1990, 253.
199 VC2, xxix; VC2, 899 & 899f.
200 E.g., Béague, 2009, 2010.
201 CD, 6 & 218; IIC, 303.
202 D&R, 18.
203 AI, 8.
204 D&R, 18.
205 CD, 110.
206 McDougall, 1969, 1.
207 EN, 119.
208 MA, 251.
209 IIC, 75.
210 Freud, 1901a, 672.
211 Freud, 1900a, 103.
212 Young-Bruehl, 1982.
213 Young-Bruehl, 1988/2008.
214 Young-Bruehl, 1998b, 3.
215 Young-Bruehl, 1998b, 3.
216 Young-Bruehl, 1998b, 44.
217 Freud, 1900a, 14.
218 Dolto & Severin, 1978, 164.
219 PM, 56.
220 QS, 64.
221 VC2, 370.
222 PS, 92.
223 PS, 61.
224 QS, 58.
225 E.g., Rostand, 1953; see VC2, 186.
226 VC2, 18; also D&R, 16; SF, 38.
227 D&R, 22.
228 D&R, 22.
229 Dolto, 1940/1965, 6.
230 MA, 93.
231 BNF, 2015.
232 For papers on this topic in Gauthier's name: Bessey, 1950, 178; Gallica, 1937.
233 Freud, 1900a, 169 & 191.
234 Dolto & Hamad, 1984/1995, 68.
235 Malandrin & Schauder, 2009, 215.
236 SS, 24 (emphasis hers).
237 SP3, 14.

238 VC2, 219; also SF, 209.
239 Dolto & Nasio, 1987, 24.
240 SP3, 129.
241 SP3, 129.
242 Malandrin & Schauder, 2009, 252.
243 SP3, 10.
244 PS, 33.
245 TL, 78.
246 AI, 192.
247 MA, 9.
248 SS, 113; also DV, 51.
249 SS, 26.
250 CD, 195–196 (emphasis hers).
251 SF, 207.
252 TL, 76.
253 CD, 196–197.
254 SP3, 236.
255 Klein, 1923/1998, 66f.
256 Freud, 1896d, 154.
257 Freud, 1908a, 149.
258 Dolto, 1985f, 531.
259 SF, 209.
260 VO, 193–194.
261 IIC, 325.
262 LF, 90.
263 IIC, 44 (parentheses hers).
264 CD, 193f.
265 VC2, 858.
266 VO, 34.
267 See Chapter 4.
268 AI, 240.
269 AI, 97; VC1, 23.
270 EN, 80.
271 AI, 240.
272 Levinas, 1982, 21.

# 8

# PHONEME

## Introduction

In July 2014, while on a research trip dedicated to Françoise Dolto, I walked around the neighborhood of L'Hôpital de la Pitié-Salpêtrière, as I thought Freud might have in his days with Charcot, in 1885–1886.[1] I began by finding the two homes where Freud lived in Paris, thanks to Bonaparte's report on a lesser-known second location on Impasse Royer-Collard, one block up from the first, at 10 Rue le Goff.[2] Both addresses are within earshot of Rue Saint-Jacques—one of the two oldest streets in Paris, antedating Roman times[3]—where Dolto lived and worked from 1942 onwards. Incidentally, Dolto's mother belonged to a metaphysical society for which Charcot was responsible for a time.[4] And in another coincidence, in the same cemetery outside of Paris, on Rue Bièvre, where Françoise Dolto lies buried, lies Pierre Janet, who inherited the responsibility for the «Pitié» from Charcot.

In fact, L'Hôpital de la Pitié-Salpêtrière is among the most outstanding treasures in Paris—a city with no shortage of wildly impressive buildings and a historical record that is abundantly archaic. For at the Salpêtrière, one locates the beginnings of psychoanalysis: the radical suggestion that psychical suffering can be healed by talking, and by a certain kind of listening. Ironically, a century later, the «Pitié» will still be a place of dreams. Enlisting subjects in modern research in neurology and "pathologies of sleep," using the most innovative methods, conclusions have a surprisingly anecdotal character: for example, that writing out or drawing nightmares, then rereading them, reduces fear.[5]

On another day, I took a photograph of Rue Sigmund Freud—a treed and circular street along the exterior of a massive defensive wall, the «Enceinte de Thiers» [homonym: «enceinte de tiers,» "pregnant of/with thirds"]. And as I did on every day of my stay, after outings in the entourage, I reentered the core of the city through a huge «porte» ["door" or "gate"; homonym: "carry"; near-homonym: «pour te,» "for you"]. This time, my feet took me through the «Porte du Pré-Saint-Gervais,» one of over 30 entranceways in the concentric layers of stone surrounding that burgeoning city for about 200 years. As ever, metaphors arrived with the force of the repressed, as the «pré» ["field"] inscribed in the name of that gate seemed like an index entry for «pré»—the precocious, pregenital, prehistory, pre-language, «pré-moi,» pre-Oedipal, «présent,» presentification, pre-subject and preverbal—in brief, a doorway of its own onto the fertile archaic field that Dolto locates through Freud's opening to psychoanalysis.

## «Huit»

But of all I experienced that summer in Paris, no place touched me more than l'Hôpital Salpêtrière. With its impressive stone «porte» on Boulevard de l'Hôpital, it is designed like a castle commune, so that Freud felt it recalled the General Hospital of Vienna.[6] And though it is in the heart of the city, near one of the busiest train stations in Europe, its grounds are remarkably still, as if holding in reserve faint whispers of 400 years of humans moving between loss and hope. Its use as an arsenal, then as a hospice for the disenfranchised—the homeless, old, mad and women—resonates in its rock walls, in the hauntingly sparse Chapelle Saint-Louis, and in faint vestiges of former gardens once nourished by an ancient river, the Bièvre, whose winding path through Paris is almost forgotten.[7] Wide billboards dot its walkways with images of periodic destruction and reconstruction, while lab coats scurry from one building to another. And it is in this return of (to) the present amid the returns of the past—ruins that become our «rue» in, just like when our journey with Dolto started—that we will begin to locate a synoptic portrait of one phoneme, «port(e)» ["port (door/carry)"],[8] as a remnant of a truly momentous archaic scene—one offering both an example and a summary of her theorization.

Before studying the astonishing movement of «port(e)» in Dolto's texts, however, we begin with an exemplary case of two other phonemes whose association seems overdetermined in her corpus: «huit jours» ["eight days"]. So frequent is its repetition that it has predictive value: whether Dolto retells or prescribes, the duration is invariably "eight days." Homonymically, the phrase is nearly «oui joue» ["yes play"]. We detour from Dolto's home to nearby Rue Pajou [homonym: «pas joue,» "no play"], to the maternal great-grandmother's house where her parents went alone every Friday. Dolto reminisces about learning time based on routines: "The days were marked by, 'This is the day when … '"[9] Many in Dolto's circle use the unit too, like her mother,[10] father,[11] brother,[12] sister-in-law,[13] maternal grandmother,[14] daughter,[15] husband[16] and Madame Chapdelot.[17] The family record also gives this as the precise time it took the maternal great-grandmother to die in 1925,[18] and how long it took Dolto's husband, Boris, to die in 1982.[19] *La Semaine de Suzette* is described as arriving every «huit jours»;[20] and in that 25-page letter to her father, three events are said to be coming in «huit jours.»[21] In four texts alone, I count 34 instances and make no claim to exhaustivity.[22] Even her young patient, Léon (age eight), is said to answer eight days later the questions she asked him eight days prior.[23] Eight o'clock also marks the time when Dolto says radio opened up her world every evening,[24] and the age she turned as she assumed her widowhood.[25]

Actually, the Romans used an eight-day week for about eight centuries from 800 BC, the «nundinae» ["no dinner"]—and its uncanny (and prolific) homonym: «non/nom dit est» ["not/name/noun said is"]. From this history, «huit jours» and «une huitaine» ["eight-ish"][26] became colloquialisms for "one week." On the one hand, then, an ordinary speech habit circulates among proximal individuals. On the other hand, something excess seems conveyed by its preponderance, as if not only its phonemes but a cycle were engrained—as if, Dolto suggests, invested dates begin in archaic rhythmic exchanges.[27] We muse, as well, that two phonemes generate a rhythm in double time. Dolto believes a «rhythme binaire» heralds uterine life,[28] leading to rhythms of displacement,[29] as we unconsciously seek a lost rhythm.[30] She also observes that some patients return about a particular pain on key dates.[31] Here, we recall Freud on Dora: "We had only *two hours* more work before us. This was the same length of time which she had spent in front of the Sistine Madonna, and ... the length of the walk which she had not made round the lake."[32]

Thus things settled in my mind for about one year until, as I walked alone one morning, a thought suddenly arrived: Jacqueline died at 18, its digits readable (as *Mititi* spoke)[33] as «dix-huit» [homonym: "say eight"]—as if it were a suggestion of play with "eight days." I scribbled it down quickly, afraid to forget. Such is learning in «après-coup»: not just the impossibility of boundaries of knowledge, subject, time or space, but the risk of losing what is so fleeting amid the thunder of reality. However, exactly «huit *mois*» ["months"; homonym: "me"] later, I discovered while sifting through my old research that the word for a male automat (evoking «automaterner»?) on a clocktower is «jacquemart» [homonym: "jacques dead" or "jacques bites"; also the abbreviation for Jacque. (line) Mar.(ette)]; while a female automat is called (curiously indeed) a «jacqueline.» And pre-modernity, uncannily, a «jacquemart» was the peasant who rang the angelus.[34] In addition, the lost nanny was said to be 18, the address (above the door) at Gustave-Zédé (the first home without her), of our infant born in 1908 (d. 1988), marked so deeply by the War of «14–18.» Left to dream, then, I hear the knell of a bell's rhythm from an archaic soundscape, entirely effacing absence. For as words flow between us, and the transference circulates wildly, it seems we each tell a finely tethered story that began long before us, that will go on when we are gone. The archaic is porous—without doors.[35]

## «À la porte»

Back in reality, though, doors are ubiquitous in both manmade and natural structures—as well as in the most prevalent drawings of any child: a house.

Doors define inside from outside, and often separate the objects of one person from another's. Doors structure many metaphors too—like "showing (someone) the door." In French, for example, «porte» expressions include the high-frequency phrase «mettre à la porte» ["put (someone) at the door," i.e., "fire someone"]. That idioms veer off divergently between languages is not irrelevant to the discovery that will present itself. At first, the Dolto reader begins to get a sense of "here and gone" from her corpus, as stories jump frames and return unexpectedly; then, of the weight of some stories around «porte»; then, of the repetition of expressions with «porte» that seem more noticeable at every pass; and then, in «après-coup,» a phoneme increasingly starts drawing attention: «porte.» But we will need to run up and down a few hallways to take in the full breadth of its archaic echoes.

In an autobiographic text, Dolto recounts how she worked at l'Hôpital des Enfants-Malades at the start of her career in a «consultation de la porte.» Over barely half-a-page, «la porte» comes up three times, always in quotes. She elaborates: "I was passionate about the consultation at/of «la porte.» I received children that other interns were fed up with."[36] We can follow the story later in that same text—but about a different hospital, l'Hôpital Armand-Trousseau:

> It is a consultation that depends on a medical service *at the* «fond» ["back" or "foundation"; homonym: «fonds,» "funds"] of the hospital; the consultation is «*à* la porte.» But it depends, administratively, *on the* «fond». It's a place where I worked without ever, ever being paid.[37]

Dolto also speaks about her work at l'Hôpital des Enfants-Malades in an interview with Roudinesco,[38] where the expression, at/of «la porte,» again in quotes, appears three times over the space of a single page—as the sliding prepositions, «à» ["at"] and «de» ["of"], uncannily augur a story to come.

But isn't there play in the idea of working at the door while not being paid—as if being put «à la porte» (fired)? Or in depending on funds yet never receiving any—like a phantasy of an economy (symbolic payment)? And doesn't it seem as if Dolto is also conveying an incidental metaphor of psychical stratification—as outer consultations are layered upon a foundation of inner resources? In one of the last descriptions (1987) of her earliest work (1937), Dolto explains how a service «à la porte» precedes any hospitalization, and how she still saw Morgenstern after shifting from being an «externe» at l'Hôpital Vaurigard (with her), to an «interne» at l'Hôpital Bretonneau (without her).[39] But in this leaving and returning (to her), in reflections blurring late and early, in being internal or external, in a practice situated midway in (or out) of facilities, and in interchangeable hospitals—each with their own huge doors—do we not begin to feel a sense of "in and out," a doorway?

The other «porte» story that acquires density is one appearing in an unassuming text of just over 100 pages, in which we find some of the last words Dolto spoke publicly. The interview is dated June 1988,[40] and on its last page (also the last page of the book), there is a touching account of the deaf child whose father (whose knock he has not heard) appears (only) for the (hearing) mother. When the child wants to see his father and opens the door, he feels "pathetic" for being unable to make him appear as his mother seems to. The phrase, «ouvrir la porte» ["open the door"] appears three times, as Dolto ends the story with these moving words: "It is indispensible to tell the child the non-perception of these signs."[41] It is a story she also tells in her interview with Jean-Pierre Winter,[42] where «à la porte» appears three times in two sentences.[43]

We could tell ourselves that this is merely a favorite expression of hers. But the word-play in Dolto's corpus awakens us to the value of lingering a little longer for what else might arrive. After all, we are in the land of paradoxes with Dolto[44]—where, as she aptly puts it, «J'enfonce les portes ouvertes»[45] [literally, "I break down (already) open doors"; colloquially, "I break down doors to open them"]. In an autobiographical text, Dolto comments on her first experience of reading about psychoanalysis, on the recommendation of her father: "I understood that there were unconscious associations that became conscious, little by little, through the force ... of being produced in a specific way, in certain circumstances."[46] And curiously, her description of her learning perfectly describes our own, as we let ourselves fall into dream-work now.

As a child of the «16e,» Dolto grew up next to the Porte de Passy—a wide opening in the trees adjoining the Jardin du Ranelagh that gives its name to her neighborhood, including the Cimétière de Passy[47] and Rue Passy, adjoining Rue Vineuse.[48] Its name is also similar in sound to the «passerelle,» where she asked her big question about death,[49] and to Mr Passe-Passe, on her grave.[50] Is it not tempting to evoke oral «passivité» here too? Further, many references that seemed to (used to) stand alone before «porte» became noticeable now appear more clearly: the minor note about a neighbor, Olga, who clacked doors;[51] the fact that Suzanne clacked doors after Jacqueline died;[52] her father's library door;[53] deliveries of *La Semaine de Suzette* (at the door);[54] walking briskly out of doors between patients;[55] forgetting her door key on Rue Dupuytren;[56] how radio gave her a «porte ouverte» on the world[57]—and, most auspiciously, that her freedom on Square Henry-Paté (in 1937) came after being «mise à la porte» of her family's home[58] (like the nanny). There is also Dolto's trip to Egypt, the neighborhood of *Babouches* (in 1956),[59] for which a postcard shows three turbaned figures (one being a boy on a donkey, like in that old text) at "Ptolemy's Door."[60] Yet moving forward from the start to the middle of the 20th Century, are we not actually (still?) moving backwards in Dolto's history?

## «Porter fruit»

The dispersal of «porte» also prevails in Dolto's clinical work. For example, in her interview with Pivot, only months before her death, he remarks that the word "solitude" comes up often in her late texts. She replies: "Solitude. It is formidable this solitude. While there is this desire to communicate, while there is this wall, this overwhelming by the weight of the flesh."[61] But do we not get a sense of a voice trapped in a body—lacking a door? In turn, this image points to several other remarks: the fetus will die if he does not go out;[62] mute kids close doors more quickly;[63] the baby knows his mother by the way she opens the door;[64] and a passive defense is like a lock on the inside of a door.[65] For the fetus is, in truth, physically waiting to go out. And regression is, practically speaking, a way to go back in psychically. Is not a door, then, the perfect metaphor for symboligenic castration?[66] In fact, Dolto will make that metaphor into a highly productive theory.

Beginning right from her dissertation, she interprets the door as a castration dream in a patient[67]—and in a seminar, she explains that if a child of seven goes in and out of the house as he wishes, castration is at stake.[68] These castrations— like walking out the door into an orchard—are precisely what allows new symbolic acquisitions. Dolto elaborates how each castation, each symbolization, will «porter fruit» ["yield fruit"]—as we pause to acknowledge «porte» as a verb now, and also note that Dolto repeats «porter fruit» five times in half-a-page.[69] But the play is more astonishing still. For "fruits of castration" are always «après-coup»[70] ["after cut" or "after hit"—a knock?]; and what is repeated is «sacré» for the child—echoing the maternal patriarch, Secrétan[71] (the door to/from the mother?)—for having «porter fruit,»[72] as we slide seamlessly from her theory into her history yet again. Two daily walks were enforced: "In the family, it was required to take in air in the morning and evening. It was sacred."[73] Then, lifelong, Dolto insists that the symbol of freedom is breathing deeply[74]—poignant indeed, given her death from pulmonary insufficiency. And while logic is far behind now, much lays ahead.

Dolto's entire conversation with Pivot feels long and heavy. They sit face-to-face in her small office on Saint-Jacques, where some 250 books are piled upon her analytic couch and spill onto chairs. Her gaze is intense, and Pivot often appears stunned by her replies. A career journalist of the highest calibre, he comments: "I was quite apprehensive. She'll stop me and say, 'Well, no, that's not the question.'"[75] And we too will have to question the question, as a panorama of family scenes begins to move more swiftly now, returning us to landmarks scattered all across her project.

Dolto shares that other than these two walks, she had to stay indoors and could not eat elsewhere (other than at her grandmother's);[76] she lived a "suffocating life,"[77] having no freedom at home,[78] and until Boris arrived, she had to honor the family tradition of being shut in through every holiday.[79] Then come recollections of Dolto being free—like running from hospital hierarchies and societies[80] and exploring and marking trails around Laforgue's.[81] And in this powerful need to be out of doors, I believe it is impossible not to "feel" something of the «allant-devenant,»[82] another influential formulation. Dolto also explains to Pivot her practice of choral witnesses,[83] and I cannot help wondering if these were helpful for Dolto too—preventing sticky fusion not only for her patients but for her—as the need for liberation seems very much her own as well. And here, a new question arrives as to what young Françoise may have overheard, behind closed doors, as her parents discussed the secret of Jacqueline's impending death,[84] and the fate of the young nanny who was stealing from them.[85] So the door invokes the «inter-dit» and the «interdit»[86]—the spoken and the forbidden.

Thereby grasping that our object—door—is neither purely symbolic nor purely real, but always a blend of both, we arrive at another weighty story. This long narration appears in that 25-page letter to her father[87]—and its impact must be assembled from autobiographical reflections 50 years later. In brief, Dolto (then 30) came home one night and asked to speak to her father privately, closing the door behind her.[88] Her mother felt the door was shut on her and imagined a secret transpiring.[89] In two pages, «porte» is repeated five times,[90] as the «prétexte de cette porte fermée»[91]—"pretext" offering an archaic play of its own for the phoneme—becomes the "pretext for the definitive rupture" with her family.[92]

Her father defends her mother in a family «roman à partir d'une porte fermée»[93] ["novel starting with a closed door"]—as word-play slips and slides on the solitary vowel blurring «part» and «port.» And it is because of this incident that Dolto will begin to see Laforgue.[94] Her mother then blames her for a «vie de trottoir»[95] [colloquially, "life of a prostitute"]—an accusation entirely unfounded yet precisely confounded, one imagines, with the accusations once leveled against the nanny. So, Dolto says, «je suis partie»[96] [colloquially, "I left"; literally, "I am/follow gone"]. Elsewhere she adds that her mother said she no longer wanted a «putain»[97] ["slut"] under her roof—an uncanny echo of Dolto's young patient.[98] As a result, Dolto says, her mother «m'a mise à la porte»[99] ["put me out"; also, "fired me"]. But again, isn't Dolto's story being conflated with the nanny's?

## «Groupe porteur»

«Porter» is a tremendously productive French verb with around 40 different meanings idiomatically. Its most frequent are "to wear," "to support," and "to transport/transmit." Dolto's use of it mostly combines the second and third, such as when she declares one day, at the *Maison verte* in Paris: "These women are anxious, and the child suffers because he doesn't know how to help his mother ... When a mother takes a baby in her arms, *he believes imaginarily that it is 'him' who carries her*" [«la porte»].[100] Here we move osmotically to somewhere between "support" and "transport," like in Dolto's notion that «toute mère porte les espoirs du monde» ["all mothers carry the hopes of the world"].[101] And by a perfect homonymic play between «mère» and «mer» ["sea"], we continue our slow entry into the watery world of primary narcissism. So we find near-thoughts in a near-form: «porteur» ["carrier"; homonym: «porte heure,» "time-carrier"]—as if the arrival of a helpful other makes possible the arrival of reality (time) itself. It also dramatically evokes (in an "organizing silence") the street immortalized in time, Rue Vineuse, and its «porteurs» ["hotel porters"].

In observations about primary narcissism, Dolto comments that erectility is related to the breast as a «porteur du sens du nom du père ... du père en général» ["carrier of the meaning of the name of the father ... the father in general"];[102] and that returning to one's narcissism is to return, unified, to one's «groupe porteur»[103]—i.e., to the archaic transference situation.[104] She also offers that her first contact with Boris was via a clinical referral, when a young girl (his patient) showed up at Trousseau «porteuse d'une lettre.»[105] Further, in discussions of multilingualism and the mother tongue (the «inter-dit» that is also the «interdit») that are well ahead of her time,[106] Dolto conceives of language as a carrier: "I think that certain children for whom the mother tongue has always been a carrier [«porteuse»] of lures, of falsities, cannot continue to use it without finding themselves trapped through this language in the projections that were made upon them."[107] Here is a note we should not miss: our lures for presentification can sometimes become traps. The relevance of this point to autism as a problem of anxiety is huge, yet this rich discussion would take us far astray from the fluid landscape of Dolto's history into which we are about to descend deeper still. Our movement is not unlike an elevator's—that object, sometimes with a porter, that ports people up and down, in groups even.

The homonymic games that proliferate even more from here are, as we will discover, carrying learning in the strangest way imaginable. For much of what Dolto teaches us about her theory is readable (i.e., decipherable) only by the transference in her texts—just as the child learns his theory of the world through the mother's corpus. As she explains it, "it is in the uterus that the unconscious image of the body truly begins,"[108] so our ears are far more implicated than our eyes. "The child hears farther than he sees," Dolto remarks, so "his space of auditory security is larger than his space of visual security."[109] In other words, audition has a much greater role than vision in early inscription, wherein *"nothing is only organic, with the human being, everything is also symbolic."*[110] So the unconscious «pré-moi»[111] first encounters reality while still, "obeying the ethic of archaic phantasms."[112] And as he is receptive to a widening soundscape of security, there remains a natural «prégnance des phonèmes les plus archaïques,»[113] as first phonemes always symbolize maternal security.[114] Conversely, any precocious or sudden loss of that auditorily securing soundscape results in a «sevrage mal symbolisé» ["poorly symbolized weaning"].[115]

The infant's experience of language *and* security will thus be an experience of language *as* security. Meanwhile, "smiles, onomatopoeia, speech ... [mark] the start of the exchanges, of the 'commerce' issued from the functional transference."[116] What is curious here, I submit, is that Dolto is also theorizing that a listener/reader who begins to enjoin homonymic plays on the invested, repetitive phonemes of a speaker/writer is engaged in the process of learning by the transference. She also theorizes, I believe, that by pronouncing the phonemes of the mother tongue, the infant "sublimates orality,"[117] this being nothing other than the child "putting into his (own) mouth what is needed either because he is hungry, or to know this object of need and of desire"[118]—i.e., automaterning.[119] That is why (how) oral castration permits «la parole.»[120] And if a child is unable to speak in the social (due to being psychogenically mute or autistic), Dolto works to analyze the poorly symbolized castration—specifically, the umbilical castration at stake:

> Language … symbolizes the castration of birth we call the umbilical castra-
> tion: this language repetitively hits the baby's hearing as an effect of his
> being in the emotional impact of his parents, at the discretion of sonar syl-
> lables, modulations and affects he perceives intuitively … It is as if all
> affects accompanied by phonemes incarnated a primary narcissistic mode
> of being.[121]

So, from behind a closed door, phonemes are softly knocking, offering reality as an opportunity.

Much of Dolto's thinking about the phoneme is in her main text on the unconscious image of the body.[122] Moreover, as we are learning with Dolto, the phoneme is what constructs the unconscious image of the body. Yet by naming the theory otherwise, the most valuable meaning (again) arrives from underneath. And as Dolto plays tentatively with its phonemes—the «i-ma-je» she describes, as if the core definition of her invaluable formulation inhered in this "simple" game of words[123]—the phonemes still (always) can only suggest thoughts from within an archaic space informed as much by silence as by sound, where saying too much might compromise the dream-work. It is as if Dolto is careful to respect the unspeakable of her own theory of the unconscious image of the body. Thus, the digressions and tangents—countless small mentions about the phoneme across her corpus in varied contexts, and innumerable stories that feel as if they continue decades later—are the only way of telling the impossible story that Dolto is relating about the psychical depths of language. It is the story of the unconscious life of the word that conscious life—and its words upon the surface—can only ever intimate.

Thus the unprecedented demonstration of the phoneme—about which she was theorizing with her unconscious image of the body—remains in the background, the undergrowth, as the hidden current in Dolto studies today. For Dolto's project manifests a wide diffusion of dream-work wherein what is not apparent in reality becomes discernible only through her unconscious associations—as she theorizes regarding her patients. Thus, slowly, we begin to grasp what has signified the dream for Dolto—or, as «Milou» once put it, how Dolto's "*sonar* letter indicated latent desire."[124] We also become aware of the importance of the other as a witness of unconscious transits that we cannot ever realize (literally) for ourselves.

## Port de Deauville

Returning to «porte» itself now, many near words come to mind—as substitutions in identification on the root, so to speak: «apporter» ["bring"], «rapporter»

["bring back"], «importance,» «supporter,» «transporter» and so on—along with «portrait,» Dolto's passion and clinical tool, and Santa's gift to every child.[125] The daunting idea of trying to follow all these derivations in her corpus gives us a sense of the dispersal to which unconscious investments are subject in time. But one variant arrives boldly on three paths: «port.» First, the "e" in «porte» is silent, making it a near-perfect homonym. Second, «porte» in French is homonymous with the English "port"—and we recall that Françoise spoke English before French.[126] Third, by a bizarre aside, «porte» symbolically invites the loss of its "e." For among Dolto's famous patients was Georges Perec (1936–1982), whom she had in analysis in 1949, after his father was killed and his mother was deported to Auschwitz. The famous writer became well-known for his lipogrammatic word play, such as his novel, *La Disparition*, in which there is not a single "e"—and another, *Les Revenentes*, in which "e" is the only vowel. And what we learn about Perec cannot help but reinforce what we learn about Suzanne, who flirted as a teenager with a Philip Marett—the same name as the man she would marry, Dolto notes, «sans e.»[127]

Yet by the removal of "e," a spectacular new landscape for dreaming opens: the thriving Port de Deauville, Deauville «sur mer»—on (by) the sea. And it is once we reach Deauville that we begin to fathom how familiar geography offers phonemes to the infant's nascent audition, and how familiar stories are what the phoneme carries as a condensation. So, like a seagull, we take in a wide pan of young Françoise in Deauville now: watching women dressed as nurses tend the sick in World War I;[128] being confused by suggestions in idiomatic language, like shrimp "asking" to be boiled alive;[129] learning to read;[130] hearing about war being declared on the big board;[131] the news seller stuttering «midi» like morse code;[132] everyone speaking English and leaving from here for Britain;[133] reading Maeterlinck;[134] goods from her grandfather's factory passing through Dives-sur-mer [homonym: "dive-on-mother"];[135] and dreaming of «Papa à Deauville.»[136]

Scattered throughout her corpus will be countless other references to Deauville that feel symbolically vested, weighty: her father at the door, leaving by train for Paris each week, uncertain to return;[137] staying there through 1914–1915, and cooking with «charbon»;[138] adults in bathing costumes on the beach looking like a «tableau»;[139] learning how to knit from Mlle;[140] and not being allowed to play with other children, but allowed to dig «trous» in the sand[141]—in new echoes of Trousseau. Dolto will visit Deauville with her family well into adulthood.[142] And an early letter from Deauville on 28 August 1914 is so rich that it offers strong evidence that the younger we are, the least dispersed our investments will be. For in five short sentences written to her father, four-year-old Françoise explains that she got mumps and stayed with the soldiers at the Royal Hotel for a few days, sharing a room with her brother Jean, "but I have already gone out (left)."[143] Her illness is a «maux d'oreilles» ["illness of the ears"; homonymically: "words of the ears"] that also invokes phantasies of incest (a shared room and the mention of Pierre), and of castration (going out). Meanwhile, the date of onset of that childhood illness will uncannily coincide with her death (25 August 1988). But we are not done yet with this place that is a condensation. For the more we hear about Deauville, the more its first phoneme—«do»—becomes audibly distinct. We pause for air, though, before our final dive.

The first digression from «do» takes us to a story about Dolto's father (Henry), when he was four years old.[144] Barely one page long and appearing only once in her entire corpus (I believe), its brevity is an apt counterpoint to its complexity—like any phoneme. Dolto describes the scene as a «tableau» akin to *Le Déjeuner sur l'herbe* ["Breakfast on the grass"] by Monet—and a "painful souvenir" from the days just before Henri (his father) died in the train fire.[145] Henry's parents loved each other, but Henri's family was ashamed that his wife was beneath their class (being the daughter of a doctor married to a midwife). The young architect lived, "in the wind of the epoch … like Monet and Manet, who were his friends." But on the last picnic, an event occurred that Henry would retell lifelong, punctuated by, "all architects are cretins." He blamed himself too: "I was an imbecile when I was four."

Little Henry was given the responsibility for cooling the refreshments, as Henri told him to put the wine «dans» ["in"] the «ruisseau» ["stream"]. So he poured every bottle out into the water. The ensuing scene of anger would be the son's last memory of his father.[146] It was the shame of his life, she says, to have been called an imbecile in public, and it left him with a lisp. Yet he was not aware he lisped until Suzanne pointed it out. No one had mentioned it before—not his mother, nor any doctor or teacher. And it was Suzanne's father who first suggested exercises. After eight days, he no longer lisped, Dolto relates. "If only someone had told me," Henry said, "I would have corrected myself sooner."

But like shrimp "asking" to be boiled,[147] the story of young Henry putting wine "in" the river exemplifies how the child entrusts literality with a suggestion. It also returns young Françoise's surprise at the contradiction of Avenue des Ternes being so colorful—i.e., «pas terne» («paterne»?).[148] Further, on the word is the devastating double-negation of a father labeled an imbecile and a grandfather deemed a cretin. Here, too, is an odd presaging of much of Dolto's theorization: the fragile edifice of reality (architecture); the wound at hearing (shame); the loss of continuity (father's death); a castration never delivered («non-dit»: no one told him); a symptom at orality (lisp); and the psychical potency of the word («dans»). Also patent is the ancient guilt inscribed by a «malentendu» ["misunderstood," also "misheard" or "evil heard"]. And with the wine-filled stream evoking libidinal flows, this story becomes a «tableau» not only of Dolto's career (combining both paternal grandparents), but of her thinking on oral passivity. It is as if her work on symbolic life originates in her father's symbolic history, reaffirming her evidence for unconscious inheritance.

The story also incidentally but perfectly narrates the child's insertion into the social as a potentially difficult one, such that not just one life but generations to follow are (shockingly) pivoting on the correct usage in a given space-time (epoch, culture, family) of a single phoneme: in this case, the preposition «dans» ["in"]. And with respect to Dolto's particular setting, the fact that «dans» is constitutive of «Dan-Mé» is portentous.[149] For what we are about to confirm is that while, "the first name is the phoneme(s) accompanying the sensorium of the child ... from birth to death,"[150] not only will his own name be invested, but all kinds of names pertinent to his survival. For by moving through Dolto's corpus anachronologically along innumerable word-associations, we rejoin what is dispersed to increase the affect of stories assumed lost that are somehow still present. It seems highly reminiscent of that famous movie, *Citizen Kane*, where a man's dying word, "Rosebud," holds his entire affective history. For it is as if the word comes first, and life gets pieced together from there.

## «Do»

In reality, we have only glimpsed Dolto's maternal grandmother up to now. But by following associations, Henriette Lucie Marguerite Secrétan (1860–1938), aka Dan-Mé, moves into the limelight, as we discover the cardinal importance of an invested phoneme to early identifications—and vice-versa. By all accounts, Dan-Mé was an impressive woman. She travels alone on the train at 64,[151] takes the Paris «métro» alone at 69,[152] and regularly attends the Grand Prix de Deauville, though skipping it in 1929.[153] She was dignified and austere, Dolto recounts, like a «nonne laïque,»[154] and she cared for her own mother, Dan-Mé Étan (1839–1925)[155]—as «dan» traces its filiation even farther back. Elsewhere, Dolto relates that Dan-Mé Étan was the first dead person she ever saw.[156] Dolto maintains daily contact with Dan-Mé, and the volumes of correspondence are replete with their exchanges. Dan-Mé's photograph is also prominent in Dolto's archives.[157] But by the start of World War II, Dan-Mé is weak. There are mentions of her hypertension, and a letter dated 19 August 1938 offers the last (public) reference to her[158]—uncannily close to the date of Françoise's death, exactly 50 years later, in August 1988.

Dan-Mé's name is a story unto itself. It seems to be an archaic version of «grand-mère» (so Dan-Mé Étan is «Grand-mère Secrétan»). In the household, both Suzanne and Henry call Dan-Mé «mère,»[159] while Dolto calls Suzanne «mère»—as the blurring of «mère» begins to evoke Dolto's clinical concern for precisely such a problem of names. It is true that Dan-Mé's middle name, Marguerite, was also Françoise's—so Françoise and Dan-Mé have the same name. As well, Dan-Mé's first name was Henriette, so Henry and Dan-Mé have similar names. I believe we thereby begin to feel an overdetermination on the name that becomes increasingly conspicuous.

Further, in public, Dan-Mé was Madame Arthur Demmler—or more commonly, Madame Demmler. But if we close our eyes and listen carefully, we hear only this: «ma dame dame leurre» ["my," "lady [bis]," "lure/the hour/their"]—with repetition built in. Do we have here a precocious «prétexte» of a whole theory on a name: the mother's repetitions as lures to reality? At least as evocative, we learn that Dan-Mé had a nickname: «Do.»[160] So that town by the sea, Deauville, that so marked young Françoise, was effectively «Do ville» ["Do's city"]. And this is how, as we begin to sense, place names inform the child's «tableau,» his coming to reality, as phonemes spread wildly by transferential coloring.[161] And by coloring just a bit outside the lines now, we come upon a most curious fact: «Do» returns us, in English, to its near-homonym: "door."

Yet by finding «Do» along so many paths, we become attuned to Dolto's critical identification to her maternal grandmother in ways that are never explicitly stated, but once detected seem obvious. So like a seagull in «Do ville» now, we pan the landscape: Dan-Mé's home is the only one where young Françoise can eat other than her own, and also where she gets into trouble with the valet;[162] Dan-Mé's German husband is the one who shames young Suzanne;[163] Dan-Mé is a widow (from 1912) who never remarries;[164] and it is Dan-Mé who explains that Saint-François is her patron saint, not Saint-Françoise—as an "e" is at stake again.[165] Dan-Mé's father is the Secrétan reverberating in Dolto's story;[166] Dan-Mé's mother is the one who went to America to marry an Irish man;[167] and Dan-Mé's son is Pierre, young Françoise's beloved «fiancé.»[168] By this much-discussed phantasy of incest, then, Dan-Mé would have been Françoise's grandmother and her «mère.» But as «mère» is also what Henry calls «Dan-Mé,» another unspoken phantasy of incest is spun by association—Henry and Françoise sharing a «mère.»

In fact, it is Dan-Mé who is most responsible for encouraging Françoise's "betrothal" to Pierre.[169] She sends measurements to the then-six-year-old for a «cache-nez» for Pierre,[170] and she sends to her son on the battlefield copies of essays by the then-eight-year-old, like «Une charge à la baïonnette.»[171] It is also Dan-Mé who gives Françoise the diamond when Pierre dies, and who gives Françoise a cross, purportedly from him, for her communion.[172] I believe it is not unfair to say that Dan-Mé perpetuates (initiates, even) the phantasy of incest and Françoise's pledge to widowhood at such a young age.[173] Yet it is the same Dan-Mé whom Françoise asks Santa for help in pleasing, in 1916.[174] And it is at Dan-Mé's house that Françoise found magazines worn with age, that she assumed had interested her mother as a child. In them were images of people dressed like her grandparents when they were younger, and her own parents as children, as she admits: "This was something enormous to help me love society."[175] It is also at Dan-Mé's house that beloved Mlle lived[176]—so we can speculate that, very likely, the lost nanny had too.

On the one hand, then, we have a child who clearly loved her grandmother. On the other hand, we observe the overdetermination of phonemes pointing to this proximal individual, Dan-Mé—and the vital role of words in the developmental process of identification. Identification is required for the earliest narrative of the self, as the psychically passive infant seeks for the sake of survival someone in his entourage to love as a «semblable»—to live with, as if, and through an other as himself. This nascent symbolization of the «pré-moi» then enables the «moi» along a phantasy of continuity with the archaic. Dolto explains:

> When a child of four or five years of age speaks of his grandparents, it is not at all a question of the real grandfather or grandmother who exist or have existed. It is at once a question *of them and of himself*, a himself of which he has no consciousness and no souvenir, that is his own childhood prior to his first souvenirs and before his first conscious relations with his parents. He thus expresses and relives the conflicts of his earliest infancy.[177]

Most uncannily, along substitutions upon identifications—in this case, backwards, via symbolic filiations on the name—Dan-Mé supplants Suzanne in (as) a «Do-ville-sur-mère,» ["Do's town on the mother"]. It is as if some extraordinary play on that place condenses theory—and we "watch," from another angle, a repetition of the supplanting of Suzanne by that beloved nanny.

Inspiring Dolto's care for infants, Dan-Mé will be the first to look after Jacques,[178] as she nurtures him pre-natally, we could say—giving Suzanne infant-rearing lessons in September 1922.[179] Then, in 1928, at the age of 68, Dan-Mé works to build a home for poor women needing treatment, in a bold feminism that cannot but evoke the *Maison verte*.[180] And when Dolto needed eyes in 1938 to start writing her dissertation,[181] it seems clear that Dan-Mé, who died in 1938, had been a valuable witness in reality until then—and that a loss of continuity will always find succour in phantasy. We also detect a deep appreciation of the archaic in Dan-Mé, who reflects in 1928 on Bagnoles-de-l'Orne: "It's the end of encrusted old Bagnoles that was without distractions, without comforts, that endeared it to me so much; there will be palaces built, routes, tennis courts ... well, at least the fir trees, woods and springs will remain."[182] It is an apt commentary on the stratification by which the present is layered upon the past, psychically and geographically. And while the evidence is already strong, we recall (from somewhere other) Dolto's explanation of Boris's name: how «Dolto» means nothing, but *Do l'oto* meant a lot.[183] For right at the porous passage between the unconscious and conscious—disguised by wild associations and substitutions—there is still the powerful love for «Do.»

## Door knock

In 1928, during a parlor game about preferences, Dolto notes that «Dominique» is her favorite man's name.[184] Other patients have names that are historically findable too: for example, «Tote»[185] is Suzanne's sister's nickname; «Jeanne»[186] is her father's favorite woman's name, in the game in 1926;[187] and «Jeanne d'Arc» is young Françoise's most admired person, in the game of 1928.[188] There is also «Agnès,»[189] after a childhood friend. So case names hold significance ironically: while the unconscious effects of any patient's most invested phonemes—his name—are lost to confidentiality in relating case material, they inevitably reveal something valuable about the clinician's historical investments. And the name of her highest-profile case is made only more portentous when we learn, in her book about "Dominique," that any child has a «dépendence mimique au rythmes de la mère»[190]—a «Do mimique»?

Refinding Dominique,[191] we note that while he can read, he cannot count or read time.[192] In the fifth session, he wishes for a name starting with «O»[193]— as if «Do» were echoing, but only partially. Yet in being reported by Dolto in the first place, this clinical material invites the observation that, while carefully listening to her young patient, Dolto is susceptible to her own archaic echoes. Dolto's attention is also on his use of doors: his putting dirty underwear in the «armoire,»[194] and toy soldiers too;[195] and his continually tidying closets.[196] She comments that the «armoire» can be a representation of the abdomen.[197] Dolto relates how the father admits that both he (the father) and Dominique's brother are timid, so they «n'ose pas frapper à une porte»[198] ["don't dare knock at a door"]. This idiom, from the first pages of the case, further blurs identifications between father and son(s) when Dominique utters, during his last session, that he will come back someday when he can pay for himself, as he still feels timid[199]— i.e., unable to knock at a door? Also included are his remarks on Italy, where rosaries «ferment les portes ... j'aimerais bien être fermier»[200] ["close doors ... I'd love to be a farmer/closer"]; and his repeating twice (in the same session) that his father closes his office door with a key.[201]

In turn, the echoes in Dolto's reporting of Dominique's case open doors into how reparation requires identification with a «semblable»—as a later edition of fusional transference, the mimic dependence on the mother—that uses the phoneme as a mediating object to progress, by association, along unconscious "slides of identifications."[202] Dolto describes this slide between Dominique's mother and maternal grandmother: "Who is this «on» ["we, someone, anyone"]?" Dolto asks, as he speaks of himself. He answers: "My grandmother, she loves me too, and my mother has always loved me."[203] As to why Dominique loves his grandmother best: "She writes everything, the restaurant, the meal, the server, the menu, she writes everything, everything we did."[204] So is Dominique's grandmother most helpful as a "script-girl"?[205]

Regarding the role of the «semblable» in identification, Dominique states: "I love playing at being a woman."[206] But somewhere here, with Dominique and the «Do mimique»—in the play of the phoneme, «ferm,» between "closing" and "farming," the pronoun «on» blurring identifications, his "script-girl" as a source of love, and his countless doors—do we not have more evidence of the role of invested phonemes in identification, and of the role of both in the transference? It is as if the reciprocity and continuity inscribing the conditions for the transference were condensed in/on this one name, «Dominique.»

## Port(e)manteau

Another patient's name is worthy of our attention: «Léon.»[207] At eight, Léon is illiterate and separates each syllable while speaking in a monocord tone, recalling Bernadette, Nicole and Jeanne. He holds walls as he walks, and he repeatedly draws the same colorless image he describes as «le-toit-le-ciel-la-porte» ["the-roof-the-sky-the-door"]. Dolto explains how he was marked profoundly by being tied to a chair as an infant, so his parents could continue the tailoring work on which their lives depended; by fearing each day the arrival of Germans at the door; and, in dissembling their Jewish heritage, by the family truncating their «patronym paternel» to its first two syllables. "Imagine using 'Karpo' for 'Karpocztski,'" Dolto explains. She concludes that he suffered from an "overdetermination of a symbolic infirmation leading to the identification of a subject to a half-individual."[208] The direct link between the phoneme and identification could not be clearer. She quips that the problem reminds her of an old song, «J'ai perdu le *do* de ma clarinette, ah, si Papa, y savait ça»[209] ["I've lost the *do* of my clarinet, ah, if papa knew that"; homonym: «dos,» "back"]. And another uncanny echo of «Do»—and the lost meaning of *Do l'oto*, with its own symbolic infirmation—thunders in.

By the sheer quantity of examples, then, we find the phoneme «do» like a seed in countless thoughts, in an unpredictable movement along wild associative journeys. Moreover, Léon's name returns us to the statue in the Jardin du Ranelagh by Léon (Longepied) that she passed during her daily walks, including after she learned to read.[210] It also evokes a scene from the Marette household during World War I, when the cook's husband, Léon, was mobilized, and Dolto says the peacocks in their yard seemed to cry, «léon-léon.»[211] They had always cried this, Dolto remarks, but the cook had not discovered the peacocks were calling her husband until he was mobilized.[212] But do peacocks really sound like this? I confess that as a child, I heard them call, "Help! Help!" So without making conscious links to theory, Dolto still enables an important one: affect influences the discernibility (and suggestion) of any phoneme.

But if affect invests the phoneme, and the phoneme invests identification, then what would it mean to lose a name—or a whole language? The disorientation at being "lost in translation" that is explored in Eva Hoffman's fine memoir is also taken up by many writers and linguists interested in language and identity.[213] And first language attrition is experienced as a "loss of the essence of the soul," as a Cree speaker puts it.[214] For the first phonemes we invest psychically are «port(e)manteau»—indelible fusions of sound and meaning. That the "e" is lost and found in translation here makes the point even more.[215] Dolto uses «portemanteau» twice after Dominique's use of it (twice) to talk about an umbrella in an abdomen. Dolto's analysis is complex, turning on «la patère» [archaic, "drinking vessel"; homonym: "not earth/not to hush"; Latin, *pater*, "father"]; «la mère-père, le père-mère … *son* (maire) (mère)» [homonyms: "mayor, mother"]; and «*sa* (père) (paire)»[216] [homonyms: "father, pair/peer"]. So we begin to fathom the auditory landscape in its fluidity, and the "polymorphous perversity" of the phoneme, to toy with Freud's words.[217] For the phoneme that is the «porteur» of history starts its symbolic life prior to space-time, or any definition.

Our final example is «Frédéric,»[218] age seven, seen only twice (perhaps). Adopted at 11 months, he is illiterate, incontinent and psychotic. Dolto notices that his draw-ings all have an "A" somewhere, upside-down or sideways. Questioning, she learns from the mother that his name at birth (never used since) was Armand. So Dolto tells him about his real name, but to no effect. Then, while all was silent, as the child was "drawing or modeling," the idea came to her to call him «à la cantonade» ["non-specifically"]. She did it without looking, she says, using a «voix sans lieu» … «voix off» ["voice without location …"]—calling as if she did not know where he was situated.[219] She called, "Armand, Armand," miming looking in cor-ners, as if trying to find him, as observed by witnesses present.[220] And as he looked towards the corners too, his eyes met hers with "exceptional intensity."[221] He then refound an «identité archaïque» lost at 11 months, Dolto says, and within two weeks, his reading and writing blocks ceased.[222]

Confirming literacy as a site (means) for oral symptoms, Dolto's material stuns. More so, since it seems as if the infant Françoise is also being called "non-specific-ally" in this story: in the use of an uncommon word («cantonade») being so close to her «cantinière» costume;[223] in «Armand, Armand» recalling «Léon, Léon,» both absent-present; in Dolto's rare use of English, that «voix off»; and in the suffering of losing a name (Armand's, the nanny's). So with only the slightest bit of associative play (and knowledge of her history), Dolto's clinical material is observed reverberat-ing between the practitioner and the patient, as the transference reveals itself and brings vital unconscious content to our attention. For the archaic can be called up to the present anytime, unpredictably, by enigmatic, unconscious conveyances that language and its silences always «porte»—"transport" and "open."

## Naming desire

By these archaic echoes without a fixed location, we knock at one last door that we cannot see but that "appears" nonetheless, as sturdy as it is ephemeral, like an unending dream: the entrance of the hotel on Rue Vineuse.[224] "Your baby carriage was always at the front *door* of that hotel," her mother states.[225] So her parents «ont *port*é plainte» ["brought a complaint"]; and though the nanny promised «de ne plus sortir» ["to never go out (the *door*) again"]—she was still «mis à la *porte*» ["fired"].[226] Dolto describes her love for the nanny: «je l'a*dor*ais.»[227] And in a sequence of sound "images"—not unlike doors clacking interminably along a long hall—I believe we can hear, with a certain kind of listening, the elevator *door*, the elevator *port*er (dressed like a soldier), the *door* man at the hotel entrance, the coat-check girl whose arm «*porte* manteaux» ["carries coats"], charming men with their open «*porte*feuilles» ["wallets"] to buy the pretty Irish girl (with a charming infant companion) a drink—and the echoes of their ironic language of love, English, in Dolto's word choice: «a*dore*» ("a *door*"?).[228]

I submit, then, that we can find in the deepest silences of Dolto's corpus, paradoxically, a phenomenal rush of sound—the wild "effect of the phantasms of the passive jouissance of a loved oral object,"[229] as she puts it. It is even tempting to play with the overdetermination in this scene to muse on the name of the nanny: Miss Porter? Miss Portman? For "Porter" is a common surname in the United Kingdom—one ironically originating in archaic French «portier» ["gatekeeper"]. But another name arrives out of nowhere, while I sit outside in a warm breeze one summer night, writing this odd chapter: Dory? After all, Dorothy and Dora were among the top 100 girls' names in 1880,[230] and her nanny would have been born around 1888. Yet as to what the nanny's name actually was, we can never know—and we need to accept that uncertainty. For what the transference delivers is not objective knowledge at all, but, rather, a doorway to the onset of the capacity for knowledge—and to the unconscious wealth from which knowledge derives.

Within the realm of linguistics, the phoneme is considered to be a unit of sound categorized by its acoustic or articulatory features, and it is deemed to have the same function in a given population. But Dolto effectively gives the phoneme a new definition and enables its phenomenal repurposing as a psychoanalytic construct: the phoneme is a unit of sound in language that does not have the same role unconsciously even between members of the same family, and whose indivisibility from its libidinal prehistory is its most potent attribute in influencing psychical structuration. Thus, with Dolto, we can infer that no dictionary of unconscious symbols is ever possible, as she warns: "Let us beware of symbolic dictionaries."[231] Rather, what we understand with Dolto is that the unconscious uses the dictionary, so to speak.

Among Dolto's artifacts is a lovely photograph of the door of Soledad, her country home in the port city of Antibes.[232] She notes in 1985 that, at the height of family life, they summered there from 1950–1970.[233] Soledad is also the birthplace of the most curious book in her corpus, *Solitude*, which she describes on the back cover: "Some facts of my private life, as well as some experiences that I had considered to be marginal, are found here better enlightened in other ways, even though they are not 'officially' part of any knowledge."[234] And inside the front cover, Dolto inscribes a perplexing dedication: "My gratitude also to the beings and to the objects animated with phantasms that populate the house of Soledad, and that helped me, them, to feel that, alone, we never are."[235] From front to back matter, then, like a breeze through open doors, Dolto arrives with a «portefeuille» full of non-knowledge from somewhere entirely other. For a psychobiographic study of Dolto discloses that every life is rooted in the primitive logic of the wish that—like a door that is neither wide open nor ever fully closed—forever makes our thoughts seekers of our long-forgotten infant dreams.

## Notes

1 Freud, 1886; Gay, 1988, 4–51.
2 Bonaparte, 1938.

3 Livius, 2011.

4 ATP, 74.

5 Arnulf, 2014, 151 & 207.

6 Freud, 1886, 6; 1893c, 17.

7 Vessier, 1999, 24 & 30.

8 Simplification of «port» ["port"] and «porte» ["door" or "carry"]. The /e/ is unstressed, so both are essentially monosyllabic (though the final vowel makes the "t" audible).

9 EN, 43.

10 PF, 40.

11 PF, 97.

12 PF, 59.

13 PF, 369.

14 PF, 109.

15 VC2, 403.

16 VC2, 422.

17 See Chapter 7.

18 AI, 102.

19 AI, 212.

20 EN, 68.

21 PF, 20; VC1, 114.

22 E.g., ATP, 89, 92, 130, 137, 157, 226 & 233; EN, 68, 73 & 86; PF, 66, 89, 114, 150, 164, 320, 331 & 454; VC2, 50, 324 & 480.

23 IIC, 297.

24 See Chapter 6.

25 See Chapter 3.

26 VC1, 454 & 484.

27 CE, 257; JD, 251; SP3, 144.

28 CE, 94–95, 257 & 350; DQ, 70; IIC, 90, PJE, 105.

29 EM, 274; LF, 61.

30 SP1, 148; also CE, 350; DV, 213; EV, 62; JD, 24.

31 D&R, Dolto & Roudinesco, 1986/1988, 17.

32 Freud, 1905a, 119 (emphasis his).

33 See Chapters 6 & 7.

34 See Chapter 7.

35 In Freud's *Da Vinci*, we locate another fine example of the word as a condensation for dream-work. Naming the bird that visits da Vinci's cradle, Freud uses *geier* (rather than normative German, *milan)* for da Vinci's *nibio* [modern, *nibbio*: "bird" or "kite"]. Freud's editors concede that, "in the face of this mistake, some readers may feel an impulse to dismiss the whole study as worthless" (Freud, 1910b, 61 & 82f). On the contrary, I believe this error makes Freud's study even more valuable. For da Vinci was forced to leave Milan, the secure home where "his position was assured" (Freud, 1910b, 65). And with Freud's use of *geier, milan* is ironically made more noticeable by its absence. Freud's translation thus hides and discloses the word-thing, *milan*, bridging the subject and biographer—the loss of a secure home: "Deeply buried within me there still lives the happy child of Freiberg, the first-born child of a youthful mother, who received his first indelible impressions from this air, from this soil" (Freud, 1931, 259). Melancholy permeates Freud's narrative, as a text he deemed, "the only beautiful thing I have ever written" (Freud in Gay, 1988, 268), continues to be derided or ignored. Yet this unique work offers another example of the transference in texts as testimony to the "co-dreaming" that happens during Freud's biographic project—and how a problem of translation is just what we would expect from such a potent investment of what is latent.

36 ATP, 137 (emphasis hers).

37 ATP, 196 (emphasis mine).
38 D&R, 14–15.
39 Nasio, 1987/1998, 36–37.
40 PJE, 91–111.
41 PJE, 111.
42 Recorded in 1986, but published in 2002.
43 DW, 94.
44 Roudinesco (2018) has recently called Dolto a "monument of paradoxes."
45 Dolto 1985/1989a, 131.
46 ATP, 104.
47 See Chapter 7.
48 See Chapter 2.
49 See Chapters 2 & 7.
50 See Chapter 5.
51 See Chapter 5.
52 ATP, 74.
53 AI, 110.
54 See Chapter 5.
55 See Chapter 5.
56 See Chapter 6.
57 See Chapter 6.
58 See Chapter 5.
59 See Chapters 5 & 7.
60 VC2, 267.
61 Ribowski, 1987/2004.
62 Dolto, 1985/1989a/1989a, 126.
63 VO, 226.
64 SS, 211.
65 LO1, 90.
66 See Chapter 6.
67 MA, 178.
68 SP2, 11.
69 DW, 71.
70 IIC, 71; also SP2, 158.
71 See Chapter 7.
72 DQ, 129.
73 ATP, 70.
74 E.g., PM, 46.
75 Ribowski, 1987/2004.
76 See Chapter 3.
77 VC1, 569.
78 VC1, 569.
79 EN, 99.
80 See Chapter 2.
81 See Chapters 5 & 7.
82 See Chapter 5.
83 1987/2004; also Chapters 4, 5 & 6.
84 See Chapter 6.
85 See Chapter 2.
86 See Chapter 6.
87 See Chapter 7.
88 PF, 91.
89 PF, 87 & 93.
90 PF, 90–92.

91  VC1, 560.
92  PF, 90–91.
93  PF, 88; VC1, 561.
94  EN, 94.
95  ATP, 90.
96  ATP, 90.
97  EN, 90.
98  See Chapter 4.
99  EN, 93.
100  Dolto, 1985b (emphasis hers).
101  LF, 66.
102  SP2, 126.
103  F. Dolto & N. Hamad, 1984/1995, 84.
104  See Chapter 5.
105  D&R, 22.
106  See Chapters 5 & 6.
107  SP1, 20–21.
108  Dolto & Nasio, 1987, 26.
109  IIC, 68.
110  IIC, 178 (emphasis hers).
111  IIC, 230.
112  IIC, 277.
113  IIC, 48.
114  LF, 62.
115  IIC, 251.
116  SS, 34 (emphasis hers).
117  LF, 108.
118  TL, 51.
119  See Chapters 3 & 5.
120  SS, 124.
121  IIC, 93.
122  I.e., «L'image inconsciente du corps» (IIC); also Chapter 7.
123  See Chapter 7, on naming the theory.
124  VC1, 454 (emphasis hers); also Chapter 7.
125  See Chapter 7.
126  See Chapter 3.
127  ATP, 218.
128  See Chapter 3.
129  See Chapter 3.
130  See Chapter 5.
131  See Chapters 5 & 6.
132  See Chapter 6.
133  See Chapter 6.
134  See Chapter 7.
135  See Chapter 7.
136  See Chapter 7.
137  EN, 26.
138  EN, 31; also Chapter 3.
139  EF, 25.
140  ATP, 81; see Chapter 3.
141  ATP, 81; see Chapter 7.
142  E.g., MF, 92.
143  EN, 29; VC1, 28.
144  Story: ATP, 231–232.

145  See Chapter 7 (for genealogical data on Henri: Garric, n.d.)

146  ATP, 231. Henry's name is twice misspelled as Henri, as Dolto reports what her grandfather said to her father: "Henri, take care of … "; and "Henri, go find … " This is likely an editing error, as the book was assembled in Dolto's last months and published posthumously. The same error occurs in many sources about Dolto (e.g., Wikipedia), and is unsurprising considering the normative French spelling is «Henri,» while "Henry" is rather English. Still, it is as if this accidental error in writing one (auditorily indistinct) letter in a single phoneme condenses (and demonstrates) Dolto's theorization on unconscious inheritance and the risks to destructuration. Further, as a record of an interview, we witness the listener as a child, for whom the fluidity of audition can easily lead to a «malentendu.»

147  See Chapter 3.

148  See Chapter 5.

149  The "s" is silent, making «dans» and «dan» perfect homonyms.

150  IIC, 46.

151  VC1, 149.

152  VC1, 232.

153  VC1, 232.

154  EN, 46.

155  VC1, 148.

156  AI, 102.

157  AI, 67; EN, 107; VC1, 135, 145, 157 & 449.

158  On Dan-mé's ill health: MF, 100; VC1, 539; VC2, 5.

159  EN, 57.

160  VC1, 33f; also MF, frontispiece & 59.

161  See Chapter 5.

162  See Chapter 3.

163  See Chapter 3.

164  See Chapter 3.

165  See Chapter 6.

166  See Chapter 7.

167  See Chapter 7.

168  See Chapter 3.

169  See Chapter 3.

170  VC1, 34; see Chapter 3.

171  VC1, 56–57.

172  See Chapter 3.

173  See Chapter 3.

174  See Chapter 7.

175  EN, 68; see Chapter 5.

176  EN, 44; see Chapters 3 & 5.

177  CE, 184 (emphasis hers).

178  See Chapters 3 & 7.

179  MF, 29.

180  VC1, 202; see Chapter 6.

181  See Chapters 7 & 9.

182  VC1, 200.

183  See Chapter 6.

184  See Chapter 4.

185  See MA.

186  See MA.

187  AI, 88.

188  AI, 88.

189  IIC, 66 and above.

190 CD, 142.
191 See Chapters 4, 5 & 7.
192 CD, 10 & 80.
193 CD, 82.
194 CD, 18.
195 CD, 48.
196 CD, 32.
197 CD, 53f.
198 CD, 36.
199 CD, 170.
200 CD, 128; also CD, 154 & 156.
201 CD, 130.
202 CD, 63.
203 CD, 99.
204 CD, 90; also CD, 62, 80, 95–97.
205 See Chapter 7.
206 CD, 96.
207 IIC, 288–325; also Chapters 7 & 9.
208 IIC, 308.
209 IIC, 308 (emphasis mine).
210 See Chapter 7.
211 ATP, 20.
212 ATP, 20.
213 See Hoffman 1989. I also recommend the excellent language memoirs of Marjorie Agosín, Gloria Anzaldúa, Patrick Chamoiseau, Evalina Chao, Isabelle de Courtivron, Ariel Dorfman, Padma Hejmadi, Nancy Huston, Alice Kaplan, Maxine Hong Kingston, Shirley G. Lim, Kyoko Mori, Richard Rodriguez, Luc Sante, Ilan Stavans, Olivier Todd and Jane Jeong Trenka; as well as a brilliant collection of languaged identities by Wendy Lesser.
214 Kouritzin, 1999, 71. "Richard" lost Cree (his hereditary language) as a child, then relearned it as an adult. Kouritzin's study offers narratives of the emotional sequelae of losing the mother tongue: Cantonese, Cree, Finnish, Hungarian, Japanese, Korean—sometimes entailing a change of birth name too. Respondents share a devastating sense of losing home and of non-belonging in their own lives. Incidentally endorsing Dolto's view of the role of the mother tongue in identity, Richard states: "You never know how beautiful you are until you know your own language" (in Kouritzin, 1999, 72).
215 "Portmanteau" has a more figurative sense than «porte-manteau,» which denotes a physical object.
216 CD, 159–161 (emphasis mine). The possessive adjective «son» is masculine, agreeing with «maire» but not «mère»; the possessive adjective «sa» is feminine, agreeing with «paire» but not «père.»
217 Freud, 1916b, 209.
218 IIC, 46–49.
219 IIC, 47 (emphasis hers).
220 IIC, 48.
221 IIC, 48.
222 IIC, 48.
223 See Chapter 7.
224 See Chapters 2 & 3.
225 EN, 63–64 (emphasis mine).
226 EN, 63–64 (emphasis mine).
227 EN, 64 (emphasis mine).
228 The emphasis throughout this sentence is mine.

229  IIC, 322.

230  British Baby Names, 2013.

231  SP1, 208. Dolto is referring to a notion attributed to Carl Jung (e.g., 1957/1990). Dolto met the aging Jung in Switzerland in 1957 (photo: VC2, 278), and she reflects: "Freud's eyes fainted (while) fixing Jung's [eyes] profoundly ... Will we ever know what Freud experienced at that moment and what there was in Jung of a *désir* for the death of Freud, who served as an Oedipal substitute for him? Jung didn't want to continue along Freud's line ... He wanted to leave the old father and create a school on the side" (VO, 110). She declares, "I did not know a single word of Jung's" (Nadal, 2006, 125). I believe Dolto effectively dismisses Jung's view of a rather undifferentiated infant: "Complexities of the infantile mind stem from its original identity with the prehistoric psyche. That 'original mind' is just as much present and still functioning in the child as the evolutionary stages are in the embryo" (Jung, 1957/1990, 139). For by the umbilical castration, Dolto argues, every subject is psychically unique and set to bring something new into the world. In a letter in 1962, Dolto also criticizes the idea of guessing of the sense of drawings from supposedly common unconscious experiences (VC2, 370). Then, in a letter in 1980 to Lacan, Dolto recalls how Laforgue believed Jung departed from Freud's thought and could not be considered a psychoanalyst (VC2, 668).

232  AI, 203.

233  AI, 203; also Dolto, 1985f, 8.

234  1985f, back matter (emphasis hers).

235  Dolto, 1985f, front matter.

# 9

# PASSIVITY

## Introduction

In 1986, somewhat weakened at 78 years of age, Dolto engages in some auto-biographical musings: "Maybe that is why I am so original in the eyes of my family, maybe it is these first eight months of love from this gifted young Irish girl, artistic and forsaken."[1] Yet the "eight"[2] contrasts with her report, only three pages prior, of nearly dying at "six" months when the nanny left.[3] Perhaps, Dolto adds, she is «pas conforme» because the nanny—who apparently had lost her own mother when she was young[4]—was «une marginale» whose punishment was to go to France.[5] Dolto is breathtakingly candid (yet surprisingly uncertain too) about what is indelible in her oeuvre: her early identification with that beloved caregiver.

Within a mere two pages of this note on marginality, Dolto recalls how her mother, depressed after Jacqueline's death, had identical clothes made for them: "So if she did not dress exactly like me, who was living … "[6] Dolto leaves her sentence unfinished, muting its inferable segue on identification between mothers and daughters. But in that ellipsis, do we not hear an echo of the "toys in the hand"[7]—that is, the deeply human need to follow life in order to have life? And are not both banned words—Vineuse and Jacqueline—pulsing together again, in a way, like in those early radio days?[8] For as time and space slip once more, I believe we observe just what Freud predicts: "Wish fulfilment is in the chain of intelligible waking mental acts,"[9] as "the secondary elaboration of dream-content is identified with the work of waking thought."[10] Thus, an invisible (but audible) seam cannot but bind the dream and the theory.

On 2 August 1988, waking with a burst of energy after three days in a coma, Dolto pens her letter to Béague,[11] closing it with a humble statement that may well hold the key to her whole project: «L'accueillant est dans la disponibilité et le *non-savoir*» ["The welcomer is in a state of availability and *non-knowledge*"].[12] Yet its perfect homonym—«nom savoir» ["know the name"]—seems to poignantly return (once more) that beloved Irish girl and Dolto's lifelong questions about lost names (Vineuse and the nanny's), underwritten in countless wordplays, that ground her convictions about the vitality of the phoneme. Dolto's obituary, three weeks later, honors her "simplicity and warmth," and her lifelong "oeuvre of listening."[13] And listening to Dolto, throughout her oeuvre, I believe we cannot but observe what Freud once said of himself: "There runs through my thoughts a continuous current of personal reference."[14] Therefore, Dolto teaches us to ask an invaluable new question of any theory: what is autobiographical about it?

## «Souffrance du livre»

Dolto's project is unique in elaborating the role of the mother tongue that is necessarily learned through the mother's emotional world. For affect and the mother tongue are co-inscribed in the psychical work of symbolization, as we ceaselessly engage in "communication through a silence inhabited by a pulsional tension."[15] Dolto affirms that, as infants, we are alive unconsciously: hearing and writing a phantastic story of our own survival in dreams where we are never alone. From here, as Freud put it, "past, present and future are strung together ... on the thread of the wish that runs through them."[16] And by "putting psychoanalysis at the service of biography," as Freud suggested, we thus "obtain information that could not be arrived at by other means."[17] For learning in the transference with Dolto is a passive education proffering decisive evidence that phonemes hold a potential for displacement, as "oral libido continues its relational modes lifelong, integrating itself little by little with other modes."[18]

Meanwhile, the animated silence of the archaic—that "origin of language as protective isolation"[19]—makes ironic the mother tongue, in the bittersweet game of reality that calls for our learning to speak and to self-mute: "In this phenomenon of the cry, incompatible with attention ... is inscribed an endogenic necessity to repress to obtain a certain pleasure. The pre-subject himself represses a pulsion of passive expression ... to focus his energy on an active pulsion, the cry."[20] Thus keeping silent in same stream by which we speak, we are all like Dolto's favourite statue, *La Marseillaise*, "mute and wailing."[21] And with Dolto, "psychoanalysis has taught us that desire can manifest by active pulses, but also by passive pulses."[22] Yet despite all that we learn from her, and with her, the absolutely unknowable inhabits Dolto's corpus. A French writer astutely notes, "the strange strangeness of meeting her"[23]—and the English reader new to Dolto will undoubtedly experience that strangeness.

Thus the offerings of Dolto's project are as hard to quantify as they are valuable, because the problem with Dolto is precisely what makes her so important: her opening onto the archaic. And it is by archaic means that Dolto conveys the infant's "reality": a non-time, non-space of inseparability, reversibility and passivity wherein we only hear with, as if and through an other. Dolto thereby reveals an intimate correspondence via the transference whereby we survive because we never actually leave the unconscious source of life—our receipt of a bequest and a debt without which life has no sense. So, narrating the archaic, we too encounter the big question of our little analyst, as the dilemma of existence is posed not only in, but of, childhood: we live in the service of a gift that cannot be understood, or repaid, or forgotten, or remembered.

And while biographers rarely consider their subject's first two years, Dolto's corpus shows convincingly that adult achievements are undeniably linked to infancy. Dolto's proposition contradicts the human narrative by giving, as Halmos describes it, the "place of a subject to the child,"[24] as a complex being engaged in a vibrant archaic history. Dolto remarks that, "one who has already unconsciously thought about his life without living it is very powerful ... this is the case with babies"—adding that theirs is a «souffrance du livre»[25] ["suffering of the book"; also, "suffering of being delivered"]. Dolto evokes here not only what life writes upon us, but narrativization itself as the work of infancy—of, "all until the confirmed conquest of mobility, that is, all that precedes Oedipus and that is inscribed in the unconscious, that the body assumes in lieu of being able to become conscious of it."[26]

In turn, Dolto explains, it is the loss of the right to know what he knows that prevents the development of mental life[27]—losing the right to one's story. Yet while Dolto's brilliance astounds, she always defers to patients: "Theory without examples serves nothing, whereas an example without theory can still serve."[28] She asks, "Is there any other pedagogy but that of the example?"[29] With Dolto, then, we observe theory as the site of accidental autobiography—and conversely, how archaic histories of love and suffering construct theory in «après-coup.» And of this transference of the autobiographical in the theoretical in Dolto, as Freud made clear—with himself as example, nowhere more than in his dream book—"the fact a theory is psychologically determined does not ... invalidate its truth."[30]

And yet, this notion of the transference in theory carries tremendous implications for cultural receptivity and transmission. For while a shared language offers common phonemes to the neonate, no two dreamers ever encounter even a single phoneme on the same intrapsychical terrain, so contingent is any libidinal history. Therefore, the unconscious predicts, paradoxically, the absolute unpredictability of the (hi)story of man: genius as a surprise, a sudden arrival, an interruption—and our groupings, as an inheritance of dream-work born of the language baths of our complicated childhoods, in endless ruptures that fold elliptically and compel our passive learning.

## «Cheminement»

The passive learning securable by reading Dolto is, as she predicts, operating somewhere beneath the surface of her conscious discourses. And while it is indirectly issued, it seems rather irrefutable. So we take up one more of her generous offers to daydream wildly inside her oeuvre, while it remains open to our senses. In a 2001 press release honouring the one-hundredth anniversary of l'Hôpital Armand-Trousseau, Catherine Dolto says that her mother invented a tunnel toy for her clinic, and that Salvador Dali tried to crawl through it but could not.[31] It is impossible to know why Dali sought a symbolic birth with Dolto (or in this way), but it is entirely possible that she invented such an object. For she was, as Freud said of Charcot, one whose "common sense was touched by genius."[32] Besides, Dolto believed children love passing through tunnels and tubes.[33]

Tunnels also transect Dolto's personal history, beginning with her question about death, at age four, as trains moved beneath the «passerelle» where she walked,[34] and she says she discovered the ignorance of adults.[35] It is also plausible that it would not occur to Dolto to file a patent, for she would have considered the concept ridiculously obvious, and she believed in the free exchange of ideas. As a case in point, Dolto never took out a patent for her remarkable «poupée-fleur.» A search reveals that a Barbara Clark filed a US application for a "Tunnel Toy" in 1931, to securitize a child, as "crawling into a hole is instinctive."[36] But Dolto had absolutely the contrary objective anyhow, as articulated elsewhere and everywhere: namely, to help a child to find his "path out of his tunnel."[37]

In another curious thread, Dali insisted that Millet's "Angelus," haunting him since childhood, was a baby's burial, so he fought for years to have it X-rayed and even wrote a book about it.[38] The original actually hung for years in the home of Dolto's maternal grandfather, Pierre-Eugène Secrétan, until it was sold at an auction in 1889.[39] Its new collector eventually donated it to the Louvre— where, in 1932, oddly enough, it was lacerated by a patient of Lacan's.[40] Through countless billboards, the painting still dominates nearby Barbizon, Millet's home town, in the forest of Fontainebleau, where Dolto's silent father spent his childhood. Françoise longed to visit him while he vacationed there in 1930, but did not,[41] only finding her way to Fontainebleau in 1939, to see Pichon.[42]

In Montmartre, a lovely museum, Espace Dali, lets the modern visitor witness the tremendous impact on Dali of Freud, whom Dali met in London in July 1938.[43] Among the critical objects for the Dolto reader is a giant sculpture, "The Snail and the Angel," that recalls «escargotage» ["snailing"][44]—Dolto's idiom for self-enclosing psychical development, akin to Freud's notion of "strangulated affect."[45] Also pertinent is Dali's "Profile of Time"—a melting watch, a theme he repeats in "The Persistence of Memory"—and how it is reminiscent of Dolto's childhood stress on the difficulty of knowing the exact time. We find her famous analysand, Dominique, telling Dolto during a session (likely in 1963, given the death of a pope upon which Dominique comments) how much he enjoyed a recent Dali exhibit.[46] He describes it as being full of «trous et puis des tiroirs dans les gens» ["holes and drawers in people"].[47] Amid echoes of «trousseau» that the attuned reader cannot miss, Dolto does not say if she has seen it, though he asks her. Yet her correspondence has many references to her own artwork,[48] and Dolto greatly valued art in her seminars and clinics.[49] So it is not so far-fetched to imagine her encounter with these iconic works and their transference—just as Dali was unconsciously moved by works from Dolto's landscape. Further, not knowing for sure if Dolto kept or changed that patient's name,[50] one notes from a perusal of the public record on Dali that it is twice his name: Salvador Domingo Felipe Jacinto Dalí i Domènech.

One hardly knows what to say about this weaving between Dolto and Dali. It is a coincidence only if one believes in such, but Dolto does not.[51] Dolto also believes about art that, "like a dream, it is a witness of the unconscious"[52]—a vehicle for the transference of latent content.[53] And from the local history of Montmartre, one learns that Espace Dali is geographically situated precisely on the first site of the *Maison Blanche*—the asylum that relocated next to Dolto's family at the turn of the century, from where it influenced her childhood and career.[54] So the effect of Espace Dali on the Dolto reader is uncanny indeed.

A somewhat related experience can be found in the Jardin du Ranelagh, whose most famous object is the statue of Jean de la Fontaine. Erected in 1985, it features a full-bodied Lafontaine looking down on a crow giving a fox a big coin.[55] Yet prior to it stood an earlier version (from 1891), which is the one young Françoise actually saw daily.[56] So a visitor familiar with Dolto has the odd impression of a reversal in time—as if the statue's revision were influenced by her "symbolic payment."[57] Dolto is correct, then: knowing the exact time is difficult in Paris.

## «Co-moi papa-maman»

The truth is that our learning with Dolto is hard to quantify and not easy to describe. Rather than yielding distinct points that might be added to a biographical database about Dolto, our education through Dolto's texts is an experience working deep inside an emotional register. It is also a subtle but indispensable example of the transference between seemingly disjoint subjects that confirms the unconscious transits beneath the surface of our conscious discourses—precisely what Dolto theorizes as "latent speech." So learning with Dolto is a fine example of our passive education and the fundamental role that words play in it. For our daydreams upon the phonemes in Dolto's corpus become testimonials of the play at the origins of thought; the indispensable role of affect in the registration of significance; the unconscious movements beneath the conscious discourse of not only proximal but distal individuals (through texts); and the absolute atemporality and aspatiality of words.

Dolto's construction of the infant in the archaic stage, as we can ascertain it now, is that of a full subject in continuity with an other in a non-time, non-space, where dreams are spun upon what arrives. And her foremost concern for instinctual life founds her radically liberating view: «C'est le foetus qui demande à naître» ["It is the fetus that asks to be born"].[58] Dolto has no need of an apologist, and she is the first to admit: "I don't write in a literary sense."[59] But if we can get beyond her words, or rather in front of them, I believe that we can finally begin to fathom the precocity of the subject position at stake in Dolto's conception of the archaic—that there is "life anterior to primary narcissism."[60] And yet, in the absence of boundaries for the «pré-moi,» the co-narcissistic state remains perplexing. Freud admits the difficulty of hypothesizing on primary narcissism, given "the importance and extensiveness of the topic,"[61] and calls his own work, "remarks ... somewhat loosely strung together."[62]

Summatively, Dolto evokes an undifferentiated, un-split, passive pre-subject: a «co-moi papa-maman» ["co-me father-mother"][63]—the mother coupled with the father and with their child[64]—for whom there is no object that is not part of the self. With Dolto, then, we are narrating the very onset of object relations wherein, as Freud explains it, "to find the object, however, is, in truth, to rediscover it."[65] The archaic's "subtle objects"[66]—sounds, including phonemes—are fluid and reversible too. They arrive in echoes that become paths to be followed, reversibly, to the dream as much as to reality—rooting our lifelong (passive) capacity for the transference. Further, the «pré-moi» begins symbolizing while without vision, without an active mode and without any distinct subjectivity. What the «pré-moi» enjoys, instead, is a primordial «rhythme binaire»[67]—an unconscious movement of presence and absence—informing the fetal environment. Put another way, human life begins as a dream of discourse with an enigmatic witness in service of the wish to live. And this unconscious discourse is the source of our «sécurité intérieur,»[68] our affective history. We are, I believe, in the wake of Freud's pertinent comment on, "the desire to go to sleep where one has slept in childhood."[69]

Of course, Dolto's elaboration of a subject that is constructed through an other—which expresses nothing other than the dominance of oral passivity during the development of primary narcissism—nonetheless hugely complicates what we mean by an object. For any object, however physical, has inseparable, unconscious symbolic significance (associated dream-work) that is idiosyncratic for one's prehistory. With Dolto, then, we arrive at a narration of primary narcissism as a state of nascent environmental impingements spun into dream-work, whereby what is affectively securing in reality (by being continuous with the archaic) acquires value in luring. And as Dolto makes clear, the most fluid, precocious, ubiquitous, repetitive—and, therefore, most likely—mediating objects (lures) for our coming to reality are phonemes.

With Dolto, I submit that we can also discern here the nascent super-ego, in the critical tasks that agency performs in developing a human secure in the world: the censorship of dreams, the capacity for auto-observation and the ideal of the self[70] that is also a "similar." And as our archaic prehistory is lived in dream-work, Dolto theorizes that it is enough to phantasize a witness. For this unconscious experience imparts a revitalizing affect of love that owes its potent origins to each human being's archaic transference situation. In turn, I suggest that we are speaking here of what Freud once called, the "incomparable strength of the first affective ties of human creatures,"[71] and the "perennial first inclinations" of dream-life.[72]

## Sublimation

I believe it is extremely helpful in comprehending infancy on Doltoian grounds to recall the value to primary narcissism of "the principle of inertia."[73] Freud expands:

> By being born we have made the step from an absolutely self-sufficient narcissism to the perception of a changing external world and the beginnings of the discovery of objects … We cannot endure the new state of things for long, [so] that we periodically revert from it, in our sleep, to our former condition of absence of stimulation and avoidance of objects.[74]

Significantly, then, object use is not comfortable at first—not until sensory modalities are sufficiently developed to enable the experience of pleasure from the side of reality (assuming it is offered).[75] For the infant, as Freud says, "sleep is his natural condition, from which he is roused only by his bodily needs. As soon as these are satisfied he falls asleep again … [and] continues his fetal state."[76] Thus the infant encounters any offer to perception (including proprioception) as an impingement—and any object he manages to use (insofar as it is invested by the transference) serves an unconscious phantasy (ironically) of the non-use of that object. It follows that the use of any object in reality will be facilitated by its closest possible relation to one's idiosyncratic phantasies. Only with maturation is there a slow migration to objects with a lesser share of phantasy, along a trail of crumbs made progressively faint by associative distance.

I submit that it is at this point that thinking through Dolto's project will bring us to an unexpected encounter with the notion of sublimation that Freud first elaborated in the context of da Vinci[77]—a concept of staggering significance to psychobiography as the vicissitudes of the pulses. As rightly noted in a dictionary of Dolto's terms, sublimation and symbolization are "close terms in the thinking of F. Dolto," linked to symboligenic castration and the displacement of aims as the capacity for "archaic pleasure to be surpassed."[78] From 1940, Dolto theorizes on sublimation as, "the utilization of libido in social activities tolerated or stimulated by the exterior world";[79] whereas "if sublimations are insufficient … there will be a tension that anxiety translates."[80] Freud explains:

> If this displaceable energy is desexualized libido, it may also be described as sublimated energy … If thought processes in the wider sense are to be included among these displacements, then the activity of thinking is also supplied from the sublimation of erotic motive forces.[81]

We pause to ponder the watershed that opens between Freud and Dolto: as the inheritor of dream-work, thinking is sublimation.

Thus, the phoneme, as a mediator for the transference, has an integral role in the process of developing culturally valorized (or at least tolerated) sublimations, as Dolto narrates:

> The mother initiates him [infant] to social life. It is this alternation in the desire to communicate, satisfied by presence and unsatisfied by absence, but from then awaited and phantasized, if I might say, followed sooner or later by the return to satisfaction of seeing the refound mother. This is what organizes in a code of language the possibilities that we are well obliged to call the *sublimation of oral pulses of desire*: because it is desire as it is organized in orality that finds there the roots of humanization, that is to say that the symbolic function is put in service of the communication of desires between human beings.[82]

Successful sublimations thus mark the subject with the capacity for fluidly displacing libido onto appropriate socio-cultural objects—including words—as environmentally contingent affective investments, thereby optimizing economic efficiencies. Freud explains sublimation in terms of primary narcissism, and he theorizes that sublimation functions to "unite and link."[83] Then again, why should we be surprised to discover that the infant is predisposed by the primary processes—under the dominion of the instinct of conservation—to precocious learning about the best means of receiving affect (i.e., surviving) in a given time-place (family, culture, nation, etc.)?

As Dolto explains it further, a subject has "a symbolic link with no one if no one knows his history or can speak it."[84] Thus parents, "hold the treasure of liberating words,"[85] and a child is "most vulnerable if he cannot get answers to his questions."[86] Again and again—evoking the difficulty of getting answers to her own early questions about death—Dolto stresses the importance to any child of being told the truth, even about his suffering.[87] She elaborates:

> Prevention ... is not to spare a child from suffering ... It is to put words on that from which he suffers, and recognize his right to suffer from it, and that we recognize with compassion that he suffers from it. But not to spare him from it, making a zone of shadow on his suffering. This will provoke a trauma that will leave a trace ... If we give him the right to suffer from the absence of his mother, we give him the right to also accept that another suffers, and that suffering is a part of humanization.[88]

It follows that Dolto is deeply concerned for the deaf: "The most phobic and most persecuted is a deaf child."[89] She will spend half her Lego prize helping deaf children,[90] remarking fondly how, from her window on Saint-Jacques, she could hear recesses at the Institute for the Deaf.[91]

I believe that Dolto is narrating the insertion of each human being into history. And from her acute valuing of words in mediating reality comes her strongest, most repeated messages: desire is a call to inter-human communication;[92] we only exist because we are linked to others in words,[93] and what is spoken soothes.[94] She quips: "Psychotherapy begins in the morning, when you live alone, when you speak to the news seller."[95] As ever, her "simple" words port phenomenal complexity: humans unconsciously securitize through a continuous passive process operating via language. Therefore, as Dolto makes patent, we arrive at subjectivity as humans only through our symbolic relations:

> The human being ... is animated without discontinuity since his birth by the symbolic function, specific to the human being. What he perceives of the interior—functional needs of his organism, that seek appeasement, and desires of his psyche, in search of communication and exchange with others—is articulated with what, perceived as coming from the exterior world, is apprehended by him as a call or as a response of others to his desire. These two sources of perception, coming from him and coming from others, weave themselves like warp and weft.[96]

## «Poupée-fleur»

In this context of deceptive simplicity dissembling remarkable complexity, I confess that when I first began reading Dolto, I believed the «poupée-fleur»[97] to be a secondary construct in her theorization—a secondary revision, as it were, of the dream-work I felt to be in circulation. But I was grievously mistaken. For the «poupée-fleur» is invaluable and central to understanding Dolto's creativity—as well as being a notion with traces to her own and her grandmother's middle name, Marguerite,[98] in the most authentic signature imaginable. So its current non-use in therapeutic work seems like a blatant overlooking of what Roudinesco calls Dolto's "prodigious clinical genius."[99]

Dolto invented the «poupée-fleur» to help Bernadette,[100] whom she met in November 1946. In one of its first issues after eight years of idle presses (1940–1948), the prestigious *Revue française de psychanalyse* includes Dolto's elaboration of her «poupée-fleur» as a means of transference for oral-stage affects.[101] The «poupée-fleur» also made an entrance at the 16e Congrès international de psychanalyse, in May 1949, in Zurich.[102] In a letter that same month to Philipp Sarasin, its Secretary, Dolto elaborates her «hypothèse» in detail:

> [This representation] provokes ... a projection onto this object of pregenital libido relating to affects lived during the epoch of the oral stage ... [for] a beneficial abreaction of oral libido that had remained pathogenic. Subjects for whom repressions lived in subsequent stages led to states of libidinal regression to pregenital stages react likewise ... [as] the disappearance of the anxiety pertaining to repressed oral-stage pulses immediately permits

the subject to address and abreact libido in pathological translations pertaining to the anal stage ... The advantage is, for the psychoanalysis of
children, the possibility of treatment in depth requiring only sessions that
are very far apart, and for the psychoanalysis of certain adults, the possibility of unblocking those who are ... incapable of directly expressing in the
transference the aggressive or 'love-interest' states of the affects of pregenital stages, characterized by the absence of logic.[103]

The «poupée-fleur» made other appearances that same year: at the SPP's 12th
annual conference on 4–5 June 1949;[104] at a meeting of the SPP on 18 October
1949;[105] and in the treatment of Nicole.[106]

The «poupée-fleur» is also mentioned in observations of ten others,[107] such as
seven-year-old Monique, for whom the «poupée-fleur» restores continence.[108]
Dolto issues prescriptions for it (with a sketch) to mothers presenting with a
child refusing food.[109] And turning to a local workshop, she has some produced
for her consultations,[110] whereby the «poupée-fleur» revives libidinal history,[111]
returns dreams and useful aggression[112] and enables patients to work on
integration.[113] It will also be used in Dolto's work with schizophrenics in asylums
for 10–15 years, "liberating affects tethered to oral-stage libidinal investments," to
achieve "unblocking" as, "thanks to the mediation of this object, they could
refind anew, going from themselves to this other, the alternating affects of emotional participation and of projection, affects that characterize personal rapports
beginning at the oral stage."[114] There is a normal need for aggression to be
invested at the oral stage, Dolto explains[115]—one that is impossible to satisfy
when met in reality with reactions of "painful aggression."[116]

Characteristically self-effacing, however, Dolto remarks: "This hypothesis is
perhaps not worth much."[117] And 15 years later, arguably the best articulation
of the «poupée-fleur» is published in the margins of her field by a pharmaceut-
ical company.[118] Then, in November 1985, nearly 40 years from the beginnings
of the «poupée-fleur» (but near the end of her own life), Dolto offers the
powerful note in a letter, that the "emotional non-reactivity" of the psychoanalyst is what achieves the "reactualization of events unknown or forgotten in his
(hi)story."[119] At SPP proceedings, Dolto names the gain as, «l'effet poupée-
fleur,»[120] adding simply that "it is usable."[121] For the «poupée-fleur» allows the
projection of "illogical affects."[122] It is also a fact that Dolto saw countless free
drawings in clinic, as children "indicated a projection of their narcissism in representations of flowers or vegetal forms."[123] The «poupée-fleur» had, in effect,
arrived in overdetermination.

Among the innumerable finds in Dolto's corpus, then, the «poupée-fleur» is, as
Muriel Djéribi-Valentin rightly notes, "one of her most stunning clinical
inventions."[124] It works in the intermediate zone between reality and phantasy, and
its design is specific: it has "no face, no hands, no feet, no back, no front,"[125] being
vegetal green with the corolla at eye level and at least seven petals.[126] I submit that
the «poupée-fleur» is functionally a kind of "always me," mediating the transference

in a regression to a perpetually findable, indestructible archaic history. And what is most operational with the «poupée-fleur» is that the object is never being destroyed, thereby addressing narcissistic injuries at the oral stage[127]—for those who are, as Dolto puts it, stuck in profound regressive symptoms.[128]

Interestingly, at the SPP meeting of 18 October 1949, Lacan took to the «poupée-fleur» quickly, elaborating on the value of its having, "no face, neither hands nor feet, neither face nor back, no articulation, no neck."[129] So we dream for a moment on Lacan's «cou» ["neck"], a perfect homonym of «coup» ["hit," or "cut"]. It is a word-play of some significance given that Lacan's theorization would provide emphasis to Freud's concept of *nachträghlichkeit*, the «après-coup»—interestingly, from the 1950s onward.[130]

## Phonemization

Dolto and Lacan are captured in an iconic photograph in 1963 that implies a parallel view[131]—even, a "theoretical couple."[132] And nowhere is the issue of Dolto's elusive legacy greater than with respect to Jacques Lacan. Lacan apparently told Dolto: "You don't need to understand what I am saying, because without theorizing, you say the same thing as me."[133] Their letters are warm and friendly, and her correspondence includes his frequent thanks for her presents.[134] Lacan apparently even sent Dolto a few of his difficult cases.[135] In fact, Dolto was «l'interlocutrice de Jacques Lacan» for many years,[136] and their historical overlap proved highly fertile for both of them. So I believe it is more sensitive to their complex relation to consider the pair widely known as «petit et grand dragon,»[137] as what Catherine calls them instead: «compagnons de route.»[138]

Dolto appreciated Lacan's efforts to dissolve linguistic rules—his independent spirit. Lacan's interventions were crucial, Dolto declares, because psychoanalytic researchers "did not pay enough attention, before him, to words and their meaning for the child's unconscious prior to reading and writing."[139] Dolto credits Lacan's capacity for «un régistre d'abstraction,»[140] and for generating great interest in psychoanalysis.[141] And consistently throughout her oeuvre, Dolto trusts Lacan's students as good listeners of children,[142] who appreciate «les plans archaïques.»[143] She also believes that only Lacan's analysands can understand what is "anterior to Oedipus."[144] So she addresses Lacanians directly: "I think that those among you who understand Lacan's formulations on the name-of-the-father will find in it what I have said about the archaic prior to phonemization and writing."[145] In Dolto's own words, she was "pro-Lacan," but "not Lacanian."[146]

Nonetheless, their views are far apart, and Dolto was unafraid to resist Lacan: "When Lacan thinks that the child … is pleased to see his own image in the mirror, and that this structures his unitariness, he is wrong. This experience is a surprise, always with the effect of an estrangement, sometimes inducing phobia, splitting."[147] Further, she vehemently opposed his efforts to close the EFP, when he issued a mock public notice on 5 January 1980 announcing the "death of the unconscious."[148] In sum, Dolto believed that Lacan erred in two ways: in thinking that everything can be put into words, while there are "auditory supports that are rhythmed and colored ... that have no words ... pulses that are non-verbalized ... and non-verbalizable"[149]—and in trying to master pulses intellectually.[150]

But perhaps no difference between them is more evident than his belief that algorithms relate to the transference. Lacan states: "The transference—I hope to approach it next time—will introduce us directly to the algorithms that I thought necessary to set out in practice."[151] Though I am not well-versed in Lacan, his approach seems to follow (from) his belief that, "the unconscious is structured like a language."[152] Yet Dolto's project affirms just the opposite: the unconscious defies structure. For Dolto confirms that language production is indelibly inscribed by the unconscious, and language reception is susceptible to being unpredictably deconstructed by it. Thus the unconscious eludes any systematization—even the distinction of presence or absence.

Not only does the transference guarantee the subversion of any narrative, but the unconscious processes at play also predict that what arrives will (must) surprise by a mismatch with respect to intention. Here we take as counterexamples Lacan's terms, such as «parlêtre»[153] and «lituraterre.»[154] His game of calculated disorthography,[155] as Soler calls it—or what Roudinesco considers, "a game of words, calculated lapsus"[156]—is a rich stimulus for thought. Dolto's good friend Alain Cuny plays this game too. Writing to Dolto on «samedi 20» ["Saturday the 20th"], he toys with the date's phonemes: «ça me dit: vain?» ["it tells me: vain?"]; and «ça me divin» [roughly, "it makes me divine"].[157] He also names his new home, «Savon noir» ["Black soap"]—in a deliberate inversion of «non-savoir» ["non-knowledge"].[158] But all these interesting counterexamples are conscious—not *un*conscious—play. In contrast, what goes on with the phoneme unconsciously is something entirely other of which we seldom become consciously aware without a laborious analysis, as this project attempts.

Of course, beyond Lacan and Cuny, languaged relations with Dolto cannot but have affected other French notables of her time—including her patients, Georges Perec (a writer)[159] and Jacques Audiberti (a playwright)[160]—or French citizens from all walks of life, some of whom were children when Dolto was in her prime. As a case in point, I respectfully submit that the work of the well-regarded psychoanalyst Olivier Douville is a superb example of how French psychoanalysis has been functioning for almost a century in a (largely unacknowledged) Doltoian climate. Douville (b. 1953) writes about «subjectivation,»[161] «phobies archaïques»[162] and «présentification»[163]—as well as the "institution of the name."[164] He sees in his Paris clinic eight-year-old Cumba, whose mutism he partly attributes to a failed "game of translations,"[165] and whose position in his office is (twice) described in reference to the "angle" of the wall.[166] Then, in a single sentence, he speaks of a «trou,» a «tiers,» the «passerelle» to the mother and "naming."[167] Perhaps the misreading is only my daydream, as I cannot help but hear Dolto everywhere now. But how is it possible *not* to hear Dolto in his citations? Yet like in countless texts by others, her name is entirely absent. For the nurturing alimentation of thought provided by Dolto has been assimilated inadvertently for decades by so many.

## «Du vécu»

Yet even while attempting summative reflections on a few treasures of Dolto's oeuvre, we come upon a new conundrum. On the one hand, words are mediating objects for the transference: i.e., words can incite dream-work. On the other hand, the watery edifice of primary narcissism is founded on the principle of inertia: i.e., the least expenditure of energy, the better. In sum, drive theory predicts that we will resist abandoning any libidinal position that satisfies. Freud explains it perfectly: "The mental apparatus is first and foremost a device for mastering the excitations that would otherwise be felt as distressing or have a pathogenic effect";[168] so "a sexual aim ... consists in replacing the projected sensation of stimulation in the erotogenic zone by an external stimulus which removes that sensation by producing a feeling of satisfaction."[169]

But the act of reading, as we now understand it with Dolto, is a provocation to dream-work that may entail a libidinal expenditure. No wonder, then, that reading resistance (or refusal) is a common educational problem—and that Dolto herself wanted to unlearn reading as a child.[170] Freud himself once remarked that, "reading is a terrible infliction imposed upon all who write."[171] Yet it is paradoxically also true, Freud notes, that "the universal and indispensable attribute of all instincts ... [is] their capacity for initiating movement"[172]—i.e., there is a "need of the unconscious for liberation."[173] For as reality inevitably encroaches, introducing environmental impingements, the resulting anxiety has to find a means of release. So there is a necessity to vent affect as, "the subjective translation of a quantity of pulsional energy."[174] And what Dolto reveals is that this need is so essential to our survival that a primary mechanism ensures its endurance lifelong, unconsciously, passively: the transference.

It is this fundamentally contradictory tension between inertia and circulation that will mark every human being's psychical life. With Freud, we also recall that dreams follow old facilitations,[175] and in an affective state, facilitation prevails.[176] For economic reasons, then, we will port investments using well-worn pathways proliferating since our prehistory. So we will naturally be lured by unconscious identifications that are continuous with those facilitations—our symbolic filiations. It is only slowly and progressively (if all goes well) that migrations of affective investments will move us towards reality, as Freud said over a century ago: "Conscious systems of thought ... are merely projections ... translations ... from the unknown, unconscious."[177]

I offer that this is why, and how, the phoneme's archaic investments are so critical: they open (facilitate) site-means of partial identification in continuity (filiation). Freud cites a patient: "'If anyone speaks, it gets light.' What he was afraid of was not the dark, but the absence of someone he loved; and he could feel sure of being soothed as soon as he had evidence of that person's presence."[178] Therefore, recalling that wishful activation produces the same result as a perception,[179] echoes of invested phonemes serve unconscious identifications to relieve that most primal human anxiety—unsurvivable, abject solitude ("no one comes").

Further, in fusion, the indissociable «semblable» is securitizing. With Dolto, then, it seems we are teasing out the phantastic origins of projection. And since it is governed by the pleasure principle, perhaps the primitive "learning" of projection stalls if there is precocious severing—the loss of the "similar" enabling progression from fusion (that phantastic co-living with, thus ready finding of a "similar"). The sequelae compel regression (even fixation) to a prior, more passive libidinal position. Yet as wishful activation is securable along facilitations, the phoneme always retains the capacity to return affect (archaic love). Thus the transference in texts enables a kind of ersatz projection. Thanks to Dolto, therefore, I believe that we can formulate a new theory of reading wherein the transference in texts serves the process of identification, as Freud notes: "The original form of emotional tie with the object ... may arise with any new perception of a common quality shared ... The more important this common quality is, the more successful may this partial identification become."[180]

Further, given that diffusion and diffraction open associative pathways for the transference, as Dolto shows, I submit that we can also infer something about the viability of identifications securable from the mediation of phonemes. It is that archaic echoes will prevail in the corpus of a beloved author, in a treasured story retold in multiple versions and even in our own disremembered scripts. Of course, the closer to one's reality any identification is, the shorter the road to sublimations. It will be easier, in other words, to migrate archaic investments to reality if our identifications are to humans (rather than animals, objects or fictions), and close to our own space-time (age, culture, geography, etc.). Thus, it is an understatement that reading influences structuration. And using Dolto's life-as-metaphor, it is in the "father's library" where, browsing passively, we can refind «repères»—the particular landmarks to which our precocious symbolization leaves us susceptible.

Dolto's notion of the script-girl also affirms the great merits of writing with, as if or through someone—on the same page, even across a gap of space-time. It is biography as continuation, as Dolto theorizes in the clinic: "The most authentic drawings are drawn on a surface already valorized by «du vécu» ["some lived"]."[181] For Dolto reveals writing to be a sponsor of dream-work that enables reading to make offers to the present, stratifying life on the already-lived—offering the most intimate identification with that enigmatic first witness, the other of primitive life. Like writing out dreams, then, biography is writing with a phantasy of a witness that makes dream-work preconscious on a terrain for exchange—a "passage for discharge,"[182] as Freud described it—as the transference is called upon, investing words as objects for thought. So the "write to think" returns the "right to think." And it is radically curative because witnessing archaic echoes makes reality feel safe. So by the transference, Freud says poignantly, "our cures are cures of love."[183]

## Desire

Dolto teaches us to attend to what is inscribed upon us in a cadence of dreaming—to how, "under the same words, each put[s] his personal experience that [is] different from that of the other,"[184] as a "human being draws from the force that filters through words."[185] And as Dolto elaborates regression to autism, she also reveals autism *as* regression: "The child needs, to assure his narcissism, a return to the securitizing base image of the body during new disappointing experiences that life procures him."[186] Further, since the transference is what exits us from infantile regression, Dolto is optimistic about recovery from autism: "All that is living is still living in language."[187] Movingly—in unspoken returns of Vineuse—Dolto adds that the observant child, "refinds roads and retains names."[188] In fact, Dolto finds so many inroads into theory that a whole new continent is discovered, as she ironically goes, "forward in a region she called 'the archaic.'"[189] So doing, Dolto underwrites the human story with a living source in the unconscious, and a means of securing reality that permits our survival by «voies» ["voices" or "paths"] of language, via the transference traversing words—mediating objects transporting and ensuring continuity with fetal audition in echo, as memorials of witnessing in a past that is ever-present.[190]

Throughout her oeuvre, Dolto makes the compelling point that while autism entails a difficulty with engaging the social actively, the autistic subject still has a potent capacity for learning, because "in passivity the child is extremely receptive, even if he is not very expressive."[191] Dolto maintains that through the securitizing witnessing of an other, even in phantasy, subjects with autism can progress, *"by living out slowly an out-of-date phase,"*[192] typically experienced in infancy, thus gradually venting affect and waking up—i.e., coming to reality.

In a relatively new genre of literature,[193] persons with autism with the capacity to write (often, by one-finger typing)—though rarely the ability to speak—share poetical texts that inadvertently confirm Dolto's propositions:

> The autistic child, for example, that is the child who looks at nothing, hears everything. He only seems to be elsewhere, and it is that which is troubling and that results, finally, in our speaking about them without addressing ourselves to their person ... We must never believe that the subject is not in full lucidity, even when the individual who is there, present, seems besotted, sleepy or even comatose.[194]

Each autistic scribe also discloses self-awareness that demuting has depended on an other, as Dolto predicts, "from which he can construct an interior unity that allows him to speak in his name, wherever he finds himself, even if it is in a manner that does not satisfy the neighbors."[195]

Dolto's understanding of autism enables the summation that whatever causes the rupture of symbolic filiation, the condition is primarily a problem of anxiety originating during the development of primary narcissism. This precocious anxiety becomes more difficult to manage economically with the inevitable progression of perception and proprioception. The result is a predisposition to regression as a defense—in Freud's words, "sleep as a defense against the external world."[196] In turn, a regressive psychical state manifests as a dependence for direction—a living for, with and through an other—that is observable in autists as a difficulty initiating action, and as a need for phantasies of being something (or someone) other. This psychical passivity is a paradoxical counterpoint to the physical aggressivity that results from the accumulation of intolerable anxiety; the inability to properly vent affect (largely due to being relatively non-verbal); and the concomitant conscious suffering of the deprivation of choice (frustration). The autistic person thus sustains an elaborate phantasy life conferring security that, ironically, diminishes affective investments in reality. Dolto thereby helps us predict that autists, seeking communicative relations but being phobic and often psychogenically (nearly) mute, will precociously (without assistance) learn to read—taking in words passively.[197]

Dolto composes one of her most classically cryptic descriptions to explain developmental mutism as an unfortunate accident of circumstance that introduces gaps in symbolic continuity that lead to a regression to autism to refind security. Doing so, she articulates from the nebulous edge of the sayable, as if struggling from an archaic silence of her own just to speak:

> Desire continues its route that develops itself as a spiral with an expansive dynamic movement through that which ... is growth and multiplication, by adjunction-disjunction-elimination, that relational life symbolizes in expressive language in its continual *mutance*[,] fruits of its partitions. This desire, when its dynamic is immured in its isolation instead of continuing in its expansive destiny, sees the spiral inflect its movement, enroll upon itself and, after phantasmatic consumptions of structures of the anterior *moi* that have become ersatz exterior elements, encyst language and the symbolic function inherent in human desire, making him scission his own potentialities taken for an elsewhere and invert, without ever ceasing, if nothing comes from the exterior of this individual to break the vicious cycle.[198]

Dolto considers the child to be highly vulnerable during the encroachment of reality: Any break in time with regards to loved persons ... [or] secure places known since birth, but especially between the age of three months and ... confirmed deliberate walking, is a rupture of the securitizing sensorium that is foundational for narcissism.[199] On Dolto's view, then, the autistic subject is one who suffers from an incomplete (or insufficient) insertion into space-time. She expands on autism in a signature passage offering a summation of her beliefs:

> Desire for interpsychic communication is the fundamental desire that above and beyond any demand for sensory objects of pleasure for the body is essential to the human being ... The link that unites them beyond their separation is an ensemble of signs that, little by little, elaborates itself in language ... Elective affinities between human beings derive from these perceptions, holders of subtle accords between them, that make them recognize each other as *semblables* and at the same time constantly new and never totally knowable.[200]

## Apprenticeship

On 11 April 1927, when she is 18 (Jacqueline's age at her death)—while on holiday in Deauville with Mlle (the nanny hired for Jacques' birth) and little Jacques (then five, when Dolto learned to read)—Dolto pens another letter to her mother.[201] A footnote remarks that the next day, 12 April, Jacqueline's birthday, will be commemorated by a mass.[202] In that piece of correspondence, Dolto muses on the title of Maeterlinck's *Les sentiers dans la montagne*: "I do not yet understand why this title. Does this mean that all these reflections on these very diverse subjects are like roads that lead to the knowledge of things, and that get nearer to the truth?"[203] Her quote, 60 years before her death, is an uncanny summation (or is it a prediction?) of the unlikely road Dolto will lead us on, as random reflections on diverse subjects get us nearest to the truth, in an availability to Dolto's latent speech—and fragrances, hints of theory, appear years ahead of time.

Through the transference in texts that is not only theorizable but demonstrable in her corpus, Dolto challenges the normative bias towards rationality to tender the powerful suggestion that associative thinking is an enduring human resource. Thus, with Dolto, we elaborate that revelation of Freud's inaugurating the 20th Century: "What is essential in dreams is the process of the dream-work."[204] For using dream-work, the archaic offers securitizing identifications in our coming to reality, via the passive movement of affect circulating continuously between us in the transferential diffusion inherent in our languaged relations—and that circulation is fundamental to good psychical health. So Dolto's project conveys the clear message that we are each conscious only because of our capacity to remain continuous with our unconscious origins. Or, as Dolto puts it in her own inimitable way: "The unconscious process of survival is to consume a partial object coming from another who represents the mother."[205]

Here, Oedipus unexpectedly returns on his riddle—symbolic of the unsaid and unspeakable of human history—as the question of origins becomes a problem of translation between the neighboring lands we all traverse: reality and phantasy. So psychoanalysis reveals a radical truth that resounds in Dolto's project: *the infant is intensely susceptible to psychical suffering.* Melancholy thus informs our unconscious heritage because, as Freud says, "satisfaction must have been previously experienced in order to have left behind a need for its repetition"[206]—recalling little Josette. The vital corollary is that whatever archaic objects secured us before can secure us again:

> The apprenticeship of the enriching or impoverishing solitude of languaged and creative means is thus linked on the one hand to the good first relation with the first guardianship, necessarily co-corporal, the mother or the same nurse, [and] on the other hand, to the inauguration and the installation, thanks to the imitation of the mother, in communication with an other than the baby (a third); languaged substitutes of means of communication, already installed in the presence of the mother in the body-to-body and the languaged exchanges with familiars associated in memory to the mother, with the other of this first other (who became such due to the fact of partition), permitting communication beyond absence and the obtaining of pleasures known, recognized and new.[207]

Dolto's project compels us to grasp that the word not only escapes any conscious story but precedes it, entering into its own free associations. Thus, reality is only ever a later edition of space-time where forgotten objects arrive unpredictably, in an uncanny circularity wherein object relations are always shored up by unconscious affects in continuity with the archaic.

There is also the inevitability of the return of lost objects to which we will remain resonant lifelong. By this, education inherits a peculiar complication in that every moment of learning is incalculable—using randomity, interruptions and silence. So the social seems strikingly collapsible: a dilemma of meaning-making from unnarratable psychical work that introduces hazards and gains we never register consciously, yet that impact our possibilities for living economically—venting rather than suffering. For Dolto demonstrates that our passive education will make our accidents into meaning, and vice-versa. And the very fact that the word is tethered to dream-work means that there is always more dream-work that the word can do.

## Notes

1 EN, 65.
2 For the prevalence of «huit,» see Chapter 8.
3 EN, 62; see Chapter 4.
4 EN, 64; Ribowski, 1987/2004.
5 EN, 118.
6 EN, 120.
7 See Chapter 6.
8 See Chapter 6.

9 Freud, 1900a, 122.
10 Freud, 1900b, 499.
11 See Chapter 7.
12 VC2, 899 (emphasis hers); also VC2, xxix.
13 Ina.fr, 1988.
14 Freud, 1901b, 24.
15 Dolto in Nasio, 1987/1998, 210.
16 Freud, 1908a, 148; also, 1900a, 184, 1900b, 621.
17 1930, 212.
18 SS, 269.
19 CD, 192.
20 JD, 284.
21 EN, 37.
22 ES, 14.
23 Dubois, 1994.
24 Halmos, 2000, 33–35.
25 Ribowski, 1987/2004.
26 VC2, 640.
27 CE, 265.
28 SP3, 8.
29 VC2, 540.
30 Freud, 1913, 179.
31 C. Dolto, 2001.
32 Freud, 1893c, 9, 1961, 196.
33 EF, 12.
34 EN, 10.
35 AI, 94f.
36 IFI Claims Patent Service, 2012.
37 Dolto, 1989c, 17; also C. Dolto & Faure-Poirée, 2008, 37.
38 AI, 248.
39 AI, 248.
40 AI, 248.
41 PF, 29 & 31.
42 VC2, 26.
43 Douville, 2009, 178.
44 E.g., Dolto, 1985f; SS, 220.
45 Freud, 1893d, 39, 1909b, 18, 1914c, 156.
46 CD, 155.
47 CD, 155.
48 E.g., AI, 120–121; PF, 26; VC1, 165, 192, 238 & 246.
49 E.g., APP; see Chapter 7.
50 See Chapter 4.
51 DW, 25; SS, 99 & 113; VC2, 495.
52 SS, 116.
53 VC2, 447.
54 Murat, 2001/2013.
55 AI, 94.
56 The first featured Lafontaine's bust, a woman with wings and clouds, a child with wings, animals, wheat and a crow with cheese in his mouth (Association le Musée Jean de la Fontaine, n.d.)—a saturation of orality.
57 ATP, 196; CE, 371; DW, 139; SS, 124 & 125f; TL, 112; VC2, 890.
58 SP1, 225.
59 AI, 217; VC2, 796.
60 SP1, 76.

61 Freud, 1914b, 100.
62 1914b.
63 EM, 39.
64 SP1, 215.
65 1907, 87; also, 1907, 108.
66 PS, 21–22 & 89; SP1, 61; SP3, 128.
67 CE, 94, 257 & 350; DQ, 70; IIC, 90; PJE, 105.
68 SP1, 215–217.
69 1907, 156.
70 Laplanche & Pontalis, 1967/2004, 471–473.
71 Freud, 1930, 209.
72 1930, 209.
73 1895, 296–297.
74 1921, 130; also, 1914b, 83 & 92.
75 As Dolto elaborates it, every object acquires (or rather, inherits) its significance in symbolic filiation with its predecessor, such that by reduction (but not to absurdity), every object is returned unconsciously to the archaic. With Freud, we also confirm that "identification is the earliest and original form of emotional tie … where the mechanisms of the unconscious are dominant, [and] object-choice is turned back into identification" (1921, 107); put another way, "during the state of narcissism, they [object-libido and ego-libido] exist together" (1914b, 76; also, 1914c, 82). The child's development makes it possible to observe his archaic heritage in his use of real objects—and the return of any object (across associative distances) to the monad of self-love, paradoxically to no objects: "The child takes himself as object of love prior to choosing external objects … of which intra-uterine life is the archetype" (Freud in Laplanche & Pontalis, 1967/2004, 264). Thus, any object from the side of reality is best conceived as an offer to perception (including proprioception), constituting what Freud described as, "disturbances to which a child's original narcissism is exposed, the reactions with which he seeks to protect himself from them, and the paths into which he is forced in doing so" (1914c, 92).
76 Freud, 1907, 222.
77 Freud, 1910b; Laplanche & Pontalis, 1967/2004, 148.
78 Ledoux, 2006, 326–327.
79 MA, 19.
80 MA, 20.
81 Freud, 1923, 45.
82 JD, 283 (emphasis hers).
83 Laplanche & Pontalis, 1967/2004, 466.
84 EM, 278.
85 Dolto, 1985d, 14.
86 PJE, 20.
87 IIC, 367; JD, 104.
88 De Mezamat, 2008b.
89 VC2, 703; also DW, 94; PJE, 85 & 111.
90 VC2, 877 & 819f.
91 Nobécourt, 2008a; Ribowski, 1987/2004.
92 E.g., JD, 272 & 283; PJE, 94; TL, 93;VO, 192.
93 E.g., CE, 256; JD, 286; PJE, 13–15 & 101; TL, 44.
94 E.g., CE, 204 & 351; DV, 40 & 89; EM, 25, 305 & 326; IIC, 213; JD, 298; NE, 211; SS, 75; TL, 46 & 84.
95 DQ, 109.
96 Dolto, 1982a, 145.
97 See Chapters 2, 3, 4, 6 & 10.
98 See Chapters 3 & 4.

99 Roudinesco, 1986, 169.
100 See Chapter 3.
101 Published in two parts: Dolto, 1949 (also in Ribas 2006, 95–108) and Dolto, 1950. For whole text: JD, 133–193. On multiple appearances: VC2, 176f.
102 VC2, 176f.
103 VC2, 177.
104 Dolto-Marette, 1949a; in JP, 19–33 (Klein attended the conference).
105 Dolto-Marette, 1949b.
106 JD, 149–174; see Chapter 3.
107 JD, 174–193.
108 JD, 176; also JD, 154 & 192.
109 E.g., VC2, 258–259; also 258f.
110 VC2, 261 & 261f.
111 JD, 191.
112 JD, 193.
113 JD, 189.
114 SS, 21.
115 Freud stresses that projection is a reaction to fear (1896c, 184 & 209), and "the mechanism is frequently employed in normal life" (1906/1962, 33). "Projective identification" is almost named by Dolto in 1940: "Thought at the anal stage is characterized by mechanisms of identification, of projection ... inherent to the sado-masochistic ambivalence of object relations" (MA, 36).
116 SS, 21f.
117 Dolto, 1950, 39; also JD, 189.
118 See JP, 43–50; by Anphar in *Phot*, see JP, 87f.
119 VC2, 799.
120 JP, 42.
121 JP, 42.
122 JP, 39.
123 VC2, 176f.
124 VC2, 176f.
125 VC2, 259.
126 JP, 46 (note the incapacity to look).
127 JD, 148 & 159.
128 JP, 11.
129 JP, 37.
130 Laplanche & Pontalis, 1967/2004, 33.
131 VC2, 389.
132 E.g., stated or implied in Golder, 2002a; Guillerault, 2003; Hivernel, 2013; Roudinesco, 1986, 274, 519 & 649.
133 2011, 97.
134 E.g., VC2, 422, 462, 554, 602.
135 Coronel & De Mezamat, 1997a.
136 E.g., De Sauverzac, 1993, 67.
137 Roudinesco, 1986, 277.
138 Pernicone & Dolto, 2002, June.
139 LF, 276.
140 LF, 276 & 287.
141 LF, 295.
142 ATP, 149; D&R, 25; DW, 79; Roudinesco, 1986, 353.
143 LF, 283.
144 D&R, 25.
145 SP2, 132.
146 VC2, 655.

147  VC2, 751; also SS, 225.
148  Lacan's notice: VC2, 667. On that fated day, Lacan ironically writes to Dolto that he speaks, "without a shred of hope of being heard" (VC2, 652). And on 13 March, Dolto writes to wish him well and tell him that she will not join his new venture («La Cause freudienne»): "But for me, I will work as in the past, for the cause, to my utmost, as long as I will have health. I do not need a constituted group and, as I have told you, which you know, I have neither the taste nor the knack for power. Good luck. I'm sending you a hug" (VC2, 668).
149  LF, 282.
150  LF, 307.
151  Lacan, 1964/1977, 19.
152  1964/1977, 149.
153  In 1979; see LF, 277.
154  In 1975; see Soler, 2008.
155  2008.
156  Roudinesco, 2011, 75.
157  VC2, 494.
158  VC2, 494f.
159  See Chapter 8.
160  VC2, 123, 129, 139 & 139f.
161  Douville, 2004, 192.
162  2004, 198.
163  2004, 196 & 215.
164  2004, 194.
165  2004, 205.
166  2004, 214.
167  2004, 200.
168  Freud, 1914b, 85.
169  1905c, 184.
170  See Chapter 5.
171  1896/1954c, 270.
172  1909a, 140–141.
173  1907, 102.
174  Laplanche & Pontalis, 1967/2004, 12.
175  Freud, 1895, 340.
176  1895, 357.
177  1907, 150.
178  1905c, 224f.
179  1895, 319.
180  1921, 107–108.
181  Dolto, 1956, 31.
182  Freud, 1895.
183  1907, 101.
184  DW, 22.
185  SP1, 136.
186  CD, 232.
187  TL, 77.
188  SP2, 68.
189  Canu, 2009, 161.
190  We locate in Frances Tustin (1981) some concordances with Dolto. However, Dolto is clear that coming to reality will be traumatic if there is a loss of *unconscious* continuity, that any infant is vulnerable to losses that might not register as trauma objectively (e.g., being left with wonderful caregivers during a mother's absence), and that all infants remain capable of what we might call an "autistic response" to

reality. For Tustin, regression may be understood as a kind of "deadness" (L. Farley, personal communication, 12 January 2016). But Dolto argues that regression is never "deadness," since unconscious life continues vibrantly and the regressed individual remains alert (susceptible) to the transference. In addition, for Dolto, there is always somewhere living to regress *to* because there is precocious symbolization from the first moments of life.

191 SP1, 114.

192 MA, 217 (emphasis hers).

193 I refer especially to works by Lucy Blackman, Temple Grandin, Naoki Higashida, Ido Kedar, Tito Mukhopadhyay and Birger Sellin; to a video project by Larry Bissonnette and Tracy Thresher (*Wretches and Jabberers*, 2016); and to parental reflections by Ron Suskind (with Owen); Arthur Fleischmann (with Carly); and Ralph Savarese (with D.J.).

194 SP1, 118.

195 SP1, 43.

196 Freud, 1907, 223.

197 I have over 5000 "contact hours" teaching young students with autism. Almost invariably, these students read precociously. Ironically, their reading is usually considered anomalous—a splinter skill or symptom (hyperlexia). Yet Dolto's theorization allows us to predict that persons with autism *will* read—and that reading holds a powerful reparative potential. Just as Dolto predicts, too, reading about themselves in specially constructed stories (i.e., as "s/he" rather than "I," and/or seeing their name in print), helps them cope with newness (reality) through an identification to the self as(-if) other.

198 PS, 88–89. Dolto coins «mutance,» in the sense of "shedding" and/or "mutation," also invoking the mute(d).

199 JD, 299.

200 SS, 243–245.

201 VC1, 171–174.

202 VC1, 174f.

203 VC1, 173 (story: Maeterlinck, 1919); also Chapter 7.

204 Freud, 1933a, 8.

205 DW, 125.

206 Freud, 1905c, 184; also Chapters 3 & 5.

207 Dolto, 1985f, 83–84.

# 10

# LEGACY

## Introduction

Dolto once famously told her daughter that a good mother is one you can leave.[1] So it is that I gesture towards ending this psychobiographic study of Françoise Dolto, whose body of evidence for the transference is, I submit, at least as convincing as da Vinci's. With Dolto, I believe we uncover the vibrancy of the infant's unconscious life and the enduring inscription of precocious symbolization in human achievement. Thereby, we obtain testimony that, as Montaigne wrote five centuries ago, a nation's government is in the hands of «nourrices» ["wetnurses" or "infant carers"].[2] Or, as Dolto puts it, in talking with Pivot: "It is the children's nursery that will make, in 30 years, the richness of this country."[3] For childhood experiences have a determining influence for the whole of later life, Freud explains[4]—with the earliest legating the most.[5]

As to this dream-work of words and where it has taken us, in this roundabout study of «Madame Dolto,» Freud's self-reflection seems fitting: "We have acquired no new fact, but only a more comprehensive view."[6] For our knowledge has grown in what is other than countable. Yet, returning to the first words cited from Dolto in this work, I believe we can confirm that she is absolutely correct: "It is a small surface with which we make our speeches, but what is living is entirely in the unconscious."[7] For as we come to understand it with Dolto, desire invokes a laborious process of becoming that writes against family and culture, as a subject achieves unit status in symbolic exchanges, interpsychically. Thus, the unconscious not only legates to thought (ergo, to theory), but sustains it through the continuous transport of prior investments and our prehistory of word-play.

Dolto's texts overturn traditional academic discourses as asides hold significance, what arrives passively is the most valuable, and just like in her clinical sessions, "in total silence, in verbal silence, there is an enormous animation of communication,"[8] as she describes it. Thereby, something that is never articulated aloud yields something that is paradoxically hearable and indispensable to listen to. With Dolto, we experience the movement between precociously invested words and thoughts that is the private driver of discovery. And we become aware of the value of surprise to insight—of the great merit of what Dolto teaches: "to question there where I feel questioned."[9]

## «Nourrisson»

Without a doubt, a survey of this psychobiographical study reveals the oddity of a vast textual terrain imbibed with homonymic word-plays and echoes in wild transits, and the absolute illogic of the transference in texts. With the phoneme, catachresis is installed deep inside language, and we meet the impossibility of saturating meaning. Seeking a reassuring perspective, I refind Dolto's good advice: "Let us begin again from Freud's discovery that libido is linked to the pleasure principle."[10] And thinking anew with Freud, I conclude that logic will necessarily have little to do with any libidinal history. After all, "dreams scarcely ever take over ordered recollections from waking life, but only details selected from them, which they tear from the psychical context in which they are usually remembered in the waking state,"[11] Freud explains. And by definition, Freud states clearly: "Libido is an expression taken from the theory of emotions."[12] Thus, by elaborating thought as the derivative of dream-work, Dolto's corpus reveals that the intellectual world is beholden to the emotional world.

I believe Dolto's project also propels psychoanalysis towards another staggering contribution of general interest, like Freud's "dream book" and "Freudian slips." It is this resounding truth: *the infant is unconsciously alert and already symbolizing.* The newborn is a wildly receptive subject making meaning of the world—even when just hours old—who seeks a witness to maintain a phantasy of continuity with his archaic prehistory. Even the word for an infant—«nourrisson» [«nouris son»: "fed sound"]—suggests a "game of forces," as he makes of words his alimentation, digesting phonemes in his archaic transference situation.

What of early reading, then—stories heard while falling asleep? Is there any practical difference if words come from life or a book? And are words that are regularly delivered (correspondence, subscriptions) a sort of punctual milk—reliable provision somewhere between reality and phantasy? For, as Freud said, "the high valuation of the word seems to contain the meaning that perceptions can become conscious only by being given a name."[13] And by theorizing the resonance of archaic echoes in psychical structuration, Dolto demonstrates that the phoneme is essential to presentification.

In every way, Dolto's theoretical work is boldly independent, original and groundbreaking. But ironically, the prominent mediatization of Dolto in France and «la francophonie» sometimes obscures her finest message. For it is a perplexing aspect of Dolto scholarship today that the phoneme is underrepresented in the secondary literature, while her notion of the unconscious image of the body carries her posterity. As a case in point, the only dictionary devoted to Dolto, while being a thoroughly researched work by a highly regarded peer, does not include the «phonème.»[14] For in an uncanny return of Dolto's theory onto itself, the phoneme only becomes detectable with an approach that presumes its existence.

Through Dolto's elaborations of the transference, the archaic and oral passivity, we begin to value the importance of waiting ardently for unconscious conveyances that arrive unpredictably to help explicate her complex work. And by being alert to the phoneme and its offers—our belief in the human capacity for passive education—we can observe its remarkable unconscious play in dreamwork: association, repetition, condensation and displacement (diffusion) over nearly 80 years, across wildly divergent works.

## Archives

Fully embracing Dolto's project as a researcher, and seeking ways to move beyond an experience primarily with texts, I spent two weeks in Paris in July 2014, as mentioned, walking in her footsteps. The journey itself had an element of the phantastic, as I am a creature of routines and seldom venture far. Yet I would end up thousands of miles from home, alone, covering the 5th and 16th «arrondissements.» I strolled through the Jardin du Ranelagh and located the first *Maison verte*, L'Église Notre Dame de Grace de Passy (where Dolto had her First Communion), her office on Rue Saint-Jacques, l'Hôpital Armand-Trousseau, l'Hôpital Bretonneau, Rue Vineuse, Rue du Ranelagh, Avenue des Ternes and so on. My two best guides were an autobiographical work, *Enfances*[15]—an interview that feels more like a journal—and her daughter's magnificent collage of a text, *Archives de l'intime*.[16] So it was that, without a laptop or reliable cell phone, I became unhooked from Canada as I followed Dolto across eight decades of life, love and work. I even placed roses on her grave at Cimétière Bourg-la-Reine one sunny morning, at a family monument covered with flowers, pebbles and tiny animal statues.

Then, on an evening when the heat soared, as if suspending time, I had a beverage on the terrace of Le Franklin—that innocuous-looking little hotel in the heart of Paris where the infant Françoise's history was forever altered by the young Irish nanny who indulged in evenings there, dressed in Suzanne's finest, towing her tiny charge, who absorbed her surroundings. Dolto was only a few months old by the time her first «nurse Irlandaise» was fired, yet the trace of that lost love is the most tangible and ubiquitous transference in Dolto's life project. Structurally triangular, Le Franklin—uncannily echoing the "Franklin" inscribed on Dolto's former home—is situated at a major roundabout in Passy where seven streets meet, including Rue Delessert, Rue Benjamin Franklin, Rue Passy—and, of course, Rue Vineuse.

While in Paris, I also had the opportunity to make two visits to the Archives Françoise Dolto, 21 Rue Cujas.[17] It was a strange sensation to have read so much about Dolto that I felt at home where I had never been before. The room was situated in the area normally occupied by a courtyard in a bourgeois Paris home. It was wood-panelled and lined with shelving that featured, floor to ceiling, a selection of Dolto's favorite books and various items that included three «poupée-fleurs,» exquisite watercolors and sculptures by Dolto, and about three dozen small owls.[18] The literature displayed also showcased conference posters; published texts; thousands of pages of unpublished notes; and the original manuscript of her medical dissertation, including Pichon's handwritten comments on her draft. In countless folders, meticulously organized by her daughter and some dedicated volunteers, one could witness how each paper was hammered out on a manual typewriter and repeatedly revised, as Dolto tirelessly reworked her material, in strata, for decades. And overlooking everything along the only wall without shelves was a photograph of Dolto almost two metres high, whose eyes follow the observer with a penetrating look (a plea?).

The archive was unofficially hosted for me that day by the archivist's infant daughter, nearly one and learning to walk.[19] Crawling from one shelf to another, she pulled herself up, looked at me and gestured to the materials with one hand and some verbalizations. It seemed so apt that a baby would be my guide, as Dolto insisted all her life that she had learned everything from babies, and that one should always regard infants as an «hôte d'honneur» ["honourable host"].[20] I believe Dolto would have wanted it just like this. For the archive, that archaic repository, is first and foremost a place of transferences—a condensation of the past in the present, whose area of influence in «après-coup» is immeasurable. So its significance can only ever make an effort at words. As it turns out, about one year to the day later, Dolto was honored by a relocation of these irreplaceable materials to the Archives Nationales in the heart of Paris, Rue des Francs Bourgeois.

As an additional testament to her generosity, Dolto openly shares her plan for the «poupée-fleur.»[21] So it seemed like good research to make one. My own is 36 cm high, and I admit to experiencing a significant return of old psychical material (in French) tethered to choosing its name, its fabric and the shade of green. After constructing it (in July 2013), I left it largely to the side. Yet I only managed to overcome a very difficult emotional impasse in starting to write my dissertation (in December 2014) by placing it on my desk—where it remains, four years on now.

## «Géographie»

In truth, I had gone to France that summer, between reading and writing Dolto, seeking a certain «je ne sais quoi.» I found it on my first full day there. I confess that I was already in a melancholy mood, after spending hours at Cimétière Père Lachaise, searching for a possible relative. It was drizzling that day and his site was unkept, so I slipped on his mossy resting spot, falling on his grave, his «tombeau»—a homonymic play of "your beautiful (male object)," "fall water" and "fall from high." Onlookers asked after me as I hobbled on, con-structively humbled. But if this was how easy it was to be symptomatic in Paris, it was going to be a long trip.

From then, I began noticing the sea of my first language, something I seldom encounter outside Quebec, my birthplace. Yet though I was in a cemetery, in the rain, alone and injured, I was entirely unafraid—whereas back home, my anxiety has such high walls to guard. And as I walked, I overheard a guide read-ing a tomb inscription to a half-dozen visitors: «Que devient le rêve quand le rêve est fini?» ["What becomes of the dream when the dream is finished?"]. It was an absolutely uncanny question. For it is my primary question—not just of the day, or of Dolto and this project, but of my whole life. So as I meandered from the cemetery to Trousseau, I began to lose my sense of the mist that had helped my foot comply with my tongue, yet I became keenly aware of having arrived at a most unusual destination. For my route, as the map suggested, was an easy trek of a few blocks. But it became, instead, a place of unmappable resonances.

Taking Avenue de Saint-Mandé ["saint-requested"; homonym: "breast-requested"], I entered a nearby church, L'Église de l'Immaculée Conception, drawn by my desire to explore landmarks upon the geography Dolto desired to return to, for free, for 40 years. So doing, I came face-to-face with an immense tree-like tapestry (behind the altar)—remarkably similar to the one in Dolto's office on Rue Saint-Jacques.[22] Once more outside, I found a street post near a «passerelle» like the one where Dolto questioned death as a child.[23] Its many signs stated that, as well as being on Saint-Mandé, I was nearing Bois de Vin-cennes [homonymically, "drink of twenty cents"], one of two large forests in Paris. I drifted absently to 1921, when a graphologist suggested that young Fran-çoise drank («boit») obstacles[24]—and I also couldn't help thinking of her sym-bolic payment.[25] I might have started worrying about my grip on reality through this bounce of sounds, except that it was not only enjoyable but thought-provoking.

So as I took in my soundscape, and words reverberated between past and pre-sent, here and elsewhere, life and texts, I began to realize that this *is* the life of a child: a wild confabulation of homonymic possibilities that are not (yet) limited by reality. Back in Canada, I would read Freud's discussion of refinding the familiar, and how a similarity of sound serves the libidinal economy through dream-work as "joke work."[26] After all, I was, that day, simply "in possession of a childish source of pleasure."[27]

Yet as I turned from Saint-Mandé to locate Trousseau, I was stunned again at the sight of three giant, elderly palm trees—surely here when Dolto was. And I was returned at once to the landscape of *Babouches*,[28] the book that made her want to learn, then unlearn, reading. For here were some of the only such trees in all of Paris. And right above them was a high clock, «l'heure juste» ["exact time"], affixed to l'Édifice de l'horloge ["clock building"].[29] «L'heure juste» is mentioned often enough in Dolto's chronicles of her early life to have become the title of a lovely children's biography about her.[30] Thus reading Dolto while standing, I sensed resonances of her autobiography in this place, until the line between theory and history blurred to a vanishing point. So while Dolto said that she kept an excellent souvenir of Trousseau,[31] I submit that Trousseau kept an excellent souvenir of Dolto.

In fact, a close reader is left with little doubt that Trousseau's «géographie» [homonymically: "I have water-written," or "I have above-written"] returns the landscape of Dolto's childhood phantasies, unconsciously sought and found—as readable on the terrain as its archaic echoes are hearable in her corpus. The walker-reader is also invited to muse that Dolto was content for all her working life at Trousseau—phonemically, «trou saut, trou (s')eau, trou seau, trou (c')haut, trousse eau, trousse haut, trousseau» [a homonymic cluster of "hole hop," "hole water," "hole bucket," "hole high," "purse/bag water," "purse/bag high" and "dowry"]. On that one word—two phonemes—we uncover holes with all kinds of means of escape (freedom), along with archaic echoes that enigmatically bring into "view" a parade of poignant silent images: the nanny's necklace (from the dowry) and the (mother's borrowed) purse; filling buckets with sand in Deauville (staring out at the English Channel); that dear angel B.A.G. (and his idiomatic evocation of theft); water- and ladder-play at the *Maison verte* (and the Armistice); and even Dominique at the Dali exhibit.

The thin mesh between reality and phantasy in this neighborhood evokes the rhythm of presence-absence infusing Dolto's entire project. This porosity of liquid objects is the ordinary stuff of childhood, a psychical working-through to which we give a deceptively simple name: listening. For safely hidden beneath our adult movements in reality, a continuous call rises from the soft bottom of our infantile origins that we always seek to refind in reality. Dolto's spectacular success in assuaging human suffering invites the conclusion that this unconscious securitization is the source of our creative potential. So I could only listen in wonder, then, on refinding my archaic security in French, a half-century after my infantile rupture. For at Trousseau, with Dolto, I learned to play again.

The truth is that I cannot deny the profound catharsis of working with Dolto's corpus. And taking my strength from Freud, who expressed, "some natural hesitation about revealing so many intimate facts about one's personal life,"[32] I will share that, post-traumatic, I spent decades feeling safe in English. But I noticed one day in the winter of 2014, during my research on Dolto, that I had just had a thought in French for the first time in 50 years. In effect, my entire psychical landscape has been permanently altered by this project. Then again, is this not the biggest risk—and benefit—of any education? For as Dolto makes evident, our history of desire is always what is at stake in any encounter with language. Ironically, I had been warned by a very well-meaning mentor that psychoanalysis would take me away from language. But I believe that it has done exactly the opposite, moving my socio-cultural inquiry as a linguist (why did I leave my mother tongue?) to the far deeper question underpinning (undermining?) linguistics: *what is a word?*

## «Collier»

It seems that while I (like her) was becoming a "doctor of education," I accidentally tumbled off the train the most loyal Dolto interpreters are riding—that of her "unconscious image of the body," the formulation for which she is most widely credited. And instead of sharing a pleasant journey with those fine colleagues, I wandered alone on ever-shifting paths through the archaic terrain for which Dolto provides a cryptic auditory map, seeking a way with, as if and through her to tell the story of the «phonème»—a tale at once so familiar to me, yet so strange.

This blurring between subjects also turns up in dreams I had in July 2014, while sleeping in the wildly different soundscape (and smells) of a warm Paris night. During that trip, I had more vivid dreams than I can usually recall. One night, Françoise, about three years old, arrived to explain, so seriously, that she asks every day: «Mais où est le collier?» ["But where is the necklace?"]. And she is heartbroken that no one ever tells her: "That's right, that's a big problem."

Of the biographer's dream, Leon Edel says: "In the last stages of the writing of his life, he [Henry James] came to me in my dream world, early one summer morning."[33] And Winnicott notes: "When I write a paper for this [British Psycho-Analytical] Society on any subject, I nearly always find myself dreaming dreams that belong to that subject."[34] Even modern scientists at the «Pitié» conclude that one gets more dreams if one asks for a journal of them.[35] Funny enough, Freud said the same thing more than a century ago, after walking along Rue Saint-Jacques to that same hospital, during a time when he was translating Charcot: "Anyone who takes an interest in dreams remembers a considerably greater number of them after waking."[36] So I cannot help but wonder: is writing biographically an asking for dreams?

Perhaps it is, and perhaps that is how the phoneme «port(e)» arrived so belatedly.[37] After three years of reading and writing Dolto (2013–2016), I began preparing for my doctoral defense, feeling the pressure of coming out of incubation to speak for the first time, like a baby, to my esteemed examiners. Aware that my memory flickers under strain, I created indices on chronologies, analysts, cases etc.[38] It was then that it hit me. Of course, my first reaction was panic—how could I have missed it? But duly humbled, I was forced to come to terms with the obvious limits of my knowledge of Dolto, or of anything. For I had foolishly thought I was done, but there is no such thing as "done." This is what the dream-work teaches, and what learning with Dolto predicts: accidental knowledge comes via the slow and unchartable psychical work of our encounters with words, and there is always more dream-work in store.

Further, although the dream-work of words is a source of play, and it harbors the power to bring us unconscious pleasure lifelong, the implications of Dolto are extremely serious. Greatest among these is the fact that the fetus is a symbolizing being. Added to this is the discovery that invested phonemes heard repeatedly in infancy affect the trajectory of our speech, texts and ingenuity. And through Dolto's study of the sequelae of the infant's nascent encounter with audition while dreaming, I believe that we get as close as we can (or ever have) to theorizing the elusive interplay between the symbolic and the biological: the relation between the unconscious precondition of human existence, and the social structures in which humans exist. We also confirm the ontogeny of thinking—and its great share in the service of survival.

Through a preponderance of evidence, Dolto's corpus reveals that the unconscious is a robust and enduring force for life inside each one of us, but it remains hidden from us by definition. So we should not be surprised that so many scholars, educators and social leaders consider it irrelevant to contemporary conversations to even think about the unconscious. By association, there may be a conscious compulsion to dismiss any spokesperson for the unconscious. Freud's project is subject to such repression. And like him, Dolto is a tremendously vigorous advocate for the necessity of considering the undeniable and ever-present role of the unconscious in human life.

Shifting to her publicly acknowledged legacy, reviews of the most recent film about Dolto offer a good glimpse of her staggering impact. Its producer, Gérard Miller (brother of Jacques-Alain Miller, Lacan's son-in-law), calls Dolto "a hero of national history" on par with Marie Curie, Simone de Beauvoir and Simone Veil.[39] Its premiere on national television was followed by a debate entitled, "Growing Up After Dolto"[40]—for there is a before and after Dolto,[41] as Miller puts it. One reviewer sustains the popular sentiment that Dolto "educated a whole generation of parents,"[42] and "succeeded in prolonging Freud's oeuvre."[43] And *Télérama* calls her "fascinating in her simplicity."[44] For it is true that while her project is incredibly complex, Dolto in person—in films, conferences, seminars and interviews—is remarkably unpretentious.

Yet those outside of France will not learn easily about Dolto from this film either, in a spectacular perpetuation of the problem of dissemination. As this manuscript goes to press, France TV still states: "This video is not available from your geographic position." And Vimeo blocks any retrieval too: "Video geo-restricted by the owner." In fact, what summation could be truer? For Dolto has been geo-restricted for 30 years at least, if not for 50, or even 80. And the recognition of her truly historical contribution keeps struggling to cross the Atlantic Ocean. It is as if that body of water offers an uncanny repetition of how the English Channel once imposed its haunting loneliness on young Françoise, alone with her questions on the sands of Deauville, digging holes, mourning the loss of her beloved nanny.

## Cohesion

In an old interview clip in Miller's film, Dolto explains her work as helping the one who suffers to reunify himself, refind his cohesion and refind his own honor.[45] The precious comment reveals Dolto's profound valuation of human liberty, while the belief that every infant is deserving of truth is a fundamental

Dolto teaching—and her most emphatic message. But a surprising slip in the film delivers another rich lesson of Dolto's corpus from underneath. For when the now-familiar anecdote about the shrimp "asking" to be boiled alive is retold by one of the analysts newly interviewed for the film, the story is said to be about «*écrevisses*» ["crayfish"] instead of «*crevettes*» ["shrimp"].[46] In the phoneme «cre,» we locate the source of the accidental word-play responsible for the error in hearing/reading Dolto, that then becomes an error in speaking. Thus, an esteemed respondent inadvertently dramatizes the hard work of childhood, as despite a carefully scripted text, we come upon an unexpected reminder that the phoneme matters.

As Dolto elaborates it like no one before her, the idiosyncratic archaic echoes of each individual's prehistory with words—the securitizing dream-work of our precocious audition—affects our identifications, our ability to love, our capacity for feeling present in reality, our facility for thinking and our potential to work for our happiness. In sum, our unconscious encounters with phonemes impact all languaged encounters and acquisitions. So the gains of a new language (beyond practical ones) will be immense for reducing anxiety by increasing the potential for venting in the social. In other words, multilingualism opens up associative possibilities. Yet any second (third, fourth... ) language introduces associative distances from the indelibly self-securing phonemes of our mother's tongue—sometimes, uncrossable chasms. So Dolto's work helps us fathom our psychical need for our first language—our capacity to access long-invested, long-forgotten filiations to the phonemes that silently carry the traces of our earliest loves and losses, and offer the best conduits to our unconscious resources for survival. Simultaneously, Dolto elaborates multilingualism—the appetite for words—as a powerful contributor to psychical resilience.

Dolto's teaching about invested phonemes is also pertinent to understanding the psychical sequelae of language migration—radically altered languaged identities—as it impacts diasporic and refugee populations around the world. Psychically speaking, the loss of language mediation is a threat to the infant akin to the mother's absence. For the infant in exile (physical and/or linguistic) leaves behind the landmarks upon which his psychical structuration depends. Everyone reassures themselves that he will manage fine for being so young—yet his losses will be the greatest of all. For Dolto demonstrates clearly that the mother tongue structures the child, contributing invaluably to discussions in many countries (like my own) with shameful histories whereby Indigenous children were forced to abandon their ancestral languages through prescribed schooling and legal prohibitions.

Following Dolto, literacy emerges as a critical field for passive education, being a site-means for unchartable flows of restorative objects that no one can help but leave behind, that others cannot help but find. For writers will necessarily, accidentally, countersign their works, folding in their libidinal prehistories as traces of the unconscious, the otherness of their texts. And since archaic phonemes confirm survival, we are each unconsciously resonant to our lost objects, whose random arrival in language offers unconscious security—an as-if proof of life. This transference of unconscious affects is an enduring source of hope securable via continuous rogue exchanges in the social because an unconscious register operates inside language (spoken or written) to silently deliver a feeling of «reconnaissance» anytime, anywhere. So reading driven by personal feelings enables returns of pleasure from an original address in phantasy via archaic echoes right off the register of consciousness. Implicitly, then, Dolto's project is a convincing argument for the human right to read freely—and a valiant defense of open libraries.

We also need to recall that archaically invested phonemes are wonderfully idiosyncratic. They are unique to any auditory, maternal, paternal, familial, linguistic, cultural, geographical or physiological prehistory. That is why explaining the movement of a phoneme in Dolto's corpus—or anyone's, for that matter—will be a laborious undertaking. For every phoneme is really slippery to the touch. Told in isolation from the corpus, a phoneme can feel as gadgetized as a pun. It is as if its ephemeral texture, like a dream, is fragilized by speaking. And there is the dreamwork of words at play too, especially condensation, so that working in reverse to tease out associations, like in analysis, it takes dozens of pages, replete with tangents, to explain a single phoneme—«port(e)» being a case in point.

Dolto's project also makes compelling offers to education, as we consider the enduring force of the unconscious in our languaged interactions. For every learner brings a forgotten yet affecting heritage with words to the scene of schooling. Even (especially) youngsters at preschool have a relatively ancient history with phonemes (and their unconscious associations) that will influence their encounters with new words as objects for their thinking. In addition, that unconscious prehistory with words will affect the transference in any pedagogical encounter, silently producing anxiety (fear) or security (love). The paradoxically rogue yet subtle "knowledge" acquired by a passive education is unintentional and unconscious for both the teacher and learner.

Passive education is a pedagogy that delivers continuous sustenance to the emotional world through unstoppable symbolic communication in the social. Thus, passive education tenders an enigmatic promise of hope—luring us to continuity (symbolic filiation) with our unconscious desires—placing much of learning entirely outside of any curriculum. These unconscious relations also turn every educational community into a rich emotional world full of unpredictable offers of significance. Adding to this, every theoretical notion presented for our instruction is an intimate inscription—the quasi-accidental product of repeated thoughts—that cannot help but be autobiographical. And because the unconscious cannot be turned off and on at will, for as long as we live, our susceptibility to the transference is perpetually assured.

## Clinic

Taking stock as I pull back, I comfort myself that despite the novelty of my textual offer, I have achieved some measurable gains. For this is the first single-author book on Dolto in English; the first full-length study of Dolto's work on the unconscious role of phonemes in identity-formation; the first text ever devoted to Dolto's groundbreaking elaboration of the archaic and the transference; and the first psychobiographic research on Dolto dedicated to demonstrating how her project is derived from the "early Freud." So as irrational as dream-work may be—and as nebulous as the transference is to sense and to show—it seems that real work gets done anyhow, moved along by an undercurrent from start to finish.

And while it is commonplace to hear that Dolto left no method, I believe she makes over a dozen direct contributions to the practical work of aiding others that meant so much to her. *One*: the therapist should seek invested phonemes through detailed anamneses to locate affectively charged names (including place names) from a patient's early history, interpreting their suggestions—and being specially attuned to changed or inherited names. *Two*: find gaps in symbolic continuity (unsymbolized castrations), such as moves, (linguistic) migration, gestational illness or trauma, a mother's absence, the loss of elders or siblings, war etc. *Three*: install choral clinics, whereby the therapist is never alone but always with at least one other—facilitating triangulation (via transferential coloring with "similars"). *Four*: require symbolic payments (rocks, stamps, coins etc.) to prevent Oedipal over-identification and over-dependency (loss of potential for psychical liberation). *Five*: use visual arts—rather than toys—to demute patients, learning from where (how) the subject feels represented (located) in the work.

*Six*: the therapist should analyze identifications, with special attention to the persistence of archaic object relations. *Seven*: organize more *Maisons vertes* to help regulate the anxiety-guilt economy in the fusional couple. *Eight*: presume competence in persons with autism (despite appearances), speaking to them intelligently and assuming comprehension. *Nine*: talk to mute children, telling them the truth and offering answers to their unspeakable questions. *Ten*: help deaf children work through gaps in languaged mediation to support their psychical structuration. *Eleven*: employ the «poupée-fleur» to speed recovery from regressive states in adults and children. *Twelve*: enable archaic identifications, restoring continuity through engagements with nature—trees, flowers, small animals and insects. *Thirteen*: write as-if biographies through correspondence on shared surfaces (preferably valorized by experience, pre-used), as a phantasy of witnessing serving triangulation.

Dolto draws us into a radically new conception of the human being as perpetually symbolizing from the beginning of life: a subject from the start, for whom associative thinking is a permanent endowment. On this view, the human is never complete but always growing through progressive liberation—never closed, but always needing affective circulation with an other. Thereby, Dolto rattles common notions of history, self and language, as she attests that the greatest source of human suffering is the loss of continuity with the archaic—so the best repair is to assist in effecting symbolic relays. For, unconsciously, as Dolto's project demonstrates without precedence, human beings need to follow life to have life.

By grounding her work in her own witness of the unconscious, Dolto helps us to reconceptualize the infant, the word, language, thought, symbolization, autism, literacy, the social and subjectivity. We learn from Dolto through an unparalleled adventure by example, via the transference, as we locate the signature of her libidinal history in all of her most fundamental notions. And though Dolto is abolutely down-to-earth in her character, our entire «lecture»—a "hearing" in English, but a "reading" in French—will necessarily be an encounter with something entirely other.

Admittedly, the means of learning with Dolto is not typical. It is necessary to sift through thousands and thousands of pages of material, to regroup ideas around word-things from her early childhood—her invested phonemes—and to welcome the symbolic continuity and play that emerges from her work. It is passive learning with, by and through the transference. There is nothing whatsoever that is logical about it. But there is, ironically, so much to be learned by it. So doing, we become witnesses to the dream-work at the origin of anyone's thoughts, and the degree to which the diffusion of dream-work leads to notions being widely dispersed in our conversations and undertakings over a lifetime, reappearing in different contexts. We also become witnesses to the secondary revision of dream-work that Freud talked about a century ago. For observing the transference in texts, it is undeniable that consciousness will spend its time beyond childhood working to justify rationally (as if by deliberate intent) what is, at its roots (routes), our unwavering devotion to our oldest wishes. Indeed, Dolto delivers a very fine elaboration of Freud's theory of emotions, in which the notion of libido originates.

Dolto's project demonstrates that the phoneme has a primary role in the transference, being essential to its exegesis—and that the vivacity of latent speech affects learning. Therefore, translation—as this project attempts—is never just about making hearable or readable someone's thoughts in another (mother's) tongue. Rather, the fact that unconscious influences subtend every author's (or speaker's) word choices impels the grave responsibility of respecting particular words as carriers of affect and heralds of authenticity—and the impossibility of doing precisely that. In other words, it seems as if the transference is what is most at stake (i.e., at risk) in translation. So while translation may be functionally possible, it is theoretically improbable.

## Work to live

The common sensation of disorientation at greeting old material in a new language—including oneself—attracts modern research into the relation between language and identity, into what happens to emotions across languages.[47] This experience is familiar to multilinguals, who endeavor to keep using the language in which they first met someone, because that person (and relationship) feels awkwardly remote in another tongue—as if the language in which the emotions between them began circulating were essential to that bond. Likewise, if we read authors in our mother tongue, we feel estranged by encounters with their works in translation. The reverse is true too: knowing a work in translation, then finding it in one's mother tongue, offers a satisfying rapprochement. Of course, every translator knows that deviation inheres in the task. But if the ideas communicated are equivalent (assuming the translator's integrity), what *is* it that is so different between versions that a profound sense of kinship might be lost— or found?

With Dolto's elaboration of the phoneme, we are helped to understand that translation can distance, dissipate, lose or even rupture symbolic filiations for each speaker-listener (reader-writer) in a languaged relation. For a chasm invariably forms that is the paradox of the «inter dit» (what becomes sayable in new ways), and the «interdit» (what becomes unsayable by the very same process). Meanwhile, millions without access to Dolto's works simply have no idea what they are missing, as her project struggles for an audience beyond «la francophonie,» the jurisdiction of French. Coming full-circle, then, we locate the problem of what is lost in non-translation, as we touch the tender (k)not of cultural transmission. And, in using the phoneme to comprehend linguistic containment, we (again) find ourselves needing Dolto to explain Dolto.

Yet while Dolto was from Paris, her project is such a significant contribution to human knowledge that it far exceeds her time and place. I believe it will take many more generations to expose what remains submerged still, in a century-long corpus of unfathomable depths. In the meantime, if I were asked to choose a half-dozen books to introduce Dolto to the reader of French, I would recommend three for her theory: *Tout est langage* (Vertiges du Nord/Carrere, 1987), *Le sentiment de soi* (Gallimard, 1997) and the diminutive *Parler juste aux enfants* (Mercure de France, 2002); and three for her autobiography: *Enfances* (Seuil, 1986), *Autoportrait d'une psychanalyste* (Seuil, 1989) and *Archives de l'intime* (Gallimard, 2008).

Even with the abundant dissemination in French, however, Dolto is often misunderstood. In an interview following Miller's film, Catherine comments that her mother is falsely credited with a notion of "baby kings" she never promoted, for example, and "abundantly criticized by people who have not even read her."[48] Catherine is right. She is joined in that interview by Caroline Eliacheff, who discusses her new book on Dolto.[49] Eliacheff considers Dolto to be underestimated as a theoretician,[50] and she too is correct. For her part, Roudinesco is critical of Miller's film, calling it "an avalanche of clichés," and full of errors.[51] Undoubtedly, despite the sincere efforts of so many, Dolto's formidable testimony about the unconscious and her affirmation of precocious human symbolization—with its astonishing ethical implications—is far easier to skew than to sanction.

In fact, the year 2018 offered multiple anniversaries for Dolto. The Archives Françoise Dolto helped organize a conference: "Françoise Dolto: Thirty Years After."[52] And another was held in Dolto's honor at the Institut National de Jeunes Sourds.[53] The Ministry of Posts issued a stamp to commemorate the

110th anniversary of her birth.[54] And in Bourg-la-Reine, where Dolto is buried, a month-long exhibit was held in conjunction with the release of that stamp.[55] In 2018 as well, Gallimard released (or rereleased) five books about Dolto, many for children[56]—including one marking 100 years since the end of World War I, contextualizing her childhood as a «veuve de guerre à sept ans» ["war widow at seven years (of age)"].[57]

Curiously, the year 2018 also heralded the eightieth anniversary of Freud's transit through Paris overnight (5 June 1938) on his way to safety in England.[58] "I never met him,"[59] Dolto reflected regretfully in 1988, as Freud remained prominent in her final thoughts. In another interview that last year of her life, Dolto adds that had she been in Paris at the time, she would gladly have gone to greet him (at Gare de l'Est).[60] For from the start of her career to the end of her life—amid countless trains and transits dotting the fine lines of her narrative—Dolto will follow Freud closely indeed. And she will not miss him again.

Within ten days of Freud's passage (15 June)—then 30 and unmarried, mired in family dramas, deep into the research for her dissertation, with Dan-Mé nearing death—Dolto penned the 25-page letter to her father that she may never have sent.[61] This letter written but perhaps never read is an apt metaphor of the *fort-da* game in Dolto's texts—the "here and gone" of an intimate history, and of all that was sent in French but has never been received in English. The game also captures our predicament as we find ourselves at the edge of the unsayable in trying to elaborate Dolto's formidable testimony about the unconscious register of language—latent speech—as an answer to the question of where the dream goes, when the dream that is infancy seems done.

In its astounding scope and implications, Dolto's project is unmatched. Yet in that letter, there is no aspiration to greatness on Dolto's part, nor any ambition to make a mark. There is only the ardent yearning that still seems to press on a young war widow wanting to earn a living:

> I say to myself that I will perhaps be happy one day to have completed my studies and to already have a little experience in my difficult speciality in case I would be obliged to continue to work to live, or I resume work after ceasing for a moment.[62]

And it is from such humility and modesty that Dolto becomes accidentally great, we could say—alleviating the suffering of so many, and bequeathing such a tremendous contribution to posterity.

Dolto's psychoanalytic project is unequivocal in its valuation of individual liberty and of the immeasurable vitality that inheres in our unique prehistories. And there is something genuinely benevolent and hopeful about Dolto's repeated assertions—and her compelling clinical evidence—that even under the most severe or precocious psychical damage, there resides in each of us a deep layer of health that can be reached and tapped. Our liberation, recovery from psychical suffering, is always possible. And by elaborating the unconscious conveyances that are in continuous circulation in language—through which we animate our enduring, archaic sources of love—Dolto reveals that we are, first and foremost, inhabitants of the emotional world.

Dolto challenges us to reconsider the human subject as a being inscribed by an intimate, archaic pedagogical relation from the first moments of life, who enters reality via reparative dream-work and who manages consciousness only as a narration that is continually sourced in the unconscious. Dolto's corpus shows how the transference of the autobiographical in our texts surprises us with what is living in us that we cannot ever know. Second only to Freud, Dolto demythologizes the unconscious, elaborating it as a limitless natural resource for every human being.

Further, Dolto's breathtaking oeuvre delivers exceptional proof of the archaic origin of language, the precocity of emotional life, the symbolic witnessing underwriting survival and the living legacy of the unconscious to human achievement. And what the present work attempts, in trying to gather some of the «après-coup» of Dolto's work and life into a given space and time, I again leave to Montaigne to explain: "I do not portray the being, I portray passing."[63] For the key truth we learn with Dolto is that the time of the dream is actually never over. So it isn't that we cannot live without the transference, but simply that we do not.

In the wake of Françoise Dolto's passage, ripples unsettle all sorts of theories about autism, biography, child development, education, identity, infancy, linguistics, literacy, narrative, psychoanalysis and translation. For the unconscious investment of phonemes with indelible significance troubles the word with a truly phantastic prehistory. Thus, arriving from elsewhere, and affecting the futurity of meaning, one word *can* change a life.

## Notes

1  AI, 12.
2  Montaigne, 1580/1958a, 114.
3  Ribowski, 1987/2004.
4  Freud, 1901b, 46, 1905c, 239, 1909b, 36.
5  Freud, 1896a, 214.
6  Freud, 1914c, 151.
7  CE, 283.
8  TL, 154.
9  IIC, 323.
10  JD, 122; also Dolto-Marette, 1947, 795.
11  Freud, 1900a, 44.
12  Freud, 1921, 90.
13  Freud, 1907/1962, 150.
14  Ledoux, 2006.
15  Dolto, 1986b, 1986c.
16  Published in 2008.
17  The scene I describe no longer exists.
18  See AI, 5 & 220–221; also AI, cover; ATP, 215 & Dolto, 1979c.

19 I thank the former archivist, Iulia Michel, and her daughter.
20 De Mezamat, 2008a; LO1, 119.
21 AI, 54 & 57; Dolto-Marette, 1949a, 546; JP, 46; VC2, 257 & 259.
22 AI, 231 & 233; VC2, 650 & 829.
23 EN, 10.
24 AI, 94; PF, 20; VC1, 114.
25 E.g., ATP, 196; CE, 371; DW, 139; SS, 124 & 125f; TL, 112; VC2, 890.
26 Freud, 1905d, 120–122.
27 Freud, 1905d, 170.
28 Balesta, 1894/1902; see ATP, 82 & Chapter 5.
29 Bel-Air Sud, 2011.
30 Farkas & Ratier, 2011.
31 ATP, 195.
32 Freud, 1900a, 105.
33 Edel, 1987, 3.
34 Winnicott, 1949, 177f.
35 Arnulf, 2014, 17.
36 Freud, 1900b, 572; Freud kept a journal of dreams.
37 See Chapter 8.
38 I also first printed my dissertation, which I was annotating.
39 Miller, 2018a.
40 France TV, 2018; France TVpro, 2018.
41 Miller, 2018a.
42 Lelièvre, 2018.
43 Lelièvre, 2018.
44 Adour, 2018.
45 Miller & Feuillette, 2018.
46 See ATP, 24–25 for Dolto's «crevettes» (emphasis mine); also Chapters 3 & 8.
47 For excellent examples, see work by linguists Aneta Pavlenko (especially) and Anna Wierzbicka.
48 C. Dolto in Gayet, 2018.
49 Eliacheff, 2018a.
50 Eliacheff, 2018b.
51 Roudinesco, 2018.
52 Archives Françoise Dolto, 2018.
53 INJS, 2018 (Institute for the young deaf).
54 Bougault, 2018.
55 Ville, 2018.
56 Gallimard, 2018.
57 Pignot & Potin, 2018.
58 Freud Museum London, 1992, 37; Gay, 1988, 629.
59 D&R, 23.
60 LF, 292 (station: Freud Museum London, 1992, 237).
61 See Chapter 7.
62 PF, 111.
63 Montaigne, 1580/1958b, 18.

# BIBLIOGRAPHY

Abraham, K. (1924/1949). "A short study of the development of the libido, viewed in the light of mental disorders." In *Selected Papers of Karl Abraham* (D. Bryan & A. Strachey, Trans., The International Psycho-Analytical Library, Ernest Jones, Ed., pp. 418–501). London: The Hogarth Press.

Abraham, N.& Torok, M. (1986). *The Wolfman's Magic Word* (N. Rand, Trans.). Minneapolis, MN: The University of Minnesota Press.

Adler, L., Delbée, A., François-Sappey, B. & Harter, H. (2006). *L'universel au féminin: Hannah Arendt, Camille Claudel, Marie Curie, Françoise Dolto, Eleanor Roosevelt, Clara Schumann.* Paris: L'Harmattan.

Administration of the President of Georgia (2016, 2 November). "The First Lady visits the psychological centre 'The Green House' with French experts." Retrieved from www.president.gov.ge/en-US/prezidenti/pirveli-ledi/maka-chichua-fsiqologiuri-momsakhurebis-centrs-fra.aspx.

Adour, M. (2018, 23 May). «Critique: La révolution Dolto.» *Télérama.* Retrieved from http://television.telerama.fr/tele/programmes-tv/la-revolution-dolto,126709766.php.

Albert-Buisson, F. (1965). «Introduction: la vie et l'oeuvre de Maurice Maeterlinck.» In M. Maeterlinck (Ed.), 1908/1965, *L'Oiseau bleu* (pp. 33–51). Paris: Éditions Rombaldi.

AlloCiné (n.d.). «Secret du tournage du film, Françoise Dolto, le désir de vivre: interview avec Joanne Balasko.» Retrieved from www.allocine.fr/film/fichefilm-139831/secrets-tournage/.

Andreas-Salomé, L. (1970). *Correspondance avec Sigmund Freud 1912–1936, suivie du Journal d'une année 1912–1913* (L. Jumel, Trans.). Paris: Gallimard.

Andreas-Salomé, L. (1977). *L'amour du narcissisme: textes psychanalytiques* (I. Hildenbrand, Trans.). Paris: Gallimard. (Original work published 1913–1933.)

Archives Françoise Dolto (2001a). «Liste des structures d'acceuil de types Maisons vertes.» Retrieved from www.dolto.fr/archives/siteWeb/liste.htm.

Archives Françoise Dolto (2001b). «Répères bibliographiques Françoise Dolto.» Retrieved from www.dolto.fr/archives/siteWeb/bio.htm.

Archives Françoise Dolto (2001c). «Titre du texte: 'Image inconsciente du corps,' Boîtes 8 à 11.» Retrieved from www.dolto.fr/archives/siteWeb/docs_a_garder/boite8%20a% 2011.htm.

Archives Françoise Dolto (2018, 1 December). Espace analytique: «Françoise Dolto, trente ans après.» [Conference poster.] Retrieved from www.dolto.fr/docs/1erDecembre2018. pdf.

Arnulf, I. (2014). *Une fenêtre sur les rêves: Neurologie et pathologie du sommeil.* Paris: Odile Jacob.

Association archives et documentation. Françoise Dolto & C. Dolto (Eds.). (1999). *Françoise Dolto aujourd'hui présente: actes du colloque de l'Unesco, 14–17 janvier, 1999.* Paris: Gallimard.

Association Françoise Dolto (Bruxelles) (1989). «L'Association.» Retrieved from www.asso ciationfdolto.be/spip.php?rubrique2.

Association le musée Jean de la Fontaine (n.d.). «La fontaine dans le seizième arrondissement de Paris.» Retrieved from www.la-fontaine-ch-thierry.net/lafseiz.htm.

Aubry, J. & Cifali, M. (1986/1988). «Entretien autour de Françoise Dolto.» In J. Aubrey et al. (Eds.), *Quelques pas sur le chemin de Françoise Dolto* (pp. 43–52). Paris: Éditions du Seuil.

Aulagnier, P. (1975/2001). *The Violence of Interpretation: From Pictogram to Statement* (A. Sheridan, Trans.). London: Brunner-Routledge.

Authier-Roux, F. (Ed.) (2000). «Frédérique Authier-Roux: entretien avec Juan-David Nasio.» In *Madame Dolto* (pp. 15–29). Paris: Erès.

Bachner, A. (2003). "Anagrams in psychoanalysis: retroping concepts by Sigmund Freud, Jacques Lacan and Jean-François Lyotard." *Comparative Literature Studies*, 40: 1, 1–25.

Bacon, R. (2013). "Listening to voices, hearing a person: Françoise Dolto and the language of the subject." *British Journal of Psychotherapy*, 29: 4, 519–531.

Balesta, H. (1894/1902). *Les babouches de Baba-Hassein* (J. Geoffroy, Illus.). Paris: C. Delagrave.

Béague, P. (Ed.) (2009). *Soif d'autre chose: Revenir à l'humain.* Bruxelles: Couleurs livres.

Béague, P. (Ed.) (2010). *Aimer à perdre la raison: Aimer, éduquer … est-ce compatible?* Bruxelles: Couleurs livres.

Bel-Air Sud (2011). «L'Horloge de l'Hôpital Armand-Trousseau.» [Photograph.] Retrieved from http://belairsud.blogspirit.com/archives/category/_l_oeil_du_quartier_/index-20. html/.

Berger, F.F. (2006). «La pratique analytique: vérité et pouvoirs de la parole.» *Cliniques Méditerranéenes*, 2006/1: 73, 255–269. Retrieved from www.cairn.info/revue-cliniques-med iterraneennes-2006-1-page-255.htm.

Bertin, C. (1982). *Marie Bonaparte: La dernière Bonaparte.* Paris: Librairie Académique Perrin.

Bessey, E.A. (1950). "Morphology and taxonomy of fungi." Philadelphia, PA: The Blakiston Company. Retrieved from http://archive.org/stream/morphologytaxono00bess/ morphologytaxono00bess_djvu.txt.

Beuve-Méry, A. (2008, 12 December). «Françoise Dolto: lorsque la biographie paraîtra.» *Le Monde.* Retrieved from www.liberation.fr/societe/2008/12/12/enattendant-dolto_295736.

Bibliothèque Nationale de France (BNF) (2015). «Anne Berman (1889–1979).» Retrieved from http://data.bnf.fr/11891454/anne_berman/.

Bibliothèque Nationale de France (BNF) (n.d.). «Notice bibliographique, Notice d'autorité personne: Marcelle Gauthier.» Retrieved from http://catalogue.bnf.fr/rechercher.do? motRecherche=marcelle+gauthier&critereRecherche=0&depart=0&facetteModifiee=ok.

Binet, E. (1999). "Françoise Dolto (1908–1988): a Christian educator out of the ordinary." *UNESCO: International Bureau of Education*, XXIX: 3, 445–454.

Binet, E. (2005). *Françoise Dolto, pédagogue.* Paris: Éditions Don Bosco.

Birksted-Breen, D., Flanders, S. & Gibeault, A. (Eds.) (2010). *Reading French Psychoanalysis*. London: Routledge.

Boehlich, W. (Ed.) (1990). *The Letters of Sigmund Freud to Eduard Silberstein, 1871–1881* (A.J. Pomerans, Trans.). Cambridge, MA: Harvard University Press.

Bonaparte, M. (1938, 15 June). «Freud à Paris.» *Marianne*. Retrieved from www.psychana lyse.lu/articles/BonaparteFreudParis.htm.

Bott Spillius, E., Milton, J., Garvey, P., Couve, C. & Steiner, D. (Eds.) (2011). *The New Dictionary of Kleinian Thought*. London: Routledge.

Bougault, S. (2018, 6 October). "Collection historique de timbre-poste français: Françoise Dolto: 1908–1988." [Postage stamp.] Retrieved from www.wikitimbres.fr/timbres/ 11361/2018-francoise-dolto-1908-1988.

Bourgeron, J.-P. (1993). *Marie Bonaparte et la psychanalyse à travers ses lettres à René Laforgue et les images de son temps*. Genève: Champion-Slatkine.

Breuer, J. & Freud, S. (1893a). "Case histories, Case 1: Fräulein Anna O." *SE*, 2: 21–47.

Breuer, J. & Freud, S. (1893b). "Case histories, Case 2: Frau Emmy von N." *SE*, 2: 48–105.

Breuer, J. & Freud, S. (1893c). "On the psychical mechanism of hysterical phenomena: preliminary communication." *SE*, 2: 3–17.

Brison, S.J. (2002). *Aftermath: Violence and the Remaking of a Self*. Princeton, NJ: Princeton University Press.

British Baby Names (2013). "Top 200 most popular names in England and Wales in 1880." Retrieved from www.britishbabynames.com/blog/2013/04/top-200-most-popular-names-in-england-and-wales-in-1880.html.

Britzman, D.P. (2003). *After-Education: Anna Freud, Melanie Klein and Psychoanalytic Histories of Learning*. Albany, NY: SUNY Press.

Britzman, D.P. (2011). *Freud and Education*. New York: Routledge.

Cabanes, B. & Piketty, G. (2007). «Sorties de guerre au XXe siècle: expériences enfantines du deuil pendant et après la Grande Guerre.» *Histoire@Politique: Politique, Culture, Sociéte*, No. 3. Retrieved from www.histoire-politique.fr/index.php?numero=03&rub=dossier&item=22.

Caldaguès, L. (Ed.). (1982). *Françoise Dolto: Séminaire de la psychanalyse d'enfants, Tome 1*. Paris: Éditions du Seuil.

Camaraire-Santoire, L. (1983). «Visite à la Maison verte avec le Dr. Françoise Dolto.» In R. Féger (Ed.), *Stage International d'études avancées sur les approches médico-psycho-socio-péd-agogiques auprès d'enfants en situations problématiques* (pp. 76–81). Montréal: GIRAPE & UQAM.

Cantet, L. (Director). (2008). «Entre les murs» ("The Class"). [Film, 128 min.] Paris: France 2 Cinéma.

Canu, A.-M. (2009). "«La Maison verte»: a place for words, personal reflections on working with Françoise Dolto." In G. Hall, F. Hivernel & S. Morgan (Eds.), *Theory and Practice in Child Psychoanalysis: An Introduction to the Work of Françoise Dolto* (pp. 143–162). London: Karnac.

Chaperot, C. & Celacu, V. (2010). «La pensée et le langage par le corps dans la schizophré-nie.» *L'évolution psychiatrique*, 75: 435–444.

Chapsal, M. (1994). *Ce que m'a appris Françoise Dolto*. Paris: Arthème Fayard.

Charcot, J.-M. (1887/1971). «L'Hystérie féminine (leçons du mardi): 1887–1888.» In E. Trillat (Ed.), *J.M. Charcot: l'hystérie: Textes choisis et présentés par E. Trillat* (pp. 25–122). Toulouse: Édouard Privat.

Charial, L., Eliacheff, C. & Valentin, J.-F. (1999). «De la transmission: voir, écouter, sentir.» In Association archives et documentation. F. Dolto & C. Dolto (Eds.), *Françoise*

*Dolto aujourd'hui présente: Actes du colloque de l'Unesco, 14–17 janvier, 1999* (pp. 48–62). Paris: Gallimard.

Charuty, G. (2015). «'Cher grand Professeur Freud': Une correspondance entre Yvette Guilbert et Sigmund Freud.» *L'homme*, 2015/3: 215, 81–102.

Chébaux, F. (Ed.) (1999a). *Françoise Dolto et l'éducation.* Paris: L'Harmattan.

Chébaux, F. (1999b). *La question du sujet entre Alain Touraine et Françoise Dolto: Archéologie de l'acte éducatif.* Paris: L'Harmattan.

Chébaux, F. (2013). *L'Éducation au désir: De Françoise Dolto à la pédagogie neuvilloise.* Paris: L'Harmattan.

Chérer, S. (2008). *Ma Dolto.* Paris: Éditions Stock.

Coronel, E. & De Mezamat, A. (Producers) (1997a). *Françoise Dolto Film 1: Tu as choisi de naître.* [Film, 53 min.] Paris: Abacaris & Gallimard.

Coronel, E. & De Mezamat, A. (Producers) (1997b). *Françoise Dolto Film 2: Parler vrai.* [Film, 55 min.] Paris: Abacaris & Gallimard.

Coronel, E. & De Mezamat, A. (Producers) (1997c). *Françoise Dolto Film 3: N'ayez pas peur* [Film, 53 min.] Paris: Abacaris & Gallimard.

Coronel, E. & De Mezamat, A. (Producers) (1997d). *Françoise Dolto Film 4: Complément, Maud Mannoni, évocations.* [Film, 22 min.] Paris: Abacaris & Gallimard.

D'Ortoli, F. & Amram, M. (1990). *L'École avec F. Dolto: Le rôle du désir dans l'éducation.* Paris: Hatier.

D'Ortoli, F. & Amram, M. (2009a). *L'année de Vienne.* [Film, 86 min.] Paris: Fremeaux & Associés.

D'Ortoli, F. & Amram, M. (2009b). *Françoise Dolto & La Neuville.* [Film, 97 min.] Paris: Fremeaux & Associés.

De Mezamat, A. (Producer) (2008a). *Françoise Dolto parle de l'éducation.* [Television broadcast, 52 min.] Vincennes: France 5/Abacaris Films.

De Mezamat, A. (2008b). *Françoise Dolto parle de l'origine.* [Television broadcast, 52 min.] Paris: France 5/Abacaris Films.

De Mezamat, A. (2008c). *Françoise Dolto parle de la psychanalyse.* [Television broadcast, 52 min.] Paris: France 5/Abacaris Films.

De Saussure, F. (1959/1974). *Course in General Linguistics* (W. Baskin, Trans.). Glasgow: William Collins Sons and Co.

De Sauverzac, J.-F. (Ed.) (1985). *Françoise Dolto: Séminaire de la psychanalyse d'enfants, Tome 2.* Paris: Éditions du Seuil.

De Sauverzac, J.-F. (Ed.) (1987). *Françoise Dolto: Dialogues québécois.* Paris: Éditions du Seuil. (Original work published 1983.)

De Sauverzac, J.-F. (Ed.) (1988). *Françoise Dolto: Séminaire de la psychanalyse d'enfants, Tome 3.* Paris: Éditions du Seuil.

De Sauverzac, J.-F. (1993). *Françoise Dolto: Itinéraire d'une psychanalyste.* Paris: Aubier.

Delphine, P. (2008, 4 December). «Catherine Dolto raconte Françoise: interview.» *L'Express.* Retrieved from www.lexpress.fr/culture/livre/catherine-dolto-raconte-francoise_823196.html.

Derrida, J. (1967a). *De la grammatologie.* Paris: Les Éditions de Minuit.

Derrida, J. (1967b). «Freud et la scène de l'écriture.» *L'Écriture et la différence* (pp. 293–340). Paris: Seuil.

Derrida, J. (1972/1987). *Positions* (A. Bass, Trans.). London: The Athlone Press.

Derrida, J. (1986a). "Foreword: fors: the anglish words of Nicolas Abraham and Maria Torok" (B. Johnson, Trans.). In N. Abraham & M. Torok (Eds.), *The Wolf Man's Magic Word: A Cryptonymy* (pp. xi–xlviii). Minneapolis, MN: University of Minnesota Press.

Derrida, J. (1986b). *Parages*. Paris: Éditions Galilée.

Derrida, J. (1987). *Feu la cendre*. Paris: Des femmes.

Derrida, J. (1991). "Circumfession" (G. Bennington, Trans.). In G. Bennington & J. Derrida (Eds.), *Jacques Derrida*. Chicago, IL: The University of Chicago Press.

Derrida, J. (1993). *Passions*. Paris: Éditions Galilée.

Derrida, J. (1997/2008). *The Animal That Therefore I Am* (D. Wills, Trans.). New York: Fordham University Press.

Derrida, J. (1999/2004). "The 'metaphoric catastrophe' (Heliopolis)." In C. Malabou & J. Derrida (Eds.), *Counterpath: Travelling with Jacques Derrida* (D. Wills, Trans., pp. 206–218). Stanford, CA: Stanford University Press.

Derrida, J. (2003). *Voyous*. Paris: Éditions Galilée.

Destombes, C. (1989). «En souvenir de … Françoise Dolto (1908–1988).» *Journal de la Psychanalyse de l'Enfant*, 6, 291–298.

Djéribi-Valentin, M. (Ed.) (2001). *Françoise Dolto: père et fille, une correspondance (1914–1938)*. Paris: Mercure de France.

Djéribi-Valentin, M. (Ed.) (2005). *Françoise Dolto: une vie de correspondances, 1938–1988*. Paris: Gallimard.

Djéribi-Valentin, M. (2008). *Françoise Dolto: mère et fille, une correspondance (1931–1962)*. Paris: Mercure de France.

Djéribi-Valentin, M. & Kouki, É. (Eds.) (1996). *Françoise Dolto, essais: sexualité féminine, la libido génitale et son destin féminin*. Paris: Gallimard. (Original work published 1960–1985.)

Djéribi-Valentin, M. & Kouki, É. (Eds.) (1998). *Françoise Dolto, Articles et conférences V: le féminin*. Paris: Gallimard. (Original work published 1959–1988.)

Dollander, N. & De Tychey, C. (2004). "Affective development, education and prevention: a psychodynamic model." *Psychoanalytic Review*, 91: 2, 257–270.

Dolto, B. (1976). *Une nouvelle kinésithérapie: le corps entre les mains*. Paris: Hermann.

Dolto, C. (1985). *Neuf mois pour naître: les aventures du bébé dans le ventre de sa maman*. Paris: Hatier.

Dolto, C. (1989). «Préface.» In S. Ramstein (Ed.), *Un pédiatre raconte: histoires de bien grandir* (pp. 9–11). Paris: Hatier.

Dolto, C. (2001). «Françoise Dolto et l'Hôpital Trousseau: au colloque pour les 100 ans de l'Hôpital Trousseau.» Retrieved from www.dolto.fr/archives/siteWeb/docs_a_garder/trouscat.htm.

Dolto, C. (2005a). «De l'Image du corps à l'haptonomie.» In C. Dolto (Ed.), *Le féminin, filiations, etc.: Actes des journées d'étude Françoise Dolto 2003 et 2004* (pp. 111–127). Paris: Gallimard.

Dolto, C. (2005b). *Le féminin, filiations, etc.: Actes des journées d'étude Françoise Dolto 2003 et 2004*. Paris: Gallimard.

Dolto, C. (2007). *Dico ado*. Paris: Gallimard Jeunesse Giboulées.

Dolto, C. (2018, 22 October). Intervention: «Pédophiles.» Retrieved from www.dolto.fr/pedophiles.php.

Dolto, C. & Faure-Poirée, C. (Eds.) (2008). *Les mots de Francoise Dolto pour les enfants et leurs parents* (L. Koechlin, Illus.). Paris: Giboulées.

Dolto, F. (1940/1965). *Psychanalyse et pédiatrie: les grandes notions de la psychanalyse, seize observations d'enfants* (troisième édition). Paris: Éditions du Seuil.

Dolto, F. (1940/1971). *Psychanalyse et pédiatrie: les grandes notions de la psychanalyse, seize observations d'enfants* (quatrième édition). Paris: Éditions du Seuil.

Dolto, F. (1940/2013). *Psychoanalysis and Paediatrics: Key Psychoanalytic Concepts with Sixteen Clinical Observations of Children* (F. Hivernel & F. Sinclair, Trans.). London: Karnac.

Dolto, F. (1949). «Cure psychanalytique à l'aide de la poupée-fleur.» *Revue française de psychanalyse*, XIII: 1, 53–69. Retrieved from https://gallica.bnf.fr/ark:/12148/bpt6k5443800r/f61.item.zoom.

Dolto, F. (1949/1981). «Cure psychanalytique à l'aide de la poupée-fleur.» In F. Dolto (Ed.), *Au jeu du désir: essais cliniques* (pp. 133–193). Paris: Éditions du Seuil.

Dolto, F. (1949/1999a). «L'enfant et la poupée-fleur: de bouche à corolle, et de corolle à oreille.» In C. Faure-Poirée & M. Djéribi-Valentin (Eds.), *Jeu de poupées* (pp. 43–50). Paris: Mercure de France.

Dolto, F. (1949/1999b). «La poupée-fleur.» In C. Faure-Poirée & M. Djéribi-Valentin (Eds.), *Jeu de poupées* (pp. 19–42). Paris: Mercure de France.

Dolto, F. (1950). «À propos des poupées-fleurs (suite).» *Revue française de psychanalyse*, Tome XIV: 1, 19–41. Retrieved from https://gallica.bnf.fr/ark:/12148/bpt6k5444467v/f25.item.zoom.

Dolto, F. (1956). «Introduction au dessin d'enfant.» *La vie médicale: arts et psychopathologie, Numéro spécial*, Noël 1956, 27–39.

Dolto, F. (1957/1997a). «Marie-Louise B. et Lionel Ségolène, deux cas de régression.» In G. Guillerault (Ed.), *Le sentiment de soi, aux sources de l'image du corps* (pp. 11–128). Paris: Gallimard.

Dolto, F. (1957/1997b). «Les premières images du corps, théorie et clinique.» In G. Guillerault (Ed.), *Le sentiment de soi, aux sources de l'image du corps* (pp. 129–235). Paris: Gallimard.

Dolto, F. (1960/1996). «Conditions narcissiques différentes de la relation d'objet chez la femme et chez l'homme. La symbolique phallique.» In M. Djéribi-Valentin & É. Kouki (Eds.), *Françoise Dolto, essais: sexualité féminine, la libido génitale et son destin féminin* (pp. 202–276). Paris: Gallimard.

Dolto, F. (1962/1999). «Le dandy, solitaire et singulier.» In M. Djéribi-Valentin (Ed.), *Françoise Dolto: le dandy, solitaire et singulier* (pp. 17–45). Paris: Mercure de France.

Dolto, F. (1965). «Préface.» In M. Mannoni (Ed.), *Le premier rendez-vous avec le psychanalyste*. Genève: Éditions Gonthier S.A.

Dolto, F. (1967). «Préface.» In A. Vasquez & F. Oury (Eds.), *Vers une pédagogie institutionelle*. Paris: F. Maspero.

Dolto, F. (1971). *Le cas Dominique*. Paris: Éditions du Seuil.

Dolto, F. (1971/1973). *Dominique: Analysis of an Adolescent* (I. Kats, Trans.). New York: Outerbridge and Lazard.

Dolto, F. (1971/1974). *Dominique: Analysis of an Adolescent* (I. Kats, Trans.). London: Souvenir Press.

Dolto, F. (1972/1981). «Au jeu du désir les dés sont pipés et les cartes truquées.» In F. Dolto (Ed.), *Le jeu du désir: essais cliniques* (pp. 268–328). Paris: Éditions du Seuil.

Dolto, F. (1977/1984). «Heures et jours qui suivent l'accouchement.» In E. Herbinet (Ed.), *Naître et ensuite?* (pp. 187–266). Paris: Stock Laurence Pernoud.

Dolto, F. (1977/1998). «La ville et l'enfant.» In *Françoise Dolto: l'enfant dans la ville* (pp. 53–89). Paris: Mercure de France.

Dolto, F. (1977a). *Lorsque l'enfant parait, Tome 1*. Paris: Éditions du Seuil.

Dolto, F. (1977b). «Préface.» In A. Muel (Ed.), *L'Éveil de l'esprit* (pp. 8–54). Paris: Aubier Montaigne.

Dolto, F. (1978). *Lorsque l'enfant parait, Tome 2*. Paris: France Loisirs.

Dolto, F. (1978/1998). *L'enfant et la fête: entretien avec André Parinaud*. Paris: Mercure de France.

Dolto, F. (1979a). *Lorsque l'enfant parait, Tome 3*. Paris: Éditions du Seuil.

Dolto, F. (1979b). «Préface.» In J. Van Den Brouck (Ed.), *Manuel à l'usage des enfants qui ont des parents difficiles*. Paris: Éditions du Seuil.

Dolto, F. (1979c). «Préface» (& Illus.). In M. Dacher & M. Weinstein (Eds.), *Histoire de Louise*. Paris: Le Seuil. Retrieved from www.psychanalyse.et.ideologie.fr/livres/pre ffrdolto.html.

Dolto, F. (1981). *Le jeu du désir: Essais cliniques*. Paris: Éditions du Seuil. (Original work published 1946–1978.)

Dolto, F. (1982a). «La boutique verte: histoire d'un lieu de rencontres et d'échanges entre adultes et enfants.» In M. Brown de Calstoun et al. (Eds.), *Enfants en souffrance* (pp. 137–156). Paris: Stock Laurence Pernoud.

Dolto, F. (1982b). *Sexualité féminine: libido, érotisme, frigidité* (deuxième édition). Paris: Scarabée & Co.

Dolto, F. (1983). «Françoise Dolto parle (*Dialogues québécois*).» [Video, 2:39 min.] Retrieved from www.youtube.com/watch?v=q_-DXyKF5RU.

Dolto, F. (1984). *L'image inconsciente du corps*. Paris: Éditions du Seuil.

Dolto, F. (1985/1998). *Parler de la mort*. Paris: Mercure de France.

Dolto, F. (1985a). *La Cause des enfants*. Paris: Robert Laffont.

Dolto, F. (1985b). «La maison verte.» Conférence au Centre de Recherches Psychanalytiques, octobre 1985. *Esquisses Psychanalytiques, No. 5, Actualités.* Retrieved from www.alaaddin.it/SITO%20DOLTO/Sito%20allegati/La%20maison%20verte%201985%20fr.pdf.

Dolto, F. (1985c). "The mirror's child" (C. Vaughn, Trans.). In S. Benvenuto & A. Molino (Eds.), *In Freud's Tracks: Conversations from the J. of European Psychoanalysis* (pp. 185–200). Lanham, MD: Jason Aronson.

Dolto, F. (1985d). «Préface.» In D. Dumas (Ed.), *L'ange et le fantôme: Introduction à la clinique de l'impensé généalogique* (pp. 9–16). Paris: Les Éditions de Minuit.

Dolto, F. (1985e). «Préface.» In A. von Feuerbach (Ed.), *Kaspar Hauser* (pp. i–xiv). Béthune: Vertiges.

Dolto, F. (1985f). *Solitude*. Paris: Vertiges du Nord/Carrere.

Dolto, F. (1986a). *La difficulté de vivre*. Paris: Vertiges du Nord/Carrere.

Dolto, F. (1986b). *Enfances* (A. de Andrade, Photographer). Paris: Éditions du Seuil.

Dolto, F. (1986c). *Enfances*. Paris: Éditions du Seuil.

Dolto, F. (1986d). *Entretiens IV: les images, les mots, le corps, Tome 4*. Paris: Gallimard.

Dolto, F. (1987). *Tout est langage*. Paris: Vertiges du Nord/Carrere.

Dolto, F. (1987/1998a). «L'enfant dans la ville.» In *Françoise Dolto: l'enfant dans la ville* (pp. 9–52). Paris: Mercure de France.

Dolto, F. (1987/1998b). «Ma reconnaissance à Sophie Morgenstern.» In J.-D. Nasio (Ed.), *Le silence en psychanalyse* (pp. 27–41). Paris: Désir/Payot.

Dolto, F. (1988a). *La cause des adolescents*. Paris: Robert Laffont.

Dolto, F. (1988b). *Quand les parents se separent*. Paris: Éditions du Seuil.

Dolto, F. (1985/1989a). «Les parents, les adultes, la société.» In F. Dolto & C. Dolto-Tolitch (Eds.), *Paroles pour adolescents ou le complexe du homard* (1989, pp. 65–74). Paris: Hatier.

Dolto, F. (1985/1989b). «Conférence de Françoise Dolto au colloque organisé par le Centre Médico-Psycho-Pégagogique de Vigneux-sur-Seine.» In F. Dolto & C. Dolto-Tolitch (Eds.), *Paroles pour adolescents ou le complexe du homard* (1989, pp. 123–137). Paris: Hatier.

Dolto, F. (1989a). *L'échec scolaire, essais sur l'éducation*. Paris: Ergo. (Original work published 1980–1986.)

Dolto, F. (1989b). *Autoportrait d'une psychanalyste 1934–1988: Entretiens avec Alain et Colette Manier*. Paris: Éditions du Seuil.

Dolto, F. (1989c). «Préface.» In E.V. Ocampo (Ed.), *L'envers de la toxicomanie: Un idéal d'indépendence* (pp. 11–22). Paris: Éditions Denoël.

Dolto, F., D'Ortoli, F. & Amram, M. (1973/1990). «Fondations: recontre entre 'La Neuville' et Françoise Dolto.» In F. D'Ortoli & M. Amram (Eds.), *L'École avec Françoise Dolto: le rôle du désir dans l'éducation* (pp. 19–28). Paris: Hatier.

Dolto, F. & Dolto-Tolitch, C. (1989). *Paroles pour adolescents ou le complexe du homard*. Paris: Hatier.

Dolto, F. & Hamad, N. (1984/1995). *Françoise Dolto, Entretiens I: destins d'enfants*. Paris: Gallimard. (Original work published 1984–1986.)

Dolto, F. & Moscovitz, J.-J. (2002). «Entretien avec Françoise Dolto, 30 décembre, 1987.» *Psychanalyse Actuelle*. Retrieved from https://sites.google.com/site/psychanalyseactuel/textes/entretien-dolto-moscovitz.

Dolto, F. & Nasio, J.-D. (1987). *L'enfant du miroir*. Paris: Rivages/Psychanalyse.

Dolto, F. & Roudinesco, E. (1986/1988). «Des jalons pour une histoire: entretien.» In J. Aubrey et al. (Eds.), *Quelques pas sur le chemin de Françoise Dolto* (pp. 11–42). Paris: Seuil.

Dolto, F. & Ruffo, A. (1983/1999). *Françoise Dolto, Entretiens 3: l'enfant, le juge, et la psychanalyse*. Paris: Gallimard. (Original work published 1986–1987.)

Dolto, F. & Severin, G. (1977). *L'évangile au risque de la psychanalyse, Tome 1*. Paris: Jean-Pierre Delarge.

Dolto, F. & Severin, G. (1978). *L'évangile au risque de la psychanalyse, Tome 2*. Paris: Jean-Pierre Delarge.

Dolto, F. & Severin, G. (1979). *A Freudian Interpretation of the Gospel: The Jesus of Psychoanalysis* (H.R. Lane, Trans.). Garden City, NY: Doubleday & Co, Inc.

Dolto, F. & This, B. (1980/2002). «Dolto et l'ange bleu: entretien de Françoise Dolto (avec Bernard This).» *ERES: Le Coq-héron*, 2002/1: 168. Retrieved from www.cairn.info/revue-le-coq-heron-2002-1-page-139.htm.

Dolto, F. & Winter, J.-P. (1986). *Les images, les mots, le corps*. Paris: Gallimard.

Dolto-Marette, F. (1947). «Hypothèse nouvelle concernant les réactions dites de jalousie à la naissance d'un puîné.» *Psyché*, 9–10: juillet–août 1947, 788–798. (Reprinted in JD, 18–59.)

Dolto-Marette, F. (1948). «Les sensations coenesthétiques de bien-être et de malaise, origines des sentiments de culpabilité.» *Psyché*, 18–19: avril–mai 1948, 468–482. (Reprinted in JD, 96–132.)

Dolto-Marette, F. (1949a). «Rapport de la 12ème Conférence des Psychanalystes de langue française (Paris, 4 et 5 juin 1949).» [Discussion.] *Revue française de psychanalyse*, XIII, 4: 545–553. Retrieved from https://gallica.bnf.fr/ark:/12148/bpt6k54444473/f99.item.zoom.

Dolto-Marette, F. (1949b). «Société de psychanalyse de Paris: Comptes-rendus, réunion du 18 octobre 1949.» [Minutes.] *Revue française de psychanalyse*, XIII, 4: 566–568. Retrieved from https://gallica.bnf.fr/ark:/12148/bpt6k54444473/f120.item.zoom.

Dolto-Tolitch, C. (1998). «Il y a 10 ans la psychanalyste des enfants disparaissait: Catherine Dolto-Tolitch parle de l'après Dolto.» *Lien Social*, No. 467, 17 décembre. Retrieved from www.lien-social.com/Il-y-a-10-ans-la-psychanalyste-des-enfants-disparaissait.

Douville, O. (2004). «Les prétendus enfants–ancêtres.» In *Che vuoi?: la psychanalyse en traductions*, No. 21 (pp. 187–217). Paris: L'Harmattan.

Douville, O. (2009). *Chronologie: situation de la psychanalyse dans le monde, du temps de la vie de Freud*. Paris: Dunod.

Dubois, C. (1994). «Introduction à la lecture de F. Dolto.» *Le Bulletin Freudien*, No. 22. Retrieved from www.association-freudienne.be/pdf/bulletins/25-BF22.07DUBOIS. pdf.

Dumas, S. (1997). «La Maison verte: une création de Françoise Dolto.» *Psychomundo*. Retrieved from www.psicomundo.org/dolto/textos/dumas.htm.

Dupont, J. (Ed.). (1985). *The Clinical Diary of Sándor Ferenczi (1932)* (M. Balint & N.Z. Jackson, Trans.). Cambridge, MA: Harvard University Press.

Durif-Varembont, J.-P., Bertrand-Oschwald, E., Boulanger, J., Fuchs, M. & Monasse, J. (1999). «Le transfert sur et dans le lieu.» In Association archives et documentation Françoise Dolto. C. Dolto (Ed.), *Françoise Dolto aujourd'hui présente: actes du colloque de l'Unesco, 14–17 janvier 1999* (pp. 295–310). Paris: Gallimard.

Edel, L. (1987). "Confessions of a biographer." In G. Moraitis & G.H. Pollock (Eds.), *Psychoanalytic Studies of Biography* (Emotions and Behaviour Monographs, No. 4, pp. 3–27). Madison, CT: International Universities Press, Inc.

Eliacheff, C. (2018a). *Françoise Dolto: une journée particulière*. Paris: Flammarion.

Eliacheff, C. (2018b). «Françoise Dolto: une journée particulière (Partie 4/4).» [Video, 38 sec.] France: Flammarion. Retrieved from www.youtube.com/watch?v=-mBWWxEdZs8.

Esterle, M. (2011). *Psychosomatique, schema corporel et image du corps*. Toulouse: Institut de formation en soins infirmiers de Toulouse Rangueil.

Farkas, M.-P. & Ratier, M. (2011). *Françoise Dolto: l'heure juste*. Paris: Naïve.

Farley, L. (2011). "Squiggle evidence: the child, the canvas, and the 'Negative Labor' of history." *History and Memory*, 23: 2, 5–39.

Faure-Poirée, C. & Djéribi-Valentin, M. (Eds.) (1999). *Jeu de poupées*. Paris: Mercure de France. (Original work published 1949 and 1964.)

Fédération Nationale du Patrimoine (1988). «Françoise Dolto.» Retrieved from www.patri moine.asso.fr/contenu/dolto/dolto.htm.

Féger, R. & Gauthier, M. (1987). *Bibliographie sur la violence à l'égard des enfants*. Montreal: Commission des écoles catholiques de Montréal.

Ferenczi, S. (1913/1950). "Stages in the development of the sense of reality." In S. Ferenczi (Ed.), *Sex in Psychoanalysis: Contributions to Psychoanalysis* (E. Jones, Trans., pp. 213–239). New York: Robert Brunner.

Ferenczi, S. (1931/1980). «Trauma et séduction: conférence de S. Ferenczi, Vienne, 1931: analyse d'enfants avec des adultes» (M. Pidoux-Payot, Trans.). *Le Coq-héron*, 75, 5–21.

Ferret-Fleury, C. (2018). *Françoise Dolto, l'enfance au coeur* (S. Martin, Illus.). Paris: Gallimard.

Fessaguet, D. (2011). «De Sophie Morgenstern l'oubliée à Françoise Dolto la tapageuse.» *L'Esprit du temps/Topique*, No. 115, 79–82.

France TV (2018, 30 May). «La révolution Dolto: diffusé le mercredi 30. 05.18 à 21h00.» [Television broadcast, 90 min.] France 3. Retrieved from www.france.tv/documen taires/societe/509779-la-revolution-dolto.html.

France TV pro (2018, 26 June). «La révolution Dolto: diffusé le mardi 26. 06.18 à 21h00.» [Television broadcast, 90 min.] France 4. Retrieved from www.francetvpro.fr/france-4/communiques-de-presse/la-revolution-dolto-14904675.

François, Y. (1990). *F. Dolto: de l'éthique à la pratique de la psychanalyse d'enfant*. Paris: Centurion.

François, Y. (1999a). *Françoise Dolto: la langue des images*. Paris: Bayard Éditions.

François, Y. (1999b). «La vraie image: du dessin d'enfant à l'image du corps.» In Association archives et documentation Françoise Dolto. C. Dolto (Ed.), *Françoise Dolto aujourd'hui présente: actes du colloque de l'Unesco, 14–17 janvier 1999* (pp. 393–405). Paris: Gallimard.

Freixa, E. (n.d.). «Quelques affirmations de Françoise Dolto.» Retrieved from http:// esteve.freixa.pagesperso-orange.fr/dolto_citations.pdf.

Frémeaux, P. & Guéno, J.-P. (2006). «Lorsque l'enfant parait: intégrale de l'anthologie radio-phonique.» Retrieved from www.fremeaux.com/index.php?page=shop.product_details&product_id=1038&option=com_virtuemart.

Freud, E. (Ed.). (1960). *Connaissance de l'inconscient: Sigmund Freud, Correspondance (1873–1939)* (A. Berman, Trans.). Paris: Gallimard.

Freud, E. (1961). *Letters of Sigmund Freud: 1873–1939* (T.& J. Stern, Trans.). London: Hogarth Press.

Freud, E. (1970). *Letters of Sigmund Freud & Arnold Zweig* (E. & W. Robson-Scott, Trans.). New York: Harcourt Brace Jovanovich, Inc. (Original work published 1927–1939.)

Freud, E.L., Freud, L. & Grubrich-Simitis, I. (Eds.) (1978). *Sigmund Freud: His Life in Pictures and Words.* New York: W.W. Norton & Company.

Freud Museum London (1992). *The Diary of Sigmund Freud: 1929–1939: A Record of the Final Decade* (M. Molnar, Trans.). New York: Charles Scribner's Sons.

Freud Museum London. (2010). "Childhood and creativity: an apprehension of the symbolic." [Conference flyer.] *Anna Freud Centre.* London. 29 May 2010. Retrieved from http://psychosheffield.blogspot.com/2010/.

Freud, S. (1886). "Report on my studies in Paris and Berlin." *SE*, 1: 1–15.

Freud, S. (1886/1974). "Letter to a Friend, 1 January 1886." In R. Byck (Ed.), *Cocaine Papers by Sigmund Freud.* New York: Stonehill Publishing Company.

Freud, S. (1888). "Hysteria." *SE*, 1: 37–59.

Freud, S. (1891/2011). *On Aphasia: A Critical Study.* New York: Literary Licensing.

Freud, S. (1893a). "Case 2: Fräu Emmy von N." *SE*, 2: 48–105.

Freud, S. (1893b). "Case 5: Fräu Elisabeth von R." *SE*, 2: 135–181.

Freud, S. (1893c). "Preface & Charcot (Obituary)." *SE*, 3: 5–23.

Freud, S. (1893d). "On the psychical mechanism of hysterical phenomena: a lecture." *SE*, 3: 25–39.

Freud, S. (1893e). "The psychotherapy of hysteria." *SE*, 2: 254–312.

Freud, S. (1895). "Project for a scientific psychology." *SE*, 1: 281–397.

Freud, S. (1896/1954a). "Letter 52, to Wilhelm Fliess, 6 December 1896." In M. Bonaparte, A. Freud & E. Kris (Eds.), *The Origins of Psycho-Analysis: Letters to Wilhelm Fliess, Drafts and Notes: 1887–1902 by Sigmund Freud* (M. Mosbacher & J. Strachey, Trans., pp. 173–181). New York: Basic Books.

Freud, S. (1896/1954b). "Letter 100, to Wilhelm Fliess, 5 December 1898." In M. Bonaparte, A. Freud & E. Kris (Eds.), *The Origins of Psycho-Analysis: Letters to Wilhelm Fliess, Drafts and Notes: 1887–1902 by Sigmund Freud* (M. Mosbacher & J. Strachey, Trans., p. 270). New York: Basic Books.

Freud, S. (1896/1954c). "Letter 131, to Wilhelm Fliess, 23 March 1900." In M. Bonaparte, A. Freud & E. Kris (Eds.), *The Origins of Psycho-Analysis: Letters to Wilhelm Fliess, Drafts and Notes: 1887–1902 by Sigmund Freud* (M. Mosbacher & J. Strachey, Trans., pp. 313–315). New York: Basic Books.

Freud, S. (1896/1954d). "Letter 137, to Wilhelm Fliess, 12 June 1900." In M. Bonaparte, A. Freud & E. Kris (Eds.), *The Origins of Psycho-Analysis: Letters to Wilhelm Fliess, Drafts and Notes: 1887–1902 by Sigmund Freud* (M. Mosbacher & J. Strachey, Trans., pp. 321–322). New York: Basic Books.

Freud, S. (1896/1954e). "Letter 140, to Wilhelm Fliess, 25 January 1901." In M. Bonaparte, A. Freud & E. Kris (Eds.), *The Origins of Psycho-Analysis: Letters to Wilhelm Fliess, Drafts and Notes: 1887–1902 by Sigmund Freud* (M. Mosbacher & J. Strachey, Trans., pp. 325–326). New York: Basic Books.

Freud, S. (1896a). "The aetiology of hysteria." *SE*, 3: 187–221.

Freud, S. (1896b). "Draft H: Paranoia." *SE*, 1: 206–212.

Freud, S. (1896c). "Draft K: The neuroses of defence (a Christmas fairy tale)." *SE*, 1: 220–229.

Freud, S. (1896c). "Further remarks on the neuro-psychoses of defence." *SE*, 3: 157–185.

Freud, S. (1896d). "Heredity and the aetiology of the neuroses." *SE*, 3: 141–156.

Freud, S. (1896e). "Letter 46, 30 May 1896." *SE*, 1: 229–232.

Freud, S. (1900a). "The interpretation of dreams (First part)." *SE*, 4: ix–338.

Freud, S. (1900b). "The interpretation of dreams (Second part)." *SE*, 5: 339–627.

Freud, S. (1901a). "On dreams." *SE*, 5: 629–685.

Freud, S. (1901b). "The psychopathology of everyday life." *SE*, 6: vii–310.

Freud, S. (1905a). "Fragment of an analysis of a case of hysteria." *SE*, 7: 1–122.

Freud, S. (1905b). "Psychical (or mental) treatment." *SE*, 7: 281–302.

Freud, S. (1905c). "Three essays on the theory of sexuality." *SE*, 7: 123–245.

Freud, S. (1905d). "Jokes and their relation to the unconscious." *SE*, 8: v–258.

Freud, S. (1906/1962). "[Freud's remarks at the Scientific Meetings]." In H. Nunberg & E. Federn (Eds.), *Minutes of the Vienna Psychoanalytic Society, Vol. I: 1906–1908* (M. Nunberg, Trans., pp. 1–80). New York: International Universities Press, Inc.

Freud, S. (1907). "Delusions and dreams in Jensen's 'Gradiva'." *SE*, 9: 1–95.

Freud, S. (1907/1962). "[Freud's remarks at the Scientific Meetings]." In H. Nunberg & E. Federn (Eds.), *Minutes of the Vienna Psychoanalytic Society, Vol. I: 1906–1908* (M. Nunberg, Trans., pp. 81–275). New York: International Universities Press, Inc.

Freud, S. (1908/1962). "[Freud's remarks at the Scientific Meetings]." In H. Nunberg & E. Federn (Eds.), *Minutes of the Vienna Psychoanalytic Society, Vol. I: 1906–1908* (M. Nunberg, Trans., pp. 276–410). New York: International Universities Press, Inc.

Freud, S. (1908a). "Creative writers and day-dreaming." *SE*, 9: 141–153.

Freud, S. (1908b). "Some general remarks on hysterical attacks." *SE*, 9: 227–234.

Freud, S. (1909/1967). "Freud's presentation to the scientific meeting of 1 December 1909: 'A Fantasy of Leonardo da Vinci'." In H. Nunberg & E. Federn (Eds.), *Minutes of the Vienna Psychoanalytic Society, Vol. II:1908–1910* (M. Nunberg, Trans., pp. 338–346). New York: International Universities Press, Inc.

Freud, S. (1909a). "Analysis of a phobia in a five-year-old boy ('Little Hans')." *SE*, 10: 1–149.

Freud, S. (1909b). "Five lectures on psycho-analysis (The Clark University Lectures)." *SE*, 11: 1–55.

Freud, S. (1910/1984). *Leonardo da Vinci: A Memory of His Childhood* (A.A. Brill, Trans.). London: Ark.

Freud, S. (1910a). "The anti-thetical meaning of primal words." *SE*, 11: 153–161.

Freud, S. (1910b). "Leonardo da Vinci and a memory of his childhood." *SE*, 11: 57–137.

Freud, S. (1911/1974). "Freud's comments on 'the problem of anxiety' at the Scientific Meeting of 15 November 1911." In H. Nunberg & E. Federn (Eds.), *Minutes of the Vienna Psychoanalytic Society, Vol. III: 1910–1911* (M. Nunberg, Trans., pp. 317–318). New York: International Universities Press, Inc.

Freud, S. (1911a). "The handling of dream–interpretation in psychoanalysis." *SE*, 12: 89–96.

Freud, S. (1911b). "Psycho-analytic notes on an autobiographical account of a case of paranoia." *SE*, 12: 1–82.

Freud, S. (1911c). "The significance of sequences of vowels." *SE*, 12: 341.

Freud, S. (1912a). "The dynamics of transference." *SE*, 12: 97–108.

Freud, S. (1912b). "A note on the unconscious in psychoanalysis." *SE*, 12: 255–266.

Freud, S. (1912c). "Recommendations to physicians practising psycho-analysis." *SE*, 12: 109–120.

Freud, S. (1913). "The claims of psychoanalysis to scientific interest." *SE*, 13: 163–190.

Freud, S. (1914a). "The Moses of Michelangelo." *SE*, 13: 209–238.

Freud, S. (1914b). "On narcissism." *SE*, 14: 67–102.

Freud, S. (1914c). "Remembering, repeating and working–through." *SE*, 12: 145–156.

Freud, S. (1915a). "Instincts and their vicissitudes." *SE*, 14: 109–140.

Freud, S. (1915b). "Observations on transference-love." *SE*, 12: 157–173.

Freud, S. (1915c). "The Unconscious." *SE*, 14: 159–215.

Freud, S. (1916a). "Introductory lectures on psycho–analysis: part I, parapraxes." *SE*, 15: 1–79.

Freud, S. (1916b). "Introductory lectures on psycho–analysis: part II, dreams." *SE*, 15: 81–239.

Freud, S. (1916c). "Introductory lectures on psycho–analysis: lecture XXV, transference." *SE*, 16: 431–447.

Freud, S. (1917a). "A childhood recollection from *Dichtung und Wahrheit* [Goethe's biography]." *SE*, 17: 147–156.

Freud, S. (1917b). "A difficulty in the path of psycho-analysis." *SE*, 17: 135–144.

Freud, S. (1917 [1916–1917]c). "General theory of the neuroses." *SE*, 16: 243–463.

Freud, S. (1917d). "A metapsychological supplement to the theory of dreams." *SE*, 14: 217–235.

Freud, S. (1917e). "Mourning and melancholia." *SE*, 14: 237–260.

Freud, S. (1918 [1914]). "From the history of an infantile neurosis." *SE*, 17: 1–122.

Freud, S. (1919). "The uncanny." *SE*, 17: 217–256.

Freud, S. (1919 [1918]a). "Lines of advance in psycho-analytic therapy." *SE*, 17: 157–168.

Freud, S. (1919 [1918]b). "On the teaching of psycho-analysis in universities." *SE*, 17: 169–173.

Freud, S. (1920). "Beyond the pleasure principle." *SE*, 18: 1–64.

Freud, S. (1921). "Group psychology and the analysis of the ego." *SE*, 18: 65–143.

Freud, S. (1923). "The ego and the id." *SE*, 19: 1–66.

Freud, S. (1924). "A short account of psychoanalysis." *SE*, 19: 189–209.

Freud, S. (1925/1969). *Le rêve et son interprétation* [translation of: *On Dreams*] (H. Legros, Trans.). Paris: Presses Universitaires de France. (Original work published 1901.)

Freud, S. (1925 [1924]). "An autobiographical study." *SE*, 20: 1–74.

Freud, S. (1926/1950). *La science des rêves* [translation of: *The Interpretation of Dreams*] (I. Meyerson, Trans.). Paris: Presses Universitaires de France. (Original work published 1900.)

Freud, S. (1927). "Humour." *SE*, 21: 159–166.

Freud, S. (1930). "The Goethe Prize." *SE*, 21: 205–212.

Freud, S. (1931). "Letter to the Burgomaster of Příbor." *SE*, 21: 259.

Freud, S. (1933a). "New introductory lectures, lecture 29: revision of the theory of dreams." *SE*, 22: 7–30.

Freud, S. (1933b). "New introductory lectures, lecture 31: dissection of the psychical personality." *SE*, 22: 57–80.

Freud, S. (1933c). "New introductory lectures, lecture 32: anxiety and instinctual life." *SE*, 22: 81–111.

Freud, S. (1936). "A disturbance of memory on the Acropolis." *SE*, 22: 239–248.

Freud, S. (1937). "Analysis terminable and interminable." *SE*, 23: 209–253.

Freud, S. (1940 [1939]). "An outline of psychoanalysis." *SE*, 23: 139–207.

Gallica. (1937). «Cryptogamie: graminella bulbosa, nouveau genre d'éntophyte parasite des larves d'Éphémérides du genre Baetis, par M. Louis Léger et Mlle Marcelle Gauthier.» *Académie des sciences, Tome 204*, janvier–juin, 1937. Retrieved from http://visualiseur. bnf.fr/ark:/12148/bpt6k31562.

Gallimard (2015). «Recherche avancée: Françoise Dolto.» Retrieved from www.gallimard. fr/searchinternet/advanced?all_title=Fran%C3%A7oise+Dolto&SearchAction=1& SearchAction=ok&SearchAction=1.

Gallimard. (2018). «Anniversaire Françoise Dolto: 1908-1988/2018.» Retrieved from www.gallimard-jeunesse.fr/Actualites/A-la-une/Anniversaire-FRANCOISE-DOLTO-1908-1988-2018.

Garric, A. (n.d.). «Henri Marette: essai de généalogie.» Retrieved from http://gw.geneanet. org/garric?lang=fr&p=henri&n=marette.

Gauthier, M. (1953). *Notice bio-bibliographique: Révérend Père Dom Raoul Hamel, O.S.* [Thesis.] Montreal: Université de Montréal.

Gauthier, M. (1962). *L'attitude de la délinquente vs Dieu: recherche pour l'obtention du certificat de Psycho-pédagogie.* [Thesis.] Montréal: Université de Montréal.

Gauthier, M. (1995). *La pensée et la personne de Françoise Dolto.* Nice: Université de Nice. [Doctoral Dissertation 1995NICE2034.]

Gay, P. (1988). *Freud: A Life for Our Time.* New York: W. W. Norton & Company.

Gayet, L. (2018, 24 August). «Catherine Dolto: Françoise Dolto a été beaucoup critiquée par des gens qui ne l'avaient pas lue.» [Interview.] France: France-Inter. Retrieved from www.franceinter.fr/emissions/l-invite-de-8h20-le-grand-entretien/l-invite-de-8h20-le-grand-entretien-24-aout-2018.

Geissmann, C. & Geissmann, P. (Eds.). (1998). *A History of Child Psychoanalysis.* London: Routledge.

Geni.com (2015). "Oliver Freud." Retrieved from www.geni.com/people/Oliver-Freud/6000000005021268044.

Gerrardyn, F. & Walleghem, P. (2005). "Françoise Dolto's clinical conception of the unconscious body image and the body schema." In H. De Preester & V. Knockaert (Eds.), *Body Image and Body Schema, Interdisciplinary Perspectives on the Body* (pp. 299–310). Amsterdam: John Benjamins Publishing.

Golder, É.-M. (2002a). «Et si on osait faire discuter Dolto avec Lacan? Quelques réflexions au sujet de l'identification et de l'invention du langage.» *Le Coq-héron,* 168: 111–124. Retrieved from www.cairn.info/revue-le-coq-heron-2002-1-page-111.htm.

Golder, É.-M. (2002b). «Quand on chasse Dolto par la porte, elle revient par la fenêtre.» In C. Schauder (Ed.), *Lire Dolto aujourd'hui* (pp. 121–129). Paris: Eres.

Goldstein, D. J. (2009). "Hannah Arendt's shared destiny with Rahel Varnhagen." *Women in Judaism: A Multidisciplinary Journal,* 6: 1, Retrieved from http://wjudaism.library.utor onto.ca/index.php/wjudaism/article/view/15801/12870.

Granger, C. A. (2004). *Silence in Second Language Learning: A Psychoanalytic Reading.* Clevedon: Multilingual Matters Ltd.

Greimas, A. J. (1969). *Dictionnaire de l'ancien français, jusqu'au milieu du XIV$^e$ siècle.* Paris: Larousse.

Grellet, I. & Kruse, C. (2004). *Des jeunes filles exemplaires: Dolto, Zaza, Beauvoir.* Paris: Hachette.

Grignon, O. (1997). «L'Apport de Françoise Dolto dans la psychanalyse: conférence à Dijon le 20 juin 1997.» *Eres/Le Coq-héron,* 168: 13–36.

Grignon, O. (2002). *Le corps des larmes.* Paris: Calmann-Lévy.

Guilbert, Y. (1927). *La chanson de ma vie (Mes mémoires)* (quinzième édn). Paris: Bernard Grasset.

Guilbert, Y. (1929). *La passante émerveillée (Mes voyages).* Paris: Bernard Grasset.

Guillerault, G. (1989). *Le corps psychique: essai sur l'image du corps selon Françoise Dolto.* Bégé-dis: Éditions universitaires Bégédis.

Guillerault, G. (1996). *Les deux corps du moi: schéma corporel et image du corps en psychanalyse.* Paris: Gallimard.

Guillerault, G. (Ed.). (1997). *Francoise Dolto: le sentiment de soi, aux sources de l'image du corps.* Paris: Gallimard. (Original work published 1956–1957.)

Guillerault, G. (1999). *L'image du corps selon Françoise Dolto: une philosophie clinique.* Paris: Institut Synthélabo pour le progrès de la connaissance.

Guillerault, G. (2002). «Dolto, Freud: du complexe de castration à la castration symboligène.» *Le Coq-héron*, 2002/1, 168: 37–46. Retrieved from www.cairn.info/revue-le-coq-heron-2002-1-page-37.htm.

Guillerault, G. (2003). *Le miroir et la psyché: Dolto, Lacan et le stade du miroir.* Paris: Gallimard.

Guillerault, G. (2007). *Dolto/Winnicott: le bébé dans la psychanalyse.* Paris: Gallimard.

Guillerault, G. (2008). *Comprendre Dolto.* Paris: Armand Colin.

Guillerault, G. (2012). *Françoise Dolto: la foi dans le désir.* Paris: Les Éditions du Cerf.

Guttmann, M. G. (2001). *The Enigma of Anna O: A Biography of Bertha Pappenheim.* Wickford: Moyer Bell.

Hall, G. (2009). «Le désir de vivre»: an introduction to the life and work of Françoise Dolto.» *British Journal of Psychotherapy*, 25: 3, 312–330.

Hall, G., Hivernel, F. & Morgan, S. (Eds.) (2009). *Theory and Practice in Child Psychoanalysis: An Introduction to the Work of Françoise Dolto.* London: Karnac.

Halmos, C. (1988). «Entre les enfants et les psychanalystes.» In J. Aubrey et al. (Ed.), *Quelques pas sur le chemin de Françoise Dolto* (pp. 81–115). Paris: Éditions du Seuil.

Halmos, C. (Ed.). (1994). *Françoise Dolto, Articles et conférences, II: les chemins de l'éducation.* Paris: Gallimard. (Original work published 1946–1989.)

Halmos, C. (2000). «Un héritage qui dérange.» In F. Authier–Roux (Ed.), *Madame Dolto* (pp. 31–38). Paris: Erès.

Halmos, C. (2008). «Françoise Dolto: une voix révolutionnaire.» Retrieved from www.psychologies.com/Therapies/Psychanalyse/Travail-psychanalytique/Articles-et-Dossiers/Francoise-Dolto-une-pensee-revolutionnaire/Francoise-Dolto-une-voix-revolutionnaire-par-Claude-Halmos.

Halmos, C. & Dolto, C. (Eds.) (1994). *Françoise Dolto, Articles et conférences, I: les étapes majeures de l'enfance.* Paris: Gallimard. (Original work published 1946–1988.)

Hamelin, A (Producer) & Rabaté, F. (Director) (2011a). «Grandir à Petits Pas.» [Video, 64 min.] *Le Monde en Face avec Carole Gaessler.* France: Les Films Grains de Sable. Retrieved from www.youtube.com/watch?v=skxuanPsBis.

Hamelin, A. (Producer) & Rabaté, F. (Director) (2011b). «La Salle des profs.» [Video, 53:39 min.] *Le Monde en Face avec Carole Gaessler.* France: Les Films Grains de Sable. Retrieved from www.youtube.com/watch?v=skxuanPsBis.

Harris, M. & Bick, E. (2011). *The Tavistock Model: Papers on Child Development and Psychoanalytic Training.* London: Karnac. (Original work published 1962–1983.)

Hesnard, A. (1926). *La vie et la mort des instincts chez l'homme.* Paris: Stock Laurence Pernoud.

Hesnard, A. (1946). *Freud dans la sociéte d'après guerre.* Genève: Éditions du Mont-Blanc.

History World (n.d.). "History of Algeria." Retrieved from www.historyworld.net/wrldhis/PlainTextHistories.asp?ParagraphID=okz.

Hitschmann, E. (1957). *Great Men.* New York: International Universities.

Hivernel, F. (2013). "'The Parental Couple': Françoise Dolto and Jacques Lacan, contributions to the mirror stage." *British Journal of Psychotherapy*, 29: 4, 505–518.

Hoffman, C. (2011). «La résistance française à la découverte freudienne: lettre du Professeur R. Morichau-Beauchant à Sigmund Freud.» *Topique*, 2/2011: 115, 13–15. Retrieved from www.cairn.info/revue-topique-2011-2-page-13.htm.

IFI Claims Patent Service (2012). "Toy Tunnel Structure, US1917018 A, Abstract." Retrieved from www.google.com/patents/US1917018.

Ina.fr (1978, 15 June).«Françoise Dolto sur l'adoption» [Video, 2:46 min.] Retrieved from www.youtube.com/watch?v=iUwWzpmn2KY.

Ina.fr (1988, 26 August). «Décès Françoise Dolto» [Video, 1:57 min.] Retrieved from www.youtube.com/watch?v=oenpf_tNZa8.

Ina.fr.2 (1998, 8 October). «La Maison verte fête ses 20 ans.» [Video, 2:32 min.] Retrieved from www.youtube.com/watch?v=Q8e2q3IDWRo.

Institut National des jeunes sourds de Paris (INJS) (201817 May). Conférence "Fenêtre sur cour": Françoise Dolto et l'INJS. Retrieved from www.injs-paris.fr/evenement/confer ence-fenetre-sur-cour-francoise-dolto-linjs.

Isaacs, S. (1948). "The nature and function of phantasy." *International Journal of Psychoanalysis*, 29: 73–97.

Janet, P. (1892/2013). *L'anasthésie hystérique*. Évreux: Imprimerie de Charles Hérisset.

Jones, E. (1953/1982). *The Life and Work of Sigmund Freud, Vol. 1*. New York: Basic Books.

Joseph, B. (1985). "Transference: the total situation." *International Journal of Psychoanalysis*, 66: 4, 447–454.

Jung, C. G. (1957/1990). *The Undiscovered Self, With Symbols and the Interpretation of Dreams* (R.F.C. Hull, Trans.). Princeton, NJ: Princeton University Press.

Kelley-Lainé, K. (1997). *Peter Pan: The Story of Lost Childhood*. Shaftesbury, MA: Element.

Klein, M. (1923/1998). "The rôle of the school in the libidinal development of the child." In M. Klein (Ed.), *Love, Guilt and Reparation, and Other Works, 1921–1945* (pp. 59–76). London: Vintage.

Kouki, É. (Ed.). (2005). *Françoise Dolto: parler de la solitude*. Paris: Mercure de France. (Original work published 1975.)

Kouritzin, S. G. (1999). *Face(t)s of Language Loss*. Mahwah, NJ: Lawrence Erlbaum Associates.

Kristeva, J. (1974). *La révolution du langage poétique*. Paris: Collection "Tel Quel" aux Éditions du Seuil.

Kristeva, J. (1996/2000). *The Sense and Non-Sense of Revolt* (J. Herman, Trans.). New York: Columbia University Press.

Krymko-Bleton, I. (2012). «Prévenir autrement: la prévention primaire à La Maison buisson-nière.» *Érudit: Nouvelles pratiques sociales, numéro 1*: 140–150. Retrieved from www.erudit. org/revue/nps/2012/v/nnps060/1008632ar.pdf.

Lacan, J. (1964/1977). *The Four Fundamental Concepts of Psycho-analysis* (A. Sheridan, Trans.). Harmondsworth: Penguin Books.

Laforgue, R. (1932/1963). *La relativité de la réalité*. Paris: Éditions du Mont-Blanc.

Laforgue, R. (1936). «La névrose familiale.» *Revue française de psychanalyse*, IX: 3, 327–355.

Landru, P. (2008). «Cimétières de France et d'ailleurs: Cimiétière de Passy, présentation générale et principales célébrités.» Retrieved from http://landrucimetieres.fr/spip/spip. php?article273.

Laplanche, J. & Pontalis, J.-B. (1964/2010). "Fantasy and the origins of sexuality." In D. Birksted-Breen, S. Flanders & A. Gibeault (Eds.), *Reading French Psychoanalysis* (pp. 310–337). London: Routledge.

Laplanche, J. & Pontalis, J.-B. (1967/2004). *Vocabulaire de la psychanalyse*. Paris: Quadrige/ Presses Universitaires de France.

Larajan (2012, November 21). "*Blogspot: Motherhood, repatriation and other fictions: 'La Maison verte' – The Green House*." Retrieved from http://larajan.blogspot.ca/2012/ 11/la-maison-verte-green-house.html.

Le Péron, S. (Director) (2008). *Françoise Dolto: Le désir de vivre*. [Film, 98 min.] France & Belgium: Radio Télévision Belge Francophone (RTBF).

Le Point (2012, 6 November). «Le secretariat du Père Noël fête ces 50 ans et ouvre mardi.» Retrieved from www.lepoint.fr/societe/la-poste-ouvre-mardi-le-traditionnel-secretariat-du-pere-noel-17-11-2014-1881861_23.php.

Le Point (2014, 17 November). «La poste ouvre mardi le traditionnel secretariat du Père Noël.» Retrieved from www.lepoint.fr/societe/la-poste-ouvre-mardi-le-traditionnel-secretariat-du-pere-noel-17-11-2014-1881861_23.php.

Leavy, S. (Ed.) (1964). *The Freud Journal of Lou Andreas-Salomé* (S. A. Leavy, Trans.). New Haven, CT: Basic Books. (Original work published 1912–1913.)

Ledoux, M.-H. (1995). *Introduction à l'oeuvre de Françoise Dolto*. Paris: Payot.

Ledoux, M.-H. (2006). *Dictionnaire raisonné de l'oeuvre de Françoise Dolto*. Paris: Payot.

Lelièvre, C. (2018, 24 May). «La révolution Dolto, un documentaire en forme d'hommage.» *Les pros de la petite enfance*. Retrieved from https://lesprosdelapetiteenfance.fr/bebes-enfants/psycho-pedagogie/lheritage-dolto/la-revolution-dolto-un-documentaire-en-forme-dhommage.

Lemisch, L. J. (Ed.) (1961/2001). *Benjamin Franklin: The Autobiography and Other Writings*. New York: Signet Classics.

Leonard, K. (2009, 4 August). "French film festival highlights differences between French and American cinema." University of Richmond and Virginia Commonwealth University: *The Collegian*. Retrieved from www.thecollegianur.com/article/2009/04/french-film-festival-highlights-differences-between-french-and-american-cinema.

Leroy, S. & Muni Toke, V. (2007). «Une date dans la description linguistique du nom propre: l'essai de grammaire de la langue française de Damourette et Pichon.» In *Lalies* 27 (Daniel Petit , Ed., pp. 115–190). Paris: ENS Éd. Retrieved from https://docplayer.fr/112016425-Une-date-dans-la-description-linguistique-du-nom-propre-l-essai-de-gram maire-de-la-langue-francaise-de-damourette-et-pichon.html.

Levinas, E. (1982). *Ethics and Infinity* (R. A. Cohen, Trans.). Pittsburgh, PA: Duquesne University Press.

Lévy, D. M. (Ed.) (2002). *Parler juste aux enfants: entretien de Françoise Dolto & D. M. Lévy*. Paris: Mercure de France. (Original work published 1978–1988.)

Lieux Insolites (2010). «La tête des faux.» Retrieved from www.lieux-insolites.fr/cicatrice/14-18/tdf/tdf.htm.

Littner, N. (1974). "An intuitive clinician but a poor theoretician." *APA: Psychcritiques*, 19: 8, 616–617.

Livingstone, A. (1984). *Lou Andreas-Salomé* (P.-E.Dauzat, Trans.). Paris: Presses Universitaires de France.

Livius (2011, 15 February). "Lutetia definition." *Ancient History Encyclopedia*. Retrieved from www.ancient.eu/Lutetia/.

Louchart, A. (2008). «Centenaire de la naissance de Françoise Dolto: lire Dolto en 2008.» *Le Figaro*, 29 décembre 2008. Retrieved from http://evene.lefigaro.fr/celebre/actualite/francoise-dolta-psychanalyse-enfants-1730.php.

Louka, J.-M. (2003). «Françoise Dolto: une psychanalyste à l'Hôpital général.» *Eres/Le coq-héron*, 174: 144–149.

Maeterlinck, M. (1908/1965). *L'Oiseau bleu*. Paris: Éditions Rombaldi.

Maeterlinck, M. (1919). *Les sentiers dans la montagne*. Paris: Bibliothèque-Charpentier.

*Maison Buissonière* (2014). "Home: more than 20 years with the little ones." Retrieved from www.maisonbuissonniere.org/en/.

*Maison Ouverte* (2011). «Acceuil: pour les enfants de moins de 4 ans accompagnés de leurs parents ou d'un adulte proche.» Retrieved from www.lamaisonouverte.ca/.

*Maison verte* (n.d.). «Acceuil: lieu d'accueil des enfants de la naissance jusqu'au 4ème anniversaire accompagnés par leurs parents, d'après une idée de Françoise Dolto.» Retrieved from www.lamaisonverte.asso.fr/.

Malandrin, M.-H. & Schauder, C. (Eds.) (2009). *Françoise Dolto: une psychanalyste dans la cité, l'aventure de la Maison verte*. Paris: Gallimard.

Manier, C. & Kouki, É. (2003). *Françoise Dolto: la vague et l'océan, séminaire sur les pulsions de mort (1970–1971)*. Paris: Gallimard.

Marc-Pezet, J. (Producer) (2004). *Françoise Dolto: anthologie radiophonique 1976–1977, Volume 1, Lorsque l'enfant parait* [3-CD Set, 190 min.] Paris: France-Inter.

Marette, F. (1940). *Psychanalyse et pédiatrie: le complexe de castration, étude générale et cas cliniques*. Paris: Amédée Legrand.

Marie, C. (2008). «Qui est la fameuse ménagère?: interview avec Joanne Balasko.» TF1, 21 octobre. Retrieved from http://lafameusemenagere.over-blog.com/article-23942781.html.

McDougall, J. (1969). *Dialogue with Sammy: A Psycho-Analytical Contribution to the Understanding of Child Psychosis*. New York: International Universities Press, Inc.

Meirieu, P. & Kübler, T. (2001). «Françoise Dolto: les bons élèves sont-ils tous névrosés?» [Video]. Retrieved from www.youtube.com/watch?v=0wYKTRQbIsY.

Miller, G. (2018a). «La révolution Dolto: note d'intention.» Retrieved from www.francetv pro.fr/france-4/communiques-de-presse/la-revolution-dolto-14904675.

Miller, G. (2018b, 30 May). «Entrevue: Françoise Dolto, la magicienne.» [Video.] *La Maison des maternelles*. Retrieved from www.youtube.com/watch?v=uYujYfLenmU.

Miller, G. & Feuillette, A. (Producers) (2018). «La révolution Dolto.» [Film, 90 min.] *Télé 7*, 30 mai 2018. Paris: France 3. Retrieved from www.programme-television.org/docu mentaires/societe/la-revolution-dolto.

Mishra Tarc, A. (2015). *Literacy of the Other: Renarrating Humanity*. Albany, NY: SUNY Press.

Montaigne, M. (1580/1958a). *Essais (Nouvelle édition conforme au texte de l'exemplaire de Bordeaux): Livre Premier*. Paris: Classiques Garnier.

Montaigne, M. (1580/1958b). *Essais (Nouvelle édition conforme au texte de l'exemplaire de Bordeaux): Livre Troisième*. Paris: Classiques Garnier.

Monteiro, A. R. (2009). «Éducation et reconnaissance chez Françoise Dolto.» *Enfances, Familles, Générations*. No. 11: 80–100. Retrieved from www.erudit.org/fr/revues/efg/ 2009-n11-efg3879/044123ar/.

Moreau Ricaud, M. (2005). "Morichau-Beauchant, Pierre Ernest René (1873–1952)." *Thomson-Gale International Dictionary of Psychoanalysis*. Retrieved from www.encyclope dia.com/psychology/dictionaries-thesauruses-pictures-and-press-releases/morichau-beauchant-pierre-ernest-rene-1873-1952.

Morgan, S. (2013). "When let's pretend goes wrong: failed transitions." *British Journal of Psychotherapy*, 29: 4, 494–504.

Morgenstern, S. (1927/2003). «Un cas de mutisme psychogène.» In *Sophie Morgenstern: Tome 3, Articles et contributions à la Revue française de psychanalyse* (Claude Tchou , Ed., pp. 9–62). Paris: Bibliothèque des introuvables.

Morgenstern, S. (1930/2003). «La psychanalyse infantile et son rôle dans l'hygiène mentale.» In *Sophie Morgenstern: Tome 2, Articles et contributions à la Revue française de psychanalyse* (Claude Tchou, Ed., pp. 245–302). Paris: Bibliothèque des introuvables.

Morgenstern, S. (1934/2003). «La pensée magique chez l'enfant.» In *Sophie Morgenstern: Tome 3, Articles et contributions à la Revue française de psychanalyse* (Claude Tchou , Ed., pp. 101–137). Paris: La Bibliothèque des introuvables.

Morgenstern, S. (1937/2003). «Psychanalyse infantile (symbolisme et valeur clinique des créations imaginatives chez l'enfant).» In *Sophie Morgenstern: Tome 2, Articles et contributions à la Revue française de psychanalyse* (Claude Tchou , Ed., pp. 15–244). Paris: La Bibliothèque des introuvables.

Morgenstern, S. (1938/2003). «La structure de la personnalité et ses déviations.» In *Sophie Morgenstern: Tome 1* (Claude Tchou , Ed., pp. 9–177). Paris: La Bibliothèque des introuvables.

Murat, L. (2001/2013). *La maison du docteur Blanche.* Paris: Gallimard.

Nadal, A. (2006). *Françoise Dolto et l'image inconsciente du corps: fondements et déplacement vers la pulsion.* Paris: De Boeck.

Nasio, J.-D. (1987/1998). «Débat: Solange Nobécourt, Jean-Pierre Dreyfuss, Françoise Dolto.» In J.D. Nasio (Ed.), *Le silence en psychanalyse* (pp. 207–212). Paris: Désir/Payot.

Neyrand, G. (1995). *Sur les pas de la Maison verte.* Paris: Syros.

Nobécourt, É. (Producer) (2008a). *Dolto par Dolto, No. 1.* [DVD, 133 min.] France: MK2.

Nobécourt, É. (Producer) (2008b). *Dolto psychanalyste, No. 2.* [DVD, 130 min.] France: MK2.

Nobécourt, É. (Producer) (2008c). *Dolto citoyenne, No. 3.* [DVD, 161 min.] France: MK2.

Nobécourt, É. (Producer) (2008d). *Parole, l'héritage Dolto, No. 4.* [DVD, 97 min.] France: MK2.

Nobécourt, É. & Simonetta, B. (Producers) (1978). *Françoise Dolto: les enfants d'abord.* [Film, 52 min.] France: Arte France.

Normandin, M. (2012). "Françoise Dolto and the preverbal 'Unconscious.'" [Lecture.] Toronto Psychoanalytic Society, Toronto, ON, September 30, 2012.

Notre Famille (2015). «Les plus belles lettres écrites au Père Noël: Texte de Françoise Dolto au dos de la carte postale.» [Image.] Retrieved from www.vosquestionsdeparents.fr/dossier/1054/lettres-au-pere-noel.

Paglia, M. (2016). "The *Maison Verte*, a transitional space: introducing the work of Françoise Dolto in the UK." *International Journal of Infant Observation and Its Applications*, 19: 3, 224–237.

Pappenheim, B. (1888/2008). *In the Junk Shop and Other Stories* (R. Latimer, Trans.). Riverside, CA: Ariadne.

Pappenheim, B. (1924/1986). *Le travail de Sisyphe.* Paris: Des femmes.

Paquis, C. (2008). «L'image inconsciente du corps: Françoise Dolto.» Retrieved from www.psychaanalyse.com/pdf/l_image_inconsciente_du_corps.pdf.

*Paris 1900* (2008, 14 July). «Blogspot Paris 1900: l'architecture art nouveau à Paris, 16e arrondissement.» Retrieved from http://paris1900.blogspot.ca/search/label/16e%20arrondissement.

Percheminier, C. (Ed.) (1991). *Françoise Dolto: correspondance, 1913–1938.* Paris: Hatier.

Pérez Foster, R. M. (2004). "Assessing the psychodynamic function of language in the bilingual patient." In R. M. Pérez Foster, M. Moskowitz & R.A. Javier (Eds.), *Reaching Across Boundaries of Culture and Class: Widening the Scope of Psychotherapy* (pp. 243–263). Lanham, MD: Jason Aronson.

Pernicone, A. & Dolto, C. (2002, June). «Interview.» *Fort-da: Revista de psicoanalisis con niños, No. 5.* Retrieved from www.fort-da.org/reportajes/dolto-fr.htm.

Pfeiffer, E. (Ed.) (1972). *Sigmund Freud and Lou Andreas-Salomé Letters* (W. & E. Robson-Scott, Trans.). New York: W.W. Norton & Company. (Original work published 1912–1936.)

Pfeiffer, E. (1979). *Lou Andreas-Salomé: ma vie* (D. Miermont & B. Vergne, Trans.). Paris: Presses Universitaires de France. (Original work published 1931–1937.)

Pfeiffer, E. (1983). *Lou Andreas-Salomé: carnets intimes des dernières années* (J. Le Rider, Trans.). Paris: Hachette. (Original work published 1934–1936.)

Pignot, M. & Potin, Y. (2018). *1914–1918: Françoise Dolto, veuve de guerre à sept ans.* Paris: Gallimard.

Portevin, C. (2008). «Françoise Dolto, psychanalyste, le tout d'une oeuvre: elle a pensé l'enfant comme personne.» *Télérama, No. 3068,* 1–7 novembre 2008, 38–40.

Postel, J. (n.d.). «René Laforgue (1894–1962).» *Encyclopædia Universalis.* Retrieved from www.universalis.fr/encyclopedie/rene-laforgue/.

Propp, V. (1965). «Morphologie du conte» (M. Derrida, Trans.). In *Morphologie du conte* (M. Derrida, T. Todorov & C. Kahn, Trans., Gérard Genette, Ed., pp. 6–144). Paris: Poétique/Seuil.

Provence, M. (1995). «Ascendance: Françoise Dolto ou la mère rêvée.» *Généalogie Magazine,* No. 144, décembre 1995, 30–38.

Psychoanalytikerinnen (2013). *"Biografisches Lexikon*: women psychoanalysts in France." Retrieved from www.psychoanalytikerinnen.de/france_biographies.html.

Puskas, D., Brien, M., Daviau, L., & Lacourse, G. (1991). «Le paiement symbolique, monnaie du désir.» *Santé mentale au Québec,* 16: 1, 139–148.

Quinodoz, J.-M. (2008). *Listening to Hanna Segal: Her Contribution to Psychoanalysis.* London: Routledge.

Radiola. (n.d.). «Histoire de Radiola: 100 ans de radio & Biographie: Michel Laporte (Radiolo).» Retrieved from http://100ansderadio.free.fr/HistoiredelaRadio/Radiola/Radiola-1922.html.

Rank, O. (1924/1993). *The Trauma of Birth.* New York: Dover Publications.

Reeves, C. (2010). "Theory and practice in child psychoanalysis: an introduction to the work of Françoise Dolto." [Book review.] *Journal of Child Psychotherapy,* 36: 3, 316–319.

Régis, E. & Hesnard, A. (1914). *La psychoanalyse des névroses et des psychoses: ses applications médicales et extramédicales.* Paris: Félix Alcan.

Reis Monteiro, A. (2009). «Éducation et reconnaissance chez Françoise Dolto.» *Enfances, Familles, Générations,* 11: 80–100.

Rekhviashvili, A. (2008, April). "Two French psychoanalysts visit Tblisi Green House." *Georgian Daily Independent Voice.* Retrieved from http://georgiandaily.com/index.php?option=com%20content&task=view&id=1429&Itemid=83.

Renders, X. (1991). «Françoise Dolto (1908–1988): la demande que se modifie l'image du corps.» In *Le jeu de la demande: une histoire de la psychanalyse d'enfants* (pp. 272–346). Bruxelles: De Boeck Université.

Ribas, D. (Ed.) (2006). *Revue française de psychanalyse: 80 ans de textes, 1926–2006.* Paris: Presses Universitaires de France.

Ribowski, N. (Producer) (1987/2004). *Apostrophes, les grands entretiens de Bernard Pivot: Françoise Dolto.* [Television Documentary, 88 min.] Paris: Gallimard/Institut National de l'Audiovisuel.

Rostand, J. (1953). *L'aventure avant la naissance (du germe au nouveau-né).* Paris: Éditions Gonthier.

Rostand, J. (1964). «Homage à René Laforgue.» Retrieved from http://users.skynet.be/fb125004/laforgue.htm.

Rotman, C. & Mallaval, C. (2008). «En attendant Dolto: interview avec Catherine Dolto.» *Libération Société,* 12 December. Retrieved from www.liberation.fr/societe/2008/12/12/enattendant-dolto_295736.

Roudinesco, É. (1975). «L'autre de la théorie.» In *L'inconscient et ses lettres* (pp. 73–86). Paris: Repères-Mame.

Roudinesco, É. (1982). *La bataille de cent ans: histoire de la psychanalyse en France, Volume 1: 1885–1939.* Paris: Éditions Ramsay.

Roudinesco, É. (1986). *La bataille de cent ans: histoire de la psychanalyse en France, Volume 2: 1925–1985.* Paris: Éditions du Seuil.

Roudinesco, É. (1999). *Pourquoi la psychanalyse?* Paris: Librairie Arthème Fayard.

Roudinesco, É. (2008, 21 October). «La cause des enfants.» *Le Monde.* Retrieved from www.lemonde.fr/societe/article/2008/10/21/la-cause-des-enfants-par-elisabeth-roudi nesco_1109370_3224.html.

Roudinesco, É. (2011). *Lacan, envers et contre tout.* Paris: Éditions du Seuil.

Roudinesco, É. (2018, 30 May). «Françoise Dolto n'est pas une 'petite fille de conte de fées.'» *Tribune.* Retrieved from www.liberation.fr/debats/2018/05/30/francoise-dolto-n-est-pas-une-petite-fille-de-conte-de-fees_1655057.

Rustin, M. (2008). "Esther Bick's legacy of infant observation at the Tavistock: some reflections 60 years on." In M. Harris & E. Bick (Eds.), *The Tavistock Model: Papers on Child Development and Psychoanalytic Training* (2011, pp. 375–390). London: Karnac.

Saint-Onge, K. (2013). *Bilingual Being: My Life as a Hyphen.* Montreal: McGill Queen's University Press.

Saint-Onge, K. (2016). *Archaic Echoes, the Word and the Transference in Texts: A Psychobiographical Study of Françoise Dolto* [Doctoral dissertation.] Toronto: York University. Retrieved from https://yorkspace.library.yorku.ca/xmlui/bitstream/handle/10315/32693/Saint-Onge_Kathleen_M_2016_PhD.pdf?sequence=2.

Schauder, C. (Ed.) (2004/2008). *Lire Dolto aujourd'hui.* Paris: Eres.

Schauder, C. (2005/2008). *Françoise Dolto et le transfert dans le travail avec les enfants.* Paris: Eres.

Scheidhauer, M. (2010). *Freud et ses visiteurs français et suisses francophones (1920–1930).* Paris: Érès.

Schiff, S. (2005). *A Great Improvisation: Franklin, France, and the Birth of America.* New York: Owl.

Schmideberg, M. (1930). "The rôle of psychotic mechanisms in cultural development." *International Journal of Psychoanalysis,* 11: 387–418.

Schmideberg, M. (1947). "Learning to talk." *Psychoanalytic Review,* 34: 296–335.

Sédat, J. (2003). «Préface.» In S. Morgenstern (Ed.), *La structure de la personnalité et ses déviations, Tome 1* (Claude Tchou, Ed., pp. 9–15). Paris: La Bibliothèque des introuvables.

Segal, H. (1957/1981). "Notes on symbol formation." In H. Segal (Ed.), *The Work of Hanna Segal: A Kleinian Approach to Clinical Practice* (pp. 49–65). Northvale, NJ: Jason Aronson.

Seuil (2015). «Recherche détaillée: Françoise Dolto.» Retrieved from www.seuil.com/recherche?s=francoise+dolto.

SHAP (Société historique d'Auteuil et de Passy) (n.d.). «Histoire générale du XVIe arrondissement de Paris.» Retrieved from www.histoire-auteuil-passy.org/histoire-du-xvie.

Shepherd, J. A. (2018). "Why it's 'I love you' or 'Je t'aime'—but not both: Language Identity Perception in Adult Survivors of Childhood Trauma in Multilingual Contexts." [Unpublished master's thesis.] Montreal: McGill University.

Soler, C. (2008). «Du parlêtre.» *L'en-je lacanien,* 2/2008: 11, 23–33. Retrieved from www.cairn.info/revue-l-en-je-lacanien-2008-2-page-23.htm.

Souslova Spiridonov, O. (2015). «La possibilité d'une Ile Verte: histoire de la Maison Verte de Paris à Saint-Pétersbourg, création et transmission d'un dispositif.» [Doctoral dissertation

188090142.] Paris: Université Paris-Sorbonne. Retrieved from https://halshs.archives-ouvertes.fr/tel-01598106/file/These%20Souslova%20Olga%20%281%29.pdf.

Stärcke, A. (1921a). "The castration complex." *International Journal of Psychoanalysis*, 2: 179–201.

Stärcke, A. (1921b). "Psychoanalysis and psychiatry." *International Journal of Psychoanalysis*, 2: 361–415.

Starobinski, J. (1964). «Les anagrammes de Ferdinant de Saussure.» In *Mercure de France: février 1964* (pp. 243–262). Paris: Le Mercure de France.

Starobinski, J. (1971). *Les mots sous les mots: les anagrammes de Ferdinand de Saussure.* Paris: Le Chemin/Gallimard.

Steel, D. (1982, 1 May). «L'amitié entre Sigmund Freud et Yvette Guilbert.» In *La Nouvelle Revue Française*, No. 352 (Georges Lambrichs , Ed., pp. 84–92). Paris: Gallimard.

Stieg, G. & Michaud, S. (Ed.). (2001). *Rilke et son amie Lou Andreas-Salomé à Paris.* Paris: Presses Sorbonne Nouvelle.

Strachey, J. (1930). "Some unconscious factors in reading." *International Journal of Psychoanalysis*, 11: 322–331.

Sudaka-Bénazéraf, J. (1987/2012). *Libres enfants de la Maison verte: sur les traces de F. Dolto.* Paris: Érès.

Sudaka-Bénazéraf, J. (n.d.). «Interview: libres enfants de la Maison verte.» [Video, 6:47 min.] *Érès 100, BB# 123.* Retrieved from www.youtube.com/watch?v=k5bSCxzwoHE.

Systemique.be (n.d.). «Eva Freud: une vie.» Retrieved from www.systemique.be/spip/IMG/article_PDF/article_a356.pdf.

Tan, L.-H. & Perfetti, C. A. (1998). "Phonological codes as early sources of constraint in Chinese word identification: a review of current discoveries and theoretical accounts." *Reading and Writing: An Interdisciplinary Journal*, 10: 165–200.

This, B. (1988). «Françoise Dolto.» *Le Coq-héron*, 109: 3–15.

This, B. (2007). *La Maison verte: créer des lieux d'acceuil.* Paris: Belin.

Turkle, S. (1995/1997). "Tough love: an Introduction to Françoise Dolto's *When Parents Separate*." In F. Dolto (Ed.), *When Parents Separate* (D. Callimanopulos, Trans., n.p.). Lincoln, MA: David R. Godine. Retrieved from web.mit.edu/sturkle/www/dolto.html.

Tustin, F. (1981). *Autistic States in Children.* London: Routledge & Kegan Paul Ltd.

Vasquez, A. (Ed.) (1976). *(Docteur X … ) S.O.S. Psychanalyste!: des consultations par les ondes. [Françoise Dolto à l'anonyme.]* Paris: Éditions Fleurus.

Vasse, D. (Ed.) (2006). *Né de l'homme et de la femme, l'enfant: chronique d'une structure Dolto.* Paris: Seuil.

Vessier, M. (1999). *La Pitié-Salpêtrière: quatre siécles d'histoire et d'histoires.* Paris: Groupe hôspitalier Pitié-Salpêtrière.

Ville, B.-L.-R. (2018). «Exposition: Françoise Dolto.» 6 octobre 2018–3 novembre 2018. Retrieved from www.bourg-la-reine.fr/Agenda/Exposition-Francoise-Dolto.

Western and Company (1892, February 27). "The Elmore Copper Depositing Company." *The Engineering and Mining Journal* 53: 248. Retrieved from https://books.google.ca/books?id=-rs-AQAAMAAJ&dq=copper+elmore+patent&source=gbs_navlinks_s.

Who's Who in France (n.d.) «Biographie de Jacques Nobécourt.» Retrieved from www.whoswho.fr/decede/biographie-jacques-nobecourt_3020.

Wiktionnaire (2018a). «Mimétiser.» Retrieved from https://fr.wiktionary.org/wiki/mim%C3%A9tiser.

Wiktionnaire (2018b). «Mythomaniser.» Retrieved from https://fr.wiktionary.org/wiki/mythomaniser.

Winnicott, D. W. (1945). "Primitive emotional development." *The International Journal of Psychoanalysis*, 26: 137–143.

Winnicott, D. W. (1949/2007). "Birth memories, birth trauma, and anxiety." In *Through Paediatrics to Psychoanalysis: Collected Papers* (pp. 174–193). London: Karnac.

Winnicott, D. W. (1956/2007). "Primary maternal preoccupation." In *Through Paediatrics to Psychoanalysis: Collected Papers* (pp. 300–305). London: Karnac.

Wittwer, J. (1992). «Critique de livre de D'Ortoli (Fabienne), Amram (Michel).—L'école avec Françoise Dolto, le rôle du désir dans l'éducation.» *Persée: Revue française de pédagogie*, 98: 1, 126–127.

Worldcat Identities (2015a). "Françoise Dolto." Retrieved from www.worldcat.org/iden tities/lccn-n79-053060/.

Worldcat.org (2015a). "Formats and editions of Françoise Dolto, *Psychanalyse et pédiatrie: Les grandes notions de la psychanalyse, seize observations*." Retrieved from www.worldcat. org/search?q=au%3ADolto%2C+Franc%CC%A7oise&fq=&dblist=638&start=11& qt=next_page.

Worldcat.org (2015b). "Worldcat identities: Marcelle Gauthier." Retrieved from http://experi mental.worldcat.org/idnetwork/searchresult.html?query=%22marcelle+gauthier%22.

Young-Bruehl, E. (1982). *Hannah Arendt: For Love of the World*. New Haven, CT: Yale University Press.

Young-Bruehl, E. (1988/2008). *Anna Freud: A Biography* (2nd edn.). New Haven, CT: Yale University Press.

Young-Bruehl, E. (1998a). "Profile of a latency woman: development for biographers." *American Imago*, 55: 2, 235–253.

Young-Bruehl, E. (1998b). *Subject to Biography: Psychoanalysis, Feminism, and Writing Women's Lives*. Cambridge, MA: Harvard University Press.

Youtube (2018, May 30). "Teaser [La révolution Dolto]." [Video, 45 sec.] Retrieved from www.youtube.com/watch?v=i846PSnNU3k.

# INDEX

Aubry, Jenny 23, 25–27, 78
Audiberti, Jacques 198
audition 5–6, 32, 58, 68–69, 72–73, 76, 82,
    95, 98–100, 103, 143, 155, 170,
    184n146; invested 73–75, 121; *see also*
    precocious
auditory 6, 26, 30, 73, 76, 83, 98–101, 129,
    170, 198, 216; climate 32, 73; focus
    40n177, 147; landscape 93, 178;
    prehistory 6, 36, 143, 219; world 3, 76
Aulagnier, Piera 117
autism 10, 48–50, 54, 104, 170, 201–203,
    209n197
auto- 33, 70, 76, 104, 115, 123, 159n103,
    165, 192; conservation 54, 76; erotic 51,
    70, 77–79, 102; materning 50, 96, 165,
    170; paterning 104
autobiographic(al) 8, 11, 20, 32, 82, 128,
    155, 166–169, 187, 212; in theoretical 7,
    143, 150, 188–191, 219–221, 224
autobiography 36, 77, 90, 105, 135n271,
    150, 155, 189, 215, 222
autonomy 79, 81, 98, 115–118
Avenue(s): Colonel Bonnet 93–95, 142; of
    language 103; Montaigne 151; Saint-
    Mandé 214; des Ternes 101–103, 173,
    212; Secrétan 140

*Les Babouches de Baba Hassein* 90–99, 105,
    123, 141, 146, 167, 214
Bacon, Roger 9, 72
B.A.G. 48, 57, 95, 215
Balint, Alice 26
Béague, Philippe 151, 187
Belgium 148, 151
Berge, André 24
Berman, Anne 152
bilingual 1, 31, 67, 101, 123, 128, 144
biography 5–8, 13, 21, 36, 44, 94, 140,
    150, 155, 200, 215, 224
blue 47–48, 118, 148–149
Bois de Vincennes 214
Bonaparte, Marie 9, 24–25, 28, 152, 163
Boulevard Delessert 123, 212
Brande(n)b(o)urg 6, 47, 123–125
breastfeed words 96
bridge 91, 96, 100, 143, 159n103

«Caillou» 113, 120
Canu, Anne-Marie 8, 15, 17n27, 17n28
castration 49, 127, 136n325, 168; complex
    127, 145, 153; door as 168, 172; failed
    127, 171, 230; lack of 58, 173; oral 49,

170; «symboligène» 125–127, 143, 168,
    193; umbilical 126, 171, 186n231
cathexis 29–31, 92, 100–102
«chameau» 98, 141
Chapdelot, Madame («Milou») 141, 150,
    164, 171
«charbon» 58, 156n1, 172
Charcot, Jean-Martin 27–29, 160n175,
    163, 190, 216
«Chasseur Alpins» 46, 127, 145, 154
«chat» 113, 141, 145, 149
«chosifiant» 68
Cimétière: Bourg-la-Reine 212; Passy 167;
    Père Lachaise 213
Cinderella 54, 58, 92, 95; *see also*
    fairy-tale(s)
circulation 1–3, 16, 94, 97, 148, 195; of
    affect 121, 152–153, 220, 224; of
    language 104, 144, 203; of libido 98, 119
climate 22, 32, 69, 96, 141; auditory 32, 73;
    of Dolto 10, 198; emotional 69, 74, 95
clinic(al) 2–3, 9, 14, 20, 23, 28–30, 33, 56,
    71, 79–80, 83, 104, 116–117, 125,
    135n288, 145, 149, 155, 167, 170–174,
    177–179, 190–191, 195–200, 210, 219,
    223; choral 79, 122, 220; note-taking
    140, 149–151; *see also* script-girl
«Club des piqués» 25, 140, 149
«collier» 81–82, 215–216
coma 4, 76, 97, 150, 187, 201
common interest 122, 153–155
communion 46, 175, 212
«co-moi papa-maman» 54, 191–192
co-narcissism 4, 74, 80, 121, 192; *see also*
    fusion
condensation(s) 31, 55, 74, 79, 84, 213;
    words as 32, 71–72, 83, 127, 172–173,
    181n35, 219
consciousness 4–5, 12, 29, 40n177, 58–59,
    71, 97–99, 111n261, 120, 140–141, 148,
    176, 219–221, 224
consolation 48, 50, 98, 102, 113, 156
continuity 14, 49–51, 77, 122, 152, 177,
    191, 199–201, 208n190, 219; archaic 5,
    104, 121, 125, 141, 152, 155, 204; loss of
    153, 173, 176, 195, 220; phantasy of 155,
    159n102, 176, 211; restoration of 98,
    124, 153, 220–221; as security 40n177,
    81, 100, 104, 121; symbolic 75, 202,
    220; *see also* unconscious
continuum (of security) 74, 77–78
contradiction 27, 32, 35, 49, 72, 139–140,
    154, 173

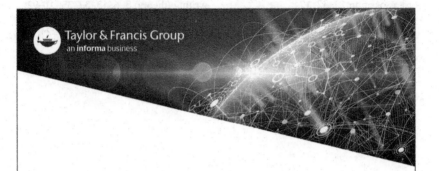